WORKBOOK

to Accompany

Understanding
Health Insurance

A Guide to Professional Billing

5th *Edition*

WORKBOOK
to Accompany
Understanding Health Insurance
A Guide to Professional Billing
5th *Edition*

JoAnn C. Rowell
Founder and Former Chairperson, Medical Assisting Department
Anne Arundel Community College, Arnold, MD

CONTRIBUTING AUTHORS
Michelle A. Green, MPS, RRA, CMA
Professor, Department of Physical & Life Sciences
State University of New York
College of Technology at Alfred, Alfred, NY

Alice Covell, CMA-A, RMA, CPC
Covell & Harwood Consultants
Kalamazoo, MI

WORKBOOK WRITTEN BY
Ruth M. Burke
Currently Medical Billing and Coding Program Specialist at
The Community College of Baltimore County, MD
Adjunct Faculty, The Community College of Baltimore County, MD
Adjunct Faculty, Harford Community College, MD
Consultant on Administrative Procedures to Health Care Practices in Maryland and Virginia
Member of the Maryland Medical Group Management Association (MGMA)

Delmar
Thomson Learning™

Africa • Australia • Canada • Denmark • Japan • Mexico • New Zealand • Phillipines
Puerto Rico • Singapore • Spain • United Kingdom • United States

COPYRIGHT © 2000
Delmar is a division of Thomson Learning. The Thomson Learning logo is a registered trademark used herein under license.

Printed in Canada
1 2 3 4 5 6 7 8 9 10 XXX 05 04 03 02 01 00 99

For more information, contact Delmar, 3 Columbia Circle, PO Box 15015, Albany, NY 12212-0515; or find us on the World Wide Web at http://www.delmar.com

Asia:
Thomson Learning
60 Albert Street, #15-01
Albert Complex
Singapore 189969
Tel: 65 336 6411
Fax: 65 336 7411

Japan:
Thomson Learning
Palaceside Building 5F
I - I - I Hitotsubashi, Chiyoda-ku
Tokyo 100 0003 Japan
Tel: 813 5218 6544
Fax: 813 5218 6551

Australia/New Zealand:
Nelson/Thomson Learning
102 Dodds Street
South Melbourne, Victoria 3205
Australia
Tel: 61 39685 4111
Fax: 61 39 685 4199

UK/Europe/Middle East
Thomson Learning
Berkshire House
168-173 High Holborn
London
WC IV 7AA United Kingdom
Tel: 44 171497 1422
Fax: 44 171497 1426
Thomas Nelson & Sons LTD
Nelson House
Mayfield Road
Walton-on-Thames
KT 12 5PL United Kingdom
Tel: 44 1932 2522111
Fax: 44 1932 246574

Latin America:
Thomson Learning
Seneca, 53
Colonia Polanco
11560 Mexico D.F. Mexico
Tel: 525-281-2906
Fax: 525-281-2656

Canada:
Nelson/Thomson Learning
1120 Birchmount Road
Scarborough, Ontario
Canada MlK 5G4
Tel: 416-752-9100
Fax: 416-752-8102

Spain:
Thomson Learning
Calle Magallanes, 25
28015-MADRID
ESPANA
Tel: 34 91446 33 50
Fax: 34 91445 62 18

International Headquarters:
Thomson Learning
International Division
290 Harbor Drive, 2nd Floor
Stamford, CT 06902-7477
Tel: 203-969-8700
Fax: 203-969-8751

Library of Congress Cataloging-in-Publication Number: 99-42099
ISBN: 0-7668-1309-6

Contents

Introduction

This workbook is designed to accompany ***Understanding Health Insurance: A Guide to Professional Billing***, 5th edition by JoAnn C. Rowell. The combination of the text and workbook is the most creative and dynamic learning system available for insurance and coding. It will help reinforce all essential competencies needed for employment in the field of medical billing.

The workbook assists the learner in reviewing the concepts and information presented in the textbook. It provides a means for the learner to achieve competency in required skills. Each chapter in the workbook correlates directly with the related text chapter. The chapter exercises are organized by the main chapter heads of the text and thus cover the basic chapter content in sequence. These exercises reinforce and apply the learner's understanding of chapter content. The workbook exercises are presented in a variety of formats to accommodate various learning styles: fill in the blank, multiple choice, true/false, and brief answers.

In Conclusion

The author hopes you will find the workbook to be both challenging and interesting. It is the author's desire that you master the content of the text to the best of your ability. This workbook is designed to assist in that process. The author wishes you success as you complete your assignments and build your skills in medical billing.

ACKNOWLEDGMENTS

I would like to express my appreciation to the following colleagues who helped gather information for me:

Rebecca L. Bechtler

Roz Laakso, ART, CCS-P

Dana J. Pierce, CCS-P

Sharon D. Whitty, CCS

Pamela J. Williams

Anita M. Zahn

In addition, I want to thank the following individuals who reviewed the manuscript for the workbook and its instructor's manual and provided valuable suggestions for improvements.

Addy Alsumidaie
Sunnyvale Cupertino Adult Education Center
Sunnyvale, CA and Santa Clara Adult Education
San Jose, CA

Michelle A. Green, MPS, RRA, CMA
Department of Physical and Life Sciences
State University of New York, College of Technology at Alfred
Alfred, NY

Virginia M. Hannan, CMA, BS
Center for Professional Advancement,
Bryant Stratton Business Institute
Williamsville, NY

Cheryl Hutchison, CMA, CPC
Belleville Area College
Belleville, IL

Eva I. Irwin, CMA
IVY Tech State College
Indianapolis, IN

Mary E. McGillivray Walker, CMT, ART, MEd
Minnesota West Community and Technical College
Jackson, MN

C H A P T E R

One

Health Insurance Specialist— Roles and Responsibilities

EMPLOYMENT OPPORTUNITIES

1. List three factors contributing to the increase in insurance specialist positions available in health care provider offices.

    a. _____

    b. _____

    c. _____

2. List six career opportunities open to health insurance specialists.

    a. _____

    b. _____

    c. _____

    d. _____

    e. _____

    f. _____

3. A consumer claim assistance professional helps private individuals _____

    _____

BASIC SKILL REQUIREMENTS

4. List six basic skills anyone who aspires to become a health insurance specialist must have.

    a. _____

    b. _____

    c. _____

    d. _____

    e. _____

    f. _____

5. A health insurance specialist must be fluent in the language of medicine in order to _____

   _____

6. Critical reading skills are needed to _____

   _____

7. Misreading of any word or diagnosis may result in the assignment of a wrong code number and the possibility of a _____ or _____ of a claim.

8. A health insurance specialist must be comfortable discussing insurance concepts and regulations with _____ and _____ _____ _____ .

9. Many companies use their websites to release _____ and _____ _____ as soon as they are adopted.

HEALTH INSURANCE SPECIALIST RESPONSIBILITIES

Critical Thinking

10. Write a paragraph describing the responsibilities of an insurance specialist.

    _____

    _____

    _____

    _____

PROFESSIONAL CERTIFICATION

11. List three professional organizations dedicated to serving health insurance specialists employed in health care providers' offices.

    a. _____

    b. _____

    c. _____

Legal Considerations

BREACH OF CONFIDENTIALITY

1. The unauthorized release of confidential patient information to a third party is known as

   _____ of _____ .

2. Match the insurance terms in the first column with the definitions in the second column. Write the correct letters in the blanks.

   _____ first party

   _____ second party

   _____ third party

   _____ contract

   _____ guardian

   a. The person or organization who is providing the service

   b. An agreement between two or more parties to perform specific services or duties

   c. The person designated in a contract to receive a contracted service

   d. The person who is legally designated to be in charge of a patient's affairs

   e. The one who has no binding interest in a specific contract

3. The answer to each of the following statements is either true or false. Indicate your choice by placing **T** for a true statement or **F** for a false statement on the line provided.

   _____ a. Breach of confidentiality cannot be charged against a health care provider if written permission to release necessary medical information to an insurance company or other third party has been obtained from the patient or guardian.

   _____ b. Patients need to sign an authorization for the release of medical information statement before completing the claim form.

   _____ c. A dated, signed release statement is generally considered to be in force for one year from the date stated on the form.

   _____ d. The authorization for release of medical information form authorizes the processing of claim forms but the phrase "signature on file" or the patient's signature still needs to appear on each form.

   _____ e The Health Care Financing Administration (HCFA) regulations allow government programs to accept only dated authorizations.

_____ f. The federal government allows two exceptions to the required authorization for release of medical information to insurance companies: patients covered by Medicare or Blue Cross and Blue Shield.

_____ g. When health care providers agree to treat either a Medicaid or a Workers' Compensation case, they agree to accept the program's payment as payment in full for covered procedures rendered to these patients.

_____ h. Patients who undergo screening for the human immunodeficiency virus (HIV) or acquired immune deficiency syndrome (AIDS) infection should not be asked to sign an additional authorization statement releasing information regarding the patient's HIV/AIDS status.

CLAIMS INFORMATION TELEPHONE QUERIES

Critical Thinking

4. It is very simple for a curious individual to place a call to a physician's office and claim to be an insurance company benefits clerk. Write a paragraph explaining how a physician's office can verify insurance company telephone inquiries.

_____

_____

_____

_____

_____

_____

_____

_____

5. Great care should be taken when attorneys request information over the telephone. Write a paragraph explaining how a physician's office can verify attorneys' inquiries.

_____

_____

_____

_____

_____

_____

_____

_____

FACSIMILE TRANSMISSION

6. Each facsimile transmission of sensitive material should have a cover sheet that includes the following information:

a. _____

b. _____

c. _____

d. _____

e. _____

INSURANCE FRAUD AND ABUSE

7. Match the terms in the first column with the definitions in the second column. Write the correct letter in each blank.

_____ fraud

_____ insurance abuse

_____ health care fraud

a. Knowingly and willfully executing, or attempting to execute, a scheme or artifact to defraud any health care benefit program; or to obtain, by false or fraudulent pretenses, representations, or promises, any of the money from, or under the custody or control of, a health care benefit program

b. An intentional deception or misrepresentation that an individual makes, knowing it to be false, which could result in some unauthorized benefit

c. Incidents or practices of providers, physicians, or suppliers of services and equipment which, while not considered fraudulent, are not consistent with accepted sound medical, business, or fiscal practices.

8. List five examples of practices that might fall in the fraud category.

a. _____

b. _____

c. _____

d. _____

e. _____

9. List three examples of practices that might fall in the abuse category.

a. _____

b. _____

c. _____

10. The Insurance Portability and Accountability Act of 1996 increases the penalty for submission of fraudulent claims up to _____ for each instance.

11. An insurance company that suspects fraud in a case has the legal right to examine the _____ _____ and _____ _____.

12. Cases of fraud are often detected when the patient receives a(n) _____ of _____ form from the insurance company.

13. To prevent inadvertent involvement in fraud, the health insurance specialist must be sure that all patient- and physician-submitted insurance information is accurate. List three things that should NEVER be done.

   a. _____

   b. _____

   c. _____

KNOW YOUR ACRONYMS

1. Define the following acronyms:

   a. HIPAA _____

   a. OIG _____

Introduction to Health Insurance

WHAT IS HEALTH INSURANCE?

1. Define the following terms:

a. insurance _____

_____

b. health insurance _____

_____

c. medical care _____

_____

d. health care _____

_____

e. preventive services _____

_____

f. disability insurance _____

_____

g. liability insurance _____

_____

MAJOR DEVELOPMENTS IN HEALTH INSURANCE

2. For the first 40 years of this century, medical practices were largely _____
_____ in _____ _____.

3. How did employer-sponsored medical or health insurance policies as employee incentives evolve?

_____

_____

_____

4. A group practice is defined by the American Medical Association as:

_____

_____

5. What happened in the early 1950s that increased paperwork resulting in practices having to increase the size of their billing staff? _____

_____

_____

6. The Physician's Current Procedural Terminology (CPT) system is published by the

_____ _____ _____

and is currently used on all outpatient claims in this country.

7. The standardization of diagnostic data on claims submitted by physicians today was achieved by adopting a diagnosis coding system known as the _____

_____ of _____ .

This system was developed by the _____ _____ _____ .

8. List three government-sponsored health care programs set up between 1965-66.

a. _____

b. _____

c. _____

9. In the late 1990s CHAMPUS was reorganized and the name was changed to _____ .

10. List the four categories of patients medical practices were dealing with by the early 1970s.

a. _____

b. _____

c. _____

d. _____

11. Define *deductible.* _____

_____

12. What attracted the attention of the general public to HMOs? _____

_____

d. HCFA _____

e. DRG _____

f. HCPCS _____

g. CCI _____

h. NPI _____

C H A P T E R

Managed Health Care

Four

WHAT IS MANAGED HEALTH CARE?

1. Write a paragraph describing managed health care.

_____

_____

_____

_____

2. Define covered lives. _____

_____

MANAGED CARE MODELS

3. List the six major MCO models in the country today.

   a. _____

   b. _____

   c. _____

   d. _____

   e. _____

   f. _____

4. A health care _____ _____ _____
   is an organization of affiliated provider sites combined under single ownership that offers the full
   spectrum of managed health care to subscribers. These affiliated provider sites include:

   a. _____

   b. _____

   c. _____

   d. _____

5. An HMO is a prepaid health care provider group practice serving a ____. (Circle the correct answer.)
   a. specific geographic area
   b. wide geographic area
   c. contracted geographic area

6. HMOs are concerned with promoting ____. (Circle the correct answer.)
   a. emergency services
   b. health and wellness
   c. easy access to medical care

7. HMOs assign all patients to a _____ _____
   _____ responsible for authorizing all referrals to other health care providers.

8. Some HMOs offer services to walk-in patients who are not members of the HMO. These nonmember patients are charged ____. (Circle the correct answer.)
   a. copay only
   b. deductible only
   c. fee-for-service

9. Which type of HMO do you belong to if the physicians are actually employees of the HMO and all health care services are provided within the corporate buildings? (Circle the correct answer.)
   a. group model HMO
   b. staff model HMO
   c. none of the above

10. Which type of HMO do you belong to if the HMO contracts with established multispecialty group practices to perform all HMO services? (Circle the correct answer.)
    a. group model HMO
    b. staff model HMO
    c. none of the above

11. HMO subscribers traveling outside the geographic area serviced by their HMO must remember to do what before obtaining nonemergency care outside the HMO? (Circle the correct answer.)
    a. contact a local HMO
    b. obtain a written referral
    c. call their HMO for authorization

12. Failure to obtain preauthorization may result in the HMO____. (Circle the correct answer.)
    a. refusing reimbursement
    b. canceling your membership
    c. transferring you to a new participating care provider (PCP)

13. The answer to each of the following statements is either true or false. Indicate your choice by placing **T** for a true statement or **F** for a false statement on the line provided.
    _____ a. IPAs are networks of individual health care providers who join together to provide prepaid health care to individuals and groups purchasing coverage.
    _____ b. Only HMOs may contract with an IPA for prepaid managed health care services for their group members.

_____ c. Health care providers in IPAs hire their own staff but may not maintain separate, private offices.

_____ d. The IPA patients are restricted to using plan ancillary service.

_____ e. IPA primary care physicians usually are paid on a fee-for-service basis.

_____ f. IPA specialists are usually paid on a negotiated fee-for-service basis.

_____ g. In the direct-contact model IPA, HMOs contract directly with the individual physicians rather than through an intermediary.

_____ h. The physicians in the direct-contact model IPA are paid only on a capitated basis.

14. In a POS plan, patients have freedom of choice to use what type of providers?

    a. _____

    b. _____

15. In an EPO plan, do the enrollees receive benefits if they opt to receive care from a provider who is not in the EPO? _____

16. PPO plans have a network of physicians and hospitals that have joined together to contract with insurance companies or regional organizations to provide health care to subscribers for a ____. (Circle the correct answer.)

    a. premium fee

    b. standard fee

    c. discounted fee

17. PPO plans usually do not have contracts for ____. (Circle the correct answer.)

    a. specialist services

    b. laboratory or pharmacy services

    c. hospital services

18. Most PPOs are _____ - _____ plans.

19. Describe a PHO. _____

_____

_____

20. Describe a PSO. _____

_____

_____

21. List three functions of the utilization review organization.

    a. _____

    b. _____

    c. _____

22. Another term for a utilization review organization is _____ - _____

_____ .

HMO ACCREDITATION

23. List the two organizations now evaluating HMOs.

    a. _____

    b. _____

24. List three ratings NCQA is required to give to plans that pass the accreditation process.

    a. _____

    b. _____

    c. _____

25. What is the status and function of the NCQA? _____

    _____

26. Describe the responsibilities of the JCAHO. _____

    _____

EFFECTS OF MANAGED CARE ON ADMINISTRATIVE PROCEDURES

27. Managed care programs have tremendous impact on a practice's administrative procedures. List a sampling of procedures that must be in place in a medical office.

    a. _____

    b. _____

    c. _____

    d. _____

    e. _____

    f. _____

Know Your Acronyms

28. Define the following acronyms:

    a. MCO _____

    b. IPA _____

    c. POS _____

    d. EPO _____

    e. PPO _____

    f. PHO _____

    g. PSO _____

    h. NCQA _____

    i. JCAHO _____

    j. URO _____

    k. TPA _____

CHAPTER 5 Five

Life Cycle of an Insurance Claim

DEVELOPMENT OF THE CLAIM

1. The development of an insurance claim begins when _____

_____

2. List three parts of insurance claim development.

   a. _____

   b. _____

   c. _____

NEW PATIENT INTERVIEW AND CHECK-IN PROCEDURES

3. Match the terms in the first column with the definitions in the second column. Write the correct letter in each blank.

   _____ primary care physician

   _____ established patient

   _____ encounter form

   _____ birthday rule

   _____ new patient

   _____ participating provider

   _____ new patient intake interview

   _____ primary care referral form

   _____ nonparticipating provider

   _____ case manager

   _____ health care specialist

   a. A person who has not received any professional service from the health care provider within the last 36 months

   b. The primary policy is the one taken out by policyholder with the earliest birthday occurring in the calendar year.

   c. This allows the office staff to gather preliminary data to check on the patient's insurance eligibility and benefit status.

   d. A medically trained person employed by a health insurance company to coordinate the health care of patients with long-term chronic conditions

   e. A form which is either hand carried by the patient or faxed to the specialist/ancillary services provider

   f. A health care provider who is not a primary care physician

   g. A provider who has no contractual relationship with the patient's insurance company, and has a legal right to expect the patient to pay the difference between the insurance allowed fee and the amount charged

   (terms continue on next page)

h. A person who has been seen within the last 36 months by the health care provider or another provider of the same specialty in the same group practice

i. The financial record source document used by the health care provider to record the patient's diagnosis and services rendered during the encounter

j. A family practitioner, internist, pediatrician, and in some insurance plans, a gynecologist, responsible for providing all routine primary health care for the patient

k. A provider who has a contract with the insurance company to provide medical services to subscribers and to accept the insurance company's determined allowed fee for the procedure performed

4. Are retroactive treatment plans valid? _____

POST CLINICAL CHECK-OUT PROCEDURES

5. Place in chronological order the following postclinical check-out procedures.

   a. Collect payment from the patient

   b. Code, if necessary, all procedures and diagnoses

   c. Post charges to the patient's ledger/account record

   d. Complete the insurance claim form

   e. Post any payment to the patient's account

   f. Enter the charges for procedures and/or services performed and total the charges

   Step 1: _____

   Step 2: _____

   Step 3: _____

   Step 4: _____

   Step 5: _____

   Step 6: _____

6. The _____ _____ is the permanent record of all the financial transactions between the patient and practice. Charges and personal or third-party payments are posted on the patient's account.

7. The manual of daily accounts receivable journal, also known as the _____ _____ is a chronological summary of all transactions posted to individual patient ledgers/accounts on a specific day.

8. What is a copay? _____

_____

9. What is a coinsurance payment? _____

_____

10. State the name of the insurance claim form used to report physician services. _____

_____

INSURANCE COMPANY PROCESSING OF A CLAIM

11. Use each of the following words or terms in a statement.

Noncovered procedure _____

_____

Unauthorized service _____

_____

Common data file _____

_____

Allowed charge _____

_____

Deductible _____

_____

Explanation of Benefits (EOB) _____

_____

12. The answer to each of the following statements is either true or false. Indicate your choice by placing **T** for a true statement or **F** for a false statement on the line provided.

_____ a. Patients may not be billed for uncovered or noncovered procedures.

_____ b. Patients may be billed for unauthorized services.

_____ c. Any service that is considered not "medically necessary" for the submitted diagnosis code may be disallowed.

_____ d. The "allowed charge" is the maximum amount the insurance company will pay for each procedure or service, according to the patient's policy.

_____ e. Payment may sometimes be greater than the fee submitted by the provider if the allowed amount is greater than the charge.

13. List five items the Explanation of Benefits (EOB) should contain.

a. _____

b. _____

c. _____

d. _____

e. _____

14. If the claim form stated that direct payment should be made to the physician, the reimbursement check and a copy of the EOB will be mailed to the physician. List three ways to accomplish this.

    a. _____

    b. _____

    c. _____

MAINTAINING PROVIDER INSURANCE CLAIM FILES

15. The federal Omnibus Budget Reconciliation Act of 1987 requires physicians to retain copies of any government insurance claim forms and all attachments filed by the provider for a period of ____. (Circle the correct answer.)

    a. 1 year

    b. 3 years

    c. 6 years

    d. forever

16. The federal Privacy Act of 1974 prohibits ____. (Circle the correct answer.)

    a. a patient from notifying the provider regarding payment or rejections of unassigned claims

    b. an insurer from notifying the provider regarding payment or rejections of unassigned claims

    c. the provider from appealing processing errors on unassigned claims

    d. an insurer from notifying the patient regarding payment or rejections of unassigned claims

Critical Thinking

17. Write a paragraph explaining the six steps that should be taken when an error in processing is found.

    _____

    _____

    _____

    _____

    _____

    _____

Know Your Acronyms

18. Define the following acronyms:

    a. PAR _____

    b. PCP _____

    c. EOB _____

Diagnosis Coding

ICD-9-CM

1. How has all coding of diagnoses on health insurance claims since 1979 been accomplished?

   _____

2. Who publishes the ICD-9-CM special edition? _____

3. Which law gives agencies the authority to levy fines against physicians found guilty of fraud and abuse?

   _____

4. Which agency has responsibility for administration of the government health care programs?

   _____

5. In 1989 HCFA required the coding of all _____ for all

   _____ - _____ medical insurance programs.

6. How often does NCHS update ICD-9-CM? _____

7. New diagnosis codes officially go into effect in what month? _____

8. What is the title of the new ICD-10?

   _____

PRIMARY VERSUS PRINCIPAL DIAGNOSIS

9. List the three general classifications of facilities in which an outpatient is treated.

   a. _____

   b. _____

   c. _____

10. Define *inpatient*. _____

    _____

11. Who stipulates the inpatient admission status? _____

12. Which type of coding uses a primary diagnosis criteria? _____

13. Which type of coding uses a principal diagnosis criteria? _____

14. To which diagnosis positions on the claim form are the concurrent or secondary conditions assigned?

    _____

15. What should be done if more than four diagnoses or symptoms are required to accurately report the conditions treated? _____

    _____

16. Define *principal diagnosis.* _____

    _____

17. What claim form is used for hospital billing? _____

Critical Thinking

18. Write a paragraph describing primary diagnosis, concurrent conditions, and secondary conditions.

    _____

    _____

    _____

    _____

    _____

PRINCIPAL VERSUS SECONDARY PROCEDURES

19. What do hospital coders use to code inpatient procedures? (Circle the correct answer.)

    a. Current Procedural Terminology coding system

    b. ICD-9-CM Volume III

    c. ICD-9-CM Volumes I & II

    d. any of the above

20. Outpatient procedures performed in the hospital are currently coded using the ____. (Circle the correct answer.)

    a. Current Procedural Terminology coding system

    b. ICD-9-CM Volume III

    c. ICD-9-CM Volumes I & II

    d. any of the above

21. The definition of a *principal procedure* is ____. (Circle the correct answer.)

    a. a procedure performed to treat a complication

    b. a procedure performed for definitive treatment

    c. a procedure performed which is most closely related to the principal diagnosis

    d. any of the above

CODING QUALIFIED DIAGNOSES

22. Define *qualified diagnosis.* _____

_____

23. List five examples of qualified diagnoses. (Do not use examples found in the textbook.)

a. _____

b. _____

c. _____

d. _____

e. _____

24. Are qualified diagnoses routinely coded on claim forms submitted from health care practitioners'

offices? _____

25. What do HCFA regulations permit on the HCFA-1500 claim form in place of qualified diagnoses?

_____

_____

ICD-9-CM CODING SYSTEM

26. Match the coding terms in the first column with the definitions in the second column. Write the correct letter in each blank.

_____ ICD-9 Volume I   a. Procedures Tabular List and Alphabetic Index

_____ ICD-9 Volume II   b. Disease Tabular List

_____ ICD-9 Volume III   c. Disease Index

27. Match the insurance terms in the first column with the definitions in the second column. Write the correct letter in each blank.

_____ V codes   a. External causes of injury and poisoning

_____ E codes   b. Tumor tissue type of neoplasms

_____ M codes   c. Factors influencing health status

28. Briefly define the three-part index to the Tabular List.

a. Section 1: _____

b. Section 2: _____

c. Section 3: _____

29. Define *Procedures Tabular List and Alphabetical Index (Volume III).*

_____

_____

DISEASE INDEX ORGANIZATION

30. Main terms are printed in _____ type and followed by the
    _____ _____ .

31. A list of _____ that qualify the main term or condition by describing differ-
    ences in site, etiology, or clinical status are indented 2 spaces under the main term.

32. Secondary qualifying conditions are indented 2 spaces under a _____ .

33. Always consult the code description in the _____ _____
    before assigning a code.

BASIC STEPS FOR USING THE INDEX

34. What is the first step for using the index? _____
    _____

35. Underline the main term in each of the following:
    a. Newborn anoxia
    b. Insect bite
    c. Radiation sickness
    d. Allergic bronchitis
    e. Infarction of brain stem
    f. Cranial nerve compression
    g. Erosion of the cornea
    h. Abdominal cramp

36. Assign codes to the following:
    a. Tension headache   _____
    b. Bronchial croup   _____
    c. Chronic conjunctivitis _____
    d. Acute confusion   _____
    e. Car sickness   _____
    f. Rosacea   _____

ORGANIZATION OF THE TABULAR LIST

37. ICD-9 codes for Chapters 1 through 17 are organized according to _____ -
    _____ category codes.

38. How is further clinical specificity achieved? _____
    _____

BASIC STEPS FOR USING THE TABULAR LIST

39. List the six basic steps for using the Tabular List.

   Step 1. _____

   Step 2. _____

   Step 3. _____

   Step 4. _____

   Step 5. _____

   Step 6. _____

INDEX CONVENTIONS

40. Match the coding terms in the first column with the definitions in the second column. Write the correct letter in each blank.

   _____ nonessential modifiers

   _____ boxed notes

   _____ cross references

   _____ eponyms

   _____ bracketed codes

   a. Warns the coder that specific fifth-digits will be required

   b. Diseases, disorders, or syndromes named after a person or place

   c. Secondary codes reported along with the primary code

   d. Main terms and subterms immediately followed by one or more terms, surrounded by parentheses

   e. Require investigation of additional main terms in the index

41. Assign codes to the following:

   a. Parkinson's disease _____

   b. Skene's gland abscess _____

   c. Stokes-Adams Syndrome _____

   d. Sprengel's Deformity _____

   e. Haglund's disease _____

42. Match the instructional cross references in the first column with the definitions in the second column. Write the correct letter in each blank.

   _____ See Category

   _____ See also

   _____ See condition

   _____ See

   a. Appears when an anatomical site is used as the main condition or the code description includes a more specific main term

   b. Indicates you have focused on the wrong term in the diagnostic statement

   c. Requires looking for a second main term before selecting a code

   d. Directs investigation of special conditions that appear in the Tabular List

43. In the index, what does NEC (not elsewhere classified) indicate?

_____

44. Assign codes to the following:

    a. Blindness due to injury NEC   _____

    b. Erythema, infectional NEC   _____

    c. Spontaneous hemorrhage NEC   _____

    d. Herpes zoster, specified site NEC   _____

    e. Eruption due to chemicals NEC   _____

45. When should you code directly from the index?

_____

46. Assign codes to the following (remember fifth-digits):

    a. Polydactyly of fingers   _____

    b. Sickle-cell crisis, NOS   _____

    c. Closed lateral dislocation of elbow _____

    d. Grand mal epilepsy without mention of
       intractable epilepsy   _____

    e. Classical migraine, intractable   _____

TABULAR LIST CONVENTIONS

47. All major disorders are printed in _____ .

48. What do bracketed numbers appearing below a fourth-digit code indicate? _____

_____

49. Assign codes to the following:

    a. Osteoarthrosis, generalized, hand   _____

    b. Chondrocalcinosis, unspecified, hand _____

    c. Allergic arthritis, multiple sites   _____

    d. Loose body in joint, shoulder region _____

    e. Loose body in knee   _____

50. Define *bracketed terms.* _____

51. Assign codes to the following:

    a. Abnormal electroencephalogram (EEG) _____

    b. Pyogenic arthritis, upper arm   _____

    c. Pediculus corporis   _____

    d. Dermatitis due to poison ivy   _____

52. Define *inclusion terms.* _____

53. Assign codes to the following:

    a. Coccidioidomysosis, unspecified   _____

    b. Splinter, cheek, without major open wound, infected   _____

    c. Sliding inguinal hernia, with gangrene, bilateral   _____

54. Define *excludes statement.* _____
_____

55. Assign codes to the following:

    a. Smokers' cough   _____

    b. Acute gingivitis   _____

    c. Anal and rectal polyp   _____

    d. Obstruction of gallbladder   _____

    e. Situs inversus   _____

56. Define *nonessential modifiers.* _____
_____

57. Assign codes to the following:

    a. Tonsillitis with influenza   _____

    b. Maxillary sinusitis   _____

    c. Hiatal hernia   _____

58. Define *brace.* _____
_____

59. Assign codes to the following:

    a. Hypertrophy of tonsils with adenoids   _____

    b. Cirrhosis of lung   _____

    c. Rupture of appendix with generalized peritonitis   _____

    d. Hiatal hernia with gangrene   _____

    e. Diverticulum of appendix   _____

60. What does each modifier found after the colon do? _____

61. Assign codes to the following:

    a. Chronic tracheobronchitis   _____

    b. Bronchopneumonia with influenza   _____

    c. Dermatitis due to acids   _____

62. What does the abbreviation NOS indicate? _____

63. Assign codes to the following:

    a. Acute sore throat NOS   _____

    b. Femoral hernia, unilateral NOS   _____

    c. Transfusion reaction NOS   _____

    d. Acute cerebrovascular insufficiency NOS   _____

    e. Unspecified peritonitis NOS   _____

64. What does a "code first" notation indicate? _____

65. When a "code first" notation appears, should the underlying disease or the disease manifestation be coded first? _____

66. Assign codes to the following case studies, giving special attention to the words "code first" and assign codes in the correct order:

	First Code	Second Code
a. Patient presents with myotonic cataract resulting from Thomsen's disease	_____	_____
b. Patient presents with postinfectious encephalitis resulting from post-measles	_____	_____
c. Patient presents with cerebral degeneration in generalized lipidoses resulting from Fabry's disease	_____	_____
d. Patient presents with parasitic infestation of eyelid caused by pediculosis	_____	_____
e. Patient presents with xanthelasma of the eyelid resulting from lipoprotein deficiencies	_____	_____

67. Assign codes to the following case studies, giving special attention to the word "and." (Some cases may require two codes; other cases require only one code.)

	First Code	Second Code
a. Patient presents with degenerative disorders of eyelid and periocular area, unspecified	_____	_____
b. Patient presents with acute and chronic conjunctivitis	_____	_____
c. Patient presents with cholesteatoma of middle ear and mastoid	_____	_____
d. Patient presents with psoriatic arthropathy and parapsoriasis	_____	_____
e. Patient presents with nausea and vomiting	_____	_____
f. Patient presents with headache and throat pain	_____	_____

68. Assign codes to the following, giving special attention to the word "with":

    a. Rheumatic fever with heart involvement   _____

    b. Diverticulosis with diverticulitis   _____

c. Acute lung edema with heart disease   _____

d. Emphysema with acute and chronic bronchitis   _____

e. Fracture fibula (closed) with tibia   _____

f. Varicose vein with inflammation and ulcer   _____

WORKING WITH INDEX TABLES

69. The answer to each of the following statements is either true or false. Indicate your choice by placing **T** for a true statement or **F** for a false statement on the line provided.

_____ a. The Hypertension/Hypertensive Table provides a complete listing of Hypertension and a list of all the various conditions normally associated with it.

_____ b. It is not always necessary to check the Tabular List before assigning a final code for hypertension/hypertensive conditions.

_____ c. When "with" separates two conditions in the diagnostic statement only one code is needed.

_____ d. Secondary hypertension is a unique and separate condition listed on the table.

_____ e. The fourth digit 9 should be used sparingly.

70. Assign codes to the following:

a. Hypertension, benign   _____

b. Chronic hypertension, malignant   _____

c. Hypertension due to brain tumor, unspecified   _____

d. Malignant hypertension with congestive heart failure   _____

e. Newborn affected by maternal hypertension   _____

71. Define the following terms:

a. neoplasms _____

b. benign _____

c. malignant _____

d. lesion _____

72. When must a lesion be coded as benign? _____

_____

73. List five examples of benign lesions.

a. _____

b. _____

c. _____

d. _____

e. _____

74. Match the neoplasm classifications in the first column with the definitions in the second column. Write the correct letter in each blank.

_____ primary malignancy	a. A malignant tumor that is localized
_____ secondary malignancy	b. There is no indication of the histology or nature of the tumor
_____ carcinoma *in situ*	
_____ uncertain behavior	c. It is not possible to predict subsequent behavior from the submitted specimen
_____ unspecified nature	d. The tumor has spread
	e. The original tumor site

75. How are M codes used? _____

_____

76. Assign codes to the following:

a. Hodgkin's sarcoma   _____

b. Ovarian fibroma   _____

c. Bronchial adenoma   _____

d. Carcinoma of oral cavity and pharynx   _____

e. Chronic lymphocytic leukemia   _____

f. Reticulosarcoma, intrathoracic   _____

g. Adenocarcinoma of rectum and anus   _____

h. Benign lymphoma of breast   _____

i. Carcinoid small intestine   _____

j. Multiple myeloma   _____

k. Lipoma, right kidney   _____

77. What is the Table of Drugs and Chemicals used for? _____

_____

78. Define *adverse effect* or *reaction*.

_____

_____

79. What are E codes used for in regard to poisoning? _____

_____

80. Describe when an E code might be used as the primary code for poisoning? _____

_____

81. Assign codes to the following, using E codes where applicable.

	First Code	Second Code
a. Poisoning due to isopropyl alcohol	_____	_____
b. Poisoning due to amino acid	_____	_____
c. Suicide attempt, overdose of tranquilizers	_____	_____
d. Accidental methadone poisoning	_____	_____
e. Poisoning due to therapeutic use of codeine	_____	_____
f. Brain damage due to allergic reaction to penicillin	_____	_____

82. V codes are supplementary classifications of factors influencing the person's _____ _____.

83. List the three types of V code categories.

a. _____

b. _____

c. _____

84. Assign codes to the following:

a. Exercise counseling _____

b. History of alcoholism _____

c. Counseling for parent/child conflict,

   unspecified _____

d. Screening, cancer, unspecified _____

e. Follow-up exam, post-surgery _____

f. Health check, not pediatric _____

g. Routine child health check _____

h. Fitting of artificial eye _____

i. Flu Shot _____

j. Family history of breast cancer _____

k. Observation for suspected tuberculosis _____

CODING SPECIAL DISORDERS

85. What precautions should a coder take before putting the HIV/AIDS code on a claim form?

_____

86. If the diagnostic statement does not specify whether a fracture is opened or closed, which one should the coder select? _____

87. Assign codes to the following:

    a. Fracture of base of skull with cerebral contusion   _____

    b. Open fracture of nasal bones   _____

    c. Fifth cervical vertebra fracture, closed   _____

    d. Open fracture coccyx with other spinal cord injury   _____

    e. Closed fracture of three ribs   _____

    f. Closed fracture of clavicle   _____

    g. Open finger fracture   _____

    h. Bennett's fracture, closed   _____

    i. Fracture of head of tibia   _____

    j. Heel bone fracture, closed   _____

88. Define *late effect*. _____

89. When coding a late effect, the primary code is the _____ condition and the secondary code represents the _____ condition or etiology of the late effect.

90. Assign codes to the following in the correct order:

	First Code	Second Code
a. Scarring due to third-degree burn of left arm	_____	_____
b. Nonunion fracture of neck of femur	_____	_____
c. Esophageal stricture due to old lye burn of esophagus	_____	_____
a. Hemiplegia due to old CVA	_____	_____

91. The percentage of total body area or surface affected by burns follows the

    " _____ _____ _____ ."

92. Assign codes to the following:

	First Code	Second Code	Third Code
a. Second-degree burn, right upper arm and shoulder	_____	_____	_____
b. Third-degree burn, trunk, 35% body surface	_____	_____	_____
c. Burn of mouth, pharynx, and esophagus	_____	_____	_____
d. Blisters on back of hand and palm	_____	_____	_____
e. Erythema on forearm and elbow	_____	_____	_____
f. Deep third-degree burn with loss of thumb	_____	_____	_____

93. Describe why a coder might use E codes on physician claims. _____

_____

94. Assign E codes to the following; adding a second code when the place of occurren

First Code

a. Assault by hanging and strangulation   _____

b. Unarmed fight   _____

c. Self-inflicted injury by crashing of motor vehicle, highway   _____   ___

d. Exposure to noise at nightclub   _____   _____

e. Struck accidentally by falling rock at quarry   _____   _____

f. Struck by thrown ball at baseball field   _____   _____

g. Caught accidentally in escalator at amusement park   _____   _____

h. Dog bite   _____   _____

i. Accidental poisoning from shellfish at restaurant   _____   _____

j. Foreign object left in body during surgical operation   _____   _____

k. Fall from ladder at home   _____   _____

l. Accident caused by hunting rifle at rifle range   _____   _____

HCFA ICD-9-CM GUIDELINES

95. Codes are to be selected according to the highest level of _____ .

96. Indicate which of the following codes need to be carried out to the highest level of specificity by writing the correct code in the space provided.

_____ a. 464.2 Acute laryngotracheitis without mention of obstruction

_____ b. 393 Chronic rheumatic pericarditis

_____ c. 690 Cradle cap

_____ d. 574.2 Calculus of gallbladder without mention of cholecystitis, without obstruction

_____ e. 570 Acute and subacute necrosis of liver

_____ f. 571.4 Chronic persistent hepatitis

_____ g. 914 Infected blister of the hand

97. Describe how diagnoses documented as "probable," "suspected," "questionable," or "ruled out" should be coded. _____

_____

98. A 45-year-old patient presents with polyuria and polydipsia. The physician documents "suspected diabetes mellitus." Circle the correct diagnoses to be coded.

a. diabetes mellitus type II (adult-onset)

b. diabetes mellitus with other specified manifestations

c. polyuria; polydipsia; diabetes mellitus

d. polyuria; polydipsia

tient presents with a blood pressure of 150/90 and is asked to rest for 10 minutes. Upon reevalu-
tion the blood pressure is 130/80. The patient is asked to return to the office in two weeks to rule
out hypertension. Circle the correct diagnosis to be coded.

   a. hypertension

   b. elevated blood pressure

   c. observation for suspected cardiovascular disease

   d. personal history of other specified circulatory disorder

100. A patient presents with wheezing and a productive cough. The physician recorded "probable bronchitis, pending chest x-ray results." X-ray results confirmed bronchitis. During this visit the patient's
glucose was checked to determine the status of his diabetes. The patient reported that his previous
indigestion and diarrhea were currently not a problem. Circle the correct diagnoses to be coded.

   a. productive cough

   b. productive cough; indigestion; diarrhea

   c. bronchitis; diabetes mellitus

   d. bronchitis; diabetes mellitus; indigestion; diarrhea

101. A patient presents complaining of tenderness in the left breast and a family history of breast cancer.
Upon examination, the physician discovers a small lump in the left breast. The patient is referred to a
breast surgeon and x-ray for a mammogram. The physician records questionable breast cancer of the
left breast. Circle the correct diagnoses to be coded.

   a. breast cancer

   b. family history of breast cancer

   c. breast pain; breast cancer

   d. breast lump; breast pain; family history of breast cancer

OFFICE PROCEDURE ERRORS CONTRIBUTING TO INACCURATE DIAGNOSIS CODING

Critical Thinking

102. Write a paragraph describing various errors contributing to inaccurate diagnosis coding.

_____

_____

_____

_____

_____

Know Your Acronyms

103. Define the following acronyms:

   a. ICD-9-CM _____

   b. NCHS _____

   c. NEC _____

   d. NOS _____

CPT™ Procedure Coding

CPT CODING SYSTEM

1. Describe circumstances in which the CPT coding system is used to report services rendered.

   _____

   _____

2. CPT is updated _____. (Circle the correct answer.)
   a. annually
   b. semi-annually
   c. every 2 years

3. The updated version of CPT is released in _____. (Circle the correct answer.)
   a. January
   b. late spring
   c. late fall

4. The CPT effective date is _____. (Circle the correct answer.)
   a. January 1
   b. June 1
   c. September 1

5. What must each procedure submitted on a claim be linked to? _____

   _____

CPT FORMAT

6. List the six sections of the CPT code. (List in the order in which they appear.)

   a. _____

   b. _____

   c. _____

   d. _____

   e. _____

   f. _____

7. Where are the Evaluation and Management codes located? _____

8. Describe the contents of the following:

    Appendix A _____

    Appendix B _____

    Appendix C _____

    Appendix D _____

    Appendix E _____

    Appendix F _____

9. The CPT coding system is based on a _____ - _____ main number that describes each type of service. (Circle the correct answer.)

    a. two-digit

    b. four-digit

    c. five-digit

10. A _____ - _____ code modifier may be added after the main number when necessary to indicate that additional factors should be considered. (Circle the correct answer.)

    a. two-digit

    b. four-digit

    c. five-digit

CPT SYMBOLS AND CONVENTIONS

11. Match the CPT symbol in the first column with the definitions in the second column. Write the correct letter in each blank.

    _____ bullet

    _____ triangle

    _____ horizontal triangles

    _____ semicolon

    _____ asterisk

    _____ circle with slash

    _____ plus symbol

    a. The code is not to be used with modifier -51

    b. A new code

    c. An add-on code

    d. Surgery is billed on a fee-for-service basis

    e. Note text to highlight changes in wording

    f. Code description has been significantly altered

    g. Separates main and subordinate clauses in code descriptions

12. Describe *section guidelines*. _____

    _____

13. What is boldface type used for? _____

CPT INDEX

14. Complete the following sentences:

    a. The CPT index is primarily organized by _____ .

    b. Cross references that begin with the word "See" provide instruction to _____

    _____

    c. Cross references followed by the phrase "See also" provide instruction to refer to a specified main term if the _____

    _____

15. Describe what *main terms* represent. _____

_____

BASIC STEPS FOR CODING PROCEDURES

16. List the seven basic steps for coding procedures.

Step 1: _____

_____

Step 2: _____

_____

Step 3: _____

Step 4: _____

_____

Step 5: _____

_____

Step 6: _____

_____

Step 7: _____

_____

17. Using only the index, write the code or range of codes to be investigated. In addition, underline the main term you referenced in the index.

    a. ankle amputation   _____

    b. lower arm biopsy   _____

    c. artery angioplasty   _____

    d. bone marrow aspiration   _____

    e. bladder aspiration   _____

    f. bladder resection   _____

    g. rib resection   _____

    h. salivary duct dilation   _____

    i. wrist disarticulation   _____

    j. drinking test for glaucoma _____

    k. Dwyer procedure   _____

    l. new patient office visit _____

    m. well-baby care   _____

    n. wound repair of pancreas _____

    o. inpatient hospital discharge _____

    p. house calls   _____

18. List five words/phrases used in the insurance industry that define a surgical procedure.

    a. _____

    b. _____

    c. _____

    d. _____

    e. _____

19. What are the three questions that must be asked to code surgeries properly?

    a. _____

    b. _____

    c. _____

20. CPT divides surgical procedures into which two main groups? _____

21. List three services/procedures included in a surgical package.

    a. _____

    b. _____

    c. _____

22. On what basis are minor surgeries to be billed? _____

23. Briefly describe *unbundling*. _____

24. Assign codes to the following: (If an asterisk appears, include it in your answer.)

    a. removal of foreign body in tendon sheath, simple   _____

    b. puncture aspiration of cyst of breast   _____

    c. incision and drainage of thyroid gland cyst   _____

    d. abrasion, single lesion   _____

    e. destruction of four flat warts   _____

    f. incision and drainage of ankle abscess   _____

    g. incision and drainage of wrist hematoma   _____

    h. aspiration thyroid cyst   _____

    i. laparoscopy with bilateral total pelvic
       lymphadenenctomy and peri-aortic lymph node biopsy   _____

25. Describe when a code qualified with the phrase "separate procedure" is used. _____

    _____

    _____

26. Assign codes to the following, giving special attention to "separate procedure."

    a. removal of impacted vaginal foreign body   _____

    b. dilation of cervical canal, instrumental   _____

    c. pleurectomy, parietal   _____

    d. thoracentesis with insertion of tube   _____

    e. laryngoscopy endoscopy, indirect   _____

    f. biopsy of testis, incisional   _____

27. Define *multiple surgical procedure.* _____

    _____

28. What is added to the CPT number for each lesser surgical procedure that does not have the symbol ∅ in front of the code? _____

Critical Thinking

29. Write a paragraph describing why multiple surgical procedures are ranked into major and lesser procedures.

    _____

    _____

    _____

    _____

NOTES FOR CODING SPECIAL SURGERY CASES

30. Define the following terms:

    a. skin lesion _____

    b. excision of a lesion _____

    c. destruction of a lesion _____

31. List five things you must know when reporting the excision or destruction of lesions.

    a. _____

    b. _____

    c. _____

    d. _____

    e. _____

32. Layered closure requires the use of two codes: one for the _____, and one for an _____ _____.

33. If a physician reports the size of a lesion in inches what must the coder do? _____

    _____

34. When converting the size of a lesion, one inch equals _____ .

35. When there are multiple lacerations, which repair should be listed first? _____

    _____

36. Assign codes to the following; then convert inches to centimeters.

    a. excision, 1 inch benign lesion, left leg   _____   _____

    b. excision, 1/2 inch malignant lesion, finger   _____   _____

    c. simple repair of a 2 inch laceration on the right foot   _____   _____

    d. intermediate repair of a 5 inch laceration of the back   _____   _____

    e. layer closure of a 3 inch wound of the neck   _____   _____

    f. repair of laceration, 2.0 cm, anterior two-thirds of tongue   _____   _____

37. What are the six questions that must be asked to code fractures/dislocations correctly?

    a. _____

    b. _____

    c. _____

    d. _____

    e. _____

    f. _____

38. Match the fracture terms in the first column with the definitions in the second column. Write the correct letter in each blank.

    _____ closed fracture treatment   a. The application of manually applied forces to restore normal anatomical alignment

    _____ open fracture treatment

    _____ manipulation of a fracture   b. Open reduction with internal fixation

    _____ reduction of a fracture   c. The fracture site was not surgically opened

    _____ ORIF   d. The fracture site was surgically opened, bone ends visualized, aligned, and internal fixation may have been applied

                                         e. A fixation device has been applied

39. When is arthrotomy considered the primary procedure? _____

_____

40. Assign codes to the following:

    a. open treatment of fracture great toe, phalanx, with external fixation   _____

    b. closed treatment of nasal bone fracture with stabilization   _____

    c. treatment of closed elbow dislocation; without anesthesia   _____

    d. closed treatment of ulnar fracture, proximal end; with manipulation   _____

    e. open treatment of maxillary fracture   _____

    f. closed treatment of shoulder dislocation, with manipulation; requiring anesthesia   _____

    g. Surgical elbow arthroscopy, with removal of loose body   _____

    h. diagnostic hip arthroscopy, with synovial biopsy   _____

41. Endoscopy codes in CPT are classified according to: (list four)

a. _____

b. _____

c. _____

d. _____

42. Complete the following sentences:

a. Endoscopies of the digestive system are always coded to the furthest site reached by the

_____ .

b. Endoscopic guidewire dilation involves the passage of a guidewire through an endoscope into the

_____ .

c. Indirect laryngoscopy means the larynx was visualized by using a warm laryngeal

_____ .

d. Direct laryngoscopy was performed by passage of a rigid or fiberoptic endoscopy into the

_____ .

43. Assign codes to the following:

a. surgical wrist endoscopy with release of
   transverse carpal ligament   _____

b. flexible esophagoscopy with single biopsy   _____

c. direct operative laryngoscopy with foreign body removal   _____

d. flexible colonoscopy with biopsy   _____

e. rigid proctosigmoidoscopy with dilation   _____

MEDICINE SECTION OVERVIEW

44. The medicine section starts with what code? _____

45. When a physician performs only one component of a test, what modifier should be added to the global code to indicate the full procedure was not performed? _____

46. The special services and reports section is a miscellaneous section which covers services considered to be _____ as _____ to basic services provided to the patient.

47. How are psychiatric consultations reported? _____

_____

48. Are psychiatric codes reserved for use only by psychiatrists? _____

49. Assign codes to the following:

a. right heart cardiac catheterization, for congenital
   cardiac anomalies   _____

b. medical testimony   _____

c. services requested between 10:00PM and 8:00AM in
   addition to basic service   _____

d. acupuncture; one or more needles, with
   electrical stimulation   _____

e. wheelchair management/propulsion training, 15 minutes _____

f. massage therapy, 45 min   _____

g. extended medical report preparation   _____

h. family psychotherapy without the patient present   _____

i. hypnotherapy   _____

j. nonpressurized inhalation treatment for acute
   airway obstruction   _____

k. educational video tapes for the patient   _____

l. one hour of psychological testing with interpretation
   and report   _____

RADIOLOGY SECTION OVERVIEW

50. Define *radiologic views.* _____

51. Describe the professional services component of a radiologic examination. _____
    _____
    _____

52. Describe the technical service component of a radiologic examination. _____
    _____

53. Assign codes to the following:

    a. complete radiologic examination of the mandible   _____

    b. urography, retrograde   _____

    c. pelvimetry   _____

    d. orthoroentgenogram, scanogram   _____

    e. chest x-ray, two views, with fluoroscopy   _____

    f. x-ray of facial bones, four views   _____

    g. CAT scan of the abdomen, with contrast   _____

    h. gastroesophageal reflux study   _____

    i. x-ray of the cervical spine, two views   _____

    j. barium enema   _____

    k. cardiac shunt detection   _____

    l. splenoportography   _____

    m. x-ray of the scapula, complete   _____

    n. x-ray of the forearm   _____

    o. hip x-ray, three views   _____

54. How would a coder locate the list of panel options? _____
_____

55. Describe the use of the following sections:

    a. drug testing _____
    _____

    b. therapeutic drug assays _____
    _____

    c. evocative/suppression testing _____
    _____

56. Assign codes to the following:

    a. red blood cell count   _____

    b. blood gases pH only   _____

    c. glucose-6-phosphate dehydrogenase screen   _____

    d. glucose tolerance test, three specimens   _____

    e. KOH prep   _____

    f. HIV antibody confirmatory test   _____

    g. leptospira   _____

    h. HDL cholesterol   _____

    i. glucose reagent strip   _____

    j. occult blood, feces   _____

    k. PKU   _____

    l. rapid test for infection, screen, each antibody   _____

    m. pregnancy test, urine   _____

    n. herpes simples virus, quantification   _____

    o. urinary potassium   _____

    p. urine dip, non-automated, without microscopy   _____

    q. triglycerides   _____

    r. cholesterol, serum, total   _____

    s. TSH   _____

EVALUATION AND MANAGEMENT SERVICES OVERVIEW

57. To properly assign an evaluation and management code, what three factors must be considered?

    a. _____
    b. _____
    c. _____

58. Define *new patient.* _____

_____

_____

59. Define *established patient.* _____

_____

_____

60. The answer to each of the following statements is either true or false. Indicate your choice by placing **T** for a true statement or **F** for a false statement on the line provided.

_____ a. The hospital is required to have a designated or official observation unit for hospital observation service codes to qualify.

_____ b. The inpatient hospital visit covers the first hospital inpatient encounter the admitting physician has with the patient for each admission.

_____ c. Subsequent hospital visits include review of the patient's chart, results of diagnostic studies, and/or reassessment of the patient's condition since the last assessment by the physician.

_____ d. The observation care discharge code is reported if the patient is admitted to that same hospital as an inpatient.

_____ e. Consultants may not initiate diagnostic and/or therapeutic services as necessary during the consultative encounter.

_____ f. There are no codes for follow-up office consultation.

_____ g. A preoperative clearance is not considered a consultation when the referring physician is the patient's primary care physician.

_____ h. A confirmatory consultation is an E&M service requested by the patient's health care provider.

_____ i. Nursing facility services do not include services performed at skilled care facilities.

_____ j. Domiciliary care covers medical services provided to patients who live in custodial care or boarding home facilities that do not provide 24-hour nursing care.

61. List four levels of complexity that are assigned to the patient history and physical examination.

a. _____

b. _____

c. _____

d. _____

62. Assign codes to the following:

a. follow-up inpatient consult, expanded _____

b. subsequent nursing facility care, problem focused _____

c. initial office visit, problem focused _____

d. follow-up office visit, comprehensive _____

e. initial observation care, detailed   _____

f. initial hospital care, low severity   _____

g. subsequent hospital care, expanded   _____

h. initial home visit, detailed   _____

i. follow-up home visit, comprehensive   _____

j. observation care discharge   _____

k. initial inpatient consult, detailed   _____

l. initial confirmatory consult, problem focused   _____

m. emergency dept. visit, comprehensive   _____

n. physician direction of EMS emergency care   _____

o. nursing facility assessment, comprehensive   _____

p. new patient rest home visit, expanded   _____

q. follow-up rest home visit, expanded   _____

r. office consult, problem focused   _____

63. Fill in the blanks using the definitions provided.

a. Medical emergency care to critically ill patients that requires the constant attendance of a physician and that is usually administered in the critical or emergency care facilities of the hospital is known as _____ .

b. _____ is used for reporting services performed by physicians for critically ill neonates/infants.

c. _____ is used in addition to the regular visit or consultation codes when the typical treatment exceeds, by 30 minutes or more, the time described in the CPT description of the visit.

d. _____ allows for the reporting of cases in which the physician spends a prolonged period of time without patient contact waiting for an event to happen that will require his/her services.

e. _____ is the process in which an attending physician coordinates and supervises the care given to a patient by other health care providers.

f. _____ covers the physician's time spent supervising a complex and multidisciplinary care treatment program for a specific patient who is under the care of a home health agency, hospice, or nursing facility.

g. Routine examinations or risk management counseling for children and adults exhibiting no overt signs or symptoms of a disorder while presenting to the medical office for a preventive medical physical are _____ .

h. Examination of normal or high-risk neonates in the hospital or other locations, subsequent newborn care in a hospital, and resuscitation of high-risk babies is _____ .

64. Assign codes to the following:

a. operative physician standby, 30 minutes   _____

b. critical care, first hour   _____

c. established well-child check-up, age 7   _____

d. prolonged office care with direct patient contact, one hour   _____

e. complex telephone call with a distraught patient   _____

f. initial inpatient history and examination of normal newborn   _____

g. periodic preventive medicine, age 52   _____

h. initial well-baby check-up, 6 months old   _____

i. telephone call to discuss test results in detail   _____

CPT MODIFIERS

65. Explain why modifiers are added to CPT codes. _____

_____

66. Assign codes and modifiers to the following:

a. bilateral partial mastectomy   _____

b. vasovasostomy discontinued after anesthesia due to
   heart arrhythmia, hospital outpatient   _____

c. decision for surgery during initial office visit, comprehensive   _____

d. expanded office visit for follow-up to mastectomy,
   new onset diabetes was discovered and treated   _____

e. cholecystectomy, postoperative management only   _____

f. difficult and complicated resection of external cardiac tumor   _____

g. hemorrhoidectomy by simple ligature discontinued prior
   to anesthesia due to severe drop in blood pressure,
   hospital outpatient   _____

h. assistant surgeon, modified radical mastectomy   _____

i. total abdominal hysterectomy, preoperative management only   _____

j. total urethrectomy, including cystostomy, female,
   surgical care only   _____

k. simple repair of a 2 inch laceration on the right foot
   discontinued due to severe dizziness, physician's office   _____

67. Assign codes to the following:

	First Code	Second Code
a. tonsillectomy and adenoidectomy, age 10 and a wart removed from the patient's neck while in the OR.	_____	_____
b. excision, malignant lesion 0.6 to 1.0 cm, face and layer closure of wounds of face, 2.0 cm	_____	_____
c. incision and drainage, perianal abscess, superficial and puncture aspiration of abscess, hematoma, cyst	_____	_____

Know Your Acronyms

68. Define the following acronyms:

    a. CPT _____

    b. ORIF _____

    c. NSF _____

    d. HPI _____

    e. ROS _____

    f. NICU _____

HCPCS Procedure Coding System

HCPCS - PROCEDURE CODE ORGANIZATION

1. How many code levels are associated with HCPCS? (Circle the correct answer.)
   a. two
   b. three
   c. four

2. Level I codes are developed and published by ____. (Circle the correct answer.)
   a. AMA
   b. HCFA
   c. LMC

3. J codes are found in which level? (Circle the correct answer.)
   a. Level I
   b. Level II
   c. Level III

4. Level II codes identify the services of ____. (Circle the correct answers.)
   a. dentists
   b. speech therapists
   c. durable medical equipment

5. J codes list ____. (Circle the correct answer.)
   a. pathology and laboratory
   b. durable medical equipment
   c. medications

6. Who is responsible for the annual updates to HCPCS Level II? (Circle the correct answer.)
   a. AMA
   b. HCFA
   c. LMC

7. Level III codes are assigned by ____. (Circle the correct answer.)
   a. AMA
   b. HCFA
   c. LMC

HCPCS NATIONAL LEVEL II CODES

8. Is HCFA responsible for errors that might occur in or from the use of private printings of HCPCS Level II Codes? _____

9. Who updates codes in the Level II D Series? _____

THE NATIONAL HCPCS INDEX

10. Because of the wide variety of services and procedures described in HCPCS Level II, the _____ _____ is very helpful in finding the correct code.

11. When looking up a code in the Level II index, it is important to verify the code in the _____ section of the codebook.

12. Assign codes to the following:

    a. injection, aminophylline, up to 250 mg _____

    b. elbow orthosis; elastic with metal joints _____

    c. ambulance service; BLS, non-emergency transport _____

    d. alcohol wipes, 2 boxes _____

    e. amputee adapter, wheelchair _____

    f. wound cleanser _____

    g. artificial larynx _____

    h. ultrasonic generator filter _____

    i. IPD supply kit _____

    j. infusion pump, insulin _____

    k. hypertonic saline solution _____

    l. ambulance oxygen _____

    m. rocking bed _____

    n. complete upper dentures _____

    o. breast prosthesis, adhesive skin support _____

    p. culture sensitivity study _____

    q. nasogastric tubing, with stylet _____

    r. pinworm examination _____

    s. plasma, single donor, fresh frozen _____

    t. frames purchases _____

    u. hearing aid, monaural, behind the ear _____

    v. routine venipuncture for collection of specimens _____

    w. assessment for hearing aid _____

    x. transportation of x-ray to nursing home, one patient _____

    y. speech screening _____

    z. noncoring needle _____

DETERMINING CARRIER RESPONSIBILITY

13. National codes beginning with D, G, M, P, or R fall under the jurisdiction of the ____. (Circle the correct answer.)

    a. DMERC

    b. LMC

    c. DMEPOS

14. The ____ is responsible for Level II codes beginning with B, E, K, and L. (Circle the correct answer.)

    a. DMERC

    b. LMC

    c. DMEPOS

15. Codes beginning with A, J, Q, and V may be assigned to the ____. (Circle the correct answers.)

    a. DMERC

    b. LMC

    c. DMEPOS

16. The answer to each of the following statements is either true or false. Indicate your choice by placing **T** for a true statement or **F** for a false statement on the line provided.

    _____ a. Because DME billings were out of control, HCFA decided to have all DME claims processed by only four regional carriers, the DMERCs.

    _____ b. Providers dispensing medical equipment and supplies must register with a DMERC.

    _____ c. When a Medicare patient is treated for a fractured leg and supplied with crutches, only one claim is generated and sent to the DMERC.

    _____ d. If the doctor is not registered with the DMERC, the patient is billed directly for the medical equipment.

    _____ e. Most dental procedures are included as Medicare benefits

    _____ f. New medical and surgical services may first be assigned a Level II code because the review procedures for adding new codes to Level II is a much shorter process.

HCPCS MODIFIERS

17. Explain why Level II and Level III modifiers are added to codes. _____

    _____

18. Assign codes and HCPCS modifiers to the following:

    a. family psychotherapy without the patient present, by a clinical psychologist   _____

    b. psychoanalysis, by a clinical social worker   _____

    c. initial office visit, problem focused, by a nurse practitioner in a rural area   _____

    d. new three-prong cane   _____

    e. tooth reimplantation of accidentally displaced tooth, emergency treatment   _____

f. emergency ambulance transport (BLS), all inclusive, from physician's office to hospital   _____

g. dental radiographs, bitewing, single film, left side   _____

h. portable whirlpool, new when rented   _____

i. chemotherapy administration by infusion technique only, physician providing service in a rural HMSA   _____

j. rented loop heel wheelchair   _____

k. initial well-adult check-up, age 67, waiver of liability statement on file   _____

l. initial home visit, detail changed to initial home visit, expanded because it was incorrect on the original claim   _____

m. non-emergency ambulance transport (BLS), all inclusive from hospital to skilled nursing home   _____

n. anesthesia for amputation of upper 2/3 of femur, complicated by total body hypothermia   _____

o. expanded follow-up inpatient consult provided by a substitute physician under a reciprocal billing arrangement   _____

p. custom made plastic prosthetic right eye   _____

q. left ankle splint for foot drop   _____

r. second opinion language screening ordered by a professional review organization   _____

s. five-minute follow-up BP check by a physician's assistant   _____

Know Your Acronyms

19. Define the following acronyms:

a. HCPCS _____

b. DME   _____

c. DMERC _____

d. DMEPOS _____

e. ABN   _____

f. CIM   _____

g. HCFA _____

h. HPSA _____

i. LMC   _____

j. MCM   _____

HCFA Reimbursement Issues

INTRODUCTION

1. Complete the following sentences:

   a. HCFA implemented the Diagnosis Related Groups Prospective Payment System to control the

   _____

   b. Medicare law requires physician payments to be based on a _____

   _____

   c. The RBRVS system divided all services into relative value units or payment components of

   _____

   d. The limiting charge placed on physicians who do not sign a Medicare participation agreement is set at 115 percent of the _____

THE MEDICARE FEE SCHEDULE

1. Match the insurance terms in the first column with the definitions in the second column. Write the correct letter in each blank.

   _____ Local Medicare Carriers

   _____ limiting charge

   _____ "J" codes

   _____ federal register

   _____ balance billing

   _____ DMEPOS

   a. The maximum fee a doctor may charge for services

   b. Publishes new payment values for procedure codes

   c. Establishes the payment schedule for supplies and equipment within HCFA specified guidelines

   d. Billing adjusted amounts to beneficiaries

   e. Medications

   f. Translates the HCPCS RVUs, GPCIs, and CF into a fee schedule and distributes it to enrolled providers

HCFA REGULATIONS

3. Who enacts Medicare legislation? (Circle the correct answer.)

    a. local Medicare carriers

    b. Congress

    c. HCFA

4. Medicare guidelines state that the ___ is responsible for knowing all rules that apply to services billed to the program. (Circle the correct answer.)

    a. patient

    b. coder

    c. provider

5. What has Medicare issued to Nurse Practitioners and Physician Assistants so that their services can be billed directly to Medicare? (Circle the correct answer.)

    a. special provider numbers

    b. a special billing address

    c. special TOS codes

6. Nurse Practitioners and Physician Assistants are paid at ___ of the Medicare fee schedule. (Circle the correct answer.)

    a. 50%

    b. 75%

    c. 85%

7. Describe *constant attendance* as it relates to Medicare. _____

_____

MEDICARE REIMBURSEMENT ISSUES

8. Define *fraud.* _____

_____

9. Describe the penalties for Medicare fraud. _____

_____

10. List the names of two manuals Medicare sends to carriers to assist in paying claims.

    a. _____

    b. _____

11. The answer to each of the following statements is either true or false. Indicate your choice by placing **T** for a true statement or **F** for a false statement on the line provided.

    _____ a. A DRG provides a fee-for-service payment dependent on the patient's diagnosis.

    _____ b. HCFA must approve a Medicare managed care plan before it is allowed to enroll Medicare beneficiaries.

    _____ c. Medicare MCOs must provide coverage that is similar to a fee-for-service program.

    _____ d. A CIM advises carriers on procedures for paying and denying claims.

_____ e. HCFA requested a change in CPT "visit" codes for office and hospital services as part of the 1992 RBRVS implementation.

_____ f. Demand for increased record keeping has resulted in increased medical practice costs while Medicare continues to decrease payments.

_____ g. Medicare regulations permit payment for preventive medicine services.

_____ h. Medicare pays for the treatment of disease.

12. List three screening services that are covered by Medicare.

a. _____

b. _____

c. _____

13. Medicare replaced the TOS indicators with _____

14. The global period for each surgery includes _____

15. During the global period, what modifier is used to indicate that a procedure is not related to the original service? (Circle the correct answer.)

a. modifier -79

b. modifier -54

c. modifier -57

16. What modifier must be used with the consultation code to report a pre-operative evaluation? (Circle the correct answer.)

a. modifier -79

b. modifier -54

c. modifier -57

17. What modifier is used with the surgical procedure code to report to Medicare that the surgeon did not provide any of the post-operative care for a surgical patient? (Circle the correct answer.)

a. modifier -79

b. modifier -54

c. modifier -57

18. What modifier would a surgeon serving as an assistant surgeon use? (Circle the correct answer.)

a. modifier -78

b. modifier -79

c. modifier -80

19. If a patient has to return to the OR for a related procedure during the postoperative period, what modifier would be appropriate? (Circle the correct answer.)

a. modifier -78

b. modifier -79

c. modifier -80

CORRECT CODING INITIATIVE

Critical Thinking

20. Write a paragraph describing the Correct Coding Initiative (CCI).

_____

_____

_____

_____

MEDICARE COMPLIANCE PLANS

21. Organizations convicted of Medicare fraud may be required to develop a _____

_____ _____ .

22. What agency handles fraud and abuse investigations? _____

23. List seven components of recommended compliance programs.

a. _____

b. _____

c. _____

d. _____

e. _____

f. _____

g. _____

Know Your Acronyms

24. Define the following acronyms:

a. RBRVS _____

b. RVU _____

c. CF _____

d. GPCI _____

e. FR _____

f. MFN _____

g. NP _____

h. PA _____

i. DRG _____

j. MCO _____

k. TOS _____

l. POS _____

m. OIG _____

n. CCI _____

CHAPTER 10 Ten

Coding from Source Documents

APPLYING ICD-9-CM CODING GUIDELINES

1. The answer to each of the following statements is either true or false. Indicate your choice by placing **T** for a true statement or **F** for a false statement on the line provided.

_____ a. Code and report conditions and procedures even if they are not documented in the medical report.

_____ b. Use the full range of ICD codes from 001 through 999.9 and V01 through V82.9, and E codes when warranted by circumstances.

_____ c. Code and report all conditions that are stated as questionable, suspected, or possible.

_____ d. Code to the highest level of specificity any disorder or injury that is known and documented at the time of the encounter.

_____ e. Documented symptoms should be coded and reported when they are manifestations of a reported disorder or injury.

_____ f. V codes are assigned when there is justification for the patient to seek health care but no disorder currently exists.

_____ g. Code only those problems treated during the encounter or that affect the treatment rendered.

_____ h. No more than six diagnoses can be reported on one claim form.

_____ i. Code and report all past conditions even if they are not currently active problems.

_____ j. Link each procedure or service to a condition that proves the medical necessity for performing that procedure/service.

2. Match the procedure/service in the first column with the diagnosis in the second column. Write the correct letter in each blank.

_____ EKG   a. Impacted cerumin

_____ urinalysis   b. Jaundice

_____ strep test   c. Hay fever

_____ wrist x-ray   d. Bronchial asthma

	venipuncture	e.	Chest pain
	removal of ear wax	f.	Strep throat
	sigmoidoscopy	g.	Fracture wrist
	inhalation treatment	h.	Hematuria
	allergy test	i.	Rectal bleeding

CODING CLINICAL SCENARIOS

3. List eight steps for abstracting and coding clinical scenarios.

a. _____

b. _____

c. _____

d. _____

e. _____

f. _____

g. _____

h. _____

4. Assign ICD-9 and CPT codes to the following scenarios. Be sure to include all necessary CPT and/or HCPCS modifiers.

a. A 35-year-old established patient came to the office for excessive menstruation and irregular menstrual cycle. The physician performed a comprehensive evaluation and cervical biopsy.

CPT Codes   **ICD-9 Codes**

_____   _____

b. Patient was referred to me by his primary care physician, Dr. Pearson, because of severe back pain. Dr. Pearson feels he should have surgery but the patient states the pain is relieved by regular chiropractic care and doesn't want to have back surgery. After a problem focused examination and a complete radiologic examination of the lumbosacral spine, including bending views, I consulted with Dr. Pearson and concluded the patient's degenerative disc disease is probably doing as well with a chiropractor as with orthopedic treatment. I did not recommend surgery at this time.

CPT Codes   **ICD-9 Codes**

_____   _____

c. Patient underwent a barium enema which included air contrast. The request form noted severe abdominal pain and diarrhea for the past two weeks. The radiology impression was diverticulitis of the colon.

CPT Codes   **ICD-9 Codes**

_____   _____

d. Patient presented for follow-up of his COPD. At this time the patient is experiencing no significant cough, no sputum, no fever, and no respiratory distress. However, there is dyspnea only with exertion, which is accompanied by angina. A detailed examination was performed and the physician spent approximately 25 minutes with the patient. Chest is clear, no wheeze or rales. Chest x-rays, frontal and lateral, were taken to determine status of COPD. No additional treatment is required at this time.

CPT Codes   **ICD-9 Codes**

_____   _____

e. A surgeon is called to the hospital by the ER physician to see a 59-year-old male who presented with an abdominal mass, left lower quadrant. The surgeon performed a comprehensive examination, admitted the patient, and scheduled an exploratory laparotomy.

CPT Codes   **ICD-9 Codes**

_____   _____

f. On 08/12/XX the patient underwent an exploratory laparotomy, a left partial hepatic resection for a malignant hepatoma, and a cholecystectomy.

CPT Codes   **ICD-9 Codes**

_____   _____

g. On 04/01/XX a 65-year-old patient underwent a bronchoscopy and biopsy for a left lower lobe lung mass. The biopsy revealed adenocarcinoma of the left lower lobe lung. On 04/05/XX the same surgeon performed a left lower lobe lobectomy and thoracic lymphadenectomy.

CPT Codes   **ICD-9 Codes**

_____   _____

_____   _____

h. On 04/01/XX a 39-year-old female presents to her GYN office with a mass and pain in the right breast. Her mother and sister died of breast cancer. A detailed history and examination was performed. The patient was referred to a surgeon for consultation.

CPT Codes   **ICD-9 Codes**

_____   _____

i. On 04/03/XX the patient presents to the surgeon's office for consultation. The patient is experiencing pain in her right breast and has noticed a lump there. She also has a family history of breast cancer. The surgeon performs a level III consultation and two breast aspirations of the right breast.

CPT Codes   **ICD-9 Codes**

_____   _____

j. On 04/09/XX the patient underwent an excision of the right breast mass in the outpatient surgery center. The pathology report revealed a malignant neoplasm, central portion of the right breast. On 04/13/XX the patient underwent a right modified radical mastectomy by the same surgeon.

CPT Codes   **ICD-9 Codes**

_____   _____

_____   _____

k. On 07/23/XX a four-month-old patient returned to the office for her routine well baby check-up. The following vaccines were administered by the medical assistant: Inactivated Poliovirus (IPV), Hepatitis B, Diphtheria, tetanus toxoids, and acellular pertussis. The patient is to return to the office in two months for her six-month check-up and vaccinations.

CPT Codes   **ICD-9 Codes**

_____   _____

l. Patient returned to the office, after a five year absence, because of abdominal pain, diarrhea, and rectal bleeding which began three weeks ago. A detailed examination revealed a tense abdomen with some guarding at the right upper quadrant. Patient to be scheduled for a flexible sigmoidoscopy to R/O colon cancer.

CPT Codes   **ICD-9 Codes**

_____   _____

CODING MEDICAL REPORTS

5. List two major formats health care providers use for documenting progress notes.

   a. _____

   b. _____

6. Match the SOAP terms in the first column with the definitions in the second column. Write the correct letter in each blank.

   _____ subjective data   a. Diagnostic statement

   _____ objective data   b. How treatment will proceed

   _____ assessment data   c. Chief complaint and description of problem

   _____ plan   d. Information not relevant to treatment

                                                e. Information gathered from the physical examination and diagnostic testing

7. Assign diagnostic codes to the following SOAP Notes:

   a. S   Patient complains of one week of severe epigastric pain and burning especially after eating.

      O   On examination there is extreme guarding and tenderness, epigastric region, no rebound. Bowel sounds normal. BP 110/70

      A   R/O gastric ulcer

      P   Patient to have upper gastrointestinal series. Start on Zantac and eliminate alcohol, fried foods, and caffeine. Return to office in one week.

   ICD-9 Codes _____

   b. S   Patient returns after undergoing an upper gastrointestinal series. She states she is still experiencing epigastric pain.

      O   Upper gastrointestinal series revealed areas of ulceration.

      A   Acute gastric ulcer

      P   Omeprazole 10mg qd. Return for follow-up visit in three weeks.

   ICD-9 Codes _____

   c. S   Patient was walking up his driveway when he slipped and fell, landing on his left arm and striking his head against his car. He was unconscious for less than ten minutes, experienced dizziness and vomiting, and felt severe pain in his left arm.

      O   Examination reveals restriction of motion of his left arm and a laceration on his head.

      A   Mild concussion. Laceration occipital region of scalp. Undisplaced fracture proximal left humerus (greater tuberosity)

     P   Laceration repair occipital region of scalp. Patient sent to Dr. Smith for fracture care.

ICD-9 Codes _____

d. S   Patient complains of rectal discomfort, rectal bleeding, and severe itching.

     O   Examination reveals multiple soft external hemorrhoids.

     A   Multiple external hemorrhoids

     P   Suppositories after each bowel movement. Return to office in four weeks.

ICD-9 Codes _____

e. S   Patient presents complaining of polyuria, polydipsia, and weight loss.

     O   Urinalysis by dip, automated, with microscopy reveals elevated glucose.

     A   Possible diabetes

     P   Patient to have a glucose tolerance test and return in three days for blood work results

ICD-9 Codes _____

CODING OPERATIVE REPORTS

8. List five items contained in an operative report.

    a. _____

    b. _____

    c. _____

    d. _____

    e. _____

9. Explain why you should make a copy of the operative report before assigning codes.

    _____

10. Explain why it is important to compare the postoperative diagnosis with the biopsy report on all excised neoplasms. _____

11. The answer to each of the following statements is either true or false. Indicate your choice by placing **T** for a true statement or **F** for a false statement on the line provided.

    _____ a. Because there is a monetary value for each CPT code, be sure to use multiple, separate codes to describe a procedure even if CPT has a single code that classifies all the individual components of the procedure described by the physician.

    _____ b. Never use a code number described in CPT as a "separate procedure" when it is performed within the same incision site as the primary procedure and is an integral part of a greater procedure.

    _____ c. The postoperative diagnosis should explain the medical necessity for performing the procedure(s).

    _____ d. When working in a medical practice you should code an excision even if the pathology report has not been received.

12. Assign ICD-9 and CPT codes to the following operative reports:

    a. PREOPERATIVE DIAGNOSIS: Pterygium of the right eye

       POSTOPERATIVE DIAGNOSIS: Pterygium of the right eye

PROCEDURE PERFORMED: Pterygium excision with conjunctival autograft of the right eye

ANESTHESIA: General endotracheal anesthesia

PROCEDURE: After the patient was prepped and draped in the usual sterile fashion, attention was directed to his right eye under the operating microscope. The area of the pterygium was viewed and an injection of lidocaine with Marcaine was placed subconjunctivally to infiltrate area of the pterygium and surrounding conjunctiva. Then, using a combination of sharp and blunt dissection with 57 Beaver blade Westcott scissors, the pterygium was lifted away from the cornea, making a plane to the cornea to achieve clarity to the cornea. Next, an area was marked with a hand held cautery nasally through the conjunctiva. A muscle hook was inserted to identify the medial rectus muscle. Then, using Westcott scissors and .12, the head and body of the pterygium were removed noting where the medial rectus muscle was at all times. Cautery was used to achieve hemostasis. An area of conjunctiva superior to the area of the prior pterygium under the lid was isolated and an incision was made through the conjunctiva. This section of conjunctiva was then transposed and placed into position over the area of the prior pterygium, thus forming an autograft. This was sutured into place with multiple single 8-0 Vicryl sutures. The autograft was noted to be in good position. Hemostasis was noted to be well achieved. The cornea was noted to be smooth and clear in the area of the prior pterygium with the epithelial defect secondary to removal of the pterygium. Maxitrol drops were placed. The patient's eye was patched. The patient tolerated the procedure well without complications and is to follow up in our office tomorrow.

CPT Codes   **ICD-9 Codes**

_____   _____

b. PREOPERATIVE DIAGNOSIS: Subcutaneous mass, posterior scalp

POSTOPERATIVE DIAGNOSIS: Subcutaneous mass, posterior scalp

PROCEDURE PERFORMED: Excision, subcutaneous mass, posterior scalp

ANESTHESIA: General

PROCEDURE: After instillation of 1% Xylocaine, a transverse incision was made directly over this elongated posterior scalp lesion. Hemostasis was obtained with electrocautery and suture ligature. A fatty tumor was encountered and sharp dissection used in completely excising this lesion. Hemostasis was obtained with ties, suture ligatures, and electrocautery. The lesion was removed in its entirety. The wound was irrigated and the incision closed in layers. The skin was closed with a running nylon suture for hemostasis.

CPT Codes   **ICD-9 Codes**

_____   _____

c. PREOPERATIVE DIAGNOSIS: Ventral hernia

POSTOPERATIVE DIAGNOSIS: Ventral hernia

PROCEDURE PERFORMED: Repair of ventral hernia with mesh

ANESTHESIA: General

PROCEDURE: The vertical midline incision was opened. Sharp and blunt dissection was used in defining the hernia sac. The hernia sac was opened and the fascia examined. The hernia defect was sizable. Careful inspection was utilized to uncover any additional adjacent fascial defects. Small defects were observed on both sides of the major hernia and were incorporated into the main hernia. The hernia sac was dissected free of the surrounding subcutaneous tissues and retained. Prolene mesh was then fashioned to size and sutured to one side with running #0 Prolene suture. Interrupted Prolene sutures were placed on the other side and tagged untied. The hernia sac was then sutured to the opposite side of the fascia with Vicryl suture. The Prolene sutures were passed through the interstices of the Prolene mesh and tied into place, insuring that the Prolene mesh was not placed under tension. Excess mesh was excised. Jackson-Pratt drains were placed, one on each side. Running subcutaneous suture utilizing Vicryl was placed, after which the skin was stapled.

CPT Codes   **ICD-9 Codes**

_____   _____

d. PREOPERATIVE DIAGNOSIS: Intermittent exotropia, alternating

Fusion with decreased stereopsis

POSTOPERATIVE DIAGNOSIS: Intermittent exotropia, alternating

Fusion with decreased stereopsis

PROCEDURE PERFORMED: Bilateral lateral rectus recession of 7.0 mm

ANESTHESIA: General endotracheal anesthesia

PROCEDURE: The patient was brought to the operating room and placed in supine position where she was prepped and draped in the usual sterile fashion for strabismus surgery. Both eyes were exposed to the surgical field. After adequate anesthesia, one drop of 2.5% Neosynephrine was placed in each eye for vasoconstriction. Forced ductions were performed on both eyes and the lateral rectus was found to be normal. An eye speculum was placed in the right eye and surgery was begun on the right eye. An inferotemporal fornix incision was performed. The right lateral rectus muscle was isolated on a muscle hook. The muscle insertion was isolated and checked ligaments were dissected back. After a series of muscle hook passes using the Steven's hook and finishing with two passes of a Green's hook, the right lateral rectus was isolated. The epimesium, as well as tenon's capsule, was dissected from the muscle insertion and the checked ligaments were lysed. The muscle was imbricated on a 6-0 Vicryl suture with an S29 needle with locking bites at either end. The muscle was detached from the globe and a distance of 7.0 mm posterior to the insertion of the muscle was marked. The muscle was then reattached 7.0 mm posterior to the original insertion using a cross-swords technique. The conjunctiva was closed using two buried sutures. Attention was then turned to the left eye where an identical procedure was performed. At the end of the case the eyes seemed slightly exotropic in position in the anesthetized state. Bounce back tests were normal. Both eyes were dressed with Tetracaine drops and Maxitrol ointment. There were no complications. The patient tolerated the procedure well, was awakened from anesthesia without difficulty, and sent to the recovery room. The patient was instructed in the use of topical antibiotics and detailed postoperative instructions were provided. The patient will be followed up within a 48-hour period in my office.

CPT Codes   **ICD-9 Codes**

_____   _____

Essential Claim Form Instructions

GENERAL BILLING GUIDELINES

1. Inpatient medical cases are billed on ___. (Circle the correct answer.)

    a. a fee-for-service basis

    b. a global fee basis

    c. an additional procedure basis

    d. none of the above

2. Inpatient or outpatient major surgery cases are billed on ___. (Circle the correct answer.)

    a. a fee-for-service basis

    b. a global fee basis

    c. an additional procedure basis

    d. none of the above

3. Postoperative complications requiring a return to the operating room for surgery related to the original procedure are billed on ___. (Circle the correct answer.)

    a. a fee-for-service basis

    b. a global fee basis

    c. an additional procedure basis

    d. none of the above

4. Minor surgery cases are billed on ___. (Circle the correct answer.)

    a. a fee-for-service basis

    b. a global fee basis

    c. an additional procedure basis

    d. none of the above

5. Some claims require attachments such as ___. (Circle the correct answer.)

    a. progress notes

    b. operative reports

    c. discharge summaries

    d. all of the above

6. List four circumstances in which a "KISS" (Keep It Short and Simple) letter should be used.

a. _____

b. _____

c. _____

d. _____

7. A claim requiring attachments for clarification should ___. (Circle the correct answer.)

a. be submitted by certified mail

b. never be submitted by electronic mail

c. always be submitted by electronic mail

d. none of the above

8. Define *electronic mail.* _____

_____

9. Data on a paper-generated claim form that runs into the adjacent data blocks or appears in the wrong block will cause _____ of _____ .

10. Before printing a claim form, a _____ _____ should be run to assist with paper alignment in the printer.

OPTICAL SCANNING GUIDELINES

11. The answer to each of the following statements is either true or false. Indicate your choice by placing **T** for a true statement or **F** for a false statement on the line provided.

_____ a. The HCFA-1500 form was designed to accommodate optical scanning of paper claims into the insurance company's computer system.

_____ b. The processing time for claims prepared for optical character readers (OCR) is a little slower than for claims that must be manually entered into the insurance company's computer system.

_____ c. The OCR guidelines were set by Medicare when the present claim form was developed.

_____ d. The OCR guidelines are now used by all insurance carriers processing claims from the official HCFA-1500 form.

_____ e. When completing a claim form, pica type (12 characters per inch) should be used.

_____ f. When completing a claim form, all alpha characters should be typed in uppercase (capital letters).

_____ g. When completing a claim form, a zero and the alpha character O should not be interchanged.

12. List five key strokes that can be substituted by a space when completing a claim form.

a. _____

b. _____

c. _____

d. _____

e. _____

13. Leave one _____ _____ between the patient/policyholder's last name, first name, and middle initial.

14. Do not use any _____ in a patient/policyholder's provider's name, except for a hyphen in a compound name.

15. Do not use a person's title or other designations such as Sr., Jr., II, or III on a claim form unless it appears on the patient's _____ _____ _____ .

16. Describe how the name on the claim form should be typed for the following patients:

    a. The name on the ID card reads: James M. Apple, II _____

    b. The name on the ID card reads: Charles T. Treebark, Jr. _____

    c. The name on the ID card reads: David J. Hurts, III _____

    d. The name on the ID card reads: Jake R. Elbow, Sr. _____

17. Describe how the birth date on the claim form should be typed for the following dates of birth:

    a. January 5, 1954: _____

    b. March 11, 1971: _____

    c. August 31, 1985: _____

    d. December 2, 1994: _____

REPORTING DIAGNOSIS: ICD-9-CM CODES

18. Diagnosis codes are placed in ___. (Circle the correct answer.)

    a. Block 24

    b. Block 33

    c. Block 21

    d. none of the above

19. The maximum number of ICD codes that may appear on a single claim form is ___. (Circle the correct answer.)

    a. four

    b. six

    c. two

    d. none of the above

20. The first ICD code listed on a claim form should be the ___. (Circle the correct answer.)

    a. qualified diagnosis

    b. possible diagnosis

    c. primary diagnosis

    d. any of the above

21. If a diagnosis not treated or addressed during an encounter is stated on the patient's record, you should ___. (Circle the correct answer.)

    a. not list the diagnosis

    b. list the diagnosis as secondary

    c. list the diagnosis as probable

    d. none of the above

22. Until a definitive diagnosis is determined, which of the following diagnoses should be used? (Circle the correct answer.)

    a. rule out
    b. suspicious for
    c. possible
    d. none of the above

INSTRUCTIONS FOR LINE 24

23. Match the blocks in the first column with the definitions in the second column. Write the correct letter in each blank.

_____	Block 24A	a. Procedures and Services
_____	Block 24B	b. Charges
_____	Block 24C	c. COB
_____	Block 24D	d. Dates of Service
_____	Block 24E	e. Days/Units
_____	Block 24F	f. EMG
_____	Block 24G	g. Reserved for Local Use
_____	Block 24H	h. Place of Service
_____	Block 24I	i. EPSDT Family Plan
_____	Block 24J	j. Diagnosis Code
_____	Block 24K	k. Type of Service

24. The maximum number of CPT codes that may appear on a single claim form is ___. (Circle the correct answer.)

    a. four
    b. six
    c. two
    d. none of the above

25. When listing multiple procedures on the claim form, the first procedure should be the ___. (Circle the correct answer.)

    a. primary procedure
    b. procedure that took the longest
    c. procedure with the highest fee
    d. any of the above

26. Identical procedures or services may be reported on one line if the following circumstances apply. (Circle the correct answer.)

    a. Procedures were performed on consecutive days in the same month.
    b. Identical code numbers apply to all procedures.
    c. Identical charges apply.
    d. all of the above

27. The maximum number of modifiers that may be added to the right of the CPT/HCPCS code is ___.
(Circle the correct answer.)

   a. four

   b. six

   c. two

   d. none of the above

Critical Thinking

28. Write a paragraph describing how to use diagnosis reference numbers.

_____

_____

_____

_____

REPORTING THE BILLING ENTITY

29. The billing entity is the _____ _____ _____ of the practice.

30. If the billing entity has a group practice identification number required by the insurance carrier, this number should be typed in box number _____ on the claim form.

PROCESSING SECONDARY CLAIMS

31. The secondary insurance claim is filed ___. (Circle the correct answer.)

   a. after the EOB from the primary claim has been received

   b. at the same time the primary claim is filed

   c. after the patient has paid his/her co-pay

   d. any of the above

32. As a general rule the secondary claim cannot be filed electronically because ___. (Circle the correct answer.)

   a. a KISS report must always accompany a secondary claim

   b. secondary insurance carriers do not accept claims electronically

   c. the primary EOB must be attached to the secondary claim

   d. all of the above

33. Supplemental plans usually cover the ___. (Circle the correct answer.)

   a. secondary procedures billed

   b. deductible and copay/coinsurance

   c. non-allowed amount

   d. none of the above

COMMON ERRORS THAT DELAY PROCESSING

34. List five common errors that delay processing of a claim.

    a. _____

    b. _____

    c. _____

    d. _____

    e. _____

FINAL PROCESSING STEPS OF PAPER CLAIMS

35. List the six final processing steps of paper claims.

    a. _____

    b. _____

    c. _____

    d. _____

    e. _____

    f. _____

MAINTAINING INSURANCE CLAIM FILES FOR THE PRACTICE

36. The federal Omnibus Budget Reconciliation Act of 1987 requires physicians to keep copies of any ___. (Circle the correct answer.)

    a. Blue Cross/Blue Shield insurance claim forms

    b. commercial insurance claim forms

    c. government insurance claim forms

    d. all of the above

37. How do providers and billing services filing claims electronically comply with the federal regulation?

    _____

    _____

    _____

38. List four examples of the way paper claim files should be set up.

    a. _____

    b. _____

    c. _____

    d. _____

39. The _____ _____ _____ of 1974 prohibits an insurance carrier from notifying the provider about payment of rejections of unassigned claims or payments sent directly to the patient/policyholder.

Critical Thinking

40. Write a paragraph describing steps that should be taken when an error in processing is found.

_____

_____

_____

_____

Know Your Acronyms

41. Define the following acronyms:

a. EMC _____

b. KISS _____

c. ASC _____

d. EMC _____

e. OCR _____

f. EIN _____

g. PIN _____

h. GRP# _____

EXERCISES

42. Using Optical Scanning Guidelines, circle the errors found in Stanley L. Fruit's claim form on the following page.

43. Using the information provided on Stanley L. Fruit's claim form, complete the blank claim form correctly.

PLEASE
DO NOT
STAPLE
IN THIS
AREA

CARRIER

HEALTH INSURANCE CLAIM FORM

PICA ▢ ▢

▢ PICA	

1. ▢ MEDICARE (Medicare #) ▢ MEDICAID (Medicaid #) ▢ CHAMPUS (Sponsor's SSN) ▢ CHAMPVA (VA File #) ▢ GROUP HEALTH PLAN (SSN or ID) ▢ FECA BLK LUNG (SSN) ☒ OTHER (ID)

1a. INSURED'S I.D. NUMBER (FOR PROGRAM IN ITEM 1)
017-09-1234

2. PATIENT'S NAME (Last Name, First Name, Middle Initial)
STANLEY L. FRUIT JR.

3. PATIENT'S BIRTH DATE MM 7 | DD 15 | YY 1954   SEX M ☒   F ▢

4. INSURED'S NAME (Last Name, First Name, Middle Initial)
SAME

5. PATIENT'S ADDRESS (No. Street)
25 S. HANSON ST.

6. PATIENT RELATIONSHIP TO INSURED
Self ☒   Spouse ▢   Child ▢   Other ▢

7. INSURED'S ADDRESS (No. Street)
SAME

CITY
ANYWHERE   STATE US

8. PATIENT STATUS
Single ☒   Married ▢   Other ▢
Employed ☒   Full-Time Student ▢   Part-Time Student ▢

CITY   STATE

ZIP CODE 12345   TELEPHONE (Include Area Code) (101) 112-2222

ZIP CODE   TELEPHONE (INCLUDE AREA CODE) ( )

9. OTHER INSURED'S NAME (Last Name, First Name, Middle Initial)
None

10. IS PATIENT'S CONDITION RELATED TO:

11. INSURED'S POLICY GROUP OR FECA NUMBER
FED 101

a. OTHER INSURED'S POLICY OR GROUP NUMBER

a. EMPLOYMENT? (CURRENT OR PREVIOUS) ▢ YES ☒ NO

a. INSURED'S DATE OF BIRTH MM | DD | YY   SEX M ▢   F ▢

b. OTHER INSURED'S DATE OF BIRTH MM | DD | YY   SEX M ▢   F ▢

b. AUTO ACCIDENT? ▢ YES ☒ NO   PLACE (State)

b. EMPLOYER'S NAME OR SCHOOL NAME
U.S. POSTAL SERVICE

c. EMPLOYER'S NAME OR SCHOOL NAME

c. OTHER ACCIDENT? ▢ YES ☒ NO

c. INSURANCE PLAN NAME OR PROGRAM NAME
MAILHANDLERS

d. INSURANCE PLAN NAME OR PROGRAM NAME

10d. RESERVED FOR LOCAL USE

d. IS THERE ANOTHER HEALTH BENEFIT PLAN? ▢ YES ☒ NO   If yes, return to and complete item 9 a – d.

READ BACK OF FORM BEFORE COMPLETING & SIGNING THIS FORM.
12. PATIENT'S OR AUTHORIZED PERSON'S SIGNATURE I authorize the release of any medical or other information necessary to process this claim. I also request payment of government benefits either to myself or to the party who accepts assignment below.

SIGNED SIGNATURE ON FILE   DATE MMDDCCYY

13. INSURED'S OR AUTHORIZED PERSON'S SIGNATURE I authorize payment of medical benefits to the undersigned physician or supplier for services described below.

SIGNED SIGNATURE ON FILE

14. DATE OF CURRENT: MM | DD | YY ILLNESS (First symptom) OR INJURY (Accident) OR PREGNANCY (LMP)

15. IF PATIENT HAS HAD SAME OR SIMILAR ILLNESS, GIVE FIRST DATE MM | DD | YY

16. DATES PATIENT UNABLE TO WORK IN CURRENT OCCUPATION MM | DD | YY FROM   TO MM | DD | YY

17. NAME OF REFERRING PHYSICIAN OR OTHER SOURCE

17a. I.D. NUMBER OF REFERRING PHYSICIAN

18. HOSPITALIZATION DATES RELATED TO CURRENT SERVICES MM | DD | YY FROM   TO MM | DD | YY

19. RESERVED FOR LOCAL USE

20. OUTSIDE LAB? ▢ YES ☒ NO $ CHARGES

21. DIAGNOSIS OR NATURE OF ILLNESS OR INJURY. (RELATE ITEMS 1, 2, 3, OR 4 TO ITEM 24E BY LINE)
1. 782.0   3. |___._|
2. 788.41   4. |___._|

22. MEDICAID RESUBMISSION CODE   ORIGINAL REF. NO.

23. PRIOR AUTHORIZATION NUMBER

24. A. DATE(S) OF SERVICE From MM DD YY	To MM DD YY	B. Place of Service	C. Type of Service	D. PROCEDURES, SERVICES, OR SUPPLIES (Explain Unusual Circumstances) CPT/HCPCS	MODIFIER	E. DIAGNOSIS CODE	F. $ CHARGES	G. DAYS OR UNITS	H. EPSDT Family Plan	I. EMG	J. COB	K. RESERVED FOR LOCAL USE
1 6 7 CCYY		3	1	99213		782.0	$ 60 00	1				
2												
3 6 7 CCYY		3	5	81001		788.41	$ 10 00	1				
4												
5												
6												

25. FEDERAL TAX I.D. NUMBER SSN ▢ EIN ☒
11-123456

26. PATIENT'S ACCOUNT NO.
123

27. ACCEPT ASSIGNMENT? (For govt. claims, see back) ☒ YES ▢ NO

28. TOTAL CHARGE $ 70.00

29. AMOUNT PAID $

30. BALANCE DUE $ 70.00

31. SIGNATURE OF PHYSICIAN OR SUPPLIER INCLUDING DEGREES OR CREDENTIALS (I certify that the statements on the reverse apply to this bill and are made a part thereof.)
R.K. PAINFREE, M.D.
SIGNED   DATE MMDDCCYY

32. NAME AND ADDRESS OF FACILITY WHERE SERVICES WERE RENDERED (If other than home or office)

33. PHYSICIAN'S, SUPPLIER'S BILLING NAME, ADDRESS, ZIP CODE & PHONE #
GOODMEDICINE CLINIC
PIN# 123-42   GRP# GC-12340

PATIENT AND INSURED INFORMATION

PHYSICIAN OR SUPPLIER INFORMATION

PLEASE PRINT OR TYPE

SAMPLE FORM 1500
SAMPLE FORM 1500 SAMPLE FORM 1500

PLEASE
DO NOT
STAPLE
IN THIS
AREA

HEALTH INSURANCE CLAIM FORM

[ ][ ] PICA   PICA [ ][ ]

1. MEDICARE	MEDICAID	CHAMPUS	CHAMPVA	GROUP HEALTH PLAN	FECA BLK LUNG	OTHER	1a. INSURED'S I.D. NUMBER (FOR PROGRAM IN ITEM 1)
[ ] (Medicare #)	[ ] (Medicaid #)	[ ] (Sponsor's SSN)	[ ] (VA File #)	[ ] (SSN or ID)	[ ] (SSN)	[ ] (ID)	

2. PATIENT'S NAME (Last Name, First Name, Middle Initial)

3. PATIENT'S BIRTH DATE   SEX
MM | DD | YY   M [ ]   F [ ]

4. INSURED'S NAME (Last Name, First Name, Middle Initial)

5. PATIENT'S ADDRESS (No. Street)

6. PATIENT RELATIONSHIP TO INSURED
Self [ ]   Spouse [ ]   Child [ ]   Other [ ]

7. INSURED'S ADDRESS (No. Street)

CITY   STATE

8. PATIENT STATUS
Single [ ]   Married [ ]   Other [ ]
Employed [ ]   Full-Time Student [ ]   Part-Time Student [ ]

CITY   STATE

ZIP CODE   TELEPHONE (Include Area Code) ( )

ZIP CODE   TELEPHONE (INCLUDE AREA CODE) ( )

9. OTHER INSURED'S NAME (Last Name, First Name, Middle Initial)

10. IS PATIENT'S CONDITION RELATED TO:

11. INSURED'S POLICY GROUP OR FECA NUMBER

a. OTHER INSURED'S POLICY OR GROUP NUMBER

a. EMPLOYMENT? (CURRENT OR PREVIOUS)
[ ] YES   [ ] NO

a. INSURED'S DATE OF BIRTH   SEX
MM | DD | YY   M [ ]   F [ ]

b. OTHER INSURED'S DATE OF BIRTH   SEX
MM | DD | YY   M [ ]   F [ ]

b. AUTO ACCIDENT?   PLACE (State)
[ ] YES   [ ] NO

b. EMPLOYER'S NAME OR SCHOOL NAME

c. EMPLOYER'S NAME OR SCHOOL NAME

c. OTHER ACCIDENT?
[ ] YES   [ ] NO

c. INSURANCE PLAN NAME OR PROGRAM NAME

d. INSURANCE PLAN NAME OR PROGRAM NAME

10d. RESERVED FOR LOCAL USE

d. IS THERE ANOTHER HEALTH BENEFIT PLAN?
[ ] YES   [ ] NO   If yes, return to and complete item 9 a – d.

READ BACK OF FORM BEFORE COMPLETING & SIGNING THIS FORM.
12. PATIENT'S OR AUTHORIZED PERSON'S SIGNATURE I authorize the release of any medical or other information necessary to process this claim. I also request payment of government benefits either to myself or to the party who accepts assignment below.

SIGNED _____   DATE _____

13. INSURED'S OR AUTHORIZED PERSON'S SIGNATURE I authorize payment of medical benefits to the undersigned physician or supplier for services described below.

SIGNED _____

14. DATE OF CURRENT: ILLNESS (First symptom) OR INJURY (Accident) OR PREGNANCY (LMP)
MM | DD | YY

15. IF PATIENT HAS HAD SAME OR SIMILAR ILLNESS, GIVE FIRST DATE   MM | DD | YY

16. DATES PATIENT UNABLE TO WORK IN CURRENT OCCUPATION
MM | DD | YY   MM | DD | YY
FROM   TO

17. NAME OF REFERRING PHYSICIAN OR OTHER SOURCE

17a. I.D. NUMBER OF REFERRING PHYSICIAN

18. HOSPITALIZATION DATES RELATED TO CURRENT SERVICES
MM | DD | YY   MM | DD | YY
FROM   TO

19. RESERVED FOR LOCAL USE

20. OUTSIDE LAB? $ CHARGES
[ ] YES   [ ] NO

21. DIAGNOSIS OR NATURE OF ILLNESS OR INJURY. (RELATE ITEMS 1, 2, 3, OR 4 TO ITEM 24E BY LINE)

1. |___|.|___| 3. |___|.|___|
2. |___|.|___| 4. |___|.|___|

22. MEDICAID RESUBMISSION CODE   ORIGINAL REF. NO.

23. PRIOR AUTHORIZATION NUMBER

24. A. DATE(S) OF SERVICE		B. Place of Service	C. Type of Service	D. PROCEDURES, SERVICES, OR SUPPLIES (Explain Unusual Circumstances)		E. DIAGNOSIS CODE	F. $ CHARGES	G. DAYS OR UNITS	H. EPSDT Family Plan	I. EMG	J. COB	K. RESERVED FOR LOCAL USE
From MM DD YY	To MM DD YY			CPT/HCPCS	MODIFIER							
1												
2												
3												
4												
5												
6												

25. FEDERAL TAX I.D. NUMBER   SSN [ ]   EIN [ ]

26. PATIENT'S ACCOUNT NO.

27. ACCEPT ASSIGNMENT? (For govt. claims, see back)
[ ] YES   [ ] NO

28. TOTAL CHARGE $

29. AMOUNT PAID $

30. BALANCE DUE $

31. SIGNATURE OF PHYSICIAN OR SUPPLIER INCLUDING DEGREES OR CREDENTIALS (I certify that the statements on the reverse apply to this bill and are made a part thereof.)

SIGNED _____   DATE _____

32. NAME AND ADDRESS OF FACILITY WHERE SERVICES WERE RENDERED (If other than home or office)

33. PHYSICIAN'S, SUPPLIER'S BILLING NAME, ADDRESS, ZIP CODE & PHONE #

PIN#   GRP#

(SAMPLE ONLY - NOT APPROVED FOR USE)   PLEASE PRINT OR TYPE   SAMPLE FORM 1500
SAMPLE FORM 1500 SAMPLE FORM 1500

44. Using Optical Scanning Guidelines, complete the blank claim form for Jane Normal. Use the step-by-step instructions provided in the textbook to properly fill out the form.

DATE	REMARKS			
02/05/XX				

PATIENT		CHART #	SEX	BIRTHDATE
Jane Normal	121-01-2179		F	02/07/1953

MAILING ADDRESS	CITY	STATE	ZIP	HOME PHONE	WORK PHONE
534 Robin St.	Anywhere	US	12345	(410) 123 1234	(301) 321 4321

EMPLOYER	ADDRESS	PATIENT STATUS
Dress Barn	576 Fleet St.	X MARRIED DIVORCED SINGLE STUDENT OTHER

INSURANCE: PRIMARY	ID#	GROUP	SECONDARY POLICY
Metropolitan	121-01-2179	C26	

POLICYHOLDER NAME	BIRTHDATE	RELATIONSHIP	POLICYHOLDER NAME	BIRTHDATE	RELATIONSHIP
		Self			

SUPPLEMENTAL PLAN	EMPLOYER

POLICYHOLDER NAME	BIRTHDATE	RELATIONSHIP	DIAGNOSIS	CODE
			1. Sinusitis, frontal	461.1
EMPLOYER			2.	
			3.	
REFERRING PHYSICIAN UPIN/SSN			4.	

PLACE OF SERVICE	Office

PROCEDURES	CODE	CHARGE
1. Established patient OV level II	99212	$65.00
2.		
3.		
4.		
5.		
6.		

SPECIAL NOTES

TOTAL CHARGES	PAYMENTS	ADJUSTMENTS	BALANCE
$65.00	0	0	$65.00

RETURN VISIT	PHYSICIAN SIGNATURE
PRN	*Donald L. Givings, M.D.*

MEDICARE D1234 MEDICAID DLG1234 BCBS 12345	**DONALD L. GIVINGS, M.D.** **11350 MEDICAL DRIVE, ANYWHERE US 12345** **PHONE NUMBER (101)111-5555**	EIN 11-123456 SSN 123-12-1234 PIN DG1234 GRP DG12345

(SAMPLE ONLY - NOT APPROVED FOR USE)

CARRIER

| | PICA

HEALTH INSURANCE CLAIM FORM

PICA | |

| 1. MEDICARE | MEDICAID | CHAMPUS | CHAMPVA | GROUP HEALTH PLAN | FECA BLK LUNG | OTHER | 1a. INSURED'S I.D. NUMBER | (FOR PROGRAM IN ITEM 1) |

☐ (Medicare #) ☐ (Medicaid #) ☐ (Sponsor's SSN) ☐ (VA File #) ☐ (SSN or ID) ☐ (SSN) ☐ (ID)

2. PATIENT'S NAME (Last Name, First Name, Middle Initial)

3. PATIENT'S BIRTH DATE MM | DD | YY   SEX   M ☐ F ☐

4. INSURED'S NAME (Last Name, First Name, Middle Initial)

5. PATIENT'S ADDRESS (No. Street)

6. PATIENT RELATIONSHIP TO INSURED   Self ☐ Spouse ☐ Child ☐ Other ☐

7. INSURED'S ADDRESS (No. Street)

CITY | STATE

8. PATIENT STATUS   Single ☐ Married ☐ Other ☐
Employed ☐ Full-Time Student ☐ Part-Time Student ☐

CITY | STATE

ZIP CODE | TELEPHONE (Include Area Code) ( )

ZIP CODE | TELEPHONE (INCLUDE AREA CODE) ( )

9. OTHER INSURED'S NAME (Last Name, First Name, Middle Initial)

10. IS PATIENT'S CONDITION RELATED TO:

11. INSURED'S POLICY GROUP OR FECA NUMBER

a. OTHER INSURED'S POLICY OR GROUP NUMBER

a. EMPLOYMENT? (CURRENT OR PREVIOUS)   ☐ YES ☐ NO

a. INSURED'S DATE OF BIRTH MM | DD | YY   SEX   M ☐ F ☐

b. OTHER INSURED'S DATE OF BIRTH MM | DD | YY   SEX   M ☐ F ☐

b. AUTO ACCIDENT?   PLACE (State)   ☐ YES ☐ NO

b. EMPLOYER'S NAME OR SCHOOL NAME

c. EMPLOYER'S NAME OR SCHOOL NAME

c. OTHER ACCIDENT?   ☐ YES ☐ NO

c. INSURANCE PLAN NAME OR PROGRAM NAME

d. INSURANCE PLAN NAME OR PROGRAM NAME

10d. RESERVED FOR LOCAL USE

d. IS THERE ANOTHER HEALTH BENEFIT PLAN?   ☐ YES ☐ NO   If yes, return to and complete item 9 a – d.

READ BACK OF FORM BEFORE COMPLETING & SIGNING THIS FORM.
12. PATIENT'S OR AUTHORIZED PERSON'S SIGNATURE I authorize the release of any medical or other information necessary to process this claim. I also request payment of government benefits either to myself or to the party who accepts assignment below.

SIGNED _____ DATE _____

13. INSURED'S OR AUTHORIZED PERSON'S SIGNATURE I authorize payment of medical benefits to the undersigned physician or supplier for services described below.

SIGNED _____

PATIENT AND INSURED INFORMATION

---

14. DATE OF CURRENT: MM | DD | YY   ILLNESS (First symptom) OR INJURY (Accident) OR PREGNANCY (LMP)

15. IF PATIENT HAS HAD SAME OR SIMILAR ILLNESS, GIVE FIRST DATE MM | DD | YY

16. DATES PATIENT UNABLE TO WORK IN CURRENT OCCUPATION FROM MM | DD | YY TO MM | DD | YY

17. NAME OF REFERRING PHYSICIAN OR OTHER SOURCE

17a. I.D. NUMBER OF REFERRING PHYSICIAN

18. HOSPITALIZATION DATES RELATED TO CURRENT SERVICES FROM MM | DD | YY TO MM | DD | YY

19. RESERVED FOR LOCAL USE

20. OUTSIDE LAB?   ☐ YES ☐ NO $ CHARGES

21. DIAGNOSIS OR NATURE OF ILLNESS OR INJURY. (RELATE ITEMS 1, 2, 3, OR 4 TO ITEM 24E BY LINE)
1. |___ . ___| 3. |___ . ___|
2. |___ . ___| 4. |___ . ___|

22. MEDICAID RESUBMISSION CODE | ORIGINAL REF. NO.

23. PRIOR AUTHORIZATION NUMBER

---

24. A DATE(S) OF SERVICE		B Place of Service	C Type of Service	D PROCEDURES, SERVICES, OR SUPPLIES (Explain Unusual Circumstances)		E DIAGNOSIS CODE	F $ CHARGES	G DAYS OR UNITS	H EPSDT Family Plan	I EMG	J COB	K RESERVED FOR LOCAL USE
From MM DD YY	To MM DD YY			CPT/HCPCS	MODIFIER							
1												
2												
3												
4												
5												
6												

25. FEDERAL TAX I.D. NUMBER   SSN ☐ EIN ☐

26. PATIENT'S ACCOUNT NO.

27. ACCEPT ASSIGNMENT? (For govt. claims, see back)   ☐ YES ☐ NO

28. TOTAL CHARGE $

29. AMOUNT PAID $

30. BALANCE DUE $

31. SIGNATURE OF PHYSICIAN OR SUPPLIER INCLUDING DEGREES OR CREDENTIALS (I certify that the statements on the reverse apply to this bill and are made a part thereof.)

SIGNED _____ DATE _____

32. NAME AND ADDRESS OF FACILITY WHERE SERVICES WERE RENDERED (If other than home or office)

33. PHYSICIAN'S, SUPPLIER'S BILLING NAME, ADDRESS, ZIP CODE & PHONE #

PIN# | GRP#

PHYSICIAN OR SUPPLIER INFORMATION

(SAMPLE ONLY - NOT APPROVED FOR USE)

PLEASE PRINT OR TYPE

SAMPLE FORM 1500
SAMPLE FORM 1500 SAMPLE FORM 1500

75

45. Using Optical Scanning Guidelines, complete the blank claim for Thomas J. Meekes. Use the step-by-step instructions provided in the textbook to properly fill out the form.

DATE 08/13/XX	REMARKS				

PATIENT			CHART #	SEX	BIRTHDATE
Thomas J. Meekes	441-44-1111			M	12/10/1949

MAILING ADDRESS	CITY	STATE	ZIP	HOME PHONE	WORK PHONE
39567 Aliceville Rd.	Anywhere	US	12345	(101) 333 4444	576 2222

EMPLOYER	ADDRESS	PATIENT STATUS
Western Auto	7928 James St.	X MARRIED DIVORCED SINGLE STUDENT OTHER

INSURANCE: PRIMARY	ID#	GROUP	SECONDARY POLICY
Atlantic Plus	411-44-1111	J276	

POLICYHOLDER NAME	BIRTHDATE	RELATIONSHIP	POLICYHOLDER NAME	BIRTHDATE	RELATIONSHIP
		Self			

SUPPLEMENTAL PLAN	EMPLOYER

POLICYHOLDER NAME	BIRTHDATE	RELATIONSHIP	DIAGNOSIS		CODE
			1. Bronchial Pneumonia		485
EMPLOYER			2.		
			3.		
REFERRING PHYSICIAN UPIN/SSN			4.		

PLACE OF SERVICE   Mercy Hospital Anywhere Street Anywhere US 12345

PROCEDURES		CODE	CHARGE
1. Initial Hospital Care Level I	08/09/XX	99221	$75.00
2. Subsequent Hospital Care Level I	08/10/XX	99231	$50.00
3. Subsequent Hospital Care Level I	08/11/XX	99231	$50.00
4. Subsequent Hospital Care Level I	08/12/XX	99231	$50.00
5. Discharge, 30 min.	08/13/XX	99238	$75.00
6.			

SPECIAL NOTES

TOTAL CHARGES	PAYMENTS	ADJUSTMENTS	BALANCE
$300.00	0	0	$300.00

RETURN VISIT	PHYSICIAN SIGNATURE
Pt will call to set up appointment within one week	Donald L. Givings, M.D.

	DONALD L. GIVINGS, M.D.	
MEDICARE D1234	11350 MEDICAL DRIVE, ANYWHERE US 12345	EIN 11-123456
MEDICAID DLG1234	PHONE NUMBER (101)111-5555	SSN 123-12-1234
BCBS 12345		PIN DG1234
		GRP DG12345

PLEASE
DO NOT
STAPLE
IN THIS
AREA

CARRIER

| | PICA

HEALTH INSURANCE CLAIM FORM

PICA | |

1. MEDICARE MEDICAID CHAMPUS CHAMPVA GROUP HEALTH PLAN FECA BLK LUNG OTHER	1a. INSURED'S I.D. NUMBER (FOR PROGRAM IN ITEM 1)
☐ (Medicare #) ☐ (Medicaid #) ☐ (Sponsor's SSN) ☐ (VA File #) ☐ (SSN or ID) ☐ (SSN) ☐ (ID)	

2. PATIENT'S NAME (Last Name, First Name, Middle Initial)	3. PATIENT'S BIRTH DATE MM DD YY SEX M ☐ F ☐	4. INSURED'S NAME (Last Name, First Name, Middle Initial)

5. PATIENT'S ADDRESS (No. Street)	6. PATIENT RELATIONSHIP TO INSURED Self ☐ Spouse ☐ Child ☐ Other ☐	7. INSURED'S ADDRESS (No. Street)

CITY	STATE	8. PATIENT STATUS Single ☐ Married ☐ Other ☐	CITY	STATE

ZIP CODE	TELEPHONE (Include Area Code) ( )	Employed ☐ Full-Time Student ☐ Part-Time Student ☐	ZIP CODE	TELEPHONE (INCLUDE AREA CODE) ( )

PATIENT AND INSURED INFORMATION

9. OTHER INSURED'S NAME (Last Name, First Name, Middle Initial)	10. IS PATIENT'S CONDITION RELATED TO:	11. INSURED'S POLICY GROUP OR FECA NUMBER

a. OTHER INSURED'S POLICY OR GROUP NUMBER	a. EMPLOYMENT? (CURRENT OR PREVIOUS) ☐ YES ☐ NO	a. INSURED'S DATE OF BIRTH MM DD YY SEX M ☐ F ☐

b. OTHER INSURED'S DATE OF BIRTH MM DD YY SEX M ☐ F ☐	b. AUTO ACCIDENT? PLACE (State) ☐ YES ☐ NO	b. EMPLOYER'S NAME OR SCHOOL NAME

c. EMPLOYER'S NAME OR SCHOOL NAME	c. OTHER ACCIDENT? ☐ YES ☐ NO	c. INSURANCE PLAN NAME OR PROGRAM NAME

d. INSURANCE PLAN NAME OR PROGRAM NAME	10d. RESERVED FOR LOCAL USE	d. IS THERE ANOTHER HEALTH BENEFIT PLAN? ☐ YES ☐ NO If yes, return to and complete item 9 a – d.

READ BACK OF FORM BEFORE COMPLETING & SIGNING THIS FORM.

12. PATIENT'S OR AUTHORIZED PERSON'S SIGNATURE I authorize the release of any medical or other information necessary to process this claim. I also request payment of government benefits either to myself or to the party who accepts assignment below.

SIGNED _____ DATE _____

13. INSURED'S OR AUTHORIZED PERSON'S SIGNATURE I authorize payment of medical benefits to the undersigned physician or supplier for services described below.

SIGNED _____

14. DATE OF CURRENT: ◄ ILLNESS (First symptom) OR MM DD YY INJURY (Accident) OR PREGNANCY (LMP)	15. IF PATIENT HAS HAD SAME OR SIMILAR ILLNESS, GIVE FIRST DATE MM DD YY	16. DATES PATIENT UNABLE TO WORK IN CURRENT OCCUPATION MM DD YY MM DD YY FROM TO

17. NAME OF REFERRING PHYSICIAN OR OTHER SOURCE	17a. I.D. NUMBER OF REFERRING PHYSICIAN	18. HOSPITALIZATION DATES RELATED TO CURRENT SERVICES MM DD YY MM DD YY FROM TO

19. RESERVED FOR LOCAL USE	20. OUTSIDE LAB? ☐ YES ☐ NO $ CHARGES

21. DIAGNOSIS OR NATURE OF ILLNESS OR INJURY. (RELATE ITEMS 1, 2, 3, OR 4 TO ITEM 24E BY LINE) 1. ⌐__ . __ 3. ⌐__ . __ 2. ⌐__ . __ 4. ⌐__ . __	22. MEDICAID RESUBMISSION CODE ORIGINAL REF. NO. 23. PRIOR AUTHORIZATION NUMBER

PHYSICIAN OR SUPPLIER INFORMATION

24. A DATE(S) OF SERVICE					B Place of Service	C Type of Service	D PROCEDURES, SERVICES, OR SUPPLIES (Explain Unusual Circumstances) CPT/HCPCS	MODIFIER	E DIAGNOSIS CODE	F $ CHARGES	G DAYS OR UNITS	H EPSDT Family Plan	I EMG	J COB	K RESERVED FOR LOCAL USE
From			To												
MM	DD	YY	MM	DD	YY												
1																
2																
3																
4																
5																
6																

25. FEDERAL TAX I.D. NUMBER SSN ☐ EIN ☐	26. PATIENT'S ACCOUNT NO.	27. ACCEPT ASSIGNMENT? (For govt. claims, see back) ☐ YES ☐ NO	28. TOTAL CHARGE $	29. AMOUNT PAID $	30. BALANCE DUE $

31. SIGNATURE OF PHYSICIAN OR SUPPLIER INCLUDING DEGREES OR CREDENTIALS (I certify that the statements on the reverse apply to this bill and are made a part thereof.) SIGNED _____ DATE _____	32. NAME AND ADDRESS OF FACILITY WHERE SERVICES WERE RENDERED (If other than home or office)	33. PHYSICIAN'S, SUPPLIER'S BILLING NAME, ADDRESS, ZIP CODE & PHONE # PIN# GRP#

CHAPTER
12
Twelve

Filing Commercial Claims

STEP-BY-STEP INSTRUCTIONS FOR PRIMARY COMMERCIAL CLAIMS

1. Describe the information to be provided in Block 4 if the patient is not the policyholder.

   _____

   _____

2. When completing Block 8, what information must be filed with the first claim when the patient is between the ages of 19 and 23, is a dependent on a family policy, and is a full-time student?

   _____

   _____

3. What does a check in the YES box of Block 10A indicate? _____

   _____

   _____

4. What does a patient's signature appearing in Block 13 authorize? _____

   _____

   _____

5. In Blocks 12 and 13, what phrase is acceptable if the patient has signed an Authorization for Release of Medical Information Form? _____

   _____

6. When would it be appropriate to complete Block 17? _____

   _____

   _____

7. When would it be appropriate to complete Block 18? _____

_____

_____

8. What does a check in the YES box of Block 20 indicate? _____

_____

_____

9. When would it be appropriate to complete Block 23? _____

_____

_____

10. Indicate the place of service code number that should appear in Block 24B if the service reported was performed in the
    a. provider's office.   _____
    b. hospital (inpatient).   _____
    c. hospital (outpatient).   _____
    d. nursing home.   _____

11. Indicate the type of service code number that should appear in Block 24C if the service reported was
    a. consultation.   _____
    b. medical care.   _____
    c. diagnostic laboratory.   _____
    d. surgery.   _____
    e. diagnostic x-ray.   _____

12. When would it be appropriate to place a check in Block 24I? _____

_____

_____

13. Describe what a check in the YES box of Block 27 would indicate. _____

_____

_____

14. Describe what a check in the NO box of Block 27 would indicate. _____

_____

_____

15. When would it be appropriate for a negative charge to appear in Block 28? _____

16. If a patient made a payment toward his/her deductible for procedures listed on the claim, which block should reflect this? _____

17. When must a provider sign Block 31? _____

_____

_____

18. When would it be appropriate to complete Block 32? _____

_____

_____

EXERCISES

19. Complete Case Studies 12-a through 12-j using the blank claim forms provided. Follow the step-by-step instructions in the textbook to properly complete the claim form. If a patient has a secondary carrier, complete an additional claim form using secondary directions in the textbook. You may choose to use a pencil so corrections can be made.

DATE 05/10/XX	REMARKS Patient prefers to be addressed as Bob			
PATIENT Robert D. Bow 444-55-6666		CHART # 12-a	SEX M	BIRTHDATE 02/12/1967

MAILING ADDRESS 663 Calabin Drive	CITY Anywhere	STATE US	ZIP 12345	HOME PHONE (101) 333 4445	WORK PHONE 576 2225

EMPLOYER Superfresh Foods	ADDRESS 187 East Avenue	PATIENT STATUS X — MARRIED DIVORCED SINGLE STUDENT OTHER

INSURANCE: PRIMARY North West Health	ID# 444-55-6666	GROUP SF123	SECONDARY POLICY

POLICYHOLDER NAME	BIRTHDATE	RELATIONSHIP Self	POLICYHOLDER NAME	BIRTHDATE	RELATIONSHIP

SUPPLEMENTAL PLAN   EMPLOYER

POLICYHOLDER NAME	BIRTHDATE	RELATIONSHIP	DIAGNOSIS	CODE
			1. Headache, facial pain	784.0
EMPLOYER			2. Cough	786.2
			3.	
REFERRING PHYSICIAN UPIN/SSN			4.	

PLACE OF SERVICE Office

PROCEDURES	CODE	CHARGE
1. Est. pt. OV level II	99212	$ 65.00
2.		
3.		
4.		
5.		
6.		

SPECIAL NOTES

TOTAL CHARGES $65.00	PAYMENTS 0	ADJUSTMENTS 0	BALANCE $65.00

RETURN VISIT 2 weeks	PHYSICIAN SIGNATURE Donald L. Givings, M.D.

DONALD L. GIVINGS, M.D.
11350 MEDICAL DRIVE, ANYWHERE US 12345
PHONE NUMBER (101)111-5555

MEDICARE D1234
MEDICAID DLG1234
BCBS 12345

EIN 11-123456
SSN 123-12-1234
PIN DG1234
GRP DG12345

(SAMPLE ONLY - NOT APPROVED FOR USE)

CARRIER

HEALTH INSURANCE CLAIM FORM

PICA		PICA

1. MEDICARE ☐ (Medicare #) MEDICAID ☐ (Medicaid #) CHAMPUS ☐ (Sponsor's SSN) CHAMPVA ☐ (VA File #) GROUP HEALTH PLAN ☐ (SSN or ID) FECA BLK LUNG ☐ (SSN) OTHER ☐ (ID)	1a. INSURED'S I.D. NUMBER (FOR PROGRAM IN ITEM 1)

2. PATIENT'S NAME (Last Name, First Name, Middle Initial)	3. PATIENT'S BIRTH DATE MM ┆ DD ┆ YY SEX M ☐ F ☐	4. INSURED'S NAME (Last Name, First Name, Middle Initial)

5. PATIENT'S ADDRESS (No. Street)	6. PATIENT RELATIONSHIP TO INSURED Self ☐ Spouse ☐ Child ☐ Other ☐	7. INSURED'S ADDRESS (No. Street)

CITY	STATE	8. PATIENT STATUS Single ☐ Married ☐ Other ☐	CITY	STATE

ZIP CODE	TELEPHONE (Include Area Code) ( )	Employed ☐ Full-Time Student ☐ Part-Time Student ☐	ZIP CODE	TELEPHONE (INCLUDE AREA CODE) ( )

9. OTHER INSURED'S NAME (Last Name, First Name, Middle Initial)	10. IS PATIENT'S CONDITION RELATED TO:	11. INSURED'S POLICY GROUP OR FECA NUMBER

a. OTHER INSURED'S POLICY OR GROUP NUMBER	a. EMPLOYMENT? (CURRENT OR PREVIOUS) YES ☐ NO ☐	a. INSURED'S DATE OF BIRTH MM ┆ DD ┆ YY SEX M ☐ F ☐

b. OTHER INSURED'S DATE OF BIRTH MM ┆ DD ┆ YY SEX M ☐ F ☐	b. AUTO ACCIDENT? PLACE (State) YES ☐ NO ☐	b. EMPLOYER'S NAME OR SCHOOL NAME

c. EMPLOYER'S NAME OR SCHOOL NAME	c. OTHER ACCIDENT? YES ☐ NO ☐	c. INSURANCE PLAN NAME OR PROGRAM NAME

d. INSURANCE PLAN NAME OR PROGRAM NAME	10d. RESERVED FOR LOCAL USE	d. IS THERE ANOTHER HEALTH BENEFIT PLAN? YES ☐ NO ☐ If yes, return to and complete item 9 a -- d.

READ BACK OF FORM BEFORE COMPLETING & SIGNING THIS FORM.
12. PATIENT'S OR AUTHORIZED PERSON'S SIGNATURE I authorize the release of any medical or other information necessary to process this claim. I also request payment of government benefits either to myself or to the party who accepts assignment below.

SIGNED _____   DATE _____

13. INSURED'S OR AUTHORIZED PERSON'S SIGNATURE I authorize payment of medical benefits to the undersigned physician or supplier for services described below.

SIGNED _____

PATIENT AND INSURED INFORMATION

14. DATE OF CURRENT: MM ┆ DD ┆ YY ILLNESS (First symptom) OR INJURY (Accident) OR PREGNANCY (LMP)	15. IF PATIENT HAS HAD SAME OR SIMILAR ILLNESS, GIVE FIRST DATE MM ┆ DD ┆ YY	16. DATES PATIENT UNABLE TO WORK IN CURRENT OCCUPATION MM ┆ DD ┆ YY MM ┆ DD ┆ YY FROM TO

17. NAME OF REFERRING PHYSICIAN OR OTHER SOURCE	17a. I.D. NUMBER OF REFERRING PHYSICIAN	18. HOSPITALIZATION DATES RELATED TO CURRENT SERVICES MM ┆ DD ┆ YY MM ┆ DD ┆ YY FROM TO

19. RESERVED FOR LOCAL USE		20. OUTSIDE LAB? $ CHARGES YES ☐ NO ☐

21. DIAGNOSIS OR NATURE OF ILLNESS OR INJURY. (RELATE ITEMS 1, 2, 3, OR 4 TO ITEM 24E BY LINE)

1. └___ . ___   3. └___ . ___
2. └___ . ___   4. └___ . ___

22. MEDICAID RESUBMISSION CODE   ORIGINAL REF. NO.

23. PRIOR AUTHORIZATION NUMBER

24. A. DATE(S) OF SERVICE From To MM DD YY MM DD YY	B. Place of Service	C. Type of Service	D. PROCEDURES, SERVICES, OR SUPPLIES (Explain Unusual Circumstances) CPT/HCPCS MODIFIER	E. DIAGNOSIS CODE	F. $ CHARGES	G. DAYS OR UNITS	H. EPSDT Family Plan	I. EMG	J. COB	K. RESERVED FOR LOCAL USE
1										
2										
3										
4										
5										
6										

25. FEDERAL TAX I.D. NUMBER SSN ☐ EIN ☐	26. PATIENT'S ACCOUNT NO.	27. ACCEPT ASSIGNMENT? (For govt. claims, see back) YES ☐ NO ☐	28. TOTAL CHARGE $	29. AMOUNT PAID $	30. BALANCE DUE $

31. SIGNATURE OF PHYSICIAN OR SUPPLIER INCLUDING DEGREES OR CREDENTIALS (I certify that the statements on the reverse apply to this bill and are made a part thereof.) SIGNED DATE	32. NAME AND ADDRESS OF FACILITY WHERE SERVICES WERE RENDERED (If other than home or office)	33. PHYSICIAN'S, SUPPLIER'S BILLING NAME, ADDRESS, ZIP CODE & PHONE # PIN# GRP#

PHYSICIAN OR SUPPLIER INFORMATION

(SAMPLE ONLY - NOT APPROVED FOR USE)   PLEASE PRINT OR TYPE   SAMPLE FORM 1500
SAMPLE FORM 1500 SAMPLE FORM 1500

DATE 12/04/XX			REMARKS				

PATIENT Bethany L. Branch	333-99-3434			CHART # 12-b	SEX F	BIRTHDATE 05/03/1986

MAILING ADDRESS 401 Cartvalley Court	CITY Anywhere	STATE US	ZIP 12345	HOME PHONE (101) 333 4466	WORK PHONE 333 5656

EMPLOYER	ADDRESS	PATIENT STATUS X MARRIED DIVORCED SINGLE STUDENT OTHER

INSURANCE: PRIMARY Metropolitan	ID# 212-22-4545	GROUP GW292	SECONDARY POLICY

POLICYHOLDER NAME John L. Branch	BIRTHDATE 10/10/54	RELATIONSHIP Father	POLICYHOLDER NAME	BIRTHDATE	RELATIONSHIP

SUPPLEMENTAL PLAN	EMPLOYER

POLICYHOLDER NAME	BIRTHDATE	RELATIONSHIP

DIAGNOSIS	CODE
1. Bronchitis	466.0
2. Strep Throat	034.0
3.	
4.	

EMPLOYER Gateway Computers Inc.

REFERRING PHYSICIAN UPIN/SSN James R. Feltbetter, M.D.   777887878

PLACE OF SERVICE   Office

PROCEDURES	CODE	CHARGE
1. Office Consult Level II	99242	$ 75.00
2. Quick Strep Test	86403	12.00
3.		
4.		
5.		
6.		

SPECIAL NOTES

TOTAL CHARGES $87.00	PAYMENTS 0	ADJUSTMENTS 0	BALANCE $87.00

RETURN VISIT PRN	PHYSICIAN SIGNATURE Donald L. Givings, M.D.

DONALD L. GIVINGS, M.D.
11350 MEDICAL DRIVE, ANYWHERE US 12345
PHONE NUMBER (101)111-5555

MEDICARE D1234
MEDICAID DLG1234
BCBS 12345

EIN 11-123456
SSN 123-12-1234
PIN DG1234
GRP DG12345

PLEASE
DO NOT
STAPLE
IN THIS
AREA

CARRIER

| | | PICA |

HEALTH INSURANCE CLAIM FORM

PICA | | |

| 1. | MEDICARE | MEDICAID | CHAMPUS | CHAMPVA | GROUP HEALTH PLAN | FECA BLK LUNG | OTHER | 1a. INSURED'S I.D. NUMBER | (FOR PROGRAM IN ITEM 1) |

☐ (Medicare #) ☐ (Medicaid #) ☐ (Sponsor's SSN) ☐ (VA File #) ☐ (SSN or ID) ☐ (SSN) ☐ (ID)

2. PATIENT'S NAME (Last Name, First Name, Middle Initial)

3. PATIENT'S BIRTH DATE MM ¦ DD ¦ YY   SEX   M ☐   F ☐

4. INSURED'S NAME (Last Name, First Name, Middle Initial)

5. PATIENT'S ADDRESS (No. Street)

6. PATIENT RELATIONSHIP TO INSURED   Self ☐   Spouse ☐   Child ☐   Other ☐

7. INSURED'S ADDRESS (No. Street)

CITY   STATE

8. PATIENT STATUS   Single ☐   Married ☐   Other ☐

CITY   STATE

ZIP CODE   TELEPHONE (Include Area Code) (   )

Employed ☐   Full-Time Student ☐   Part-Time Student ☐

ZIP CODE   TELEPHONE (INCLUDE AREA CODE) (   )

9. OTHER INSURED'S NAME (Last Name, First Name, Middle Initial)

10. IS PATIENT'S CONDITION RELATED TO:

11. INSURED'S POLICY GROUP OR FECA NUMBER

a. OTHER INSURED'S POLICY OR GROUP NUMBER

a. EMPLOYMENT? (CURRENT OR PREVIOUS)   YES ☐   NO ☐

a. INSURED'S DATE OF BIRTH MM ¦ DD ¦ YY   SEX   M ☐   F ☐

b. OTHER INSURED'S DATE OF BIRTH MM ¦ DD ¦ YY   SEX   M ☐   F ☐

b. AUTO ACCIDENT?   PLACE (State)   YES ☐   NO ☐

b. EMPLOYER'S NAME OR SCHOOL NAME

c. EMPLOYER'S NAME OR SCHOOL NAME

c. OTHER ACCIDENT?   YES ☐   NO ☐

c. INSURANCE PLAN NAME OR PROGRAM NAME

d. INSURANCE PLAN NAME OR PROGRAM NAME

10d. RESERVED FOR LOCAL USE

d. IS THERE ANOTHER HEALTH BENEFIT PLAN?   YES ☐   NO ☐   If yes, return to and complete item 9 a – d.

READ BACK OF FORM BEFORE COMPLETING & SIGNING THIS FORM.
12. PATIENT'S OR AUTHORIZED PERSON'S SIGNATURE I authorize the release of any medical or other information necessary to process this claim. I also request payment of government benefits either to myself or to the party who accepts assignment below.

SIGNED _____   DATE _____

13. INSURED'S OR AUTHORIZED PERSON'S SIGNATURE I authorize payment of medical benefits to the undersigned physician or supplier for services described below.

SIGNED _____

PATIENT AND INSURED INFORMATION

14. DATE OF CURRENT: MM ¦ DD ¦ YY   ILLNESS (First symptom) OR INJURY (Accident) OR PREGNANCY (LMP)

15. IF PATIENT HAS HAD SAME OR SIMILAR ILLNESS, GIVE FIRST DATE MM ¦ DD ¦ YY

16. DATES PATIENT UNABLE TO WORK IN CURRENT OCCUPATION   FROM MM ¦ DD ¦ YY   TO MM ¦ DD ¦ YY

17. NAME OF REFERRING PHYSICIAN OR OTHER SOURCE

17a. I.D. NUMBER OF REFERRING PHYSICIAN

18. HOSPITALIZATION DATES RELATED TO CURRENT SERVICES   FROM MM ¦ DD ¦ YY   TO MM ¦ DD ¦ YY

19. RESERVED FOR LOCAL USE

20. OUTSIDE LAB? $ CHARGES   YES ☐   NO ☐

21. DIAGNOSIS OR NATURE OF ILLNESS OR INJURY. (RELATE ITEMS 1, 2, 3, OR 4 TO ITEM 24E BY LINE)

1. |___ . ___   3. |___ . ___

2. |___ . ___   4. |___ . ___

22. MEDICAID RESUBMISSION CODE   ORIGINAL REF. NO.

23. PRIOR AUTHORIZATION NUMBER

24.	A				B	C	D	E	F	G	H	I	J	K
	DATE(S) OF SERVICE				Place of Service	Type of Service	PROCEDURES, SERVICES, OR SUPPLIES (Explain Unusual Circumstances) CPT/HCPCS ¦ MODIFIER	DIAGNOSIS CODE	$ CHARGES	DAYS OR UNITS	EPSDT Family Plan	EMG	COB	RESERVED FOR LOCAL USE
	From MM DD YY		To MM DD YY											
1														
2														
3														
4														
5														
6														

25. FEDERAL TAX I.D. NUMBER   SSN ☐   EIN ☐

26. PATIENT'S ACCOUNT NO.

27. ACCEPT ASSIGNMENT? (For govt. claims, see back)   YES ☐   NO ☐

28. TOTAL CHARGE $

29. AMOUNT PAID $

30. BALANCE DUE $

31. SIGNATURE OF PHYSICIAN OR SUPPLIER INCLUDING DEGREES OR CREDENTIALS (I certify that the statements on the reverse apply to this bill and are made a part thereof.)

SIGNED _____   DATE _____

32. NAME AND ADDRESS OF FACILITY WHERE SERVICES WERE RENDERED (If other than home or office)

33. PHYSICIAN'S, SUPPLIER'S BILLING NAME, ADDRESS, ZIP CODE & PHONE #

PIN# _____   GRP# _____

PHYSICIAN OR SUPPLIER INFORMATION

(SAMPLE ONLY - NOT APPROVED FOR USE)

PLEASE PRINT OR TYPE

SAMPLE FORM 1500
SAMPLE FORM 1500 SAMPLE FORM 1500

DATE 10/28/XX	REMARKS			
PATIENT Laurie P. Reed 456-78-6969		CHART # 12-c	SEX F	BIRTHDATE 06/05/1964
MAILING ADDRESS 579 Vacation Drive	CITY Anywhere	STATE US	ZIP 12345 HOME PHONE (101) 333 5555	WORK PHONE 444 5555
EMPLOYER The Learning Center	ADDRESS Anywhere, US	PATIENT STATUS X MARRIED DIVORCED SINGLE STUDENT OTHER		
INSURANCE: PRIMARY US Health	ID# C748593	GROUP TLC45	SECONDARY POLICY	

POLICYHOLDER NAME	BIRTHDATE	RELATIONSHIP Self	POLICYHOLDER NAME	BIRTHDATE	RELATIONSHIP
SUPPLEMENTAL PLAN			EMPLOYER		
POLICYHOLDER NAME	BIRTHDATE	RELATIONSHIP	DIAGNOSIS CODE 1. Allergic Rhinitis 477.9		
EMPLOYER			2.		
			3.		
REFERRING PHYSICIAN UPIN/SSN			4.		

PLACE OF SERVICE Office

PROCEDURES	CODE	CHARGE
1. Est. pt. OV level I	99211	$ 55.00
2.		
3.		
4.		
5.		
6.		

SPECIAL NOTES

TOTAL CHARGES $55.00	PAYMENTS $55.00	ADJUSTMENTS -0-	BALANCE -0-
RETURN VISIT PRN	PHYSICIAN SIGNATURE *Donald L. Givings, M.D.*		

	DONALD L. GIVINGS, M.D.	EIN 11-123456
MEDICARE D1234 MEDICAID DLG1234 BCBS 12345	11350 MEDICAL DRIVE, ANYWHERE US 12345 PHONE NUMBER (101)111-5555	SSN 123-12-1234 PIN DG1234 GRP DG12345

(SAMPLE ONLY - NOT APPROVED FOR USE)

CARRIER

[ ][ ] PICA

HEALTH INSURANCE CLAIM FORM

PICA [ ][ ]

1. MEDICARE [ ] (Medicare #)	MEDICAID [ ] (Medicaid #)	CHAMPUS [ ] (Sponsor's SSN)	CHAMPVA [ ] (VA File #)	GROUP HEALTH PLAN [ ] (SSN or ID)	FECA BLK LUNG [ ] (SSN)	OTHER [ ] (ID)	1a. INSURED'S I.D. NUMBER (FOR PROGRAM IN ITEM 1)

2. PATIENT'S NAME (Last Name, First Name, Middle Initial)

3. PATIENT'S BIRTH DATE MM | DD | YY   SEX M [ ]   F [ ]

4. INSURED'S NAME (Last Name, First Name, Middle Initial)

5. PATIENT'S ADDRESS (No. Street)

6. PATIENT RELATIONSHIP TO INSURED Self [ ] Spouse [ ] Child [ ] Other [ ]

7. INSURED'S ADDRESS (No. Street)

CITY   STATE

8. PATIENT STATUS Single [ ] Married [ ] Other [ ]

CITY   STATE

ZIP CODE   TELEPHONE (Include Area Code) ( )

Employed [ ] Full-Time Student [ ] Part-Time Student [ ]

ZIP CODE   TELEPHONE (INCLUDE AREA CODE) ( )

9. OTHER INSURED'S NAME (Last Name, First Name, Middle Initial)

10. IS PATIENT'S CONDITION RELATED TO:

11. INSURED'S POLICY GROUP OR FECA NUMBER

a. OTHER INSURED'S POLICY OR GROUP NUMBER

a. EMPLOYMENT? (CURRENT OR PREVIOUS) YES [ ] NO [ ]

a. INSURED'S DATE OF BIRTH MM | DD | YY   SEX M [ ] F [ ]

b. OTHER INSURED'S DATE OF BIRTH MM | DD | YY   SEX M [ ] F [ ]

b. AUTO ACCIDENT? PLACE (State) YES [ ] NO [ ]

b. EMPLOYER'S NAME OR SCHOOL NAME

c. EMPLOYER'S NAME OR SCHOOL NAME

c. OTHER ACCIDENT? YES [ ] NO [ ]

c. INSURANCE PLAN NAME OR PROGRAM NAME

d. INSURANCE PLAN NAME OR PROGRAM NAME

10d. RESERVED FOR LOCAL USE

d. IS THERE ANOTHER HEALTH BENEFIT PLAN? YES [ ] NO [ ] If yes, return to and complete item 9 a – d.

READ BACK OF FORM BEFORE COMPLETING & SIGNING THIS FORM.
12. PATIENT'S OR AUTHORIZED PERSON'S SIGNATURE I authorize the release of any medical or other information necessary to process this claim. I also request payment of government benefits either to myself or to the party who accepts assignment below.

SIGNED _____ DATE _____

13. INSURED'S OR AUTHORIZED PERSON'S SIGNATURE I authorize payment of medical benefits to the undersigned physician or supplier for services described below.

SIGNED _____

PATIENT AND INSURED INFORMATION

14. DATE OF CURRENT: MM | DD | YY ◄ ILLNESS (First symptom) OR INJURY (Accident) OR PREGNANCY (LMP)

15. IF PATIENT HAS HAD SAME OR SIMILAR ILLNESS, GIVE FIRST DATE MM | DD | YY

16. DATES PATIENT UNABLE TO WORK IN CURRENT OCCUPATION MM | DD | YY   MM | DD | YY FROM   TO

17. NAME OF REFERRING PHYSICIAN OR OTHER SOURCE

17a. I.D. NUMBER OF REFERRING PHYSICIAN

18. HOSPITALIZATION DATES RELATED TO CURRENT SERVICES MM | DD | YY   MM | DD | YY FROM   TO

19. RESERVED FOR LOCAL USE

20. OUTSIDE LAB? YES [ ] NO [ ] $ CHARGES

21. DIAGNOSIS OR NATURE OF ILLNESS OR INJURY. (RELATE ITEMS 1, 2, 3, OR 4 TO ITEM 24E BY LINE)
1. |___|.|___|
2. |___|.|___|
3. |___|.|___|
4. |___|.|___|

22. MEDICAID RESUBMISSION CODE   ORIGINAL REF. NO.

23. PRIOR AUTHORIZATION NUMBER

24. A DATE(S) OF SERVICE					B Place of Service	C Type of Service	D PROCEDURES, SERVICES, OR SUPPLIES (Explain Unusual Circumstances) CPT/HCPCS MODIFIER	E DIAGNOSIS CODE	F $ CHARGES	G DAYS OR UNITS	H EPSDT Family Plan	I EMG	J COB	K RESERVED FOR LOCAL USE
From MM	DD	YY	To MM	DD	YY										
1														
2														
3														
4														
5														
6														

25. FEDERAL TAX I.D. NUMBER   SSN [ ] EIN [ ]

26. PATIENT'S ACCOUNT NO.

27. ACCEPT ASSIGNMENT? (For govt. claims, see back) YES [ ] NO [ ]

28. TOTAL CHARGE $

29. AMOUNT PAID $

30. BALANCE DUE $

31. SIGNATURE OF PHYSICIAN OR SUPPLIER INCLUDING DEGREES OR CREDENTIALS (I certify that the statements on the reverse apply to this bill and are made a part thereof.)

SIGNED _____ DATE _____

32. NAME AND ADDRESS OF FACILITY WHERE SERVICES WERE RENDERED (If other than home or office)

33. PHYSICIAN'S, SUPPLIER'S BILLING NAME, ADDRESS, ZIP CODE & PHONE #

PIN# _____ GRP# _____

PHYSICIAN OR SUPPLIER INFORMATION

(SAMPLE ONLY - NOT APPROVED FOR USE)

PLEASE PRINT OR TYPE

SAMPLE FORM 1500
SAMPLE FORM 1500 SAMPLE FORM 1500

DATE	REMARKS			
07/04/XX	Prior Authorization #27901			

PATIENT			CHART #	SEX	BIRTHDATE
Pamela Sharp	212-77-8989		12-d	F	05/09/1970

MAILING ADDRESS	CITY	STATE	ZIP	HOME PHONE	WORK PHONE
678 Heather Avenue	Anywhere	US	12345	(101) 333 5559	444 5556

EMPLOYER	ADDRESS	PATIENT STATUS				
Design Consultants	Anywhere US			X		
		MARRIED	DIVORCED	SINGLE	STUDENT	OTHER

INSURANCE: PRIMARY	ID#	GROUP	SECONDARY POLICY
Cigna	123-66-6666	DC22	

POLICYHOLDER NAME	BIRTHDATE	RELATIONSHIP	POLICYHOLDER NAME	BIRTHDATE	RELATIONSHIP
		Self			

SUPPLEMENTAL PLAN	EMPLOYER

POLICYHOLDER NAME	BIRTHDATE	RELATIONSHIP	DIAGNOSIS	CODE
			1. Chronic Obstructive Asthma	493.21
EMPLOYER			2. Bronchial Pneumonia	485
			3.	
REFERRING PHYSICIAN UPIN/SSN			4.	
Ledger Masters, M.D.	595-33-4959			

PLACE OF SERVICE   Office

PROCEDURES		CODE	CHARGE
1. Initial Hospital Level I	06/28/XX	99221	$ 75.00
2. Subsequent Hospital Level I	06/29/XX	99231	50.00
3. Subsequent Hospital Level I	06/30/XX	99231	50.00
4. Subsequent Hospital Level I	07/01/XX	99231	50.00
5. Subsequent Hospital Level I	07/02/XX	99231	50.00
6. Discharge 30 Min.	07/03/XX	99238	75.00

SPECIAL NOTES

TOTAL CHARGES	PAYMENTS	ADJUSTMENTS	BALANCE
$350.00	0	0	$350.00

RETURN VISIT	PHYSICIAN SIGNATURE
	Donald L. Givings, M.D.

	DONALD L. GIVINGS, M.D.	EIN 11-123456
MEDICARE D1234	11350 MEDICAL DRIVE, ANYWHERE US 12345	SSN 123-12-1234
MEDICAID DLG1234	PHONE NUMBER (101)111-5555	PIN DG1234
BCBS 12345		GRP DG12345

PLEASE
DO NOT
STAPLE
IN THIS
AREA

CARRIER

	PICA		

HEALTH INSURANCE CLAIM FORM

PICA | | |

1. MEDICARE ☐ (Medicare #) MEDICAID ☐ (Medicaid #) CHAMPUS ☐ (Sponsor's SSN) CHAMPVA ☐ (VA File #) GROUP HEALTH PLAN ☐ (SSN or ID) FECA BLK LUNG ☐ (SSN) OTHER ☐ (ID)

1a. INSURED'S I.D. NUMBER   (FOR PROGRAM IN ITEM 1)

2. PATIENT'S NAME (Last Name, First Name, Middle Initial)

3. PATIENT'S BIRTH DATE MM ┊ DD ┊ YY   SEX M ☐ F ☐

4. INSURED'S NAME (Last Name, First Name, Middle Initial)

5. PATIENT'S ADDRESS (No. Street)

6. PATIENT RELATIONSHIP TO INSURED Self ☐ Spouse ☐ Child ☐ Other ☐

7. INSURED'S ADDRESS (No. Street)

CITY   STATE

8. PATIENT STATUS Single ☐ Married ☐ Other ☐

CITY   STATE

ZIP CODE   TELEPHONE (Include Area Code) (   )

Employed ☐ Full-Time Student ☐ Part-Time Student ☐

ZIP CODE   TELEPHONE (INCLUDE AREA CODE) (   )

9. OTHER INSURED'S NAME (Last Name, First Name, Middle Initial)

10. IS PATIENT'S CONDITION RELATED TO:

11. INSURED'S POLICY GROUP OR FECA NUMBER

a. OTHER INSURED'S POLICY OR GROUP NUMBER

a. EMPLOYMENT? (CURRENT OR PREVIOUS) ☐ YES ☐ NO

a. INSURED'S DATE OF BIRTH MM ┊ DD ┊ YY   SEX M ☐ F ☐

b. OTHER INSURED'S DATE OF BIRTH MM ┊ DD ┊ YY   SEX M ☐ F ☐

b. AUTO ACCIDENT?   PLACE (State) ☐ YES ☐ NO

b. EMPLOYER'S NAME OR SCHOOL NAME

c. EMPLOYER'S NAME OR SCHOOL NAME

c. OTHER ACCIDENT? ☐ YES ☐ NO

c. INSURANCE PLAN NAME OR PROGRAM NAME

d. INSURANCE PLAN NAME OR PROGRAM NAME

10d. RESERVED FOR LOCAL USE

d. IS THERE ANOTHER HEALTH BENEFIT PLAN? ☐ YES ☐ NO If yes, return to and complete item 9 a – d.

READ BACK OF FORM BEFORE COMPLETING & SIGNING THIS FORM.

12. PATIENT'S OR AUTHORIZED PERSON'S SIGNATURE I authorize the release of any medical or other information necessary to process this claim. I also request payment of government benefits either to myself or to the party who accepts assignment below.

SIGNED _____ DATE _____

13. INSURED'S OR AUTHORIZED PERSON'S SIGNATURE I authorize payment of medical benefits to the undersigned physician or supplier for services described below.

SIGNED _____

PATIENT AND INSURED INFORMATION

14. DATE OF CURRENT: MM ┊ DD ┊ YY ◄ ILLNESS (First symptom) OR INJURY (Accident) OR PREGNANCY (LMP)

15. IF PATIENT HAS HAD SAME OR SIMILAR ILLNESS, GIVE FIRST DATE MM ┊ DD ┊ YY

16. DATES PATIENT UNABLE TO WORK IN CURRENT OCCUPATION FROM MM ┊ DD ┊ YY TO MM ┊ DD ┊ YY

17. NAME OF REFERRING PHYSICIAN OR OTHER SOURCE

17a. I.D. NUMBER OF REFERRING PHYSICIAN

18. HOSPITALIZATION DATES RELATED TO CURRENT SERVICES FROM MM ┊ DD ┊ YY TO MM ┊ DD ┊ YY

19. RESERVED FOR LOCAL USE

20. OUTSIDE LAB? ☐ YES ☐ NO $ CHARGES

21. DIAGNOSIS OR NATURE OF ILLNESS OR INJURY. (RELATE ITEMS 1, 2, 3, OR 4 TO ITEM 24E BY LINE)

1. └___ . ___   3. └___ . ___

2. └___ . ___   4. └___ . ___

22. MEDICAID RESUBMISSION CODE   ORIGINAL REF. NO.

23. PRIOR AUTHORIZATION NUMBER

24. A. DATE(S) OF SERVICE			B. Place of Service	C. Type of Service	D. PROCEDURES, SERVICES, OR SUPPLIES (Explain Unusual Circumstances)		E. DIAGNOSIS CODE	F. $ CHARGES	G. DAYS OR UNITS	H. EPSDT Family Plan	I. EMG	J. COB	K. RESERVED FOR LOCAL USE
From MM DD YY	To MM DD YY				CPT/HCPCS	MODIFIER							
1													
2													
3													
4													
5													
6													

25. FEDERAL TAX I.D. NUMBER SSN ☐ EIN ☐

26. PATIENT'S ACCOUNT NO.

27. ACCEPT ASSIGNMENT? (For govt. claims, see back) ☐ YES ☐ NO

28. TOTAL CHARGE $

29. AMOUNT PAID $

30. BALANCE DUE $

31. SIGNATURE OF PHYSICIAN OR SUPPLIER INCLUDING DEGREES OR CREDENTIALS (I certify that the statements on the reverse apply to this bill and are made a part thereof.)

SIGNED _____ DATE _____

32. NAME AND ADDRESS OF FACILITY WHERE SERVICES WERE RENDERED (If other than home or office)

33. PHYSICIAN'S, SUPPLIER'S BILLING NAME, ADDRESS, ZIP CODE & PHONE #

PIN#   GRP#

PHYSICIAN OR SUPPLIER INFORMATION

PLEASE PRINT OR TYPE

SAMPLE FORM 1500
SAMPLE FORM 1500 SAMPLE FORM 1500

DATE	REMARKS				
02/03/XX					

PATIENT		CHART #	SEX	BIRTHDATE
James R. Brandt 576-66-9997		12-e	M	12/05/1948

MAILING ADDRESS	CITY	STATE	ZIP	HOME PHONE	WORK PHONE
95 Commission Circle Anywhere		US	12345	(101) 223 5555	224 5555

EMPLOYER	ADDRESS	PATIENT STATUS
The Yard Guard	Anywhere US	X MARRIED DIVORCED SINGLE STUDENT OTHER

INSURANCE: PRIMARY	ID#	GROUP	SECONDARY POLICY
Prudential	555-66-7777	YG4	

POLICYHOLDER NAME	BIRTHDATE	RELATIONSHIP	POLICYHOLDER NAME	BIRTHDATE	RELATIONSHIP
		Self			

SUPPLEMENTAL PLAN	EMPLOYER

POLICYHOLDER NAME	BIRTHDATE	RELATIONSHIP

DIAGNOSIS / CODE

1. Diabetes, Type II — 250.00
2. Hypertension, Benign — 401.1
3. Gout — 274.0
4.

EMPLOYER

REFERRING PHYSICIAN UPIN/SSN
Rita M. Michaels, M.D.   343-54-7979

PLACE OF SERVICE   Office

PROCEDURES		CODE	CHARGE
1. New pt. OV level IV	02/02/XX	99204	$ 100.00
2. EKG	02/02/XX	93000	50.00
3. Glucose	02/02/XX	82947	10.00
4. Est. Pt. OV Level III	02/03/XX	99213	75.00
5. Glucose	02/03/XX	82947	10.00
6.			

SPECIAL NOTES

Onset 02/02/XX

TOTAL CHARGES	PAYMENTS	ADJUSTMENTS	BALANCE
$245.00	0	0	$245.00

RETURN VISIT	PHYSICIAN SIGNATURE
2 weeks	*Donald L. Givings, M.D.*

DONALD L. GIVINGS, M.D.
11350 MEDICAL DRIVE, ANYWHERE US 12345
PHONE NUMBER (101)111-5555

MEDICARE D1234
MEDICAID DLG1234
BCBS 12345

EIN 11-123456
SSN 123-12-1234
PIN DG1234
GRP DG12345

PLEASE
DO NOT
STAPLE
IN THIS
AREA

CARRIER

□□ PICA

HEALTH INSURANCE CLAIM FORM

PICA □□□

1.	MEDICARE	MEDICAID	CHAMPUS	CHAMPVA	GROUP HEALTH PLAN	FECA BLK LUNG	OTHER	1a. INSURED'S I.D. NUMBER (FOR PROGRAM IN ITEM 1)
	□ (Medicare #)	□ (Medicaid #)	□ (Sponsor's SSN)	□ (VA File #)	□ (SSN or ID)	□ (SSN)	□ (ID)	

2. PATIENT'S NAME (Last Name, First Name, Middle Initial)

3. PATIENT'S BIRTH DATE
MM | DD | YY   SEX   M □ F □

4. INSURED'S NAME (Last Name, First Name, Middle Initial)

5. PATIENT'S ADDRESS (No. Street)

6. PATIENT RELATIONSHIP TO INSURED
Self □   Spouse □   Child □   Other □

7. INSURED'S ADDRESS (No. Street)

CITY   STATE

8. PATIENT STATUS
Single □   Married □   Other □
Employed □   Full-Time Student □   Part-Time Student □

CITY   STATE

ZIP CODE   TELEPHONE (Include Area Code)
( )

ZIP CODE   TELEPHONE (INCLUDE AREA CODE)
( )

9. OTHER INSURED'S NAME (Last Name, First Name, Middle Initial)

10. IS PATIENT'S CONDITION RELATED TO:

11. INSURED'S POLICY GROUP OR FECA NUMBER

a. OTHER INSURED'S POLICY OR GROUP NUMBER

a. EMPLOYMENT? (CURRENT OR PREVIOUS)
□ YES   □ NO

a. INSURED'S DATE OF BIRTH
MM | DD | YY   SEX   M □ F □

b. OTHER INSURED'S DATE OF BIRTH
MM | DD | YY   SEX   M □ F □

b. AUTO ACCIDENT?   PLACE (State)
□ YES   □ NO

b. EMPLOYER'S NAME OR SCHOOL NAME

c. EMPLOYER'S NAME OR SCHOOL NAME

c. OTHER ACCIDENT?
□ YES   □ NO

c. INSURANCE PLAN NAME OR PROGRAM NAME

d. INSURANCE PLAN NAME OR PROGRAM NAME

10d. RESERVED FOR LOCAL USE

d. IS THERE ANOTHER HEALTH BENEFIT PLAN?
□ YES   □ NO   If yes, return to and complete item 9 a – d.

READ BACK OF FORM BEFORE COMPLETING & SIGNING THIS FORM.
12. PATIENT'S OR AUTHORIZED PERSON'S SIGNATURE I authorize the release of any medical or other information necessary to process this claim. I also request payment of government benefits either to myself or to the party who accepts assignment below.

SIGNED _____ DATE _____

13. INSURED'S OR AUTHORIZED PERSON'S SIGNATURE I authorize payment of medical benefits to the undersigned physician or supplier for services described below.

SIGNED _____

PATIENT AND INSURED INFORMATION

14. DATE OF CURRENT: ◄ ILLNESS (First symptom) OR INJURY (Accident) OR PREGNANCY (LMP)
MM | DD | YY

15. IF PATIENT HAS HAD SAME OR SIMILAR ILLNESS, GIVE FIRST DATE   MM | DD | YY

16. DATES PATIENT UNABLE TO WORK IN CURRENT OCCUPATION
MM | DD | YY   MM | DD | YY
FROM   TO

17. NAME OF REFERRING PHYSICIAN OR OTHER SOURCE

17a. I.D. NUMBER OF REFERRING PHYSICIAN

18. HOSPITALIZATION DATES RELATED TO CURRENT SERVICES
MM | DD | YY   MM | DD | YY
FROM   TO

19. RESERVED FOR LOCAL USE

20. OUTSIDE LAB? $ CHARGES
□ YES   □ NO

21. DIAGNOSIS OR NATURE OF ILLNESS OR INJURY. (RELATE ITEMS 1, 2, 3, OR 4 TO ITEM 24E BY LINE)
1. |___.___| 3. |___.___|
2. |___.___| 4. |___.___|

22. MEDICAID RESUBMISSION
CODE   ORIGINAL REF. NO.

23. PRIOR AUTHORIZATION NUMBER

24. A DATE(S) OF SERVICE						B Place of Service	C Type of Service	D PROCEDURES, SERVICES, OR SUPPLIES (Explain Unusual Circumstances)		E DIAGNOSIS CODE	F $ CHARGES	G DAYS OR UNITS	H EPSDT Family Plan	I EMG	J COB	K RESERVED FOR LOCAL USE
From MM	DD	YY	To MM	DD	YY			CPT/HCPCS	MODIFIER							
1																
2																
3																
4																
5																
6																

25. FEDERAL TAX I.D. NUMBER   SSN □ EIN □

26. PATIENT'S ACCOUNT NO.

27. ACCEPT ASSIGNMENT? (For govt. claims, see back)
□ YES   □ NO

28. TOTAL CHARGE
$

29. AMOUNT PAID
$

30. BALANCE DUE
$

31. SIGNATURE OF PHYSICIAN OR SUPPLIER INCLUDING DEGREES OR CREDENTIALS
(I certify that the statements on the reverse apply to this bill and are made a part thereof.)

SIGNED _____ DATE _____

32. NAME AND ADDRESS OF FACILITY WHERE SERVICES WERE RENDERED (If other than home or office)

33. PHYSICIAN'S, SUPPLIER'S BILLING NAME, ADDRESS, ZIP CODE & PHONE #

PIN#   GRP#

PHYSICIAN OR SUPPLIER INFORMATION

PLEASE PRINT OR TYPE

SAMPLE FORM 1500
SAMPLE FORM 1500 SAMPLE FORM 1500

DATE	REMARKS			
04/23/XX	Patient has a $10 Copay			

PATIENT		CHART #	SEX	BIRTHDATE
Lois R. Jamison	212-34-1414	12-f	F	03/28/1950

MAILING ADDRESS	CITY	STATE	ZIP	HOME PHONE	WORK PHONE
548 Dayton Terr.	Anywhere	US	12345	(101) 333 5555	444 5555

EMPLOYER	ADDRESS	PATIENT STATUS
Printers "R" Us	Anywhere, US	X MARRIED DIVORCED SINGLE STUDENT OTHER

INSURANCE: PRIMARY	ID#	GROUP	SECONDARY POLICY
Great West	21785		

POLICYHOLDER NAME	BIRTHDATE	RELATIONSHIP	POLICYHOLDER NAME	BIRTHDATE	RELATIONSHIP
		Self			

SUPPLEMENTAL PLAN	EMPLOYER

POLICYHOLDER NAME	BIRTHDATE	RELATIONSHIP	DIAGNOSIS	CODE
			1. Incontinence of urine	788.30
EMPLOYER			2. Polyuria	788.42
			3.	
REFERRING PHYSICIAN UPIN/SSN			4.	

PLACE OF SERVICE	Office

PROCEDURES	CODE	CHARGE
1. Est. Pt. OV Level II	99212	$ 65.00
2. Urinalysis	81000	10.00
3.		
4.		
5.		
6.		

SPECIAL NOTES
Patient to be scheduled at St. John's Hospital for surgery

TOTAL CHARGES	PAYMENTS	ADJUSTMENTS	BALANCE
$75.00	$10.00	-0-	$65.00

RETURN VISIT	PHYSICIAN SIGNATURE
Refer to Dr. Stream	Donald L. Givings, M.D.

MEDICARE D1234 MEDICAID DLG1234 BCBS 12345	DONALD L. GIVINGS, M.D. 11350 MEDICAL DRIVE, ANYWHERE US 12345 PHONE NUMBER (101)111-5555	EIN 11-123456 SSN 123-12-1234 PIN DG1234 GRP DG12345

(SAMPLE ONLY - NOT APPROVED FOR USE)

CARRIER

| | PICA

HEALTH INSURANCE CLAIM FORM

PICA | |

1. MEDICARE MEDICAID CHAMPUS CHAMPVA GROUP HEALTH PLAN FECA BLK LUNG OTHER	1a. INSURED'S I.D. NUMBER (FOR PROGRAM IN ITEM 1)
☐ (Medicare #) ☐ (Medicaid #) ☐ (Sponsor's SSN) ☐ (VA File #) ☐ (SSN or ID) ☐ (SSN) ☐ (ID)	

2. PATIENT'S NAME (Last Name, First Name, Middle Initial)	3. PATIENT'S BIRTH DATE MM DD YY SEX M ☐ F ☐	4. INSURED'S NAME (Last Name, First Name, Middle Initial)

5. PATIENT'S ADDRESS (No. Street)	6. PATIENT RELATIONSHIP TO INSURED Self ☐ Spouse ☐ Child ☐ Other ☐	7. INSURED'S ADDRESS (No. Street)
CITY STATE	8. PATIENT STATUS Single ☐ Married ☐ Other ☐	CITY STATE
ZIP CODE TELEPHONE (Include Area Code) ( )	Employed ☐ Full-Time Student ☐ Part-Time Student ☐	ZIP CODE TELEPHONE (INCLUDE AREA CODE) ( )

9. OTHER INSURED'S NAME (Last Name, First Name, Middle Initial)	10. IS PATIENT'S CONDITION RELATED TO:	11. INSURED'S POLICY GROUP OR FECA NUMBER
a. OTHER INSURED'S POLICY OR GROUP NUMBER	a. EMPLOYMENT? (CURRENT OR PREVIOUS) ☐ YES ☐ NO	a. INSURED'S DATE OF BIRTH MM DD YY SEX M ☐ F ☐
b. OTHER INSURED'S DATE OF BIRTH MM DD YY SEX M ☐ F ☐	b. AUTO ACCIDENT? PLACE (State) ☐ YES ☐ NO	b. EMPLOYER'S NAME OR SCHOOL NAME
c. EMPLOYER'S NAME OR SCHOOL NAME	c. OTHER ACCIDENT? ☐ YES ☐ NO	c. INSURANCE PLAN NAME OR PROGRAM NAME
d. INSURANCE PLAN NAME OR PROGRAM NAME	10d. RESERVED FOR LOCAL USE	d. IS THERE ANOTHER HEALTH BENEFIT PLAN? ☐ YES ☐ NO If yes, return to and complete item 9 a – d.

READ BACK OF FORM BEFORE COMPLETING & SIGNING THIS FORM.
12. PATIENT'S OR AUTHORIZED PERSON'S SIGNATURE I authorize the release of any medical or other information necessary to process this claim. I also request payment of government benefits either to myself or to the party who accepts assignment below.

SIGNED _____ DATE _____

13. INSURED'S OR AUTHORIZED PERSON'S SIGNATURE I authorize payment of medical benefits to the undersigned physician or supplier for services described below.

SIGNED _____

PATIENT AND INSURED INFORMATION

14. DATE OF CURRENT: ILLNESS (First symptom) OR INJURY (Accident) OR PREGNANCY (LMP) MM DD YY	15. IF PATIENT HAS HAD SAME OR SIMILAR ILLNESS, GIVE FIRST DATE MM DD YY	16. DATES PATIENT UNABLE TO WORK IN CURRENT OCCUPATION MM DD YY MM DD YY FROM TO
17. NAME OF REFERRING PHYSICIAN OR OTHER SOURCE	17a. I.D. NUMBER OF REFERRING PHYSICIAN	18. HOSPITALIZATION DATES RELATED TO CURRENT SERVICES MM DD YY MM DD YY FROM TO
19. RESERVED FOR LOCAL USE		20. OUTSIDE LAB? ☐ YES ☐ NO $ CHARGES

21. DIAGNOSIS OR NATURE OF ILLNESS OR INJURY. (RELATE ITEMS 1, 2, 3, OR 4 TO ITEM 24E BY LINE)	22. MEDICAID RESUBMISSION CODE ORIGINAL REF. NO.
1. L___ . ___ 3. L___ . ___ 2. L___ . ___ 4. L___ . ___	23. PRIOR AUTHORIZATION NUMBER

24. A DATE(S) OF SERVICE						B Place of Service	C Type of Service	D PROCEDURES, SERVICES, OR SUPPLIES (Explain Unusual Circumstances) CPT/HCPCS	MODIFIER	E DIAGNOSIS CODE	F $ CHARGES	G DAYS OR UNITS	H EPSDT Family Plan	I EMG	J COB	K RESERVED FOR LOCAL USE
From MM	DD	YY	To MM	DD	YY											
1																
2																
3																
4																
5																
6																

25. FEDERAL TAX I.D. NUMBER SSN ☐ EIN ☐	26. PATIENT'S ACCOUNT NO.	27. ACCEPT ASSIGNMENT? (For govt. claims, see back) ☐ YES ☐ NO	28. TOTAL CHARGE $	29. AMOUNT PAID $	30. BALANCE DUE $

31. SIGNATURE OF PHYSICIAN OR SUPPLIER INCLUDING DEGREES OR CREDENTIALS (I certify that the statements on the reverse apply to this bill and are made a part thereof.) SIGNED DATE	32. NAME AND ADDRESS OF FACILITY WHERE SERVICES WERE RENDERED (If other than home or office)	33. PHYSICIAN'S, SUPPLIER'S BILLING NAME, ADDRESS, ZIP CODE & PHONE # PIN# GRP#

PHYSICIAN OR SUPPLIER INFORMATION

(SAMPLE ONLY - NOT APPROVED FOR USE)

PLEASE PRINT OR TYPE

SAMPLE FORM 1500
SAMPLE FORM 1500 SAMPLE FORM 1500

93

DATE	REMARKS			
05/12/XX	Prior Authorization #29704/Onset of symptoms 4/23/XX			

PATIENT		CHART #	SEX	BIRTHDATE
Lois R. Jamison 212-34-1414		12-g	F	03/28/1950

MAILING ADDRESS	CITY	STATE	ZIP	HOME PHONE	WORK PHONE
548 Dayton Terr.	Anywhere	US	12345	(101) 333 5555	444 5555

EMPLOYER	ADDRESS	PATIENT STATUS
Printers "R" Us	Anywhere, US	X
		MARRIED DIVORCED SINGLE STUDENT OTHER

INSURANCE: PRIMARY	ID#	GROUP	SECONDARY POLICY
Great West	21785		

POLICYHOLDER NAME	BIRTHDATE	RELATIONSHIP	POLICYHOLDER NAME	BIRTHDATE	RELATIONSHIP
		Self			

SUPPLEMENTAL PLAN	EMPLOYER

POLICYHOLDER NAME	BIRTHDATE	RELATIONSHIP

DIAGNOSIS   **CODE**

1. Incontinence of urine   788.30
2. Polyuria   788.42
3.
4.

EMPLOYER

REFERRING PHYSICIAN UPIN/SSN	
Donald L. Givings, MD	123-12-1234

PLACE OF SERVICE   Office

PROCEDURES	CODE	CHARGE
1. Office Consultation Level III	99243	$ 85.00
2. Urinalysis, with Micro.	81001	10.00
3.		
4.		
5.		
6.		

SPECIAL NOTES

Patient to be scheduled at St. John's Hospital for surgery

TOTAL CHARGES	PAYMENTS	ADJUSTMENTS	BALANCE
$95.00	-0-	-0-	$95.00

RETURN VISIT	PHYSICIAN SIGNATURE
	Paul R. Stream, M.D.

MEDICARE P1234 MEDICAID PRS1234 BCBS 12345	**PAUL R. STREAM, M.D. UROLOGY** **456 HOSPITAL DRIVE, ANYWHERE US 12345** **PHONE NUMBER (101)111-5555**	EIN 11223344 SSN 555-12-1234 PIN PS1234 GRP PS12345

PLEASE
DO NOT
STAPLE
IN THIS
AREA

CARRIER

| | PICA | |

HEALTH INSURANCE CLAIM FORM

PICA | | |

1. MEDICARE	MEDICAID	CHAMPUS	CHAMPVA	GROUP HEALTH PLAN	FECA BLK LUNG	OTHER	1a. INSURED'S I.D. NUMBER	(FOR PROGRAM IN ITEM 1)
(Medicare #)	(Medicaid #)	(Sponsor's SSN)	(VA File #)	(SSN or ID)	(SSN)	(ID)		

2. PATIENT'S NAME (Last Name, First Name, Middle Initial)

3. PATIENT'S BIRTH DATE MM | DD | YY SEX M | F

4. INSURED'S NAME (Last Name, First Name, Middle Initial)

5. PATIENT'S ADDRESS (No. Street)

6. PATIENT RELATIONSHIP TO INSURED Self | Spouse | Child | Other

7. INSURED'S ADDRESS (No. Street)

CITY | STATE

8. PATIENT STATUS Single | Married | Other

CITY | STATE

ZIP CODE | TELEPHONE (Include Area Code) ( )

Employed | Full-Time Student | Part-Time Student

ZIP CODE | TELEPHONE (INCLUDE AREA CODE) ( )

9. OTHER INSURED'S NAME (Last Name, First Name, Middle Initial)

10. IS PATIENT'S CONDITION RELATED TO:

11. INSURED'S POLICY GROUP OR FECA NUMBER

a. OTHER INSURED'S POLICY OR GROUP NUMBER

a. EMPLOYMENT? (CURRENT OR PREVIOUS) YES | NO

a. INSURED'S DATE OF BIRTH MM | DD | YY SEX M | F

b. OTHER INSURED'S DATE OF BIRTH MM | DD | YY SEX M | F

b. AUTO ACCIDENT? PLACE (State) YES | NO

b. EMPLOYER'S NAME OR SCHOOL NAME

c. EMPLOYER'S NAME OR SCHOOL NAME

c. OTHER ACCIDENT? YES | NO

c. INSURANCE PLAN NAME OR PROGRAM NAME

d. INSURANCE PLAN NAME OR PROGRAM NAME

10d. RESERVED FOR LOCAL USE

d. IS THERE ANOTHER HEALTH BENEFIT PLAN? YES | NO If yes, return to and complete item 9 a – d.

READ BACK OF FORM BEFORE COMPLETING & SIGNING THIS FORM.
12. PATIENT'S OR AUTHORIZED PERSON'S SIGNATURE. I authorize the release of any medical or other information necessary to process this claim. I also request payment of government benefits either to myself or to the party who accepts assignment below.

SIGNED _____ DATE _____

13. INSURED'S OR AUTHORIZED PERSON'S SIGNATURE. I authorize payment of medical benefits to the undersigned physician or supplier for services described below.

SIGNED _____

PATIENT AND INSURED INFORMATION

14. DATE OF CURRENT: MM | DD | YY ILLNESS (First symptom) OR INJURY (Accident) OR PREGNANCY (LMP)

15. IF PATIENT HAS HAD SAME OR SIMILAR ILLNESS, GIVE FIRST DATE MM | DD | YY

16. DATES PATIENT UNABLE TO WORK IN CURRENT OCCUPATION MM | DD | YY FROM TO MM | DD | YY

17. NAME OF REFERRING PHYSICIAN OR OTHER SOURCE

17a. I.D. NUMBER OF REFERRING PHYSICIAN

18. HOSPITALIZATION DATES RELATED TO CURRENT SERVICES MM | DD | YY FROM TO MM | DD | YY

19. RESERVED FOR LOCAL USE

20. OUTSIDE LAB? YES | NO $ CHARGES

21. DIAGNOSIS OR NATURE OF ILLNESS OR INJURY. (RELATE ITEMS 1, 2, 3, OR 4 TO ITEM 24E BY LINE)
1. ___ . ___   3. ___ . ___
2. ___ . ___   4. ___ . ___

22. MEDICAID RESUBMISSION CODE ORIGINAL REF. NO.

23. PRIOR AUTHORIZATION NUMBER

24. A DATE(S) OF SERVICE						B Place of Service	C Type of Service	D PROCEDURES, SERVICES, OR SUPPLIES (Explain Unusual Circumstances) CPT/HCPCS	MODIFIER	E DIAGNOSIS CODE	F $ CHARGES	G DAYS OR UNITS	H EPSDT Family Plan	I EMG	J COB	K RESERVED FOR LOCAL USE
From MM	DD	YY	To MM	DD	YY											
1																
2																
3																
4																
5																
6																

25. FEDERAL TAX I.D. NUMBER SSN | EIN

26. PATIENT'S ACCOUNT NO.

27. ACCEPT ASSIGNMENT? (For govt. claims, see back) YES | NO

28. TOTAL CHARGE $

29. AMOUNT PAID $

30. BALANCE DUE $

31. SIGNATURE OF PHYSICIAN OR SUPPLIER INCLUDING DEGREES OR CREDENTIALS (I certify that the statements on the reverse apply to this bill and are made a part thereof.)

SIGNED _____ DATE _____

32. NAME AND ADDRESS OF FACILITY WHERE SERVICES WERE RENDERED (If other than home or office)

33. PHYSICIAN'S, SUPPLIER'S BILLING NAME, ADDRESS, ZIP CODE & PHONE #

PIN# | GRP#

PHYSICIAN OR SUPPLIER INFORMATION

PLEASE PRINT OR TYPE

SAMPLE FORM 1500
SAMPLE FORM 1500 SAMPLE FORM 1500

95

DATE	REMARKS
05/19/XX	Prior Authorization #29948/Onset of symptoms 4/23/XX

PATIENT			CHART #	SEX	BIRTHDATE
Lois R. Jamison	212-34-1414		12-h	F	03/28/1950

MAILING ADDRESS	CITY	STATE	ZIP	HOME PHONE	WORK PHONE
548 Dayton Terr.	Anywhere	US	12345	(101) 333 5555	444 5555

EMPLOYER	ADDRESS	PATIENT STATUS
Printers "R" Us	Anywhere, US	X MARRIED DIVORCED SINGLE STUDENT OTHER

INSURANCE: PRIMARY	ID#	GROUP	SECONDARY POLICY
Great West	21785		

POLICYHOLDER NAME	BIRTHDATE	RELATIONSHIP	POLICYHOLDER NAME	BIRTHDATE	RELATIONSHIP
		Self			

SUPPLEMENTAL PLAN	EMPLOYER

POLICYHOLDER NAME	BIRTHDATE	RELATIONSHIP	DIAGNOSIS		CODE
			1. Bladder tumor, anterior wall		239.4
EMPLOYER			2.		
			3.		
REFERRING PHYSICIAN UPIN/SSN			4.		
Donald L. Givings, MD	123-12-1234				

PLACE OF SERVICE	St. Johns Hospital 456 Hospital Drive Anywhere US 12345

PROCEDURES	CODE	CHARGE
1. Cystourethroscopy w/ fulguration of bladder tumor 05/19/XX	52235	$ 1200.00
2.		
3.		
4.		
5.		
6.		

SPECIAL NOTES

TOTAL CHARGES	PAYMENTS	ADJUSTMENTS	BALANCE
$1200.00	0	0	$1200.00

RETURN VISIT	PHYSICIAN SIGNATURE
	Paul R. Stream, M.D.

MEDICARE P1234 MEDICAID PRS1234 BCBS 12345	**PAUL R. STREAM, M.D. UROLOGY** **456 HOSPITAL DRIVE, ANYWHERE US 12345** **PHONE NUMBER (101)111-5555**	EIN 11223344 SSN 555-12-1234 PIN PS1234 GRP PS12345

(SAMPLE ONLY - NOT APPROVED FOR USE)

CARRIER

HEALTH INSURANCE CLAIM FORM

PICA		PICA	

1. MEDICARE ☐ (Medicare #) MEDICAID ☐ (Medicaid #) CHAMPUS ☐ (Sponsor's SSN) CHAMPVA ☐ (VA File #) GROUP HEALTH PLAN ☐ (SSN or ID) FECA BLK LUNG ☐ (SSN) OTHER ☐ (ID)

1a. INSURED'S I.D. NUMBER   (FOR PROGRAM IN ITEM 1)

2. PATIENT'S NAME (Last Name, First Name, Middle Initial)

3. PATIENT'S BIRTH DATE   MM | DD | YY   SEX   M ☐   F ☐

4. INSURED'S NAME (Last Name, First Name, Middle Initial)

5. PATIENT'S ADDRESS (No. Street)

6. PATIENT RELATIONSHIP TO INSURED   Self ☐   Spouse ☐   Child ☐   Other ☐

7. INSURED'S ADDRESS (No. Street)

CITY   STATE

8. PATIENT STATUS   Single ☐   Married ☐   Other ☐   Employed ☐   Full-Time Student ☐   Part-Time Student ☐

CITY   STATE

ZIP CODE   TELEPHONE (Include Area Code) ( )

ZIP CODE   TELEPHONE (INCLUDE AREA CODE) ( )

9. OTHER INSURED'S NAME (Last Name, First Name, Middle Initial)

10. IS PATIENT'S CONDITION RELATED TO:

11. INSURED'S POLICY GROUP OR FECA NUMBER

a. OTHER INSURED'S POLICY OR GROUP NUMBER

a. EMPLOYMENT? (CURRENT OR PREVIOUS)   YES ☐   NO ☐

a. INSURED'S DATE OF BIRTH   MM | DD | YY   SEX   M ☐   F ☐

b. OTHER INSURED'S DATE OF BIRTH   MM | DD | YY   SEX   M ☐   F ☐

b. AUTO ACCIDENT?   PLACE (State)   YES ☐   NO ☐

b. EMPLOYER'S NAME OR SCHOOL NAME

c. EMPLOYER'S NAME OR SCHOOL NAME

c. OTHER ACCIDENT?   YES ☐   NO ☐

c. INSURANCE PLAN NAME OR PROGRAM NAME

d. INSURANCE PLAN NAME OR PROGRAM NAME

10d. RESERVED FOR LOCAL USE

d. IS THERE ANOTHER HEALTH BENEFIT PLAN?   YES ☐   NO ☐   If yes, return to and complete item 9 a – d.

READ BACK OF FORM BEFORE COMPLETING & SIGNING THIS FORM.
12. PATIENT'S OR AUTHORIZED PERSON'S SIGNATURE I authorize the release of any medical or other information necessary to process this claim. I also request payment of government benefits either to myself or to the party who accepts assignment below.

SIGNED _____ DATE _____

13. INSURED'S OR AUTHORIZED PERSON'S SIGNATURE I authorize payment of medical benefits to the undersigned physician or supplier for services described below.

SIGNED _____

PATIENT AND INSURED INFORMATION

14. DATE OF CURRENT: ILLNESS (First symptom) OR INJURY (Accident) OR PREGNANCY (LMP)   MM | DD | YY

15. IF PATIENT HAS HAD SAME OR SIMILAR ILLNESS, GIVE FIRST DATE   MM | DD | YY

16. DATES PATIENT UNABLE TO WORK IN CURRENT OCCUPATION   MM | DD | YY   FROM   TO   MM | DD | YY

17. NAME OF REFERRING PHYSICIAN OR OTHER SOURCE

17a. I.D. NUMBER OF REFERRING PHYSICIAN

18. HOSPITALIZATION DATES RELATED TO CURRENT SERVICES   MM | DD | YY   FROM   TO   MM | DD | YY

19. RESERVED FOR LOCAL USE

20. OUTSIDE LAB?   YES ☐   NO ☐ $ CHARGES

21. DIAGNOSIS OR NATURE OF ILLNESS OR INJURY. (RELATE ITEMS 1, 2, 3, OR 4 TO ITEM 24E BY LINE)

1. |___.___|
2. |___.___|
3. |___.___|
4. |___.___|

22. MEDICAID RESUBMISSION CODE   ORIGINAL REF. NO.

23. PRIOR AUTHORIZATION NUMBER

24. A DATE(S) OF SERVICE						B Place of Service	C Type of Service	D PROCEDURES, SERVICES, OR SUPPLIES (Explain Unusual Circumstances)		E DIAGNOSIS CODE	F $ CHARGES	G DAYS OR UNITS	H EPSDT Family Plan	I EMG	J COB	K RESERVED FOR LOCAL USE
From MM	DD	YY	To MM	DD	YY			CPT/HCPCS	MODIFIER							
1																
2																
3																
4																
5																
6																

25. FEDERAL TAX I.D. NUMBER   SSN ☐   EIN ☐

26. PATIENT'S ACCOUNT NO.

27. ACCEPT ASSIGNMENT? (For govt. claims, see back)   YES ☐   NO ☐

28. TOTAL CHARGE $

29. AMOUNT PAID $

30. BALANCE DUE $

31. SIGNATURE OF PHYSICIAN OR SUPPLIER INCLUDING DEGREES OR CREDENTIALS (I certify that the statements on the reverse apply to this bill and are made a part thereof.)

SIGNED _____ DATE _____

32. NAME AND ADDRESS OF FACILITY WHERE SERVICES WERE RENDERED (If other than home or office)

33. PHYSICIAN'S, SUPPLIER'S BILLING NAME, ADDRESS, ZIP CODE & PHONE #

PIN#   GRP#

PHYSICIAN OR SUPPLIER INFORMATION

PLEASE PRINT OR TYPE

SAMPLE FORM 1500
SAMPLE FORM 1500 SAMPLE FORM 1500

DATE	REMARKS			
09/03/XX				

PATIENT			CHART #	SEX	BIRTHDATE
Ben A. Hanson	334-55-8686		12-i	M	08/09/1975

MAILING ADDRESS	CITY	STATE	ZIP	HOME PHONE	WORK PHONE
632 Greenvalley Ct.	Anywhere	US	12345	(101) 333 5555	444 5555

EMPLOYER	ADDRESS	PATIENT STATUS
Ace Plumbing Service	Anywhere, US	X MARRIED DIVORCED SINGLE STUDENT OTHER

INSURANCE: PRIMARY	ID#	GROUP	SECONDARY POLICY	ID#	GROUP
Guardian	334-55-8686	4596	Liberty Mutual	334-88-7788	DD12

POLICYHOLDER NAME	BIRTHDATE	RELATIONSHIP	POLICYHOLDER NAME	BIRTHDATE	RELATIONSHIP
		Self	Joy M. Hanson	10/10/77	Wife

SUPPLEMENTAL PLAN	EMPLOYER
	Dew Drop Inn

POLICYHOLDER NAME	BIRTHDATE	RELATIONSHIP	DIAGNOSIS	CODE
			1. Painful respiration	786.52
EMPLOYER			2. Chest tightness	786.59
			3.	
REFERRING PHYSICIAN UPIN/SSN			4.	

PLACE OF SERVICE	Office

PROCEDURES	CODE	CHARGE
1. Est. Pt. OV Level III	99213	$ 75.00
2. EKG	93000	50.00
3.		
4.		
5.		
6.		

SPECIAL NOTES

Refer to Dr. Stanley M. Hart

TOTAL CHARGES	PAYMENTS	ADJUSTMENTS	BALANCE
$125.00	-0-	-0-	$125.00

RETURN VISIT	PHYSICIAN SIGNATURE
2 weeks after seeing Dr. Hart	*Donald L. Givings, M.D.*

	DONALD L. GIVINGS, M.D.	
MEDICARE D1234	11350 MEDICAL DRIVE, ANYWHERE US 12345	EIN 11-123456
MEDICAID DLG1234	PHONE NUMBER (101)111-5555	SSN 123-12-1234
BCBS 12345		PIN DG1234
		GRP DG12345

PLEASE
DO NOT
STAPLE
IN THIS
AREA

(SAMPLE ONLY - NOT APPROVED FOR USE)

CARRIER

HEALTH INSURANCE CLAIM FORM

PICA [ ] [ ]   PICA [ ] [ ]

1. MEDICARE MEDICAID CHAMPUS CHAMPVA GROUP HEALTH PLAN FECA BLK LUNG OTHER	1a. INSURED'S I.D. NUMBER (FOR PROGRAM IN ITEM 1)
[ ] (Medicare #) [ ] (Medicaid #) [ ] (Sponsor's SSN) [ ] (VA File #) [ ] (SSN or ID) [ ] (SSN) [ ] (ID)	

2. PATIENT'S NAME (Last Name, First Name, Middle Initial)

3. PATIENT'S BIRTH DATE MM | DD | YY   SEX M [ ] F [ ]

4. INSURED'S NAME (Last Name, First Name, Middle Initial)

5. PATIENT'S ADDRESS (No. Street)

6. PATIENT RELATIONSHIP TO INSURED Self [ ] Spouse [ ] Child [ ] Other [ ]

7. INSURED'S ADDRESS (No. Street)

CITY   STATE

8. PATIENT STATUS Single [ ] Married [ ] Other [ ]

CITY   STATE

ZIP CODE   TELEPHONE (Include Area Code) (   )

Employed [ ] Full-Time Student [ ] Part-Time Student [ ]

ZIP CODE   TELEPHONE (INCLUDE AREA CODE) (   )

9. OTHER INSURED'S NAME (Last Name, First Name, Middle Initial)

10. IS PATIENT'S CONDITION RELATED TO:

11. INSURED'S POLICY GROUP OR FECA NUMBER

a. OTHER INSURED'S POLICY OR GROUP NUMBER

a. EMPLOYMENT? (CURRENT OR PREVIOUS) YES [ ] NO [ ]

a. INSURED'S DATE OF BIRTH MM | DD | YY   SEX M [ ] F [ ]

b. OTHER INSURED'S DATE OF BIRTH MM | DD | YY   SEX M [ ] F [ ]

b. AUTO ACCIDENT? PLACE (State) YES [ ] NO [ ]

b. EMPLOYER'S NAME OR SCHOOL NAME

c. EMPLOYER'S NAME OR SCHOOL NAME

c. OTHER ACCIDENT? YES [ ] NO [ ]

c. INSURANCE PLAN NAME OR PROGRAM NAME

d. INSURANCE PLAN NAME OR PROGRAM NAME

10d. RESERVED FOR LOCAL USE

d. IS THERE ANOTHER HEALTH BENEFIT PLAN? YES [ ] NO [ ] If yes, return to and complete item 9 a – d.

READ BACK OF FORM BEFORE COMPLETING & SIGNING THIS FORM.
12. PATIENT'S OR AUTHORIZED PERSON'S SIGNATURE I authorize the release of any medical or other information necessary to process this claim. I also request payment of government benefits either to myself or to the party who accepts assignment below.

SIGNED _____ DATE _____

13. INSURED'S OR AUTHORIZED PERSON'S SIGNATURE I authorize payment of medical benefits to the undersigned physician or supplier for services described below.

SIGNED _____

PATIENT AND INSURED INFORMATION

14. DATE OF CURRENT: MM | DD | YY ILLNESS (First symptom) OR INJURY (Accident) OR PREGNANCY (LMP)

15. IF PATIENT HAS HAD SAME OR SIMILAR ILLNESS, GIVE FIRST DATE MM | DD | YY

16. DATES PATIENT UNABLE TO WORK IN CURRENT OCCUPATION MM | DD | YY FROM TO MM | DD | YY

17. NAME OF REFERRING PHYSICIAN OR OTHER SOURCE

17a. I.D. NUMBER OF REFERRING PHYSICIAN

18. HOSPITALIZATION DATES RELATED TO CURRENT SERVICES MM | DD | YY FROM TO MM | DD | YY

19. RESERVED FOR LOCAL USE

20. OUTSIDE LAB? YES [ ] NO [ ] $ CHARGES

21. DIAGNOSIS OR NATURE OF ILLNESS OR INJURY. (RELATE ITEMS 1, 2, 3, OR 4 TO ITEM 24E BY LINE)

1. |___.___| 3. |___.___|
2. |___.___| 4. |___.___|

22. MEDICAID RESUBMISSION CODE   ORIGINAL REF. NO.

23. PRIOR AUTHORIZATION NUMBER

24. A DATE(S) OF SERVICE						B Place of Service	C Type of Service	D PROCEDURES, SERVICES, OR SUPPLIES (Explain Unusual Circumstances)		E DIAGNOSIS CODE	F $ CHARGES	G DAYS OR UNITS	H EPSDT Family Plan	I EMG	J COB	K RESERVED FOR LOCAL USE
From MM	DD	YY	To MM	DD	YY			CPT/HCPCS	MODIFIER							
1																
2																
3																
4																
5																
6																

25. FEDERAL TAX I.D. NUMBER SSN [ ] EIN [ ]

26. PATIENT'S ACCOUNT NO.

27. ACCEPT ASSIGNMENT? (For govt. claims, see back) YES [ ] NO [ ]

28. TOTAL CHARGE $

29. AMOUNT PAID $

30. BALANCE DUE $

31. SIGNATURE OF PHYSICIAN OR SUPPLIER INCLUDING DEGREES OR CREDENTIALS (I certify that the statements on the reverse apply to this bill and are made a part thereof.)

SIGNED _____ DATE _____

32. NAME AND ADDRESS OF FACILITY WHERE SERVICES WERE RENDERED (If other than home or office)

33. PHYSICIAN'S, SUPPLIER'S BILLING NAME, ADDRESS, ZIP CODE & PHONE #

PIN# _____   GRP# _____

PHYSICIAN OR SUPPLIER INFORMATION

(SAMPLE ONLY - NOT APPROVED FOR USE)

PLEASE PRINT OR TYPE

SAMPLE FORM 1500
SAMPLE FORM 1500 SAMPLE FORM 1500

PLEASE
DO NOT
STAPLE
IN THIS
AREA

(SAMPLE ONLY - NOT APPROVED FOR USE)

CARRIER

HEALTH INSURANCE CLAIM FORM

PICA ☐☐   PICA ☐☐

1. MEDICARE ☐ (Medicare #) MEDICAID ☐ (Medicaid #) CHAMPUS ☐ (Sponsor's SSN) CHAMPVA ☐ (VA File #) GROUP HEALTH PLAN ☐ (SSN or ID) FECA BLK LUNG ☐ (SSN) OTHER ☐ (ID)	1a. INSURED'S I.D. NUMBER (FOR PROGRAM IN ITEM 1)

2. PATIENT'S NAME (Last Name, First Name, Middle Initial)	3. PATIENT'S BIRTH DATE MM DD YY SEX M☐ F☐	4. INSURED'S NAME (Last Name, First Name, Middle Initial)

5. PATIENT'S ADDRESS (No. Street)

6. PATIENT RELATIONSHIP TO INSURED
Self ☐ Spouse ☐ Child ☐ Other ☐

7. INSURED'S ADDRESS (No. Street)

CITY   STATE

8. PATIENT STATUS
Single ☐ Married ☐ Other ☐

CITY   STATE

ZIP CODE   TELEPHONE (Include Area Code)
(   )

Employed ☐ Full-Time Student ☐ Part-Time Student ☐

ZIP CODE   TELEPHONE (INCLUDE AREA CODE)
(   )

9. OTHER INSURED'S NAME (Last Name, First Name, Middle Initial)

10. IS PATIENT'S CONDITION RELATED TO:

11. INSURED'S POLICY GROUP OR FECA NUMBER

a. OTHER INSURED'S POLICY OR GROUP NUMBER

a. EMPLOYMENT? (CURRENT OR PREVIOUS)
YES ☐ NO ☐

a. INSURED'S DATE OF BIRTH
MM DD YY   SEX
M☐ F☐

b. OTHER INSURED'S DATE OF BIRTH
MM DD YY SEX M☐ F☐

b. AUTO ACCIDENT?   PLACE (State)
YES ☐ NO ☐

b. EMPLOYER'S NAME OR SCHOOL NAME

c. EMPLOYER'S NAME OR SCHOOL NAME

c. OTHER ACCIDENT?
YES ☐ NO ☐

c. INSURANCE PLAN NAME OR PROGRAM NAME

d. INSURANCE PLAN NAME OR PROGRAM NAME

10d. RESERVED FOR LOCAL USE

d. IS THERE ANOTHER HEALTH BENEFIT PLAN?
YES ☐ NO ☐ If yes, return to and complete item 9 a – d.

READ BACK OF FORM BEFORE COMPLETING & SIGNING THIS FORM.
12. PATIENT'S OR AUTHORIZED PERSON'S SIGNATURE I authorize the release of any medical or other information necessary to process this claim. I also request payment of government benefits either to myself or to the party who accepts assignment below.

SIGNED _____ DATE _____

13. INSURED'S OR AUTHORIZED PERSON'S SIGNATURE I authorize payment of medical benefits to the undersigned physician or supplier for services described below.

SIGNED _____

PATIENT AND INSURED INFORMATION

14. DATE OF CURRENT: ILLNESS (First symptom) OR INJURY (Accident) OR PREGNANCY (LMP) MM DD YY	15. IF PATIENT HAS HAD SAME OR SIMILAR ILLNESS, GIVE FIRST DATE MM DD YY	16. DATES PATIENT UNABLE TO WORK IN CURRENT OCCUPATION MM DD YY MM DD YY FROM TO

17. NAME OF REFERRING PHYSICIAN OR OTHER SOURCE

17a. I.D. NUMBER OF REFERRING PHYSICIAN

18. HOSPITALIZATION DATES RELATED TO CURRENT SERVICES
MM DD YY   MM DD YY FROM   TO

19. RESERVED FOR LOCAL USE

20. OUTSIDE LAB? $ CHARGES
YES ☐ NO ☐

21. DIAGNOSIS OR NATURE OF ILLNESS OR INJURY. (RELATE ITEMS 1, 2, 3, OR 4 TO ITEM 24E BY LINE)
1. _____   3. _____
2. _____   4. _____

22. MEDICAID RESUBMISSION
CODE ____ ORIGINAL REF. NO. ____

23. PRIOR AUTHORIZATION NUMBER

24. A. DATE(S) OF SERVICE		B. Place of Service	C. Type of Service	D. PROCEDURES, SERVICES, OR SUPPLIES (Explain Unusual Circumstances)		E. DIAGNOSIS CODE	F. $ CHARGES	G. DAYS OR UNITS	H. EPSDT Family Plan	I. EMG	J. COB	K. RESERVED FOR LOCAL USE
From MM DD YY	To MM DD YY			CPT/HCPCS	MODIFIER							
1												
2												
3												
4												
5												
6												

25. FEDERAL TAX I.D. NUMBER SSN ☐ EIN ☐	26. PATIENT'S ACCOUNT NO.	27. ACCEPT ASSIGNMENT? (For govt. claims, see back) YES ☐ NO ☐	28. TOTAL CHARGE $	29. AMOUNT PAID $	30. BALANCE DUE $

31. SIGNATURE OF PHYSICIAN OR SUPPLIER INCLUDING DEGREES OR CREDENTIALS (I certify that the statements on the reverse apply to this bill and are made a part thereof.)

SIGNED _____ DATE _____

32. NAME AND ADDRESS OF FACILITY WHERE SERVICES WERE RENDERED (If other than home or office)

33. PHYSICIAN'S, SUPPLIER'S BILLING NAME, ADDRESS, ZIP CODE & PHONE #

PIN# ____   GRP# ____

PHYSICIAN OR SUPPLIER INFORMATION

(SAMPLE ONLY - NOT APPROVED FOR USE)   *PLEASE PRINT OR TYPE*

SAMPLE FORM 1500
SAMPLE FORM 1500 SAMPLE FORM 1500

DATE	REMARKS				
09/03/XX	Prior Authorization #659427				

PATIENT		CHART #	SEX	BIRTHDATE	
Ben A. Hanson	334-55-8686	12-j	M	08/09/1975	

MAILING ADDRESS	CITY	STATE	ZIP	HOME PHONE	WORK PHONE
632 Greenvalley Ct.	Anywhere	US	12345	(101) 333 5555	444 5555

EMPLOYER	ADDRESS	PATIENT STATUS
Ace Plumbing Service	Anywhere, US	X MARRIED DIVORCED SINGLE STUDENT OTHER

INSURANCE: PRIMARY	ID#	GROUP	SECONDARY POLICY	ID#	GROUP
Guardian	334-55-8686	4596	Liberty Mutual	334-88-7788	DD12

POLICYHOLDER NAME	BIRTHDATE	RELATIONSHIP	POLICYHOLDER NAME	BIRTHDATE	RELATIONSHIP
		Self	Joy M. Hanson	10/10/77	Wife

SUPPLEMENTAL PLAN	EMPLOYER
	Dew Drop Inn

POLICYHOLDER NAME	BIRTHDATE	RELATIONSHIP	DIAGNOSIS	CODE
			1. Painful respiration	786.52
EMPLOYER			2. Chest tightness	786.59
			3. Abnormal chest sounds	786.7
REFERRING PHYSICIAN UPIN/SSN Donald L. Givings, M.D.			4.	

PLACE OF SERVICE	Office	

PROCEDURES	CODE	CHARGE
1. Office consult level II	99242	$ 75.00
2. Cardiovascular stress test, with interpretation and report	93015	150.00
3.		
4.		
5.		
6.		

SPECIAL NOTES

TOTAL CHARGES	PAYMENTS	ADJUSTMENTS	BALANCE
$225.00	-0-	-0-	$225.00

RETURN VISIT	PHYSICIAN SIGNATURE
PRN	*Stanley M. Hart, M.D.*

MEDICARE S1234 MEDICAID SMH1234 BCBS 12388	**STANLEY M. HART, M.D. CARDIOLOGY** **316 GRACE WAY, SUITE 102, ANYWHERE US 12345** **PHONE NUMBER (101)111-5555**	EIN 11785678 SSN 133-12-1254 PIN SH1234 GRP SH12345

PLEASE
DO NOT
STAPLE
IN THIS
AREA

CARRIER

(SAMPLE ONLY - NOT APPROVED FOR USE)

[ ] [ ] PICA

HEALTH INSURANCE CLAIM FORM

PICA [ ] [ ]

1. MEDICARE   MEDICAID   CHAMPUS   CHAMPVA   GROUP HEALTH PLAN   FECA BLK LUNG   OTHER
[ ] (Medicare #) [ ] (Medicaid #) [ ] (Sponsor's SSN) [ ] (VA File #) [ ] (SSN or ID) [ ] (SSN) [ ] (ID)

1a. INSURED'S I.D. NUMBER   (FOR PROGRAM IN ITEM 1)

2. PATIENT'S NAME (Last Name, First Name, Middle Initial)

3. PATIENT'S BIRTH DATE   MM   DD   YY   SEX   M [ ] F [ ]

4. INSURED'S NAME (Last Name, First Name, Middle Initial)

5. PATIENT'S ADDRESS (No. Street)

6. PATIENT RELATIONSHIP TO INSURED
Self [ ] Spouse [ ] Child [ ] Other [ ]

7. INSURED'S ADDRESS (No. Street)

CITY   STATE

8. PATIENT STATUS
Single [ ]   Married [ ]   Other [ ]
Employed [ ]   Full-Time Student [ ]   Part-Time Student [ ]

CITY   STATE

ZIP CODE   TELEPHONE (Include Area Code)
(   )

ZIP CODE   TELEPHONE (INCLUDE AREA CODE)
(   )

9. OTHER INSURED'S NAME (Last Name, First Name, Middle Initial)

10. IS PATIENT'S CONDITION RELATED TO:

11. INSURED'S POLICY GROUP OR FECA NUMBER

a. OTHER INSURED'S POLICY OR GROUP NUMBER

a. EMPLOYMENT? (CURRENT OR PREVIOUS)
[ ] YES [ ] NO

a. INSURED'S DATE OF BIRTH   MM   DD   YY   SEX   M [ ] F [ ]

b. OTHER INSURED'S DATE OF BIRTH   MM   DD   YY   SEX   M [ ] F [ ]

b. AUTO ACCIDENT?   PLACE (State)
[ ] YES [ ] NO

b. EMPLOYER'S NAME OR SCHOOL NAME

c. EMPLOYER'S NAME OR SCHOOL NAME

c. OTHER ACCIDENT?
[ ] YES [ ] NO

c. INSURANCE PLAN NAME OR PROGRAM NAME

d. INSURANCE PLAN NAME OR PROGRAM NAME

10d. RESERVED FOR LOCAL USE

d. IS THERE ANOTHER HEALTH BENEFIT PLAN?
[ ] YES [ ] NO   If yes, return to and complete item 9 a – d.

READ BACK OF FORM BEFORE COMPLETING & SIGNING THIS FORM.
12. PATIENT'S OR AUTHORIZED PERSON'S SIGNATURE I authorize the release of any medical or other information necessary to process this claim. I also request payment of government benefits either to myself or to the party who accepts assignment below.

SIGNED _____   DATE _____

13. INSURED'S OR AUTHORIZED PERSON'S SIGNATURE I authorize payment of medical benefits to the undersigned physician or supplier for services described below.

SIGNED _____

14. DATE OF CURRENT: ILLNESS (First symptom) OR   MM DD YY   INJURY (Accident) OR   PREGNANCY (LMP)

15. IF PATIENT HAS HAD SAME OR SIMILAR ILLNESS, GIVE FIRST DATE   MM DD YY

16. DATES PATIENT UNABLE TO WORK IN CURRENT OCCUPATION
MM DD YY   FROM   TO   MM DD YY

17. NAME OF REFERRING PHYSICIAN OR OTHER SOURCE

17a. I.D. NUMBER OF REFERRING PHYSICIAN

18. HOSPITALIZATION DATES RELATED TO CURRENT SERVICES
MM DD YY   FROM   TO   MM DD YY

19. RESERVED FOR LOCAL USE

20. OUTSIDE LAB? $ CHARGES
[ ] YES [ ] NO

21. DIAGNOSIS OR NATURE OF ILLNESS OR INJURY. (RELATE ITEMS 1, 2, 3, OR 4 TO ITEM 24E BY LINE)
1. |___.___| 3. |___.___|
2. |___.___| 4. |___.___|

22. MEDICAID RESUBMISSION CODE   ORIGINAL REF. NO.

23. PRIOR AUTHORIZATION NUMBER

24.	A		B	C	D		E	F	G	H	I	J	K
	DATE(S) OF SERVICE		Place of Service	Type of Service	PROCEDURES, SERVICES, OR SUPPLIES (Explain Unusual Circumstances)		DIAGNOSIS CODE	$ CHARGES	DAYS OR UNITS	EPSDT Family Plan	EMG	COB	RESERVED FOR LOCAL USE
	From MM DD YY	To MM DD YY			CPT/HCPCS	MODIFIER							
1													
2													
3													
4													
5													
6													

25. FEDERAL TAX I.D. NUMBER   SSN [ ] EIN [ ]

26. PATIENT'S ACCOUNT NO.

27. ACCEPT ASSIGNMENT? (For govt. claims, see back)
[ ] YES [ ] NO

28. TOTAL CHARGE $

29. AMOUNT PAID $

30. BALANCE DUE $

31. SIGNATURE OF PHYSICIAN OR SUPPLIER INCLUDING DEGREES OR CREDENTIALS (I certify that the statements on the reverse apply to this bill and are made a part thereof.)

SIGNED _____   DATE _____

32. NAME AND ADDRESS OF FACILITY WHERE SERVICES WERE RENDERED (If other than home or office)

33. PHYSICIAN'S, SUPPLIER'S BILLING NAME, ADDRESS, ZIP CODE & PHONE #

PIN#   GRP#

(SAMPLE ONLY - NOT APPROVED FOR USE)

PLEASE PRINT OR TYPE

SAMPLE FORM 1500
SAMPLE FORM 1500 SAMPLE FORM 1500

PATIENT AND INSURED INFORMATION

PHYSICIAN OR SUPPLIER INFORMATION

PLEASE
DO NOT
STAPLE
IN THIS
AREA

(SAMPLE ONLY - NOT APPROVED FOR USE)

CARRIER

HEALTH INSURANCE CLAIM FORM

	PICA		PICA		

1.
MEDICARE	MEDICAID	CHAMPUS	CHAMPVA	GROUP HEALTH PLAN	FECA BLK LUNG	OTHER
☐ (Medicare #)	☐ (Medicaid #)	☐ (Sponsor's SSN)	☐ (VA File #)	☐ (SSN or ID)	☐ (SSN)	☐ (ID)

1a. INSURED'S I.D. NUMBER   (FOR PROGRAM IN ITEM 1)

2. PATIENT'S NAME (Last Name, First Name, Middle Initial)

3. PATIENT'S BIRTH DATE
MM | DD | YY   SEX   M ☐   F ☐

4. INSURED'S NAME (Last Name, First Name, Middle Initial)

5. PATIENT'S ADDRESS (No. Street)

6. PATIENT RELATIONSHIP TO INSURED
Self ☐   Spouse ☐   Child ☐   Other ☐

7. INSURED'S ADDRESS (No. Street)

CITY   STATE

8. PATIENT STATUS
Single ☐   Married ☐   Other ☐

CITY   STATE

ZIP CODE   TELEPHONE (Include Area Code)
(   )

Employed ☐   Full-Time Student ☐   Part-Time Student ☐

ZIP CODE   TELEPHONE (INCLUDE AREA CODE)
(   )

9. OTHER INSURED'S NAME (Last Name, First Name, Middle Initial)

10. IS PATIENT'S CONDITION RELATED TO:

11. INSURED'S POLICY GROUP OR FECA NUMBER

a. OTHER INSURED'S POLICY OR GROUP NUMBER

a. EMPLOYMENT? (CURRENT OR PREVIOUS)
☐ YES   ☐ NO

a. INSURED'S DATE OF BIRTH
MM | DD | YY   SEX   M ☐   F ☐

b. OTHER INSURED'S DATE OF BIRTH
MM | DD | YY   SEX   M ☐   F ☐

b. AUTO ACCIDENT?   PLACE (State)
☐ YES   ☐ NO

b. EMPLOYER'S NAME OR SCHOOL NAME

c. EMPLOYER'S NAME OR SCHOOL NAME

c. OTHER ACCIDENT?
☐ YES   ☐ NO

c. INSURANCE PLAN NAME OR PROGRAM NAME

d. INSURANCE PLAN NAME OR PROGRAM NAME

10d. RESERVED FOR LOCAL USE

d. IS THERE ANOTHER HEALTH BENEFIT PLAN?
☐ YES   ☐ NO   If yes, return to and complete item 9 a – d.

READ BACK OF FORM BEFORE COMPLETING & SIGNING THIS FORM.
12. PATIENT'S OR AUTHORIZED PERSON'S SIGNATURE I authorize the release of any medical or other information necessary to process this claim. I also request payment of government benefits either to myself or to the party who accepts assignment below.

SIGNED _____   DATE _____

13. INSURED'S OR AUTHORIZED PERSON'S SIGNATURE I authorize payment of medical benefits to the undersigned physician or supplier for services described below.

SIGNED _____

PATIENT AND INSURED INFORMATION

14. DATE OF CURRENT: ILLNESS (First symptom) OR
MM | DD | YY   INJURY (Accident) OR
                PREGNANCY (LMP)

15. IF PATIENT HAS HAD SAME OR SIMILAR ILLNESS,
GIVE FIRST DATE MM | DD | YY

16. DATES PATIENT UNABLE TO WORK IN CURRENT OCCUPATION
MM | DD | YY   MM | DD | YY
FROM   TO

17. NAME OF REFERRING PHYSICIAN OR OTHER SOURCE

17a. I.D. NUMBER OF REFERRING PHYSICIAN

18. HOSPITALIZATION DATES RELATED TO CURRENT SERVICES
MM | DD | YY   MM | DD | YY
FROM   TO

19. RESERVED FOR LOCAL USE

20. OUTSIDE LAB? $ CHARGES
☐ YES   ☐ NO

21. DIAGNOSIS OR NATURE OF ILLNESS OR INJURY. (RELATE ITEMS 1, 2, 3, OR 4 TO ITEM 24E BY LINE)
1. L___ . ___   3. L___ . ___
2. L___ . ___   4. L___ . ___

22. MEDICAID RESUBMISSION
CODE   ORIGINAL REF. NO.

23. PRIOR AUTHORIZATION NUMBER

24. A						B	C	D		E	F	G	H	I	J	K
DATE(S) OF SERVICE						Place of Service	Type of Service	PROCEDURES, SERVICES, OR SUPPLIES (Explain Unusual Circumstances)		DIAGNOSIS CODE	$ CHARGES	DAYS OR UNITS	EPSDT Family Plan	EMG	COB	RESERVED FOR LOCAL USE
From			To					CPT/HCPCS	MODIFIER							
MM	DD	YY	MM	DD	YY											
1																
2																
3																
4																
5																
6																

25. FEDERAL TAX I.D. NUMBER   SSN ☐ EIN ☐

26. PATIENT'S ACCOUNT NO.

27. ACCEPT ASSIGNMENT?
(For govt. claims, see back)
☐ YES   ☐ NO

28. TOTAL CHARGE
$

29. AMOUNT PAID
$

30. BALANCE DUE
$

31. SIGNATURE OF PHYSICIAN OR SUPPLIER INCLUDING DEGREES OR CREDENTIALS
(I certify that the statements on the reverse apply to this bill and are made a part thereof.)

SIGNED _____   DATE _____

32. NAME AND ADDRESS OF FACILITY WHERE SERVICES WERE RENDERED (If other than home or office)

33. PHYSICIAN'S, SUPPLIER'S BILLING NAME, ADDRESS, ZIP CODE & PHONE #

PIN#   GRP#

PHYSICIAN OR SUPPLIER INFORMATION

(SAMPLE ONLY - NOT APPROVED FOR USE)

PLEASE PRINT OR TYPE

SAMPLE FORM 1500
SAMPLE FORM 1500 SAMPLE FORM 1500

13
Thirteen

Blue Cross and Blue Shield Plans

BRIEF HISTORY

1. The forerunner of what is known today as the Blue Cross plan began when Baylor University Hospital approached ___. (Circle the correct answer.)

   a. doctors

   b. teachers

   c. hospital employees

   d. none of the above

2. The Blue Cross Association grew out of what need? (Circle the correct answer.)

   a. more national coordination between plans

   b. more member hospitals

   c. more participating physicians

   d. all of the above

3. The Blue Shield plans trace their beginning to a resolution passed by the House of Delegates at a meeting of the ___. (Circle the correct answer.)

   a. Blue Cross Association

   b. American Hospital Association

   c. American Medical Association

   d. none of the above

4. The first Blue Shield plan was formed in 1939 and was known as ___. (Circle the correct answer.)

   a. California Physicians' Service

   b. Blue Shield of California

   c. Blue Cross Association

   d. none of the above

5. The Blue Shield design was first used as a trademark by the ___. (Circle the correct answer.)

   a. California Physicians' Service

   b. Buffalo, New York plan

   c. American Medical Association

   d. none of the above

6. Blue Cross plans originally covered only _____ bills.

7. Blue Shield plans were set up to cover fees for _____ services.

8. Define *nonprofit corporation*. _____

_____

9. Define *for-profit corporation*. _____

_____

BCBS ASSOCIATION

10. List four functions of the Blue Cross and Blue Shield Association (BCBSA).

    a. _____

    b. _____

    c. _____

    d. _____

11. BCBSA is the registered owner of the BC and BS _____

BCBS DISTINCTIVE FEATURES

12. The "Blues" were pioneers in ___, prepaid health care. (Circle the correct answer.)

    a. profit

    b. nonprofit

    c. premium

    d. all of the above

13. The "Blues" agreed to perform the following service. (Circle the correct answer.)

    a. make prompt, direct payments of claims

    b. maintain regional professional representatives to assist participating providers with claim problems

    c. provide educational seminars, workshops, billing manuals, and newsletters

    d. all of the above

14. BCBS plans are forbidden by state law from _____ _____ for
    an individual because he or she is in poor health or BCBS payments to providers have far
    exceeded the average.

15. Describe when a BCBS policy can be canceled or an individual disenrolled. _____

_____

_____

16. BCBS plans must obtain approval for any rate increase or benefit change from the ___. (Circle the correct answer.)

    a. State Insurance Commissioner

    b. American Hospital Association

    c. American Medical Association

    d. all of the above

PARTICIPATING PROVIDERS

17. When a health care provider elects to become a participating provider (PAR), that provider enters into a contract with a BCBS corporation and agrees to ___. (Circle the correct answer.)

    a. submit insurance claims for all BCBS subscribers

    b. write off the difference between the amount charged and the approved fee

    c. bill patients for only the deductible and copay/coinsurance amounts and the full charge fee for any uncovered service

    d. all of the above

18. List five services BCBS agrees to provide to PAR providers.

    a. _____

    b. _____

    c. _____

    d. _____

    e. _____

NONPARTICIPATING PROVIDERS

19. Nonparticipating Providers are providers who ___. (Circle the correct answer.)

    a. have not signed participating provider contracts

    b. expect to be paid the full amount of the fee charged for services they perform

    c. understand the insurance company will send payment for claims directly to the patient

    d. all of the above

Critical Thinking

20. Write a paragraph describing the basic differences between a participating provider and a nonparticipating provider.

_____

_____

_____

_____

_____

TRADITIONAL FEE-FOR-SERVICE COVERAGE

21. Name two types of coverage into which many of the large group contracts are subdivided.

    a. _____

    b. _____

22. List seven benefits routinely included under BCBS basic coverage.

    a. _____

    b. _____

    c. _____

    d. _____

    e. _____

    f. _____

    g. _____

23. List seven benefits routinely included under the BCBS major medical plan.

    a. _____

    b. _____

    c. _____

    d. _____

    e. _____

    f. _____

    g. _____

24. Major Medical services are usually subject to patient _____ and _____ requirements.

Critical Thinking

25. Write a paragraph describing riders; include special accidental injury riders and medical emergency care riders.

    _____

    _____

    _____

    _____

    _____

    _____

    _____

    _____

    _____

26. Match the insurance terms in the first column with the definitions in the second column. Write the correct letter in each blank.

_____ nationwide account   a. provider's local plan

_____ home plan   b. eases the processing of claims when patients are enrolled in

_____ BlueCard program   plans outside the local service area

_____ host plan   c. patient's out-of-area plan

     d. companies with employees in more than one local plan area

27. Describe how you might be able to identify a National Account. _____

_____

_____

_____

28. National Accounts claims are filed with the ___. (Circle the correct answer.)

a. provider's local corporation

b. national Blue Cross and Blue Shield Association in Chicago

c. state insurance commissioner's office

d. all of the above

29. By dialing 1-800-676-BLUE, the health care provider has quick access to information about the patient's ___. (Circle the correct answer.)

a. eligibility

b. deductible

c. copay

d. all of the above

30. BlueCard patients have identification numbers that begin with a(n) ___. (Circle the correct answer.)

a. numerical prefix

b. asterisk as a prefix

c. alpha prefix

d. none of the above

31. List four benefits that are not covered by the BlueCard program.

a. _____

b. _____

c. _____

d. _____

32. Claims for the services listed in Question 31 must be mailed or sent electronically to the ___. (Circle the correct answer.)

    a. providers local plan

    b. patient's home plan

    c. BlueCard program

    d. none of the above

BCBS AND MANAGED CARE

33. Match the insurance terms in the first column with the definitions in the second column. Write the correct letter in each blank.

    _____ Preferred Provider Plan

    _____ Preferred Provider Network

    _____ subscriber

    _____ Point-of-Service Plan

    _____ primary care physician

    _____ Federal Employee Program

    a. assumes responsibility for coordinating all the subscriber's medical care

    b. subscriber-driven program

    c. the largest BCBS national account

    d. policyholder

    e. provider-driven program

    f. managed care plan that provides a full range of inpatient and outpatient services

34. The primary care physician is often referred to as the _____ of the patient's medical care.

35. The answer to each of the following statements is either true or false. Indicate your choice by placing **T** for a true statement or **F** for a false statement on the line provided below.

    _____ a. The subscriber is responsible for staying within the network of PPO providers.

    _____ b. The provider is responsible for adhering to the managed care provisions of the PPN plan.

    _____ c. In the POS plan, each subscriber must choose a PCP from the local telephone directory.

    _____ d. Written referral notices issued by the PCP must be attached to all paper claims for services.

    _____ e. In the POS plan, the patient is responsible for obtaining authorizations for all inpatient hospitalizations.

    _____ f. The BCBS Federal Employee Program ID number begins with the letter "F" followed by eight digits.

    _____ g. FEP cards contain the phrase "Government-Wide Service Benefit Plan."

36. The Outpatient Pretreatment Authorization Plan requires preauthorization of outpatient ___. (Circle the correct answer.)

    a. physical therapy services

    b. occupational therapy services

    c. speech therapy services

    d. all of the above

37. The Mandatory Second Surgical Opinion requirement is necessary when a patient is considering ___. (Circle the correct answer.)

   a. emergency surgical care

   b. elective, non-emergency surgical care

   c. non-emergency surgical care

   d. all of the above

38. The Coordinated Home Health and Hospice Care plan allows patients with this option to elect an alternative to the ___. (Circle the correct answer.)

   a. acute care setting

   b. second surgical opinion requirement

   c. urgent care center

   d. none of the above

BCBS HEALTH MAINTENANCE ORGANIZATION PLAN

39. All BCBS corporations offer at least one _____ _____ _____ plan.

MEDICARE SUPPLEMENTAL PLANS

40. BCBS corporations carry several of the federally-designed and regulated Medicare Supplemental plans which augment the Medicare program by paying for Medicare _____ and _____ .

41. These plans are better known throughout the industry as _____ _____ .

BILLING INFORMATION SUMMARY

42. The deadline for filing claims is customarily ___ from the date of service, unless otherwise specified in the subscriber's or provider's contracts. (Circle the correct answer.)

   a. five years

   b. 90 days

   c. one year

   d. none of the above

43. Most corporations currently accept the ___. (Circle the correct answer.)

   a. BCBS form

   b. HCFA-1500 form

   c. HCFA-1450 form

   d. none of the above

44. The most common coinsurance amounts are ___. (Circle the correct answer.)

    a. 20 or 25 percent

    b. 5 or 10 percent

    c. 50 or 75 percent

    d. none of the above

45. The Explanation of Benefits sent to PAR and PPN providers clearly states the patient's ___. (Circle the correct answer.)

    a. coinsurance

    b. deductible

    c. copayment

    d. all of the above

46. Participating providers must accept the allowable rate on all _____ _____ .

47. NonPARs may collect the _____ _____ from the patient. BCBS payments are then sent directly to the _____ .

48. All claims filed by participating providers qualify for an assignment of benefits to the

_____ .

49. The answer to each of the following statements is either true or false. Indicate your choice by placing **T** for a true statement or **F** for a false statement on the line provided below.

    _____ a. You need to retain a current photocopy of only the front of all patient ID cards.

    _____ b. Claims for BlueCard patients with more than one insurance policy must be billed directly to the plan from which the program originated.

    _____ c. NonPARs must bill the home plan for all nonnational account patients with BlueCards.

    _____ d. Rebill claims not paid within 60 days.

    _____ e. Some mental health claims are forwarded to a third-party administrator specializing in mental health case management.

Know Your Acronyms

50. Define the following acronyms:

    a. BS _____

    b. BS _____

    c. AHA _____

    d. BCBS _____

    e. BCBSA _____

    f. PAR _____

    g. PPN _____

    h. MM _____

    i. DME _____

j. PPO   _____

k. POS   _____

l. FEP   _____

m. OPAP _____

n. SSO   _____

EXERCISES

50. Complete Case Studies 13-a through 13-h using the blank claim form provided. Follow the step-by-step instructions in the textbook to properly complete the claim form. If a patient has a secondary carrier, complete an additional claim form using secondary directions in the textbook. You may choose to use a pencil so corrections can be made.

DATE	REMARKS				
01/19/XX					

PATIENT			CHART #	SEX	BIRTHDATE
Monty L. Booker	678-22-3434		13-a	M	12/25/66

MAILING ADDRESS	CITY	STATE	ZIP	HOME PHONE	WORK PHONE
47 Snowflake Road	Anywhere	US	12345	(101) 333 5555	444 5555

EMPLOYER	ADDRESS	PATIENT STATUS
Atlanta Publisher	Anywhere, US	X MARRIED DIVORCED SINGLE STUDENT OTHER

INSURANCE: PRIMARY	ID#	GROUP	SECONDARY POLICY	ID#	GROUP
BCBS US	NXY 678-22-3434	678			

POLICYHOLDER NAME	BIRTHDATE	RELATIONSHIP	POLICYHOLDER NAME	BIRTHDATE	RELATIONSHIP
		Self			

SUPPLEMENTAL PLAN	EMPLOYER

POLICYHOLDER NAME BIRTHDATE RELATIONSHIP	DIAGNOSIS	CODE
	1. Abnormal loss of weight	783.2
EMPLOYER	2. Polydipsia	783.5
	3. Polyphagia	783.6
REFERRING PHYSICIAN UPIN/SSN	4.	

PLACE OF SERVICE	Office	

PROCEDURES	CODE	CHARGE
1. New pt. OV Level IV	99204	$ 100.00
2. Urinalysis, with micro.	81001	10.00
3.		
4.		
5.		
6.		

SPECIAL NOTES

TOTAL CHARGES	PAYMENTS	ADJUSTMENTS	BALANCE
$110.00	0	0	$110.00

RETURN VISIT	PHYSICIAN SIGNATURE
3 weeks	*Donald L. Givings, M.D.*

	DONALD L. GIVINGS, M.D.	EIN 11-123456
MEDICARE D1234 MEDICAID DLG1234 BCBS 12345	11350 MEDICAL DRIVE, ANYWHERE US 12345 PHONE NUMBER (101)111-5555	SSN 123-12-1234 PIN DG1234 GRP DG12345

(SAMPLE ONLY - NOT APPROVED FOR USE)

CARRIER

☐☐ PICA

HEALTH INSURANCE CLAIM FORM

PICA ☐☐

1. MEDICARE ☐ (Medicare #)	MEDICAID ☐ (Medicaid #)	CHAMPUS ☐ (Sponsor's SSN)	CHAMPVA ☐ (VA File #)	GROUP HEALTH PLAN ☐ (SSN or ID)	FECA BLK LUNG ☐ (SSN)	OTHER ☐ (ID)	1a. INSURED'S I.D. NUMBER (FOR PROGRAM IN ITEM 1)

2. PATIENT'S NAME (Last Name, First Name, Middle Initial)

3. PATIENT'S BIRTH DATE   MM ¦ DD ¦ YY   SEX   M ☐   F ☐

4. INSURED'S NAME (Last Name, First Name, Middle Initial)

5. PATIENT'S ADDRESS (No. Street)

6. PATIENT RELATIONSHIP TO INSURED   Self ☐   Spouse ☐   Child ☐   Other ☐

7. INSURED'S ADDRESS (No. Street)

CITY   STATE

8. PATIENT STATUS   Single ☐   Married ☐   Other ☐

CITY   STATE

ZIP CODE   TELEPHONE (Include Area Code) (   )

Employed ☐   Full-Time Student ☐   Part-Time Student ☐

ZIP CODE   TELEPHONE (INCLUDE AREA CODE) (   )

9. OTHER INSURED'S NAME (Last Name, First Name, Middle Initial)

10. IS PATIENT'S CONDITION RELATED TO:

11. INSURED'S POLICY GROUP OR FECA NUMBER

a. OTHER INSURED'S POLICY OR GROUP NUMBER

a. EMPLOYMENT? (CURRENT OR PREVIOUS)   ☐ YES   ☐ NO

a. INSURED'S DATE OF BIRTH   MM ¦ DD ¦ YY   SEX   M ☐   F ☐

b. OTHER INSURED'S DATE OF BIRTH   MM ¦ DD ¦ YY   SEX   M ☐   F ☐

b. AUTO ACCIDENT?   PLACE (State)   ☐ YES   ☐ NO

b. EMPLOYER'S NAME OR SCHOOL NAME

c. EMPLOYER'S NAME OR SCHOOL NAME

c. OTHER ACCIDENT?   ☐ YES   ☐ NO

c. INSURANCE PLAN NAME OR PROGRAM NAME

d. INSURANCE PLAN NAME OR PROGRAM NAME

10d. RESERVED FOR LOCAL USE

d. IS THERE ANOTHER HEALTH BENEFIT PLAN?   ☐ YES   ☐ NO   If yes, return to and complete item 9 a – d.

READ BACK OF FORM BEFORE COMPLETING & SIGNING THIS FORM.
12. PATIENT'S OR AUTHORIZED PERSON'S SIGNATURE I authorize the release of any medical or other information necessary to process this claim. I also request payment of government benefits either to myself or to the party who accepts assignment below.

SIGNED _____   DATE _____

13. INSURED'S OR AUTHORIZED PERSON'S SIGNATURE I authorize payment of medical benefits to the undersigned physician or supplier for services described below.

SIGNED _____

PATIENT AND INSURED INFORMATION

14. DATE OF CURRENT: MM ¦ DD ¦ YY   ILLNESS (First symptom) OR INJURY (Accident) OR PREGNANCY (LMP)

15. IF PATIENT HAS HAD SAME OR SIMILAR ILLNESS, GIVE FIRST DATE   MM ¦ DD ¦ YY

16. DATES PATIENT UNABLE TO WORK IN CURRENT OCCUPATION   FROM MM ¦ DD ¦ YY   TO MM ¦ DD ¦ YY

17. NAME OF REFERRING PHYSICIAN OR OTHER SOURCE

17a. I.D. NUMBER OF REFERRING PHYSICIAN

18. HOSPITALIZATION DATES RELATED TO CURRENT SERVICES   FROM MM ¦ DD ¦ YY   TO MM ¦ DD ¦ YY

19. RESERVED FOR LOCAL USE

20. OUTSIDE LAB?   ☐ YES   ☐ NO $ CHARGES

21. DIAGNOSIS OR NATURE OF ILLNESS OR INJURY. (RELATE ITEMS 1, 2, 3, OR 4 TO ITEM 24E BY LINE)

1. |___.___   3. |___.___

2. |___.___   4. |___.___

22. MEDICAID RESUBMISSION CODE   ORIGINAL REF. NO.

23. PRIOR AUTHORIZATION NUMBER

24. A DATE(S) OF SERVICE						B Place of Service	C Type of Service	D PROCEDURES, SERVICES, OR SUPPLIES (Explain Unusual Circumstances) CPT/HCPCS MODIFIER	E DIAGNOSIS CODE	F $ CHARGES	G DAYS OR UNITS	H EPSDT Family Plan	I EMG	J COB	K RESERVED FOR LOCAL USE
From MM	DD	YY	To MM	DD	YY										
1															
2															
3															
4															
5															
6															

25. FEDERAL TAX I.D. NUMBER   SSN ☐   EIN ☐

26. PATIENT'S ACCOUNT NO.

27. ACCEPT ASSIGNMENT? (For govt. claims, see back)   ☐ YES   ☐ NO

28. TOTAL CHARGE $

29. AMOUNT PAID $

30. BALANCE DUE $

31. SIGNATURE OF PHYSICIAN OR SUPPLIER INCLUDING DEGREES OR CREDENTIALS (I certify that the statements on the reverse apply to this bill and are made a part thereof.)

SIGNED _____   DATE _____

32. NAME AND ADDRESS OF FACILITY WHERE SERVICES WERE RENDERED (If other than home or office)

33. PHYSICIAN'S, SUPPLIER'S BILLING NAME, ADDRESS, ZIP CODE & PHONE #

PIN# _____   GRP# _____

PHYSICIAN OR SUPPLIER INFORMATION

(SAMPLE ONLY - NOT APPROVED FOR USE)

PLEASE PRINT OR TYPE

SAMPLE FORM 1500
SAMPLE FORM 1500   SAMPLE FORM 1500

DATE	REMARKS			
11/07/XX	Patient has a $20 copay			

PATIENT		CHART #	SEX	BIRTHDATE
Anita B. Strong 214-55-6666		13-b	F	04/25/59

MAILING ADDRESS	CITY	STATE	ZIP	HOME PHONE	WORK PHONE
124 Prosper Way	Anywhere	US	12345	(101) 333 5555	444 5555

EMPLOYER	ADDRESS	PATIENT STATUS
Self	Anywhere, US	X MARRIED DIVORCED SINGLE STUDENT OTHER

INSURANCE: PRIMARY	ID#	GROUP	SECONDARY POLICY	ID#	GROUP
BCBS US	XWG 214-55-6666	1357			

POLICYHOLDER NAME	BIRTHDATE	RELATIONSHIP	POLICYHOLDER NAME	BIRTHDATE	RELATIONSHIP
		Self			

SUPPLEMENTAL PLAN	EMPLOYER

POLICYHOLDER NAME	BIRTHDATE	RELATIONSHIP	DIAGNOSIS	CODE
			1. Migraine, classical	346.01
EMPLOYER			2.	
			3.	
REFERRING PHYSICIAN UPIN/SSN			4.	

PLACE OF SERVICE   **Office**

PROCEDURES	CODE	CHARGE
1. Est. pt. OV level I	99211	$ 55.00
2.		
3.		
4.		
5.		
6.		

SPECIAL NOTES

TOTAL CHARGES	PAYMENTS	ADJUSTMENTS	BALANCE
$55.00	$20.00	-0-	$35.00

RETURN VISIT	PHYSICIAN SIGNATURE
PRN	*Donald L. Givings, M.D.*

MEDICARE D1234
MEDICAID DLG1234
BCBS 12345

DONALD L. GIVINGS, M.D.
11350 MEDICAL DRIVE, ANYWHERE US 12345
PHONE NUMBER (101)111-5555

EIN 11-123456
SSN 123-12-1234
PIN DG1234
GRP DG12345

(SAMPLE ONLY - NOT APPROVED FOR USE)

CARRIER

☐☐ PICA

HEALTH INSURANCE CLAIM FORM

PICA ☐☐☐

1. MEDICARE	MEDICAID	CHAMPUS	CHAMPVA	GROUP HEALTH PLAN	FECA BLK LUNG	OTHER	1a. INSURED'S I.D. NUMBER (FOR PROGRAM IN ITEM 1)
☐ (Medicare #)	☐ (Medicaid #)	☐ (Sponsor's SSN)	☐ (VA File #)	☐ (SSN or ID)	☐ (SSN)	☐ (ID)	

2. PATIENT'S NAME (Last Name, First Name, Middle Initial)

3. PATIENT'S BIRTH DATE MM DD YY   SEX   M ☐ F ☐

4. INSURED'S NAME (Last Name, First Name, Middle Initial)

5. PATIENT'S ADDRESS (No. Street)

6. PATIENT RELATIONSHIP TO INSURED   Self ☐ Spouse ☐ Child ☐ Other ☐

7. INSURED'S ADDRESS (No. Street)

CITY   STATE

8. PATIENT STATUS   Single ☐   Married ☐   Other ☐

CITY   STATE

ZIP CODE   TELEPHONE (Include Area Code) (   )

Employed ☐   Full-Time Student ☐   Part-Time Student ☐

ZIP CODE   TELEPHONE (INCLUDE AREA CODE) (   )

9. OTHER INSURED'S NAME (Last Name, First Name, Middle Initial)

10. IS PATIENT'S CONDITION RELATED TO:

11. INSURED'S POLICY GROUP OR FECA NUMBER

a. OTHER INSURED'S POLICY OR GROUP NUMBER

a. EMPLOYMENT? (CURRENT OR PREVIOUS)   YES ☐   NO ☐

a. INSURED'S DATE OF BIRTH MM DD YY   SEX   M ☐   F ☐

b. OTHER INSURED'S DATE OF BIRTH MM DD YY   SEX   M ☐ F ☐

b. AUTO ACCIDENT?   PLACE (State)   YES ☐   NO ☐

b. EMPLOYER'S NAME OR SCHOOL NAME

c. EMPLOYER'S NAME OR SCHOOL NAME

c. OTHER ACCIDENT?   YES ☐   NO ☐

c. INSURANCE PLAN NAME OR PROGRAM NAME

d. INSURANCE PLAN NAME OR PROGRAM NAME

10d. RESERVED FOR LOCAL USE

d. IS THERE ANOTHER HEALTH BENEFIT PLAN?   YES ☐   NO ☐   If yes, return to and complete item 9 a – d.

READ BACK OF FORM BEFORE COMPLETING & SIGNING THIS FORM.
12. PATIENT'S OR AUTHORIZED PERSON'S SIGNATURE I authorize the release of any medical or other information necessary to process this claim. I also request payment of government benefits either to myself or to the party who accepts assignment below.

SIGNED _____ DATE _____

13. INSURED'S OR AUTHORIZED PERSON'S SIGNATURE I authorize payment of medical benefits to the undersigned physician or supplier for services described below.

SIGNED _____

14. DATE OF CURRENT: MM DD YY ◄ ILLNESS (First symptom) OR INJURY (Accident) OR PREGNANCY (LMP)

15. IF PATIENT HAS HAD SAME OR SIMILAR ILLNESS, GIVE FIRST DATE MM DD YY

16. DATES PATIENT UNABLE TO WORK IN CURRENT OCCUPATION MM DD YY   MM DD YY FROM   TO

17. NAME OF REFERRING PHYSICIAN OR OTHER SOURCE

17a. I.D. NUMBER OF REFERRING PHYSICIAN

18. HOSPITALIZATION DATES RELATED TO CURRENT SERVICES MM DD YY   MM DD YY FROM   TO

19. RESERVED FOR LOCAL USE

20. OUTSIDE LAB?   YES ☐   NO ☐ $ CHARGES

21. DIAGNOSIS OR NATURE OF ILLNESS OR INJURY. (RELATE ITEMS 1, 2, 3, OR 4 TO ITEM 24E BY LINE)

1. ____   3. ____

2. ____   4. ____

22. MEDICAID RESUBMISSION CODE   ORIGINAL REF. NO.

23. PRIOR AUTHORIZATION NUMBER

24. A DATE(S) OF SERVICE						B Place of Service	C Type of Service	D PROCEDURES, SERVICES, OR SUPPLIES (Explain Unusual Circumstances)		E DIAGNOSIS CODE	F $ CHARGES	G DAYS OR UNITS	H EPSDT Family Plan	I EMG	J COB	K RESERVED FOR LOCAL USE
From MM	DD	YY	To MM	DD	YY			CPT/HCPCS	MODIFIER							
1																
2																
3																
4																
5																
6																

25. FEDERAL TAX I.D. NUMBER   SSN ☐ EIN ☐

26. PATIENT'S ACCOUNT NO.

27. ACCEPT ASSIGNMENT? (For govt. claims, see back)   YES ☐   NO ☐

28. TOTAL CHARGE $

29. AMOUNT PAID $

30. BALANCE DUE $

31. SIGNATURE OF PHYSICIAN OR SUPPLIER INCLUDING DEGREES OR CREDENTIALS (I certify that the statements on the reverse apply to this bill and are made a part thereof.)

SIGNED _____ DATE _____

32. NAME AND ADDRESS OF FACILITY WHERE SERVICES WERE RENDERED (If other than home or office)

33. PHYSICIAN'S, SUPPLIER'S BILLING NAME, ADDRESS, ZIP CODE & PHONE #

PIN#   GRP#

PHYSICIAN OR SUPPLIER INFORMATION

PATIENT AND INSURED INFORMATION

(SAMPLE ONLY - NOT APPROVED FOR USE)

PLEASE PRINT OR TYPE

SAMPLE FORM 1500
SAMPLE FORM 1500 SAMPLE FORM 1500

DATE 07/03/XX				REMARKS						
PATIENT Virginia A. Love		212-44-6161			CHART # 13-c	SEX F		BIRTHDATE 07/04/62		
MAILING ADDRESS 61 Isaiah Circle		CITY Anywhere		STATE US	ZIP 12345	HOME PHONE (101) 333 5555		WORK PHONE 444 5555		
EMPLOYER None		ADDRESS		PATIENT STATUS X MARRIED DIVORCED SINGLE STUDENT OTHER						
INSURANCE: PRIMARY BCBS POS		ID# XWN 212-56-7972		GROUP 123	SECONDARY POLICY			ID#		GROUP
POLICYHOLDER NAME Charles L. Love	BIRTHDATE 10/06/60	RELATIONSHIP Spouse		POLICYHOLDER NAME		BIRTHDATE		RELATIONSHIP		
SUPPLEMENTAL PLAN				EMPLOYER						

POLICYHOLDER NAME	BIRTHDATE	RELATIONSHIP	DIAGNOSIS		CODE
			1. Chronic conjunctivitis		372.10
EMPLOYER Imperial Bayliners			2. Contact dermatitis		692.9
			3.		
REFERRING PHYSICIAN UPIN/SSN			4.		

PLACE OF SERVICE Office

PROCEDURES	CODE	CHARGE
1. Est. pt. OV level I	99211	$ 55.00
2.		
3.		
4.		
5.		
6.		

SPECIAL NOTES

If the conjunctivitis does not clear within one week refer to Dr. Glance

TOTAL CHARGES $55.00	PAYMENTS 0	ADJUSTMENTS 0	BALANCE $55.00
RETURN VISIT PRN		PHYSICIAN SIGNATURE Donald L. Givings, M.D.	

MEDICARE D1234
MEDICAID DLG1234
BCBS 12345

DONALD L. GIVINGS, M.D.
11350 MEDICAL DRIVE, ANYWHERE US 12345
PHONE NUMBER (101)111-5555

EIN 11-123456
SSN 123-12-1234
PIN DG1234
GRP DG12345

CARRIER

☐☐ PICA

HEALTH INSURANCE CLAIM FORM

PICA ☐☐

1. MEDICARE	MEDICAID	CHAMPUS	CHAMPVA	GROUP HEALTH PLAN	FECA BLK LUNG	OTHER	1a. INSURED'S I.D. NUMBER	(FOR PROGRAM IN ITEM 1)
☐ (Medicare #)	☐ (Medicaid #)	☐ (Sponsor's SSN)	☐ (VA File #)	☐ (SSN or ID)	☐ (SSN)	☐ (ID)		

2. PATIENT'S NAME (Last Name, First Name, Middle Initial)		3. PATIENT'S BIRTH DATE MM ¦ DD ¦ YY SEX M ☐ F ☐	4. INSURED'S NAME (Last Name, First Name, Middle Initial)

5. PATIENT'S ADDRESS (No. Street)	6. PATIENT RELATIONSHIP TO INSURED Self ☐ Spouse ☐ Child ☐ Other ☐	7. INSURED'S ADDRESS (No. Street)
CITY STATE	8. PATIENT STATUS Single ☐ Married ☐ Other ☐	CITY STATE
ZIP CODE TELEPHONE (Include Area Code) ( )	Employed ☐ Full-Time Student ☐ Part-Time Student ☐	ZIP CODE TELEPHONE (INCLUDE AREA CODE) ( )

9. OTHER INSURED'S NAME (Last Name, First Name, Middle Initial)	10. IS PATIENT'S CONDITION RELATED TO:	11. INSURED'S POLICY GROUP OR FECA NUMBER
a. OTHER INSURED'S POLICY OR GROUP NUMBER	a. EMPLOYMENT? (CURRENT OR PREVIOUS) ☐ YES ☐ NO	a. INSURED'S DATE OF BIRTH MM ¦ DD ¦ YY SEX M ☐ F ☐
b. OTHER INSURED'S DATE OF BIRTH MM ¦ DD ¦ YY SEX M ☐ F ☐	b. AUTO ACCIDENT? PLACE (State) ☐ YES ☐ NO	b. EMPLOYER'S NAME OR SCHOOL NAME
c. EMPLOYER'S NAME OR SCHOOL NAME	c. OTHER ACCIDENT? ☐ YES ☐ NO	c. INSURANCE PLAN NAME OR PROGRAM NAME
d. INSURANCE PLAN NAME OR PROGRAM NAME	10d. RESERVED FOR LOCAL USE	d. IS THERE ANOTHER HEALTH BENEFIT PLAN? ☐ YES ☐ NO If yes, return to and complete item 9 a – d.

READ BACK OF FORM BEFORE COMPLETING & SIGNING THIS FORM.
12. PATIENT'S OR AUTHORIZED PERSON'S SIGNATURE I authorize the release of any medical or other information necessary to process this claim. I also request payment of government benefits either to myself or to the party who accepts assignment below.

SIGNED _____ DATE _____

13. INSURED'S OR AUTHORIZED PERSON'S SIGNATURE I authorize payment of medical benefits to the undersigned physician or supplier for services described below.

SIGNED _____

PATIENT AND INSURED INFORMATION

14. DATE OF CURRENT: MM ¦ DD ¦ YY ◀ ILLNESS (First symptom) OR INJURY (Accident) OR PREGNANCY (LMP)	15. IF PATIENT HAS HAD SAME OR SIMILAR ILLNESS, GIVE FIRST DATE MM ¦ DD ¦ YY	16. DATES PATIENT UNABLE TO WORK IN CURRENT OCCUPATION MM ¦ DD ¦ YY MM ¦ DD ¦ YY FROM TO
17. NAME OF REFERRING PHYSICIAN OR OTHER SOURCE	17a. I.D. NUMBER OF REFERRING PHYSICIAN	18. HOSPITALIZATION DATES RELATED TO CURRENT SERVICES MM ¦ DD ¦ YY MM ¦ DD ¦ YY FROM TO
19. RESERVED FOR LOCAL USE		20. OUTSIDE LAB? $ CHARGES ☐ YES ☐ NO

21. DIAGNOSIS OR NATURE OF ILLNESS OR INJURY. (RELATE ITEMS 1, 2, 3, OR 4 TO ITEM 24E BY LINE)	22. MEDICAID RESUBMISSION CODE ORIGINAL REF. NO.
1. ∟__.__ 3. ∟__.__ 2. ∟__.__ 4. ∟__.__	23. PRIOR AUTHORIZATION NUMBER

24. A DATE(S) OF SERVICE					B Place of Service	C Type of Service	D PROCEDURES, SERVICES, OR SUPPLIES (Explain Unusual Circumstances)		E DIAGNOSIS CODE	F $ CHARGES	G DAYS OR UNITS	H EPSDT Family Plan	I EMG	J COB	K RESERVED FOR LOCAL USE
From MM	DD	YY	To MM	DD	YY			CPT/HCPCS	MODIFIER							
1																
2																
3																
4																
5																
6																

25. FEDERAL TAX I.D. NUMBER SSN ☐ EIN ☐	26. PATIENT'S ACCOUNT NO.	27. ACCEPT ASSIGNMENT? (For govt. claims, see back) ☐ YES ☐ NO	28. TOTAL CHARGE $	29. AMOUNT PAID $	30. BALANCE DUE $

31. SIGNATURE OF PHYSICIAN OR SUPPLIER INCLUDING DEGREES OR CREDENTIALS (I certify that the statements on the reverse apply to this bill and are made a part thereof.) SIGNED _____ DATE _____	32. NAME AND ADDRESS OF FACILITY WHERE SERVICES WERE RENDERED (If other than home or office)	33. PHYSICIAN'S, SUPPLIER'S BILLING NAME, ADDRESS, ZIP CODE & PHONE # PIN# GRP#

PHYSICIAN OR SUPPLIER INFORMATION

PLEASE PRINT OR TYPE

SAMPLE FORM 1500
SAMPLE FORM 1500 SAMPLE FORM 1500

DATE	REMARKS			
07/03/XX	Prior Authorization #79254			

PATIENT			CHART #	SEX	BIRTHDATE
Virginia A. Love	212-44-6161		13-d	F	07/04/62

MAILING ADDRESS	CITY	STATE	ZIP	HOME PHONE	WORK PHONE
61 Isaiah Circle	Anywhere	US	12345	(101) 333 5555	444 5555

EMPLOYER	ADDRESS	PATIENT STATUS
None		X MARRIED DIVORCED SINGLE STUDENT OTHER

INSURANCE: PRIMARY	ID#	GROUP	SECONDARY POLICY	ID#	GROUP
BCBS POS	XWN 212-56-7972	123			

POLICYHOLDER NAME	BIRTHDATE	RELATIONSHIP	POLICYHOLDER NAME	BIRTHDATE	RELATIONSHIP
Charles L. Love	10/06/60	Spouse			

SUPPLEMENTAL PLAN	EMPLOYER

POLICYHOLDER NAME	BIRTHDATE	RELATIONSHIP	DIAGNOSIS	CODE
			1. Chronic conjunctivitis	372.10
EMPLOYER			2. Conjunctival degeneration	372.50
Imperial Bayliners			3. ,	
REFERRING PHYSICIAN UPIN/SSN			4.	
Donald L. Givings, M.D.	123-12-1234			

PLACE OF SERVICE   Office

PROCEDURES	CODE	CHARGE
1. Office consult level I	99241	$ 65.00
2.		
3.		
4.		
5.		
6.		

SPECIAL NOTES

TOTAL CHARGES	PAYMENTS	ADJUSTMENTS	BALANCE
$65.00	0	0	$65.00

RETURN VISIT	PHYSICIAN SIGNATURE
	Iris A. Glance, M.D.

MEDICARE I1234 MEDICAID IG1234 BCBS 45678	**IRIS A. GLANCE, M.D. OPTHALMOLOGIST** **66 GRANITE DRIVE, ANYWHERE US 12345** **PHONE NUMBER (101)111-5555**	EIN 11616161 SSN 166-12-1234 PIN IG1234 GRP IG12345

PLEASE
DO NOT
STAPLE
IN THIS
AREA

CARRIER

(SAMPLE ONLY - NOT APPROVED FOR USE)

| | PICA

HEALTH INSURANCE CLAIM FORM

PICA | |

1. MEDICARE	MEDICAID	CHAMPUS	CHAMPVA	GROUP HEALTH PLAN	FECA BLK LUNG	OTHER	1a. INSURED'S I.D. NUMBER	(FOR PROGRAM IN ITEM 1)
☐ (Medicare #)	☐ (Medicaid #)	☐ (Sponsor's SSN)	☐ (VA File #)	☐ (SSN or ID)	☐ (SSN)	☐ (ID)		

2. PATIENT'S NAME (Last Name, First Name, Middle Initial)

3. PATIENT'S BIRTH DATE   MM   DD   YY   SEX   M ☐   F ☐

4. INSURED'S NAME (Last Name, First Name, Middle Initial)

5. PATIENT'S ADDRESS (No. Street)

6. PATIENT RELATIONSHIP TO INSURED   Self ☐   Spouse ☐   Child ☐   Other ☐

7. INSURED'S ADDRESS (No. Street)

CITY   STATE

8. PATIENT STATUS   Single ☐   Married ☐   Other ☐

CITY   STATE

ZIP CODE   TELEPHONE (Include Area Code)   (   )

Employed ☐   Full-Time Student ☐   Part-Time Student ☐

ZIP CODE   TELEPHONE (INCLUDE AREA CODE)   (   )

9. OTHER INSURED'S NAME (Last Name, First Name, Middle Initial)

10. IS PATIENT'S CONDITION RELATED TO:

11. INSURED'S POLICY GROUP OR FECA NUMBER

a. OTHER INSURED'S POLICY OR GROUP NUMBER

a. EMPLOYMENT? (CURRENT OR PREVIOUS)   ☐ YES   ☐ NO

a. INSURED'S DATE OF BIRTH   MM   DD   YY   SEX   M ☐   F ☐

b. OTHER INSURED'S DATE OF BIRTH   MM   DD   YY   SEX   M ☐   F ☐

b. AUTO ACCIDENT?   PLACE (State)   ☐ YES   ☐ NO

b. EMPLOYER'S NAME OR SCHOOL NAME

c. EMPLOYER'S NAME OR SCHOOL NAME

c. OTHER ACCIDENT?   ☐ YES   ☐ NO

c. INSURANCE PLAN NAME OR PROGRAM NAME

d. INSURANCE PLAN NAME OR PROGRAM NAME

10d. RESERVED FOR LOCAL USE

d. IS THERE ANOTHER HEALTH BENEFIT PLAN?   ☐ YES   ☐ NO   If yes, return to and complete item 9 a – d.

READ BACK OF FORM BEFORE COMPLETING & SIGNING THIS FORM.
12. PATIENT'S OR AUTHORIZED PERSON'S SIGNATURE   I authorize the release of any medical or other information necessary to process this claim. I also request payment of government benefits either to myself or to the party who accepts assignment below.

SIGNED _____   DATE _____

13. INSURED'S OR AUTHORIZED PERSON'S SIGNATURE   I authorize payment of medical benefits to the undersigned physician or supplier for services described below.

SIGNED _____

PATIENT AND INSURED INFORMATION

14. DATE OF CURRENT: MM   DD   YY   ◄ ILLNESS (First symptom) OR INJURY (Accident) OR PREGNANCY (LMP)

15. IF PATIENT HAS HAD SAME OR SIMILAR ILLNESS, GIVE FIRST DATE   MM   DD   YY

16. DATES PATIENT UNABLE TO WORK IN CURRENT OCCUPATION   MM   DD   YY   FROM   TO   MM   DD   YY

17. NAME OF REFERRING PHYSICIAN OR OTHER SOURCE

17a. I.D. NUMBER OF REFERRING PHYSICIAN

18. HOSPITALIZATION DATES RELATED TO CURRENT SERVICES   MM   DD   YY   FROM   TO   MM   DD   YY

19. RESERVED FOR LOCAL USE

20. OUTSIDE LAB?   ☐ YES   ☐ NO $ CHARGES

21. DIAGNOSIS OR NATURE OF ILLNESS OR INJURY. (RELATE ITEMS 1, 2, 3, OR 4 TO ITEM 24E BY LINE)

1. |___ . ___| 3. |___ . ___|

2. |___ . ___| 4. |___ . ___|

22. MEDICAID RESUBMISSION CODE   ORIGINAL REF. NO.

23. PRIOR AUTHORIZATION NUMBER

24. A DATE(S) OF SERVICE						B Place of Service	C Type of Service	D PROCEDURES, SERVICES, OR SUPPLIES (Explain Unusual Circumstances) CPT/HCPCS MODIFIER	E DIAGNOSIS CODE	F $ CHARGES	G DAYS OR UNITS	H EPSDT Family Plan	I EMG	J COB	K RESERVED FOR LOCAL USE
From			To												
MM	DD	YY	MM	DD	YY										
1															
2															
3															
4															
5															
6															

25. FEDERAL TAX I.D. NUMBER   SSN ☐   EIN ☐

26. PATIENT'S ACCOUNT NO.

27. ACCEPT ASSIGNMENT? (For govt. claims, see back)   YES ☐   NO ☐

28. TOTAL CHARGE $

29. AMOUNT PAID $

30. BALANCE DUE $

31. SIGNATURE OF PHYSICIAN OR SUPPLIER INCLUDING DEGREES OR CREDENTIALS (I certify that the statements on the reverse apply to this bill and are made a part thereof.)

SIGNED _____   DATE _____

32. NAME AND ADDRESS OF FACILITY WHERE SERVICES WERE RENDERED (If other than home or office)

33. PHYSICIAN'S, SUPPLIER'S BILLING NAME, ADDRESS, ZIP CODE & PHONE #

PIN#   GRP#

PHYSICIAN OR SUPPLIER INFORMATION

(SAMPLE ONLY - NOT APPROVED FOR USE)

PLEASE PRINT OR TYPE

SAMPLE FORM 1500
SAMPLE FORM 1500   SAMPLE FORM 1500

121

DATE	REMARKS			
09/03/XX				

PATIENT			CHART #	SEX	BIRTHDATE
Keith S. Kutter		313-99-7777	13-e	M	12/01/55

MAILING ADDRESS	CITY	STATE	ZIP	HOME PHONE	WORK PHONE
22 Pinewood Avenue	Anywhere	US	12345	(101) 333 5555	444 5555

EMPLOYER	ADDRESS		PATIENT STATUS
First League	Anywhere	US	X MARRIED DIVORCED SINGLE STUDENT OTHER

INSURANCE: PRIMARY	ID#	GROUP	SECONDARY POLICY	ID#	GROUP
BCBS US FLX 313-99-7777	567	Aetna	212-44-6868	S234	

POLICYHOLDER NAME	BIRTHDATE	RELATIONSHIP	POLICYHOLDER NAME	BIRTHDATE	RELATIONSHIP
		Self	Linda Kutter	05/22/56	Spouse

SUPPLEMENTAL PLAN	EMPLOYER
	Anderson Music & Sound

POLICYHOLDER NAME	BIRTHDATE	RELATIONSHIP	DIAGNOSIS	CODE
			1. Muscle Spasms	728.85
EMPLOYER			2.	
			3.	
REFERRING PHYSICIAN UPIN/SSN			4.	

PLACE OF SERVICE	Office

PROCEDURES	CODE	CHARGE
1. Est. pt. OV level II	99212	$ 65.00
2.		
3.		
4.		
5.		
6.		

SPECIAL NOTES
Refer to a chiropractor

TOTAL CHARGES	PAYMENTS	ADJUSTMENTS	BALANCE
$65.00	0	0	$65.00

RETURN VISIT	PHYSICIAN SIGNATURE
	Donald L. Givings, M.D.

MEDICARE D1234
MEDICAID DLG1234
BCBS 12345

DONALD L. GIVINGS, M.D.
11350 MEDICAL DRIVE, ANYWHERE US 12345
PHONE NUMBER (101)111-5555

EIN 11-123456
SSN 123-12-1234
PIN DG1234
GRP DG12345

(SAMPLE ONLY - NOT APPROVED FOR USE)

CARRIER

HEALTH INSURANCE CLAIM FORM

| PICA | | PICA | |

1. MEDICARE ☐ (Medicare #) MEDICAID ☐ (Medicaid #) CHAMPUS ☐ (Sponsor's SSN) CHAMPVA ☐ (VA File #) GROUP HEALTH PLAN ☐ (SSN or ID) FECA BLK LUNG ☐ (SSN) OTHER ☐ (ID)

1a. INSURED'S I.D. NUMBER   (FOR PROGRAM IN ITEM 1)

2. PATIENT'S NAME (Last Name, First Name, Middle Initial)

3. PATIENT'S BIRTH DATE MM | DD | YY   SEX M ☐ F ☐

4. INSURED'S NAME (Last Name, First Name, Middle Initial)

5. PATIENT'S ADDRESS (No. Street)

6. PATIENT RELATIONSHIP TO INSURED   Self ☐ Spouse ☐ Child ☐ Other ☐

7. INSURED'S ADDRESS (No. Street)

CITY   STATE

8. PATIENT STATUS   Single ☐ Married ☐ Other ☐   Employed ☐ Full-Time Student ☐ Part-Time Student ☐

CITY   STATE

ZIP CODE   TELEPHONE (Include Area Code) (   )

ZIP CODE   TELEPHONE (INCLUDE AREA CODE) (   )

9. OTHER INSURED'S NAME (Last Name, First Name, Middle Initial)

10. IS PATIENT'S CONDITION RELATED TO:

11. INSURED'S POLICY GROUP OR FECA NUMBER

a. OTHER INSURED'S POLICY OR GROUP NUMBER

a. EMPLOYMENT? (CURRENT OR PREVIOUS) ☐ YES ☐ NO

a. INSURED'S DATE OF BIRTH MM | DD | YY   SEX M ☐ F ☐

b. OTHER INSURED'S DATE OF BIRTH MM | DD | YY   SEX M ☐ F ☐

b. AUTO ACCIDENT? ☐ YES ☐ NO   PLACE (State)

b. EMPLOYER'S NAME OR SCHOOL NAME

c. EMPLOYER'S NAME OR SCHOOL NAME

c. OTHER ACCIDENT? ☐ YES ☐ NO

c. INSURANCE PLAN NAME OR PROGRAM NAME

d. INSURANCE PLAN NAME OR PROGRAM NAME

10d. RESERVED FOR LOCAL USE

d. IS THERE ANOTHER HEALTH BENEFIT PLAN? ☐ YES ☐ NO   If yes, return to and complete item 9 a – d.

READ BACK OF FORM BEFORE COMPLETING & SIGNING THIS FORM.
12. PATIENT'S OR AUTHORIZED PERSON'S SIGNATURE I authorize the release of any medical or other information necessary to process this claim. I also request payment of government benefits either to myself or to the party who accepts assignment below.

SIGNED _____   DATE _____

13. INSURED'S OR AUTHORIZED PERSON'S SIGNATURE I authorize payment of medical benefits to the undersigned physician or supplier for services described below.

SIGNED _____

PATIENT AND INSURED INFORMATION

14. DATE OF CURRENT: ILLNESS (First symptom) OR INJURY (Accident) OR PREGNANCY (LMP) MM | DD | YY

15. IF PATIENT HAS HAD SAME OR SIMILAR ILLNESS, GIVE FIRST DATE MM | DD | YY

16. DATES PATIENT UNABLE TO WORK IN CURRENT OCCUPATION FROM MM | DD | YY TO MM | DD | YY

17. NAME OF REFERRING PHYSICIAN OR OTHER SOURCE

17a. I.D. NUMBER OF REFERRING PHYSICIAN

18. HOSPITALIZATION DATES RELATED TO CURRENT SERVICES FROM MM | DD | YY TO MM | DD | YY

19. RESERVED FOR LOCAL USE

20. OUTSIDE LAB? ☐ YES ☐ NO $ CHARGES

21. DIAGNOSIS OR NATURE OF ILLNESS OR INJURY. (RELATE ITEMS 1, 2, 3, OR 4 TO ITEM 24E BY LINE)

1. L___ . ___   3. L___ . ___
2. L___ . ___   4. L___ . ___

22. MEDICAID RESUBMISSION CODE   ORIGINAL REF. NO.

23. PRIOR AUTHORIZATION NUMBER

24. A						B	C	D		E	F		G	H	I	J	K	
DATE(S) OF SERVICE						Place of Service	Type of Service	PROCEDURES, SERVICES, OR SUPPLIES (Explain Unusual Circumstances)		DIAGNOSIS CODE	$ CHARGES		DAYS OR UNITS	EPSDT Family Plan	EMG	COB	RESERVED FOR LOCAL USE	
From MM	DD	YY	To MM	DD	YY			CPT/HCPCS	MODIFIER									
1																		
2																		
3																		
4																		
5																		
6																		

25. FEDERAL TAX I.D. NUMBER   SSN ☐ EIN ☐

26. PATIENT'S ACCOUNT NO.

27. ACCEPT ASSIGNMENT? (For govt. claims, see back) ☐ YES ☐ NO

28. TOTAL CHARGE $

29. AMOUNT PAID $

30. BALANCE DUE $

31. SIGNATURE OF PHYSICIAN OR SUPPLIER INCLUDING DEGREES OR CREDENTIALS (I certify that the statements on the reverse apply to this bill and are made a part thereof.)

SIGNED _____   DATE _____

32. NAME AND ADDRESS OF FACILITY WHERE SERVICES WERE RENDERED (If other than home or office)

33. PHYSICIAN'S, SUPPLIER'S BILLING NAME, ADDRESS, ZIP CODE & PHONE #

PIN#   GRP#

PHYSICIAN OR SUPPLIER INFORMATION

(SAMPLE ONLY - NOT APPROVED FOR USE)   *PLEASE PRINT OR TYPE*   SAMPLE FORM 1500 SAMPLE FORM 1500 SAMPLE FORM 1500

(SAMPLE ONLY - NOT APPROVED FOR USE)

CARRIER

| | | | PICA | | |

HEALTH INSURANCE CLAIM FORM

PICA | | |

1. MEDICARE MEDICAID CHAMPUS CHAMPVA GROUP HEALTH PLAN FECA BLK LUNG OTHER	1a. INSURED'S I.D. NUMBER (FOR PROGRAM IN ITEM 1)
☐ (Medicare #) ☐ (Medicaid #) ☐ (Sponsor's SSN) ☐ (VA File #) ☐ (SSN or ID) ☐ (SSN) ☐ (ID)	

2. PATIENT'S NAME (Last Name, First Name, Middle Initial)	3. PATIENT'S BIRTH DATE MM DD YY SEX M ☐ F ☐	4. INSURED'S NAME (Last Name, First Name, Middle Initial)

5. PATIENT'S ADDRESS (No. Street)	6. PATIENT RELATIONSHIP TO INSURED Self ☐ Spouse ☐ Child ☐ Other ☐	7. INSURED'S ADDRESS (No. Street)
CITY STATE	8. PATIENT STATUS Single ☐ Married ☐ Other ☐ Employed ☐ Full-Time Student ☐ Part-Time Student ☐	CITY STATE
ZIP CODE TELEPHONE (Include Area Code) ( )		ZIP CODE TELEPHONE (INCLUDE AREA CODE) ( )

9. OTHER INSURED'S NAME (Last Name, First Name, Middle Initial)	10. IS PATIENT'S CONDITION RELATED TO:	11. INSURED'S POLICY GROUP OR FECA NUMBER
a. OTHER INSURED'S POLICY OR GROUP NUMBER	a. EMPLOYMENT? (CURRENT OR PREVIOUS) ☐ YES ☐ NO	a. INSURED'S DATE OF BIRTH MM DD YY SEX M ☐ F ☐
b. OTHER INSURED'S DATE OF BIRTH MM DD YY SEX M ☐ F ☐	b. AUTO ACCIDENT? PLACE (State) ☐ YES ☐ NO	b. EMPLOYER'S NAME OR SCHOOL NAME
c. EMPLOYER'S NAME OR SCHOOL NAME	c. OTHER ACCIDENT? ☐ YES ☐ NO	c. INSURANCE PLAN NAME OR PROGRAM NAME
d. INSURANCE PLAN NAME OR PROGRAM NAME	10d. RESERVED FOR LOCAL USE	d. IS THERE ANOTHER HEALTH BENEFIT PLAN? ☐ YES ☐ NO If yes, return to and complete item 9 a – d.

READ BACK OF FORM BEFORE COMPLETING & SIGNING THIS FORM.

12. PATIENT'S OR AUTHORIZED PERSON'S SIGNATURE I authorize the release of any medical or other information necessary to process this claim. I also request payment of government benefits either to myself or to the party who accepts assignment below. SIGNED _____ DATE _____	13. INSURED'S OR AUTHORIZED PERSON'S SIGNATURE I authorize payment of medical benefits to the undersigned physician or supplier for services described below. SIGNED _____

14. DATE OF CURRENT: ILLNESS (First symptom) OR INJURY (Accident) OR PREGNANCY (LMP) MM DD YY	15. IF PATIENT HAS HAD SAME OR SIMILAR ILLNESS, GIVE FIRST DATE MM DD YY	16. DATES PATIENT UNABLE TO WORK IN CURRENT OCCUPATION MM DD YY MM DD YY FROM TO
17. NAME OF REFERRING PHYSICIAN OR OTHER SOURCE	17a. I.D. NUMBER OF REFERRING PHYSICIAN	18. HOSPITALIZATION DATES RELATED TO CURRENT SERVICES MM DD YY MM DD YY FROM TO
19. RESERVED FOR LOCAL USE		20. OUTSIDE LAB? ☐ YES ☐ NO $ CHARGES

21. DIAGNOSIS OR NATURE OF ILLNESS OR INJURY. (RELATE ITEMS 1, 2, 3, OR 4 TO ITEM 24E BY LINE) 1. _____ 2. _____ 3. _____ 4. _____	22. MEDICAID RESUBMISSION CODE ORIGINAL REF. NO. 23. PRIOR AUTHORIZATION NUMBER

24. A. DATE(S) OF SERVICE From To MM DD YY MM DD YY	B. Place of Service	C. Type of Service	D. PROCEDURES, SERVICES, OR SUPPLIES (Explain Unusual Circumstances) CPT/HCPCS MODIFIER	E. DIAGNOSIS CODE	F. $ CHARGES	G. DAYS OR UNITS	H. EPSDT Family Plan	I. EMG	J. COB	K. RESERVED FOR LOCAL USE
1										
2										
3										
4										
5										
6										

25. FEDERAL TAX I.D. NUMBER SSN ☐ EIN ☐	26. PATIENT'S ACCOUNT NO.	27. ACCEPT ASSIGNMENT? (For govt. claims, see back) ☐ YES ☐ NO	28. TOTAL CHARGE $	29. AMOUNT PAID $	30. BALANCE DUE $

31. SIGNATURE OF PHYSICIAN OR SUPPLIER INCLUDING DEGREES OR CREDENTIALS (I certify that the statements on the reverse apply to this bill and are made a part thereof.) SIGNED _____ DATE _____	32. NAME AND ADDRESS OF FACILITY WHERE SERVICES WERE RENDERED (If other than home or office)	33. PHYSICIAN'S, SUPPLIER'S BILLING NAME, ADDRESS, ZIP CODE & PHONE # PIN# GRP#

PATIENT AND INSURED INFORMATION

PHYSICIAN OR SUPPLIER INFORMATION

(SAMPLE ONLY - NOT APPROVED FOR USE)

PLEASE PRINT OR TYPE

SAMPLE FORM 1500
SAMPLE FORM 1500 SAMPLE FORM 1500

DATE 09/10/XX		REMARKS			
PATIENT Keith S. Kutter	313-99-7777		CHART # 13-f	SEX M	BIRTHDATE 12/01/55

MAILING ADDRESS	CITY	STATE	ZIP	HOME PHONE	WORK PHONE
22 Pinewood Avenue	Anywhere	US	12345	(101) 333 5555	444 5555

EMPLOYER First League	ADDRESS Anywhere US	PATIENT STATUS X MARRIED DIVORCED SINGLE STUDENT OTHER

INSURANCE: PRIMARY BCBS US	ID# FLX 313-99-7777	GROUP 567	SECONDARY POLICY Aetna	ID# 212-44-6868	GROUP S234

POLICYHOLDER NAME	BIRTHDATE	RELATIONSHIP Self	POLICYHOLDER NAME Linda Kutter	BIRTHDATE 05/22/56	RELATIONSHIP Spouse

SUPPLEMENTAL PLAN	EMPLOYER Anderson Music & Sound

POLICYHOLDER NAME	BIRTHDATE	RELATIONSHIP	DIAGNOSIS	CODE
			1. Cervical lesion	739.1
EMPLOYER			2. Rib cage lesion	739.8
			3. Disorder of soft tissue	729.1
REFERRING PHYSICIAN UPIN/SSN Donald L. Givings M.D. 123-12-1234			4. Muscle spasms	728.85

PLACE OF SERVICE **Office**

PROCEDURES	CODE	CHARGE
1. Manipulation 3-4 region	98941	$ 55.00
2. Manipulation extra spinal	98943-51	35.00
3. Massage	97124	30.00
4. Mechanical traction	97012	27.00
5. Electrical stimulation	97014	25.00
6.		

SPECIAL NOTES

TOTAL CHARGES $172.00	PAYMENTS 0	ADJUSTMENTS 0	BALANCE $172.00

RETURN VISIT PRN	PHYSICIAN SIGNATURE *Robert Strain, D.C.*

MEDICARE R1234 MEDICAID RSD1234 BCBS 98765	**ROBERT STRAIN, D.C. CHIROPRACTOR** **234 WINDING BEND ROAD, ANYWHERE, US 12345** **PHONE NUMBER (101)111-5555**	EIN 11446688 SSN 222-12-1234 PIN RS1234 GRP RS12345

PLEASE
DO NOT
STAPLE
IN THIS
AREA

CARRIER

| | PICA | | | | |

HEALTH INSURANCE CLAIM FORM

PICA | | |

1. MEDICARE	MEDICAID	CHAMPUS	CHAMPVA	GROUP HEALTH PLAN	FECA BLK LUNG	OTHER	1a. INSURED'S I.D. NUMBER	(FOR PROGRAM IN ITEM 1)
☐ (Medicare #)	☐ (Medicaid #)	☐ (Sponsor's SSN)	☐ (VA File #)	☐ (SSN or ID)	☐ (SSN)	☐ (ID)		

2. PATIENT'S NAME (Last Name, First Name, Middle Initial)

3. PATIENT'S BIRTH DATE MM ¦ DD ¦ YY   SEX   M ☐   F ☐

4. INSURED'S NAME (Last Name, First Name, Middle Initial)

5. PATIENT'S ADDRESS (No. Street)

6. PATIENT RELATIONSHIP TO INSURED   Self ☐ Spouse ☐ Child ☐ Other ☐

7. INSURED'S ADDRESS (No. Street)

CITY | STATE

8. PATIENT STATUS   Single ☐   Married ☐   Other ☐

CITY | STATE

ZIP CODE | TELEPHONE (Include Area Code) (   )

Employed ☐   Full-Time Student ☐   Part-Time Student ☐

ZIP CODE | TELEPHONE (INCLUDE AREA CODE) (   )

9. OTHER INSURED'S NAME (Last Name, First Name, Middle Initial)

10. IS PATIENT'S CONDITION RELATED TO:

11. INSURED'S POLICY GROUP OR FECA NUMBER

a. OTHER INSURED'S POLICY OR GROUP NUMBER

a. EMPLOYMENT? (CURRENT OR PREVIOUS)   YES ☐   NO ☐

a. INSURED'S DATE OF BIRTH MM ¦ DD ¦ YY   SEX   M ☐   F ☐

b. OTHER INSURED'S DATE OF BIRTH MM ¦ DD ¦ YY   SEX   M ☐   F ☐

b. AUTO ACCIDENT?   PLACE (State)   YES ☐   NO ☐

b. EMPLOYER'S NAME OR SCHOOL NAME

c. EMPLOYER'S NAME OR SCHOOL NAME

c. OTHER ACCIDENT?   YES ☐   NO ☐

c. INSURANCE PLAN NAME OR PROGRAM NAME

d. INSURANCE PLAN NAME OR PROGRAM NAME

10d. RESERVED FOR LOCAL USE

d. IS THERE ANOTHER HEALTH BENEFIT PLAN?   YES ☐   NO ☐   If yes, return to and complete item 9 a – d.

READ BACK OF FORM BEFORE COMPLETING & SIGNING THIS FORM.

12. PATIENT'S OR AUTHORIZED PERSON'S SIGNATURE I authorize the release of any medical or other information necessary to process this claim. I also request payment of government benefits either to myself or to the party who accepts assignment below.

SIGNED _____   DATE _____

13. INSURED'S OR AUTHORIZED PERSON'S SIGNATURE I authorize payment of medical benefits to the undersigned physician or supplier for services described below.

SIGNED _____

PATIENT AND INSURED INFORMATION

14. DATE OF CURRENT: MM ¦ DD ¦ YY   ◄ ILLNESS (First symptom) OR INJURY (Accident) OR PREGNANCY (LMP)

15. IF PATIENT HAS HAD SAME OR SIMILAR ILLNESS, GIVE FIRST DATE MM ¦ DD ¦ YY

16. DATES PATIENT UNABLE TO WORK IN CURRENT OCCUPATION MM ¦ DD ¦ YY   FROM   TO   MM ¦ DD ¦ YY

17. NAME OF REFERRING PHYSICIAN OR OTHER SOURCE

17a. I.D. NUMBER OF REFERRING PHYSICIAN

18. HOSPITALIZATION DATES RELATED TO CURRENT SERVICES MM ¦ DD ¦ YY   FROM   TO   MM ¦ DD ¦ YY

19. RESERVED FOR LOCAL USE

20. OUTSIDE LAB?   YES ☐   NO ☐ $ CHARGES

21. DIAGNOSIS OR NATURE OF ILLNESS OR INJURY. (RELATE ITEMS 1, 2, 3, OR 4 TO ITEM 24E BY LINE)

1. ⌐___ . ___   3. ⌐___ . ___
2. ⌐___ . ___   4. ⌐___ . ___

22. MEDICAID RESUBMISSION CODE   ORIGINAL REF. NO.

23. PRIOR AUTHORIZATION NUMBER

24. A DATE(S) OF SERVICE						B Place of Service	C Type of Service	D PROCEDURES, SERVICES, OR SUPPLIES (Explain Unusual Circumstances)		E DIAGNOSIS CODE	F $ CHARGES	G DAYS OR UNITS	H EPSDT Family Plan	I EMG	J COB	K RESERVED FOR LOCAL USE
From MM	DD	YY	To MM	DD	YY			CPT/HCPCS	MODIFIER							
1																
2																
3																
4																
5																
6																

25. FEDERAL TAX I.D. NUMBER   SSN ☐ EIN ☐

26. PATIENT'S ACCOUNT NO.

27. ACCEPT ASSIGNMENT? (For govt. claims, see back)   YES ☐   NO ☐

28. TOTAL CHARGE $

29. AMOUNT PAID $

30. BALANCE DUE $

31. SIGNATURE OF PHYSICIAN OR SUPPLIER INCLUDING DEGREES OR CREDENTIALS (I certify that the statements on the reverse apply to this bill and are made a part thereof.)

SIGNED _____   DATE _____

32. NAME AND ADDRESS OF FACILITY WHERE SERVICES WERE RENDERED (If other than home or office)

33. PHYSICIAN'S, SUPPLIER'S BILLING NAME, ADDRESS, ZIP CODE & PHONE #

PIN# _____   GRP# _____

PHYSICIAN OR SUPPLIER INFORMATION

(SAMPLE ONLY - NOT APPROVED FOR USE)

CARRIER

| | PICA

HEALTH INSURANCE CLAIM FORM

PICA | | |

| 1. | MEDICARE | MEDICAID | CHAMPUS | CHAMPVA | GROUP HEALTH PLAN | FECA BLK LUNG | OTHER | 1a. INSURED'S I.D. NUMBER | (FOR PROGRAM IN ITEM 1) |

| (Medicare #) | (Medicaid #) | (Sponsor's SSN) | (VA File #) | (SSN or ID) | (SSN) | (ID) |

2. PATIENT'S NAME (Last Name, First Name, Middle Initial)

3. PATIENT'S BIRTH DATE MM | DD | YY   SEX M [ ] F [ ]

4. INSURED'S NAME (Last Name, First Name, Middle Initial)

5. PATIENT'S ADDRESS (No. Street)

6. PATIENT RELATIONSHIP TO INSURED
Self [ ]   Spouse [ ]   Child [ ]   Other [ ]

7. INSURED'S ADDRESS (No. Street)

CITY   STATE

8. PATIENT STATUS
Single [ ]   Married [ ]   Other [ ]

CITY   STATE

ZIP CODE   TELEPHONE (Include Area Code) ( )

Employed [ ]   Full-Time Student [ ]   Part-Time Student [ ]

ZIP CODE   TELEPHONE (INCLUDE AREA CODE) ( )

9. OTHER INSURED'S NAME (Last Name, First Name, Middle Initial)

10. IS PATIENT'S CONDITION RELATED TO:

11. INSURED'S POLICY GROUP OR FECA NUMBER

a. OTHER INSURED'S POLICY OR GROUP NUMBER

a. EMPLOYMENT? (CURRENT OR PREVIOUS)
YES [ ]   NO [ ]

a. INSURED'S DATE OF BIRTH MM | DD | YY   SEX M [ ] F [ ]

b. OTHER INSURED'S DATE OF BIRTH MM | DD | YY   SEX M [ ] F [ ]

b. AUTO ACCIDENT?   PLACE (State)
YES [ ]   NO [ ]

b. EMPLOYER'S NAME OR SCHOOL NAME

c. EMPLOYER'S NAME OR SCHOOL NAME

c. OTHER ACCIDENT?
YES [ ]   NO [ ]

c. INSURANCE PLAN NAME OR PROGRAM NAME

d. INSURANCE PLAN NAME OR PROGRAM NAME

10d. RESERVED FOR LOCAL USE

d. IS THERE ANOTHER HEALTH BENEFIT PLAN?
YES [ ]   NO [ ]   If yes, return to and complete item 9 a – d.

READ BACK OF FORM BEFORE COMPLETING & SIGNING THIS FORM.
12. PATIENT'S OR AUTHORIZED PERSON'S SIGNATURE I authorize the release of any medical or other information necessary to process this claim. I also request payment of government benefits either to myself or to the party who accepts assignment below.

SIGNED _____ DATE _____

13. INSURED'S OR AUTHORIZED PERSON'S SIGNATURE I authorize payment of medical benefits to the undersigned physician or supplier for services described below.

SIGNED _____

PATIENT AND INSURED INFORMATION

---

14. DATE OF CURRENT: ◄ ILLNESS (First symptom) OR INJURY (Accident) OR PREGNANCY (LMP)   MM | DD | YY

15. IF PATIENT HAS HAD SAME OR SIMILAR ILLNESS, GIVE FIRST DATE   MM | DD | YY

16. DATES PATIENT UNABLE TO WORK IN CURRENT OCCUPATION   MM | DD | YY   FROM   TO   MM | DD | YY

17. NAME OF REFERRING PHYSICIAN OR OTHER SOURCE

17a. I.D. NUMBER OF REFERRING PHYSICIAN

18. HOSPITALIZATION DATES RELATED TO CURRENT SERVICES   MM | DD | YY   FROM   TO   MM | DD | YY

19. RESERVED FOR LOCAL USE

20. OUTSIDE LAB? $ CHARGES
YES [ ]   NO [ ]

21. DIAGNOSIS OR NATURE OF ILLNESS OR INJURY. (RELATE ITEMS 1, 2, 3, OR 4 TO ITEM 24E BY LINE)

1. |___ . ___| 3. |___ . ___|

2. |___ . ___| 4. |___ . ___|

22. MEDICAID RESUBMISSION CODE   ORIGINAL REF. NO.

23. PRIOR AUTHORIZATION NUMBER

24. A DATE(S) OF SERVICE			B Place of Service	C Type of Service	D PROCEDURES, SERVICES, OR SUPPLIES (Explain Unusual Circumstances)		E DIAGNOSIS CODE	F $ CHARGES	G DAYS OR UNITS	H EPSDT Family Plan	I EMG	J COB	K RESERVED FOR LOCAL USE
From MM DD YY	To MM DD YY				CPT/HCPCS	MODIFIER							
1													
2													
3													
4													
5													
6													

25. FEDERAL TAX I.D. NUMBER   SSN [ ]   EIN [ ]

26. PATIENT'S ACCOUNT NO.

27. ACCEPT ASSIGNMENT? (For govt. claims, see back)
YES [ ]   NO [ ]

28. TOTAL CHARGE $

29. AMOUNT PAID $

30. BALANCE DUE $

31. SIGNATURE OF PHYSICIAN OR SUPPLIER INCLUDING DEGREES OR CREDENTIALS (I certify that the statements on the reverse apply to this bill and are made a part thereof.)

SIGNED _____ DATE _____

32. NAME AND ADDRESS OF FACILITY WHERE SERVICES WERE RENDERED (If other than home or office)

33. PHYSICIAN'S, SUPPLIER'S BILLING NAME, ADDRESS, ZIP CODE & PHONE #

PIN#   GRP#

PHYSICIAN OR SUPPLIER INFORMATION

PLEASE PRINT OR TYPE

SAMPLE FORM 1500
SAMPLE FORM 1500 SAMPLE FORM 1500

DATE	REMARKS			
10/23/XX	Patient has a $15 copay			

PATIENT			CHART #	SEX	BIRTHDATE
Kristen A. Wonder	556-78-7986		13-g	F	04/16/99

MAILING ADDRESS	CITY	STATE	ZIP	HOME PHONE	WORK PHONE
1654 Willow Tree Dr.	Anywhere	US	12345	(101) 333 5555	444 5555

EMPLOYER	ADDRESS	PATIENT STATUS
None		X MARRIED DIVORCED SINGLE STUDENT OTHER

INSURANCE: PRIMARY	ID#	GROUP	SECONDARY POLICY	ID#	GROUP
BCBS US	NYV 415-55-6767	678			

POLICYHOLDER NAME	BIRTHDATE	RELATIONSHIP	POLICYHOLDER NAME	BIRTHDATE	RELATIONSHIP
John F. Wonder	05/22/75	Father			

SUPPLEMENTAL PLAN	EMPLOYER

POLICYHOLDER NAME	BIRTHDATE	RELATIONSHIP	DIAGNOSIS	CODE
			1. Impacted wax	380.4
EMPLOYER			2.	
White Water Sales			3.	
REFERRING PHYSICIAN UPIN/SSN			4.	

PLACE OF SERVICE	Office

PROCEDURES	CODE	CHARGE
1. Est. pt. OV level II	99212	$ 65.00
2. Removal impacted cerumen	69210	25.00
3.		
4.		
5.		
6.		

SPECIAL NOTES

TOTAL CHARGES	PAYMENTS	ADJUSTMENTS	BALANCE
$90.00	$15.00	0	$75.00

RETURN VISIT	PHYSICIAN SIGNATURE
PRN	*Donald L. Givings, M.D.*

	DONALD L. GIVINGS, M.D.	
MEDICARE D1234 MEDICAID DLG1234 BCBS 12345	11350 MEDICAL DRIVE, ANYWHERE US 12345 PHONE NUMBER (101)111-5555	EIN 11-123456 SSN 123-12-1234 PIN DG1234 GRP DG12345

(SAMPLE ONLY - NOT APPROVED FOR USE)

CARRIER

HEALTH INSURANCE CLAIM FORM

[ ][ ] PICA

PICA [ ][ ]

1. MEDICARE MEDICAID CHAMPUS CHAMPVA GROUP HEALTH PLAN FECA BLK LUNG OTHER	1a. INSURED'S I.D. NUMBER (FOR PROGRAM IN ITEM 1)

1. MEDICARE [ ] (Medicare #) MEDICAID [ ] (Medicaid #) CHAMPUS [ ] (Sponsor's SSN) CHAMPVA [ ] (VA File #) GROUP HEALTH PLAN [ ] (SSN or ID) FECA BLK LUNG [ ] (SSN) OTHER [ ] (ID)

1a. INSURED'S I.D. NUMBER (FOR PROGRAM IN ITEM 1)

2. PATIENT'S NAME (Last Name, First Name, Middle Initial)

3. PATIENT'S BIRTH DATE MM | DD | YY SEX M [ ] F [ ]

4. INSURED'S NAME (Last Name, First Name, Middle Initial)

5. PATIENT'S ADDRESS (No. Street)

6. PATIENT RELATIONSHIP TO INSURED Self [ ] Spouse [ ] Child [ ] Other [ ]

7. INSURED'S ADDRESS (No. Street)

CITY | STATE

8. PATIENT STATUS Single [ ] Married [ ] Other [ ] Employed [ ] Full-Time Student [ ] Part-Time Student [ ]

CITY | STATE

ZIP CODE | TELEPHONE (Include Area Code) ( )

ZIP CODE | TELEPHONE (INCLUDE AREA CODE) ( )

9. OTHER INSURED'S NAME (Last Name, First Name, Middle Initial)

10. IS PATIENT'S CONDITION RELATED TO:

11. INSURED'S POLICY GROUP OR FECA NUMBER

a. OTHER INSURED'S POLICY OR GROUP NUMBER

a. EMPLOYMENT? (CURRENT OR PREVIOUS) YES [ ] NO [ ]

a. INSURED'S DATE OF BIRTH MM | DD | YY SEX M [ ] F [ ]

b. OTHER INSURED'S DATE OF BIRTH MM | DD | YY SEX M [ ] F [ ]

b. AUTO ACCIDENT? PLACE (State) YES [ ] NO [ ]

b. EMPLOYER'S NAME OR SCHOOL NAME

c. EMPLOYER'S NAME OR SCHOOL NAME

c. OTHER ACCIDENT? YES [ ] NO [ ]

c. INSURANCE PLAN NAME OR PROGRAM NAME

d. INSURANCE PLAN NAME OR PROGRAM NAME

10d. RESERVED FOR LOCAL USE

d. IS THERE ANOTHER HEALTH BENEFIT PLAN? YES [ ] NO [ ] If yes, return to and complete item 9 a – d.

READ BACK OF FORM BEFORE COMPLETING & SIGNING THIS FORM.

12. PATIENT'S OR AUTHORIZED PERSON'S SIGNATURE I authorize the release of any medical or other information necessary to process this claim. I also request payment of government benefits either to myself or to the party who accepts assignment below.

SIGNED _____ DATE _____

13. INSURED'S OR AUTHORIZED PERSON'S SIGNATURE I authorize payment of medical benefits to the undersigned physician or supplier for services described below.

SIGNED _____

PATIENT AND INSURED INFORMATION

14. DATE OF CURRENT: MM | DD | YY ILLNESS (First symptom) OR INJURY (Accident) OR PREGNANCY (LMP)

15. IF PATIENT HAS HAD SAME OR SIMILAR ILLNESS, GIVE FIRST DATE MM | DD | YY

16. DATES PATIENT UNABLE TO WORK IN CURRENT OCCUPATION FROM MM | DD | YY TO MM | DD | YY

17. NAME OF REFERRING PHYSICIAN OR OTHER SOURCE

17a. I.D. NUMBER OF REFERRING PHYSICIAN

18. HOSPITALIZATION DATES RELATED TO CURRENT SERVICES FROM MM | DD | YY TO MM | DD | YY

19. RESERVED FOR LOCAL USE

20. OUTSIDE LAB? YES [ ] NO [ ] $ CHARGES

21. DIAGNOSIS OR NATURE OF ILLNESS OR INJURY. (RELATE ITEMS 1, 2, 3, OR 4 TO ITEM 24E BY LINE)

1. |___ . ___| 3. |___ . ___|

2. |___ . ___| 4. |___ . ___|

22. MEDICAID RESUBMISSION CODE | ORIGINAL REF. NO.

23. PRIOR AUTHORIZATION NUMBER

24. A DATE(S) OF SERVICE		B Place of Service	C Type of Service	D PROCEDURES, SERVICES, OR SUPPLIES (Explain Unusual Circumstances)		E DIAGNOSIS CODE	F $ CHARGES	G DAYS OR UNITS	H EPSDT Family Plan	I EMG	J COB	K RESERVED FOR LOCAL USE
From MM DD YY	To MM DD YY			CPT/HCPCS	MODIFIER							
1												
2												
3												
4												
5												
6												

25. FEDERAL TAX I.D. NUMBER SSN [ ] EIN [ ]

26. PATIENT'S ACCOUNT NO.

27. ACCEPT ASSIGNMENT? (For govt. claims, see back) YES [ ] NO [ ]

28. TOTAL CHARGE $

29. AMOUNT PAID $

30. BALANCE DUE $

31. SIGNATURE OF PHYSICIAN OR SUPPLIER INCLUDING DEGREES OR CREDENTIALS (I certify that the statements on the reverse apply to this bill and are made a part thereof.) SIGNED _____ DATE _____

32. NAME AND ADDRESS OF FACILITY WHERE SERVICES WERE RENDERED (If other than home or office)

33. PHYSICIAN'S, SUPPLIER'S BILLING NAME, ADDRESS, ZIP CODE & PHONE # PIN# _____ GRP# _____

PHYSICIAN OR SUPPLIER INFORMATION

(SAMPLE ONLY - NOT APPROVED FOR USE)

PLEASE PRINT OR TYPE

SAMPLE FORM 1500
SAMPLE FORM 1500 SAMPLE FORM 1500

DATE 04/16/XX			REMARKS							

PATIENT					CHART #	SEX	BIRTHDATE			
Edward R. Turtle		NXG 444-55-2323			13-h	M	09/15/49			

MAILING ADDRESS	CITY	STATE	ZIP	HOME PHONE	WORK PHONE
68 North Street	Anywhere	US	12345	(101) 333 5555	444 5555

EMPLOYER	ADDRESS	PATIENT STATUS
Carpet Pro	Anywhere US	X MARRIED DIVORCED SINGLE · STUDENT OTHER

INSURANCE: PRIMARY	ID#	GROUP	SECONDARY POLICY		ID#	GROUP
BCBS Federal	R12345678	105				

POLICYHOLDER NAME	BIRTHDATE	RELATIONSHIP	POLICYHOLDER NAME	BIRTHDATE	RELATIONSHIP
		Self			

SUPPLEMENTAL PLAN	EMPLOYER

POLICYHOLDER NAME	BIRTHDATE	RELATIONSHIP	DIAGNOSIS	CODE
			1. Rectal bleeding	569.3
EMPLOYER			2. Irritable bowel	564.1
Carpet Pro			3. Abdominal pain	789.00
REFERRING PHYSICIAN UPIN/SSN			4.	

PLACE OF SERVICE   Mercy Hospital   Anywhere Street   Anywhere US   12345

PROCEDURES		CODE	CHARGE
1. Init. hospital level IV	04/14/XX	99224	$175.00
2. Subsq. hospital level III	04/15/XX	99233	85.00
3. Hospital discharge 30 min.	04/16/XX	99238	75.00
4.			
5.			
6.			

SPECIAL NOTES
Onset 04/07/XX

TOTAL CHARGES	PAYMENTS	ADJUSTMENTS	BALANCE
$335.00	-0-	-0-	$335.00

RETURN VISIT	PHYSICIAN SIGNATURE
4 weeks	*Donald L. Givings, M.D.*

	DONALD L. GIVINGS, M.D.	
MEDICARE D1234	11350 MEDICAL DRIVE, ANYWHERE US 12345	EIN 11-123456
MEDICAID DLG1234	PHONE NUMBER (101)111-5555	SSN 123-12-1234
BCBS 12345		PIN DG1234
		GRP DG12345

PLEASE
DO NOT
STAPLE
IN THIS
AREA

CARRIER

☐☐ PICA

HEALTH INSURANCE CLAIM FORM

PICA ☐☐☐

1.	MEDICARE	MEDICAID	CHAMPUS	CHAMPVA	GROUP HEALTH PLAN	FECA BLK LUNG	OTHER	1a. INSURED'S I.D. NUMBER	(FOR PROGRAM IN ITEM 1)
	☐ (Medicare #)	☐ (Medicaid #)	☐ (Sponsor's SSN)	☐ (VA File #)	☐ (SSN or ID)	☐ (SSN)	☐ (ID)		

2. PATIENT'S NAME (Last Name, First Name, Middle Initial)

3. PATIENT'S BIRTH DATE
MM | DD | YY   SEX   M ☐   F ☐

4. INSURED'S NAME (Last Name, First Name, Middle Initial)

5. PATIENT'S ADDRESS (No. Street)

6. PATIENT RELATIONSHIP TO INSURED
Self ☐   Spouse ☐   Child ☐   Other ☐

7. INSURED'S ADDRESS (No. Street)

CITY   STATE

8. PATIENT STATUS
Single ☐   Married ☐   Other ☐
Employed ☐   Full-Time Student ☐   Part-Time Student ☐

CITY   STATE

ZIP CODE   TELEPHONE (Include Area Code)
(   )

ZIP CODE   TELEPHONE (INCLUDE AREA CODE)
(   )

9. OTHER INSURED'S NAME (Last Name, First Name, Middle Initial)

10. IS PATIENT'S CONDITION RELATED TO:

11. INSURED'S POLICY GROUP OR FECA NUMBER

a. OTHER INSURED'S POLICY OR GROUP NUMBER

a. EMPLOYMENT? (CURRENT OR PREVIOUS)
☐ YES   ☐ NO

a. INSURED'S DATE OF BIRTH
MM | DD | YY   SEX   M ☐   F ☐

b. OTHER INSURED'S DATE OF BIRTH
MM | DD | YY   SEX   M ☐   F ☐

b. AUTO ACCIDENT?   PLACE (State)
☐ YES   ☐ NO

b. EMPLOYER'S NAME OR SCHOOL NAME

c. EMPLOYER'S NAME OR SCHOOL NAME

c. OTHER ACCIDENT?
☐ YES   ☐ NO

c. INSURANCE PLAN NAME OR PROGRAM NAME

d. INSURANCE PLAN NAME OR PROGRAM NAME

10d. RESERVED FOR LOCAL USE

d. IS THERE ANOTHER HEALTH BENEFIT PLAN?
☐ YES   ☐ NO   If yes, return to and complete item 9 a – d.

READ BACK OF FORM BEFORE COMPLETING & SIGNING THIS FORM.
12. PATIENT'S OR AUTHORIZED PERSON'S SIGNATURE I authorize the release of any medical or other information necessary to process this claim. I also request payment of government benefits either to myself or to the party who accepts assignment below.

SIGNED _____   DATE _____

13. INSURED'S OR AUTHORIZED PERSON'S SIGNATURE I authorize payment of medical benefits to the undersigned physician or supplier for services described below.

SIGNED _____

PATIENT AND INSURED INFORMATION

14. DATE OF CURRENT: ◄ ILLNESS (First symptom) OR INJURY (Accident) OR PREGNANCY (LMP)
MM | DD | YY

15. IF PATIENT HAS HAD SAME OR SIMILAR ILLNESS, GIVE FIRST DATE   MM | DD | YY

16. DATES PATIENT UNABLE TO WORK IN CURRENT OCCUPATION
MM | DD | YY   TO   MM | DD | YY
FROM

17. NAME OF REFERRING PHYSICIAN OR OTHER SOURCE

17a. I.D. NUMBER OF REFERRING PHYSICIAN

18. HOSPITALIZATION DATES RELATED TO CURRENT SERVICES
MM | DD | YY   TO   MM | DD | YY
FROM

19. RESERVED FOR LOCAL USE

20. OUTSIDE LAB? $ CHARGES
☐ YES   ☐ NO

21. DIAGNOSIS OR NATURE OF ILLNESS OR INJURY. (RELATE ITEMS 1, 2, 3, OR 4 TO ITEM 24E BY LINE)
1. ⌐___ . ___
2. ⌐___ . ___
3. ⌐___ . ___
4. ⌐___ . ___

22. MEDICAID RESUBMISSION
CODE   ORIGINAL REF. NO.

23. PRIOR AUTHORIZATION NUMBER

24. A DATE(S) OF SERVICE						B Place of Service	C Type of Service	D PROCEDURES, SERVICES, OR SUPPLIES (Explain Unusual Circumstances) CPT/HCPCS	MODIFIER	E DIAGNOSIS CODE	F $ CHARGES	G DAYS OR UNITS	H EPSDT Family Plan	I EMG	J COB	K RESERVED FOR LOCAL USE
From MM	DD	YY	To MM	DD	YY											
1																
2																
3																
4																
5																
6																

25. FEDERAL TAX I.D. NUMBER   SSN ☐ EIN ☐

26. PATIENT'S ACCOUNT NO.

27. ACCEPT ASSIGNMENT? (For govt. claims, see back)
☐ YES   ☐ NO

28. TOTAL CHARGE
$

29. AMOUNT PAID
$

30. BALANCE DUE
$

31. SIGNATURE OF PHYSICIAN OR SUPPLIER INCLUDING DEGREES OR CREDENTIALS
(I certify that the statements on the reverse apply to this bill and are made a part thereof.)

SIGNED _____   DATE _____

32. NAME AND ADDRESS OF FACILITY WHERE SERVICES WERE RENDERED (If other than home or office)

33. PHYSICIAN'S, SUPPLIER'S BILLING NAME, ADDRESS, ZIP CODE & PHONE #

PIN#   GRP#

PHYSICIAN OR SUPPLIER INFORMATION

CHAPTER 14 Fourteen

Medicare

MEDICARE ELIGIBILITY

1. Persons eligible for Medicare services include: (Fill in the blanks.)

   a. All persons age sixty-five or older, _____ on Social Security Administration benefits.

   b. All persons age sixty-five or older on Railroad Retirement, and their _____ age sixty-five or older.

   c. Spouses, age _____ or older, of persons who regularly pay into the Social Security Administration program, whether or not the worker is retired.

   d. All persons who have received Social Security Disability Insurance benefits for _____ years.

2. Special eligibility has been established for the following cases: (Fill in the blanks.)

   a. All workers afflicted with end-stage _____ disease who pay Social Security tax either through payroll deduction or self-employment tax.

   b. Affected spouses and affected dependent _____ of workers who pay Social Security taxes.

   c. Donors of _____ transplanted into persons with end-stage _____ disease are covered for all medical expenses directly related to the donation of a _____ .

   d. Retired _____ employees enrolled in the Civil Service Retirement System and their spouses over age sixty-five.

MEDICARE ENROLLMENT

3. The answer to each of the following statements is either true or false. Indicate your choice by placing **T** for a true statement or **F** for a false statement on the line provided.

   _____ a. Everyone eligible for Social Security benefits and federal workers enrolled in the CSRS program are automatically enrolled in Medicare Part B.

   _____ b. Persons age sixty-two and over who do not qualify for Social Security benefits may "buy in" to Part A.

   _____ c. Anyone eligible for Part A may elect to enroll in Part B by paying premiums to Medicare.

   _____ d. Persons should enroll in the Medicare program prior to the first of the month in which they turn sixty-five years old.

   _____ e. New monthly premium rates are announced each October and go into effect the following February.

CRITICAL THINKING

4. Write a paragraph describing the difference between the **Qualified Medicare Beneficiary program** and the **Specified Low-Income Medicare Beneficiary program**.

_____

_____

_____

_____

PART A COVERAGE

5. Medicare pays only a portion of a patient's acute care hospitalization expenses, and the patient's out-of-pocket expenses are calculated on a ___. (Circle the correct answer.)

   a. spell-of-illness basis

   b. benefit period basis

   c. spell-of-sickness basis

   d. all of the above

6. A benefit period begins on the first day of hospitalization and ends when the patient has been out of the hospital for ___. (Circle the correct answer.)

   a. 30 consecutive days

   b. 60 consecutive days

   c. 90 consecutive days

   d. none of the above

7. After ninety continuous days of hospitalization, the patient may elect to use his/her ___. (Circle the correct answer.)

   a. ninety-day lifetime reserve days

   b. thirty-day lifetime reserve days

   c. sixty-day lifetime reserve days

   d. none of the above

8. Persons confined to a psychiatric hospital are allowed ___. (Circle the correct answer.)

   a. 190 lifetime reserve days

   b. 160 lifetime reserve days

   c. 90 lifetime reserve days

   d. none of the above

9. Persons who become inpatients at a skilled nursing facility after a three-day minimum acute hospital stay, and who meet Medicare's qualified diagnosis and comprehensive treatment plan requirements pay 1999 rates of: (Fill in the blanks.)

   a. Days 1-20   _____

   b. Days 21-100   _____

   c. Days 101+   _____

10. Match the insurance terms in the first column with the definitions in the second column. Write the correct letter in each blank.

_____ Medicare Part A	a. used only once during a patient's lifetime
_____ hospice care	b. the temporary hospitalization of a hospice patient
_____ ESRD coverage	c. covers institutional care
_____ lifetime reserve days	d. all terminally ill patients qualify for this
_____ home health services	e. available to patients confined to the home
_____ respite care	f. used by persons in need of renal dialysis or transplant

11. Kidney donor coverage includes ___. (Circle the correct answer.)
   a. preoperative testing
   b. surgery
   c. postoperative services
   d. all of the above

12. All payments for medical expenses incurred by a kidney donor are made directly to the ___. (Circle the correct answer.)
   a. health care providers
   b. kidney donor
   c. kidney recipient
   d. any of the above

13. Heart and heart-lung transplants are now covered if the person is Medicare-eligible and the transplant takes place in a Medicare-certified regional ___. (Circle the correct answer.)
   a. hospital
   b. medical center
   c. transplant center
   d. any of the above

14. Liver transplants for adults are covered if the person is Medicare-eligible and does not have the following two diagnoses.
   a. _____
   b. _____

PART B COVERAGE

15. Medicare Part B does not cover ___. (Circle the correct answer.)
   a. diagnostic testing
   b. routine physicals
   c. ambulance services
   d. physician services

16. Which of the following statements about Medicare Part B is NOT true? (Circle the correct answer.)
   a. Medicare pays for therapeutic shoes for hypertensive patients.
   b. Medicare pays for influenza, hepatitis B, and pneumonococcal vaccines.
   c. Medicare pays for drugs that are not self-administered.
   d. none of the above

17. The following preventive screening services were added to the benefits under the Balanced Budget Act of 1997: (Fill in the blanks.)

a. annual _____ screening for women over age 39

b. annual colorectal screening/fecal-occult blood for patients age _____ and older

c. colorectal screening/flexible sigmoidoscopies every _____ _____ for patients age 50 and over

d. colorectal screening/colonoscopies every two years if the patient is at high risk for

_____ _____

e. screening _____ and clinical _____ examinations every three years

18. The patient is required to pay a $ _____ annual deductible and _____ percent of the Medicare allowed charges on all covered benefits for traditional Medicare Part B.

19. Describe the possible consequences for providers who are in violation of Medicare regulations by routinely refraining from collecting the patient's deductible and coinsurance.

_____

20. The coinsurance for outpatient mental health treatments is ___. (Circle the correct answer.)

a. 20 percent of allowed charges

b. 50 percent of allowed charges

c. 75 percent of allowed charges

d. There is no coinsurance.

PARTICIPATING/NONPARTICIPATING PROVIDERS

21. Indicate whether each of the following applies to **PAR** or **NonPAR** providers on the line provided.

a. _____ providers must accept assignment on clinical laboratory charges

b. _____ bonuses provided to carriers for recruitment and enrollment of PARs

c. _____ direct payment of all claims

d. _____ balance billing of the patient is forbidden

e. _____ faster processing of assigned claims

f. _____ patient must sign a Surgical Disclosure form for all nonassigned surgical fees over $500.

g. _____ provider fees are restricted to no more than the "limiting charge" on nonassigned claims

h. _____ a five percent high fee schedule

i. _____ collections are restricted to only the deductible and coinsurance due at the time of service on an assigned claim

22. Fill in the blanks using the example provided.

NonPAR charges "limiting fee"	$95
NonPAR approved rate	$80
The patient owes NonPAR provider	$_____
Total payment to NonPAR provider	$_____

23. Fill in the blanks using the example provided.

PAR charges usual fee $100

PARMedicare approved rate $ 75

PAR adjustment $_____

Patient payment to PAR provider $_____

Total payment to PAR provider $_____

24. If a NonPAR provider does not heed the carrier's warnings to desist from flagrant abuse of the "limiting charge" rules, the potential fine has been increased to ___. (Circle the correct answer.)

   a. $2,000

   b. $5,000

   c. $10,000

   d. $20,000

25. When is a NonPAR not restricted to billing the "limiting fee" on a specific claim?

_____

CRITICAL THINKING

26. Write a paragraph describing the use of the Surgery Disclosure form and the penalties for not using this form.

_____

_____

_____

_____

_____

_____

27. Federal law requires that all providers submit claims to Medicare if they provide a Medicare-covered service to a patient enrolled in Medicare Part B. This regulation does not apply if ___. (Circle the correct answer.)

   a. the patient disenrolled before the service was furnished

   b. the patient has not enrolled in Part B

   c. the patient or the patient's legal representative refuses to sign an authorization for release of medical information

   d. all of the above

28. The Privacy Act of 1979 forbids the regional carrier from disclosing the status of any unassigned claim beyond the ___. (Circle the correct answer.)

   a. date the claim was received by the carrier

   b. date the claim was paid, denied, or suspended

   c. general reason the claim was suspended

   d. all of the above

29. On all clinical laboratory charges, federal law mandates the _____ of _____ .

30. Which of the following statements about Medicare Part B is NOT true? (Circle the correct answer.)

    a. Medicare requires that assignment be accepted on all claims for services performed in an outpatient setting by physicians.

    b. Medicare requires that assignment be accepted on all claims for services performed in an outpatient setting by nurse practitioners.

    c. Medicare requires that assignment be accepted on all claims for services performed in an outpatient setting by physician assistants.

    d. Medicare requires that assignment be accepted on all claims for services performed in an outpatient setting by clinical social workers.

31. Define *balance billing*. _____

_____

MEDICARE FEE SCHEDULE (MFS)

32. List five factors on which the RBRVS or MFS formula is based.

    a. _____

    b. _____

    c. _____

    d. _____

    e. _____

33. The answer to each of the following statements is either true or false. Indicate your choice by placing **T** for a true statement or **F** for a false statement on the line provided.

    _____ a. Medicare law requires payment only for services or supplies that are considered reasonable and necessary for the stated diagnosis.

    _____ b. Medicare may cover procedures deemed to be unproved, experimental, or investigational in nature.

    _____ c. The patient must pay the full cost of the procedures denied by Medicare as not medically necessary.

    _____ d. The patient must agree in writing, after receiving the services, to personally pay for services denied by Medicare as not medically necessary.

    _____ e. The provider must refund any payment received from a patient for a service denied by Medicare as not medically necessary unless the patient agreed verbally to personally pay for such services.

    _____ f. A refund is not required if the provider could not have known a specific treatment would be ruled unnecessary.

MEDICARE AS A SECONDARY PAYOR

34. What should a provider do to prevent fines and penalties for routinely billing Medicare as primary payor when it is the secondary payor? _____

_____

35. The following statements apply to Medicare Secondary Payor fee schedule rules. (Fill in the blanks.)

    a. The primary insurance fee schedule overrules the Medicare schedule on _____ claims only

    b. NonPARs who do not accept assignment are _____ from collecting amounts above the applicable limiting charge

    c. Providers are not required to file Medicare secondary claims unless the _____ specifically requests it.

36. Employees who leave a company with employer-sponsored group health insurance have the right to continue health insurance coverage for up to eighteen months if they are willing to pay the entire cost of the premiums. This continuation plan is known as _____ _____ _____ _____ _____ insurance.

MEDICARE SUPPLEMENTAL PLANS

37. List two forms of additional insurance persons who are eligible for Medicare often purchase.

    a. _____

    b. _____

38. Which of the following statements about a Medigap policy is NOT true? (Circle the correct answer.)

    a. A Medigap policy is a private, commercial plan that collects the premiums directly from the patient.

    b. Medigap premiums can widely vary even within the same geographic area.

    c. NonPAR providers are required to include Medigap information on the claim form.

    d. The NonPAR provider does not receive an EOB directly from Medicare for nonassigned claims.

39. The answer to each of the following statements is either yes or no. Indicate your choice by placing **Y** for yes or **N** for no on the line provided.

    _____ a. Is an Employer-Sponsored Retirement Plan regulated by the federal government?

    _____ b. Are premiums for an Employer-Sponsored Retirement Plan paid by the employer?

    _____ c. Are health care providers required to file Employer-Sponsored Retirement Plan claims?

    _____ d. If the employer-sponsored retirement claim is not forwarded electronically, will the patient need to file for benefits after the Medicare EOB is received?

40. The Medicare-Medicaid Crossover program is: (Fill in the blanks.)

    a. a combination of the _____ / _____ programs.

    b. available to Medicare-eligible persons with incomes below the federal _____ level.

MEDICARE AND MANAGED CARE

41. List five advantages of HMO-Medicare enrollment.

    a. _____

    b. _____

    c. _____

    d. _____

    e. _____

42. Beneficiaries have the right to disenroll from a Medicare-HMO ___. (Circle the correct answer.)

    a. at any time

    b. for personal reasons

    c. for medical reasons

    d. all of the above

43. When written notification of disenrollment is given, ___ should be allowed to ensure that proper transfer from the HMO has occurred. (Circle the correct answer.)

    a. 15 days

    b. 30 days

    c. 60 days

    d. none of the above

44. For HMO-authorized fee-for-service specialty care, the claim is sent directly to ___. (Circle the correct answer.)

    a. the HMO

    b. the patient

    c. Medicare

    d. none of the above

45. What is the deadline for filing Medicare-HMO claims? (Circle the correct answer.)

    a. 45 days

    b. 90 days

    c. one year

    d. HMO specific

CRITICAL THINKING

46. Why is it important that a practice's billing department be aware of each HMO's timely filing restrictions?

_____

_____

MEDICARE+CHOICE

47. List three options Medicare+Choice offers.

    a. _____

    b. _____

    c. _____

48. In a private fee-for-service plan, the Medicare beneficiary may elect to use a regular fee-for-service insurance plan and _____ will help pay the premium.

49. Provider Sponsored Organizations are managed care organizations owned and operated by a network of _____ and _____ rather than by an insurance company.

50. Explain how the regional carrier for traditional Medicare claims is selected by HCFA.

_____

51. Complete the following sentences:

   a. The words that appear on a Railroad Retirement Medicare card are _____

   _____ .

   b. On the Railroad Retirement Medicare card, there appears a nine-digit identification number which has an _____ .

   c. Coal miners' claims are sent to the _____ .

   d. The claim filing deadline for both regular Medicare and Railroad Retirement claims is

   _____ .

   e. A claim for services performed in late November of 2000 must be postmarked on or before

   _____ .

   f. The claim form that all paper claims must be filed on is the _____ .

   g. All providers are required to file Medicare claims for their _____ .

   h. When Medicare is the secondary payor, the _____
   must be attached to the Medicare claim.

Know Your Acronyms

52. Define the following acronyms:

   a. SSA _____

   b. SSDI _____

   c. ESRD _____

   d. CSRS _____

   e. QMB _____

   f. SLMB _____

   g. NonPAR _____

   h. LLP _____

   i. MFS _____

   j. RBRVS _____

   k. MSP _____

   l. COBRA _____

   m. PSO _____

   n. MSA _____

   o. DMERC _____

   p. UPIN _____

   q. NPI _____

   r. PIN _____

   s. PAYERID _____

   t. CLIA _____

EXERCISES

1. Complete Case Studies 14-a through 14-l using the blank claim form provided. Follow the step-by-step instructions given in the textbook to properly complete the claim form. If a patient has a secondary carrier, complete an additional claim form using secondary directions given in the textbook. You may choose to use a pencil so corrections can be made.

Case Study 14-a

DATE 07/12/XX	REMARKS				
PATIENT Alice E. Worthington 444-22-3333		CHART # 14-a	SEX F	BIRTHDATE 02/16/26	
MAILING ADDRESS 3301 Sunny Day Dr.	CITY Anywhere	STATE US	ZIP 12345	HOME PHONE (101) 333-5555	WORK PHONE
EMPLOYER	ADDRESS Anywhere US	PATIENT STATUS X MARRIED DIVORCED SINGLE STUDENT OTHER			
INSURANCE: PRIMARY Medicare	ID# 444-22-3333A	GROUP	SECONDARY POLICY		
POLICYHOLDER NAME	BIRTHDATE	RELATIONSHIP Self	POLICYHOLDER NAME	BIRTHDATE	RELATIONSHIP
SUPPLEMENTAL PLAN			EMPLOYER		

POLICYHOLDER NAME	BIRTHDATE	RELATIONSHIP	DIAGNOSIS	CODE
			1. Breast lump	611.72
EMPLOYER			2. Breast pain	611.71
			3. Family history breast cancer	V16.3
REFERRING PHYSICIAN UPIN/SSN			4.	

PLACE OF SERVICE	Office	
PROCEDURES	CODE	CHARGE
1. Ext. Pt. OV Level II	99212	$65.00
2.		
3.		
4.		
5.		
6.		

SPECIAL NOTES Refer to Dr. Kutter

TOTAL CHARGES $65.00	PAYMENTS 0	ADJUSTMENTS 0	BALANCE $65.00
RETURN VISIT		PHYSICIAN SIGNATURE *Donald L. Givings, M.D.*	

MEDICARE # D1234 MEDICAID # DLG1234 BCBS # 12345	DONALD L. GIVINGS, M.D. 11350 MEDICAL DRIVE, ANYWHERE, US 12345 PHONE NUMBER (101)111-5555	EIN # 11123456 SSN # 123-12-1234 UPIN # DG1234 GRP # DG12345

(SAMPLE ONLY - NOT APPROVED FOR USE)

HEALTH INSURANCE CLAIM FORM

| | PICA | | PICA | | |

CARRIER

1. MEDICARE ☐ (Medicare #) MEDICAID ☐ (Medicaid #) CHAMPUS ☐ (Sponsor's SSN) CHAMPVA ☐ (VA File #) GROUP HEALTH PLAN ☐ (SSN or ID) FECA BLK LUNG ☐ (SSN) OTHER ☐ (ID)	1a. INSURED'S I.D. NUMBER (FOR PROGRAM IN ITEM 1)	
2. PATIENT'S NAME (Last Name, First Name, Middle Initial)	3. PATIENT'S BIRTH DATE MM DD YY SEX M ☐ F ☐	4. INSURED'S NAME (Last Name, First Name, Middle Initial)
5. PATIENT'S ADDRESS (No. Street)	6. PATIENT RELATIONSHIP TO INSURED Self ☐ Spouse ☐ Child ☐ Other ☐	7. INSURED'S ADDRESS (No. Street)
CITY STATE	8. PATIENT STATUS Single ☐ Married ☐ Other ☐	CITY STATE
ZIP CODE TELEPHONE (Include Area Code) ( )	Employed ☐ Full-Time Student ☐ Part-Time Student ☐	ZIP CODE TELEPHONE (INCLUDE AREA CODE) ( )
9. OTHER INSURED'S NAME (Last Name, First Name, Middle Initial)	10. IS PATIENT'S CONDITION RELATED TO:	11. INSURED'S POLICY GROUP OR FECA NUMBER
a. OTHER INSURED'S POLICY OR GROUP NUMBER	a. EMPLOYMENT? (CURRENT OR PREVIOUS) ☐ YES ☐ NO	a. INSURED'S DATE OF BIRTH MM DD YY SEX M ☐ F ☐
b. OTHER INSURED'S DATE OF BIRTH MM DD YY SEX M ☐ F ☐	b. AUTO ACCIDENT? PLACE (State) ☐ YES ☐ NO	b. EMPLOYER'S NAME OR SCHOOL NAME
c. EMPLOYER'S NAME OR SCHOOL NAME	c. OTHER ACCIDENT? ☐ YES ☐ NO	c. INSURANCE PLAN NAME OR PROGRAM NAME
d. INSURANCE PLAN NAME OR PROGRAM NAME	10d. RESERVED FOR LOCAL USE	d. IS THERE ANOTHER HEALTH BENEFIT PLAN? ☐ YES ☐ NO If yes, return to and complete item 9 a - d.

PATIENT AND INSURED INFORMATION

READ BACK OF FORM BEFORE COMPLETING & SIGNING THIS FORM.

12. PATIENT'S OR AUTHORIZED PERSON'S SIGNATURE I authorize the release of any medical or other information necessary to process this claim. I also request payment of government benefits either to myself or to the party who accepts assignment below.

SIGNED _____ DATE _____

13. INSURED'S OR AUTHORIZED PERSON'S SIGNATURE I authorize payment of medical benefits to the undersigned physician or supplier for services described below.

SIGNED _____

14. DATE OF CURRENT: MM DD YY ILLNESS (First symptom) OR INJURY (Accident) OR PREGNANCY (LMP)	15. IF PATIENT HAS HAD SAME OR SIMILAR ILLNESS, GIVE FIRST DATE MM DD YY	16. DATES PATIENT UNABLE TO WORK IN CURRENT OCCUPATION MM DD YY MM DD YY FROM TO
17. NAME OF REFERRING PHYSICIAN OR OTHER SOURCE	17a. I.D. NUMBER OF REFERRING PHYSICIAN	18. HOSPITALIZATION DATES RELATED TO CURRENT SERVICES MM DD YY MM DD YY FROM TO
19. RESERVED FOR LOCAL USE		20. OUTSIDE LAB? ☐ YES ☐ NO $ CHARGES
21. DIAGNOSIS OR NATURE OF ILLNESS OR INJURY. (RELATE ITEMS 1, 2, 3, OR 4 TO ITEM 24E BY LINE) 1. ___.___ 3. ___.___ 2. ___.___ 4. ___.___		22. MEDICAID RESUBMISSION CODE ORIGINAL REF. NO. 23. PRIOR AUTHORIZATION NUMBER

PHYSICIAN OR SUPPLIER INFORMATION

24.

A. DATE(S) OF SERVICE		B. Place of Service	C. Type of Service	D. PROCEDURES, SERVICES, OR SUPPLIES (Explain Unusual Circumstances) CPT/HCPCS MODIFIER	E. DIAGNOSIS CODE	F. $ CHARGES	G. DAYS OR UNITS	H. EPSDT Family Plan	I. EMG	J. COB	K. RESERVED FOR LOCAL USE
From MM DD YY	To MM DD YY										
1											
2											
3											
4											
5											
6											

25. FEDERAL TAX I.D. NUMBER SSN ☐ EIN ☐	26. PATIENT'S ACCOUNT NO.	27. ACCEPT ASSIGNMENT? (For govt. claims, see back) ☐ YES ☐ NO	28. TOTAL CHARGE $	29. AMOUNT PAID $	30. BALANCE DUE $
31. SIGNATURE OF PHYSICIAN OR SUPPLIER INCLUDING DEGREES OR CREDENTIALS (I certify that the statements on the reverse apply to this bill and are made a part thereof.) SIGNED DATE	32. NAME AND ADDRESS OF FACILITY WHERE SERVICES WERE RENDERED (If other than home or office)	33. PHYSICIAN'S, SUPPLIER'S BILLING NAME, ADDRESS, ZIP CODE & PHONE # PIN# GRP#

(SAMPLE ONLY - NOT APPROVED FOR USE)

PLEASE PRINT OR TYPE

SAMPLE FORM 1500
SAMPLE FORM 1500 SAMPLE FORM 1500

DATE	REMARKS					
07/15/XX						

PATIENT			CHART #	SEX	BIRTHDATE
Alice E. Worthington	444-22-3333		14-b	F	02/16/26

MAILING ADDRESS	CITY	STATE	ZIP	HOME PHONE	WORK PHONE
3301 Sunny Day Dr.	Anywhere	US	12345	(101) 333-5555	

EMPLOYER	ADDRESS	PATIENT STATUS
		X
		MARRIED DIVORCED SINGLE STUDENT OTHER

INSURANCE: PRIMARY	ID#	GROUP	SECONDARY POLICY
Medicare	444-22-3333A		

POLICYHOLDER NAME	BIRTHDATE	RELATIONSHIP	POLICYHOLDER NAME	BIRTHDATE	RELATIONSHIP
		Self			

SUPPLEMENTAL PLAN	EMPLOYER

POLICYHOLDER NAME	BIRTHDATE	RELATIONSHIP	DIAGNOSIS		CODE
			1. Breast lump		611.72
EMPLOYER			2. Breast pain		611.71
			3. Family history breast cancer		V16.3
REFERRING PHYSICIAN UPIN/SSN			4.		
Donald L. Givings, M.D.	123-12-1234				

PLACE OF SERVICE	Office

PROCEDURES	CODE	CHARGE
1. Office Consult Level II	99242	$75.00
2.		
3.		
4.		
5.		
6.		

SPECIAL NOTES

TOTAL CHARGES	PAYMENTS	ADJUSTMENTS	BALANCE
$75.00	-0-	-0-	$75.00

RETURN VISIT	PHYSICIAN SIGNATURE
	Jonathan B. Kutter, M.D.

MEDICARE # J1234
MEDICAID # JBK1234
BCBS # 12885

JONATHAN B. KUTTER, M.D. SURGERY
339 WOODLAND PLACE, ANYWHERE, US 12345
PHONE NUMBER (101)111-5555

EIN # 11556677
SSN # 245-12-1234
UPIN # JK1234
GRP # JK12345

(SAMPLE ONLY - NOT APPROVED FOR USE)

CARRIER

PICA

HEALTH INSURANCE CLAIM FORM   PICA

1. MEDICARE MEDICAID CHAMPUS CHAMPVA GROUP HEALTH PLAN FECA BLK LUNG OTHER	1a. INSURED'S I.D. NUMBER (FOR PROGRAM IN ITEM 1)
(Medicare #) (Medicaid #) (Sponsor's SSN) (VA File #) (SSN or ID) (SSN) (ID)	

2. PATIENT'S NAME (Last Name, First Name, Middle Initial)	3. PATIENT'S BIRTH DATE MM DD YY SEX M F	4. INSURED'S NAME (Last Name, First Name, Middle Initial)

5. PATIENT'S ADDRESS (No. Street)	6. PATIENT RELATIONSHIP TO INSURED Self Spouse Child Other	7. INSURED'S ADDRESS (No. Street)

CITY	STATE	8. PATIENT STATUS Single Married Other	CITY	STATE

ZIP CODE	TELEPHONE (Include Area Code) ( )	Employed Full-Time Student Part-Time Student	ZIP CODE	TELEPHONE (INCLUDE AREA CODE) ( )

9. OTHER INSURED'S NAME (Last Name, First Name, Middle Initial)	10. IS PATIENT'S CONDITION RELATED TO:	11. INSURED'S POLICY GROUP OR FECA NUMBER
a. OTHER INSURED'S POLICY OR GROUP NUMBER	a. EMPLOYMENT? (CURRENT OR PREVIOUS) YES NO	a. INSURED'S DATE OF BIRTH MM DD YY SEX M F
b. OTHER INSURED'S DATE OF BIRTH MM DD YY SEX M F	b. AUTO ACCIDENT? PLACE (State) YES NO	b. EMPLOYER'S NAME OR SCHOOL NAME
c. EMPLOYER'S NAME OR SCHOOL NAME	c. OTHER ACCIDENT? YES NO	c. INSURANCE PLAN NAME OR PROGRAM NAME
d. INSURANCE PLAN NAME OR PROGRAM NAME	10d. RESERVED FOR LOCAL USE	d. IS THERE ANOTHER HEALTH BENEFIT PLAN? YES NO If yes, return to and complete item 9 a – d.

READ BACK OF FORM BEFORE COMPLETING & SIGNING THIS FORM. 12. PATIENT'S OR AUTHORIZED PERSON'S SIGNATURE I authorize the release of any medical or other information necessary to process this claim. I also request payment of government benefits either to myself or to the party who accepts assignment below. SIGNED _____ DATE _____	13. INSURED'S OR AUTHORIZED PERSON'S SIGNATURE I authorize payment of medical benefits to the undersigned physician or supplier for services described below. SIGNED _____

14. DATE OF CURRENT: MM DD YY ILLNESS (First symptom) OR INJURY (Accident) OR PREGNANCY (LMP)	15. IF PATIENT HAS HAD SAME OR SIMILAR ILLNESS, GIVE FIRST DATE MM DD YY	16. DATES PATIENT UNABLE TO WORK IN CURRENT OCCUPATION MM DD YY MM DD YY FROM TO
17. NAME OF REFERRING PHYSICIAN OR OTHER SOURCE	17a. I.D. NUMBER OF REFERRING PHYSICIAN	18. HOSPITALIZATION DATES RELATED TO CURRENT SERVICES MM DD YY MM DD YY FROM TO
19. RESERVED FOR LOCAL USE		20. OUTSIDE LAB? $ CHARGES YES NO
21. DIAGNOSIS OR NATURE OF ILLNESS OR INJURY. (RELATE ITEMS 1, 2, 3, OR 4 TO ITEM 24E BY LINE) 1. ____ . ____ 3. ____ . ____ 2. ____ . ____ 4. ____ . ____		22. MEDICAID RESUBMISSION CODE ORIGINAL REF. NO. 23. PRIOR AUTHORIZATION NUMBER

24. A DATE(S) OF SERVICE From To MM DD YY MM DD YY	B Place of Service	C Type of Service	D PROCEDURES, SERVICES, OR SUPPLIES (Explain Unusual Circumstances) CPT/HCPCS MODIFIER	E DIAGNOSIS CODE	F $ CHARGES	G DAYS OR UNITS	H EPSDT Family Plan	I EMG	J COB	K RESERVED FOR LOCAL USE
1										
2										
3										
4										
5										
6										

25. FEDERAL TAX I.D. NUMBER SSN EIN	26. PATIENT'S ACCOUNT NO.	27. ACCEPT ASSIGNMENT? (For govt. claims, see back) YES NO	28. TOTAL CHARGE $	29. AMOUNT PAID $	30. BALANCE DUE $

31. SIGNATURE OF PHYSICIAN OR SUPPLIER INCLUDING DEGREES OR CREDENTIALS (I certify that the statements on the reverse apply to this bill and are made a part thereof.) SIGNED DATE	32. NAME AND ADDRESS OF FACILITY WHERE SERVICES WERE RENDERED (If other than home or office)	33. PHYSICIAN'S, SUPPLIER'S BILLING NAME, ADDRESS, ZIP CODE & PHONE # PIN# GRP#

(SAMPLE ONLY - NOT APPROVED FOR USE)   *PLEASE PRINT OR TYPE*   SAMPLE FORM 1500
SAMPLE FORM 1500   SAMPLE FORM 1500

DATE	REMARKS			
07/22/XX	Alice was in the hospital from July 22 through July 25			

PATIENT		CHART #	SEX	BIRTHDATE
Alice E. Worthington 444-22-3333		14-c	F	02/16/26

MAILING ADDRESS	CITY	STATE	ZIP	HOME PHONE	WORK PHONE
3301 Sunny Day Dr.	Anywhere	US	12345	(101) 333-5555	

EMPLOYER	ADDRESS	PATIENT STATUS
	Anywhere US	MARRIED DIVORCED **X** SINGLE STUDENT OTHER

INSURANCE: PRIMARY	ID#	GROUP	SECONDARY POLICY
Medicare	444-22-3333A		

POLICYHOLDER NAME	BIRTHDATE	RELATIONSHIP	POLICYHOLDER NAME	BIRTHDATE	RELATIONSHIP
		Self			

SUPPLEMENTAL PLAN	EMPLOYER

POLICYHOLDER NAME	BIRTHDATE	RELATIONSHIP	DIAGNOSIS	CODE
			1. Breast cancer	174.8
EMPLOYER			2.	
			3.	
REFERRING PHYSICIAN UPIN/SSN			4.	
Donald L. Givings, M.D. 123-12-1234				

PLACE OF SERVICE	Mercy Hospital, Anywhere St., Anywhere, US 12345 PIN# M1234

PROCEDURES	CODE	CHARGE
1. Mastectomy, Simple, Complete 07/22/XX	19180	$1,200.00
2.		
3.		
4.		
5.		
6.		

SPECIAL NOTES

TOTAL CHARGES	PAYMENTS	ADJUSTMENTS	BALANCE
$1,200.00	0	0	$1,200.00

RETURN VISIT	PHYSICIAN SIGNATURE
	Jonathan B. Kutter, M.D.

JONATHAN B. KUTTER, M.D. SURGERY
339 WOODLAND PLACE, ANYWHERE, US 12345
PHONE NUMBER (101)111-5555

MEDICARE # J1234
MEDICAID # JBK1234
BCBS # 12885

EIN # 11556677
SSN # 245-12-1234
UPIN # JK1234
GRP # JK12345

(SAMPLE ONLY - NOT APPROVED FOR USE)

CARRIER

| | PICA

HEALTH INSURANCE CLAIM FORM

PICA | |

1. MEDICARE   MEDICAID   CHAMPUS   CHAMPVA   GROUP HEALTH PLAN   FECA BLK LUNG   OTHER
☐ (Medicare #) ☐ (Medicaid #) ☐ (Sponsor's SSN) ☐ (VA File #) ☐ (SSN or ID) ☐ (SSN) ☐ (ID)

1a. INSURED'S I.D. NUMBER   (FOR PROGRAM IN ITEM 1)

2. PATIENT'S NAME (Last Name, First Name, Middle Initial)

3. PATIENT'S BIRTH DATE
MM | DD | YY   SEX
M ☐   F ☐

4. INSURED'S NAME (Last Name, First Name, Middle Initial)

5. PATIENT'S ADDRESS (No. Street)

6. PATIENT RELATIONSHIP TO INSURED
Self ☐   Spouse ☐   Child ☐   Other ☐

7. INSURED'S ADDRESS (No. Street)

CITY   STATE

8. PATIENT STATUS
Single ☐   Married ☐   Other ☐

CITY   STATE

ZIP CODE   TELEPHONE (Include Area Code)
( )

Employed ☐   Full-Time Student ☐   Part-Time Student ☐

ZIP CODE   TELEPHONE (INCLUDE AREA CODE)
( )

9. OTHER INSURED'S NAME (Last Name, First Name, Middle Initial)

10. IS PATIENT'S CONDITION RELATED TO:

11. INSURED'S POLICY GROUP OR FECA NUMBER

a. OTHER INSURED'S POLICY OR GROUP NUMBER

a. EMPLOYMENT? (CURRENT OR PREVIOUS)
☐ YES   ☐ NO

a. INSURED'S DATE OF BIRTH
MM | DD | YY   SEX
M ☐   F ☐

b. OTHER INSURED'S DATE OF BIRTH
MM | DD | YY   SEX
M ☐   F ☐

b. AUTO ACCIDENT?   PLACE (State)
☐ YES   ☐ NO

b. EMPLOYER'S NAME OR SCHOOL NAME

c. EMPLOYER'S NAME OR SCHOOL NAME

c. OTHER ACCIDENT?
☐ YES   ☐ NO

c. INSURANCE PLAN NAME OR PROGRAM NAME

d. INSURANCE PLAN NAME OR PROGRAM NAME

10d. RESERVED FOR LOCAL USE

d. IS THERE ANOTHER HEALTH BENEFIT PLAN?
☐ YES   ☐ NO   If yes, return to and complete item 9 a – d.

READ BACK OF FORM BEFORE COMPLETING & SIGNING THIS FORM.
12. PATIENT'S OR AUTHORIZED PERSON'S SIGNATURE I authorize the release of any medical or other information necessary to process this claim. I also request payment of government benefits either to myself or to the party who accepts assignment below.

SIGNED _____   DATE _____

13. INSURED'S OR AUTHORIZED PERSON'S SIGNATURE I authorize payment of medical benefits to the undersigned physician or supplier for services described below.

SIGNED _____

PATIENT AND INSURED INFORMATION

14. DATE OF CURRENT: ◄ ILLNESS (First symptom) OR
MM | DD | YY   INJURY (Accident) OR
PREGNANCY (LMP)

15. IF PATIENT HAS HAD SAME OR SIMILAR ILLNESS, GIVE FIRST DATE   MM | DD | YY

16. DATES PATIENT UNABLE TO WORK IN CURRENT OCCUPATION
MM | DD | YY   MM | DD | YY
FROM   TO

17. NAME OF REFERRING PHYSICIAN OR OTHER SOURCE

17a. I.D. NUMBER OF REFERRING PHYSICIAN

18. HOSPITALIZATION DATES RELATED TO CURRENT SERVICES
MM | DD | YY   MM | DD | YY
FROM   TO

19. RESERVED FOR LOCAL USE

20. OUTSIDE LAB? $ CHARGES
☐ YES   ☐ NO

21. DIAGNOSIS OR NATURE OF ILLNESS OR INJURY. (RELATE ITEMS 1, 2, 3, OR 4 TO ITEM 24E BY LINE) ————
1. L___ . ___   3. L___ . ___
2. L___ . ___   4. L___ . ___

22. MEDICAID RESUBMISSION
CODE   ORIGINAL REF. NO.

23. PRIOR AUTHORIZATION NUMBER

24. A DATE(S) OF SERVICE						B	C	D PROCEDURES, SERVICES, OR SUPPLIES		E	F	G	H	I	J	K
From			To			Place of Service	Type of Service	(Explain Unusual Circumstances)		DIAGNOSIS CODE	$ CHARGES	DAYS OR UNITS	EPSDT Family Plan	EMG	COB	RESERVED FOR LOCAL USE
MM	DD	YY	MM	DD	YY			CPT/HCPCS	MODIFIER							
1																
2																
3																
4																
5																
6																

25. FEDERAL TAX I.D. NUMBER   SSN EIN
☐ ☐

26. PATIENT'S ACCOUNT NO.

27. ACCEPT ASSIGNMENT?
(For govt. claims, see back)
☐ YES   ☐ NO

28. TOTAL CHARGE
$

29. AMOUNT PAID
$

30. BALANCE DUE
$

31. SIGNATURE OF PHYSICIAN OR SUPPLIER INCLUDING DEGREES OR CREDENTIALS
(I certify that the statements on the reverse apply to this bill and are made a part thereof.)

SIGNED _____ DATE _____

32. NAME AND ADDRESS OF FACILITY WHERE SERVICES WERE RENDERED (If other than home or office)

33. PHYSICIAN'S, SUPPLIER'S BILLING NAME, ADDRESS, ZIP CODE & PHONE #

PIN#   GRP#

PHYSICIAN OR SUPPLIER INFORMATION

(SAMPLE ONLY - NOT APPROVED FOR USE)

PLEASE PRINT OR TYPE

SAMPLE FORM 1500
SAMPLE FORM 1500 SAMPLE FORM 1500

147

DATE	REMARKS			
08/25/XX	Today's visit is included in global surgery			

PATIENT			CHART #	SEX	BIRTHDATE
Alice E. Worthington	444-22-3333		14-d	F	02/16/26

MAILING ADDRESS	CITY	STATE	ZIP	HOME PHONE	WORK PHONE
3301 Sunny Day Dr.	Anywhere	US	12345	(101) 333-5555	

EMPLOYER	ADDRESS	PATIENT STATUS			
	Anywhere US	X			
		MARRIED DIVORCED SINGLE STUDENT OTHER			

INSURANCE: PRIMARY	ID#	GROUP	SECONDARY POLICY
Medicare	444-22-3333A		

POLICYHOLDER NAME	BIRTHDATE	RELATIONSHIP	POLICYHOLDER NAME	BIRTHDATE	RELATIONSHIP
		Self			

SUPPLEMENTAL PLAN	EMPLOYER

POLICYHOLDER NAME	BIRTHDATE	RELATIONSHIP	DIAGNOSIS	CODE
			1. Breast cancer	174.8
EMPLOYER			2.	
			3.	
REFERRING PHYSICIAN UPIN/SSN			4.	
Donald L. Givings, M.D.	123-12-1234			

PLACE OF SERVICE   Office

PROCEDURES	CODE	CHARGE
1. Postoperative follow-up visit	99024	$0.00
2.		
3.		
4.		
5.		
6.		

SPECIAL NOTES

TOTAL CHARGES	PAYMENTS	ADJUSTMENTS	BALANCE
$0.00	0	0	$0.00

RETURN VISIT	PHYSICIAN SIGNATURE
	Jonathan B. Kutter, M.D.

	JONATHAN B. KUTTER, M.D. SURGERY	
MEDICARE # J1234	339 WOODLAND PLACE, ANYWHERE, US 12345	EIN # 11556677
MEDICAID # JBK1234	PHONE NUMBER (101)111-5555	SSN # 245-12-1234
BCBS # 12885		UPIN # JK1234
		GRP # JK12345

(SAMPLE ONLY - NOT APPROVED FOR USE)

CARRIER

| | PICA | | **HEALTH INSURANCE CLAIM FORM** | PICA | | |

1. MEDICARE	MEDICAID	CHAMPUS	CHAMPVA	GROUP HEALTH PLAN	FECA BLK LUNG	OTHER	1a. INSURED'S I.D. NUMBER	(FOR PROGRAM IN ITEM 1)
(Medicare #)	(Medicaid #)	(Sponsor's SSN)	(VA File #)	(SSN or ID)	(SSN)	(ID)		

2. PATIENT'S NAME (Last Name, First Name, Middle Initial)

3. PATIENT'S BIRTH DATE MM | DD | YY   SEX M ☐ F ☐

4. INSURED'S NAME (Last Name, First Name, Middle Initial)

5. PATIENT'S ADDRESS (No. Street)

6. PATIENT RELATIONSHIP TO INSURED
Self ☐ Spouse ☐ Child ☐ Other ☐

7. INSURED'S ADDRESS (No. Street)

CITY   STATE

8. PATIENT STATUS
Single ☐ Married ☐ Other ☐

CITY   STATE

ZIP CODE   TELEPHONE (Include Area Code) ( )

Employed ☐ Full-Time Student ☐ Part-Time Student ☐

ZIP CODE   TELEPHONE (INCLUDE AREA CODE) ( )

9. OTHER INSURED'S NAME (Last Name, First Name, Middle Initial)

10. IS PATIENT'S CONDITION RELATED TO:

11. INSURED'S POLICY GROUP OR FECA NUMBER

a. OTHER INSURED'S POLICY OR GROUP NUMBER

a. EMPLOYMENT? (CURRENT OR PREVIOUS)
YES ☐ NO ☐

a. INSURED'S DATE OF BIRTH MM | DD | YY   SEX M ☐ F ☐

b. OTHER INSURED'S DATE OF BIRTH MM | DD | YY   SEX M ☐ F ☐

b. AUTO ACCIDENT?   PLACE (State)
YES ☐ NO ☐

b. EMPLOYER'S NAME OR SCHOOL NAME

c. EMPLOYER'S NAME OR SCHOOL NAME

c. OTHER ACCIDENT?
YES ☐ NO ☐

c. INSURANCE PLAN NAME OR PROGRAM NAME

d. INSURANCE PLAN NAME OR PROGRAM NAME

10d. RESERVED FOR LOCAL USE

d. IS THERE ANOTHER HEALTH BENEFIT PLAN?
YES ☐ NO ☐   If yes, return to and complete item 9 a – d.

READ BACK OF FORM BEFORE COMPLETING & SIGNING THIS FORM.
12. PATIENT'S OR AUTHORIZED PERSON'S SIGNATURE I authorize the release of any medical or other information necessary to process this claim. I also request payment of government benefits either to myself or to the party who accepts assignment below.

SIGNED _____ DATE _____

13. INSURED'S OR AUTHORIZED PERSON'S SIGNATURE I authorize payment of medical benefits to the undersigned physician or supplier for services described below.

SIGNED _____

PATIENT AND INSURED INFORMATION

14. DATE OF CURRENT: ▶ ILLNESS (First symptom) OR INJURY (Accident) OR PREGNANCY (LMP) MM | DD | YY

15. IF PATIENT HAS HAD SAME OR SIMILAR ILLNESS, GIVE FIRST DATE MM | DD | YY

16. DATES PATIENT UNABLE TO WORK IN CURRENT OCCUPATION MM | DD | YY   MM | DD | YY
FROM   TO

17. NAME OF REFERRING PHYSICIAN OR OTHER SOURCE

17a. I.D. NUMBER OF REFERRING PHYSICIAN

18. HOSPITALIZATION DATES RELATED TO CURRENT SERVICES MM | DD | YY   MM | DD | YY
FROM   TO

19. RESERVED FOR LOCAL USE

20. OUTSIDE LAB? $ CHARGES
YES ☐ NO ☐

21. DIAGNOSIS OR NATURE OF ILLNESS OR INJURY. (RELATE ITEMS 1, 2, 3, OR 4 TO ITEM 24E BY LINE)
1. |___.___| 3. |___.___|
2. |___.___| 4. |___.___|

22. MEDICAID RESUBMISSION CODE   ORIGINAL REF. NO.

23. PRIOR AUTHORIZATION NUMBER

24. A DATE(S) OF SERVICE						B Place of Service	C Type of Service	D PROCEDURES, SERVICES, OR SUPPLIES (Explain Unusual Circumstances) CPT/HCPCS	MODIFIER	E DIAGNOSIS CODE	F $ CHARGES	G DAYS OR UNITS	H EPSDT Family Plan	I EMG	J COB	K RESERVED FOR LOCAL USE
From MM	DD	YY	To MM	DD	YY												
1																
2																
3																
4																
5																
6																

25. FEDERAL TAX I.D. NUMBER   SSN ☐ EIN ☐

26. PATIENT'S ACCOUNT NO.

27. ACCEPT ASSIGNMENT? (For govt. claims, see back)
YES ☐ NO ☐

28. TOTAL CHARGE $

29. AMOUNT PAID $

30. BALANCE DUE $

31. SIGNATURE OF PHYSICIAN OR SUPPLIER INCLUDING DEGREES OR CREDENTIALS (I certify that the statements on the reverse apply to this bill and are made a part thereof.)

SIGNED _____ DATE _____

32. NAME AND ADDRESS OF FACILITY WHERE SERVICES WERE RENDERED (If other than home or office)

33. PHYSICIAN'S, SUPPLIER'S BILLING NAME, ADDRESS, ZIP CODE & PHONE #

PIN# _____   GRP# _____

PHYSICIAN OR SUPPLIER INFORMATION

(SAMPLE ONLY - NOT APPROVED FOR USE)

PLEASE PRINT OR TYPE

SAMPLE FORM 1500
SAMPLE FORM 1500 SAMPLE FORM 1500

149

DATE 08/10/XX		REMARKS				

PATIENT				CHART #	SEX	BIRTHDATE
Rebecca Nichols		667-14-3344		14-e	F	10/12/25

MAILING ADDRESS	CITY	STATE	ZIP	HOME PHONE	WORK PHONE
384 Dean Street	Anywhere	US	12345	(101) 333-5555	

EMPLOYER	ADDRESS	PATIENT STATUS
	Anywhere US	X
		MARRIED DIVORCED SINGLE STUDENT OTHER

INSURANCE: PRIMARY	ID#	GROUP	SECONDARY POLICY
Medicare	667-14-3344A		

POLICYHOLDER NAME	BIRTHDATE	RELATIONSHIP	POLICYHOLDER NAME	BIRTHDATE	RELATIONSHIP
		Self			

SUPPLEMENTAL PLAN	EMPLOYER

POLICYHOLDER NAME	BIRTHDATE	RELATIONSHIP	DIAGNOSIS	CODE
			1. Rectal bleeding	569.3
EMPLOYER			2. Diarrhea	787.91
			3. Abnormal loss of weight	783.2
REFERRING PHYSICIAN UPIN/SSN			4.	

PLACE OF SERVICE   Mercy Hospital, Anywhere St., Anywhere, US 12345 PIN# M1234

PROCEDURES		CODE	CHARGE
1. Initial Hosp Level IV	08/06/XX	99224	$175.00
2. Subsq. Hosp. Level III	08/07/XX	99233	$85.00
3. Subsq. Hosp. Level III	08/08/XX	99233	$85.00
4. Subsq. Hosp. Level II	08/09/XX	99232	$75.00
5. Hosp. Discharge 30 min.	08/10/XX	99238	$75.00
6.			

SPECIAL NOTES

Dr. Gestive saw the patient for a consult on August 7 & August 8

TOTAL CHARGES	PAYMENTS	ADJUSTMENTS	BALANCE
$495.00	-0-	-0-	$495.00

RETURN VISIT	PHYSICIAN SIGNATURE
	Donald L. Givings, M.D.

MEDICARE # D1234 MEDICAID # DLG1234 BCBS # 12345	**DONALD L. GIVINGS, M.D.** **11350 MEDICAL DRIVE, ANYWHERE, US 12345** **PHONE NUMBER (101)111-5555**	EIN # 11123456 SSN # 123-12-1234 UPIN # DG1234 GRP # DG12345

(SAMPLE ONLY - NOT APPROVED FOR USE)

CARRIER

□□ PICA

HEALTH INSURANCE CLAIM FORM

PICA □□

1. MEDICARE	MEDICAID	CHAMPUS	CHAMPVA	GROUP HEALTH PLAN	FECA BLK LUNG	OTHER	1a. INSURED'S I.D. NUMBER	(FOR PROGRAM IN ITEM 1)
□ (Medicare #)	□ (Medicaid #)	□ (Sponsor's SSN)	□ (VA File #)	□ (SSN or ID)	□ (SSN)	□ (ID)		

2. PATIENT'S NAME (Last Name, First Name, Middle Initial)

3. PATIENT'S BIRTH DATE
MM | DD | YY   SEX M □ F □

4. INSURED'S NAME (Last Name, First Name, Middle Initial)

5. PATIENT'S ADDRESS (No. Street)

6. PATIENT RELATIONSHIP TO INSURED
Self □ Spouse □ Child □ Other □

7. INSURED'S ADDRESS (No. Street)

CITY   STATE

8. PATIENT STATUS
Single □   Married □   Other □

CITY   STATE

ZIP CODE   TELEPHONE (Include Area Code) ( )

Employed □   Full-Time Student □   Part-Time Student □

ZIP CODE   TELEPHONE (INCLUDE AREA CODE) ( )

9. OTHER INSURED'S NAME (Last Name, First Name, Middle Initial)

10. IS PATIENT'S CONDITION RELATED TO:

11. INSURED'S POLICY GROUP OR FECA NUMBER

a. OTHER INSURED'S POLICY OR GROUP NUMBER

a. EMPLOYMENT? (CURRENT OR PREVIOUS)
□ YES □ NO

a. INSURED'S DATE OF BIRTH
MM | DD | YY   SEX M □ F □

b. OTHER INSURED'S DATE OF BIRTH
MM | DD | YY   SEX M □ F □

b. AUTO ACCIDENT?   PLACE (State)
□ YES □ NO

b. EMPLOYER'S NAME OR SCHOOL NAME

c. EMPLOYER'S NAME OR SCHOOL NAME

c. OTHER ACCIDENT?
□ YES □ NO

c. INSURANCE PLAN NAME OR PROGRAM NAME

d. INSURANCE PLAN NAME OR PROGRAM NAME

10d. RESERVED FOR LOCAL USE

d. IS THERE ANOTHER HEALTH BENEFIT PLAN?
□ YES □ NO   If yes, return to and complete item 9 a – d.

READ BACK OF FORM BEFORE COMPLETING & SIGNING THIS FORM.
12. PATIENT'S OR AUTHORIZED PERSON'S SIGNATURE I authorize the release of any medical or other information necessary to process this claim. I also request payment of government benefits either to myself or to the party who accepts assignment below.

SIGNED _____ DATE _____

13. INSURED'S OR AUTHORIZED PERSON'S SIGNATURE I authorize payment of medical benefits to the undersigned physician or supplier for services described below.

SIGNED _____

PATIENT AND INSURED INFORMATION

14. DATE OF CURRENT: ILLNESS (First symptom) OR INJURY (Accident) OR PREGNANCY (LMP)
MM | DD | YY

15. IF PATIENT HAS HAD SAME OR SIMILAR ILLNESS, GIVE FIRST DATE
MM | DD | YY

16. DATES PATIENT UNABLE TO WORK IN CURRENT OCCUPATION
FROM MM | DD | YY TO MM | DD | YY

17. NAME OF REFERRING PHYSICIAN OR OTHER SOURCE

17a. I.D. NUMBER OF REFERRING PHYSICIAN

18. HOSPITALIZATION DATES RELATED TO CURRENT SERVICES
FROM MM | DD | YY TO MM | DD | YY

19. RESERVED FOR LOCAL USE

20. OUTSIDE LAB? $ CHARGES
□ YES □ NO

21. DIAGNOSIS OR NATURE OF ILLNESS OR INJURY. (RELATE ITEMS 1, 2, 3, OR 4 TO ITEM 24E BY LINE)

1. ____.__   3. ____.__

2. ____.__   4. ____.__

22. MEDICAID RESUBMISSION CODE   ORIGINAL REF. NO.

23. PRIOR AUTHORIZATION NUMBER

24. A DATE(S) OF SERVICE						B Place of Service	C Type of Service	D PROCEDURES, SERVICES, OR SUPPLIES (Explain Unusual Circumstances) CPT/HCPCS	MODIFIER	E DIAGNOSIS CODE	F $ CHARGES	G DAYS OR UNITS	H EPSDT Family Plan	I EMG	J COB	K RESERVED FOR LOCAL USE
From MM	DD	YY	To MM	DD	YY											
1																
2																
3																
4																
5																
6																

25. FEDERAL TAX I.D. NUMBER   SSN □ EIN □

26. PATIENT'S ACCOUNT NO.

27. ACCEPT ASSIGNMENT? (For govt. claims, see back)
□ YES □ NO

28. TOTAL CHARGE $

29. AMOUNT PAID $

30. BALANCE DUE $

31. SIGNATURE OF PHYSICIAN OR SUPPLIER INCLUDING DEGREES OR CREDENTIALS (I certify that the statements on the reverse apply to this bill and are made a part thereof.)

SIGNED _____ DATE _____

32. NAME AND ADDRESS OF FACILITY WHERE SERVICES WERE RENDERED (If other than home or office)

33. PHYSICIAN'S, SUPPLIER'S BILLING NAME, ADDRESS, ZIP CODE & PHONE #

PIN#   GRP#

PHYSICIAN OR SUPPLIER INFORMATION

(SAMPLE ONLY - NOT APPROVED FOR USE)

PLEASE PRINT OR TYPE

SAMPLE FORM 1500
SAMPLE FORM 1500 SAMPLE FORM 1500

151

DATE	REMARKS
08/07/XX	Miss Nichols was in the hospital from August 6 through August 10

PATIENT			CHART #	SEX	BIRTHDATE
Rebecca Nichols	667-14-3344		14-f	F	10/12/25

MAILING ADDRESS	CITY	STATE	ZIP	HOME PHONE	WORK PHONE
384 Dean Street	Anywhere	US	12345	(101) 333-5555	

EMPLOYER	ADDRESS	PATIENT STATUS
	Anywhere US	X
		MARRIED DIVORCED SINGLE STUDENT OTHER

INSURANCE: PRIMARY	ID#	GROUP	SECONDARY POLICY
Medicare	667-14-3344A		

POLICYHOLDER NAME	BIRTHDATE	RELATIONSHIP	POLICYHOLDER NAME	BIRTHDATE	RELATIONSHIP
		Self			

SUPPLEMENTAL PLAN	EMPLOYER

POLICYHOLDER NAME	BIRTHDATE	RELATIONSHIP	DIAGNOSIS	CODE
			1. Diverticulitis of the colon with hemorrhage	562.13
EMPLOYER			2.	
			3.	
REFERRING PHYSICIAN UPIN/SSN			4.	
Donald L. Givings, M.D. 123-12-1234				

PLACE OF SERVICE Mercy Hospital, Anywhere St., Anywhere, US 12345 PIN# M1234

PROCEDURES		CODE	CHARGE
1. Initial Inpatient Consult Level IV	08/07/XX	99254	$220.00
2. Follow-up Inpatient Consult Level III	08/08/XX	99263	$80.00
3.			
4.			
5.			
6.			

SPECIAL NOTES

TOTAL CHARGES	PAYMENTS	ADJUSTMENTS	BALANCE
$300.00	-0-	-0-	$300.00

RETURN VISIT	PHYSICIAN SIGNATURE
	Colin D. Gestive, M.D.

(SAMPLE ONLY - NOT APPROVED FOR USE)

CARRIER

HEALTH INSURANCE CLAIM FORM

PICA ☐ ☐

☐ ☐ PICA

1. MEDICARE	MEDICAID	CHAMPUS	CHAMPVA	GROUP HEALTH PLAN	FECA BLK LUNG	OTHER	1a. INSURED'S I.D. NUMBER	(FOR PROGRAM IN ITEM 1)
☐ (Medicare #)	☐ (Medicaid #)	☐ (Sponsor's SSN)	☐ (VA File #)	☐ (SSN or ID)	☐ (SSN)	☐ (ID)		

2. PATIENT'S NAME (Last Name, First Name, Middle Initial)

3. PATIENT'S BIRTH DATE MM | DD | YY   SEX M ☐ F ☐

4. INSURED'S NAME (Last Name, First Name, Middle Initial)

5. PATIENT'S ADDRESS (No. Street)

6. PATIENT RELATIONSHIP TO INSURED Self ☐ Spouse ☐ Child ☐ Other ☐

7. INSURED'S ADDRESS (No. Street)

CITY   STATE

8. PATIENT STATUS Single ☐ Married ☐ Other ☐   Employed ☐ Full-Time Student ☐ Part-Time Student ☐

CITY   STATE

ZIP CODE   TELEPHONE (Include Area Code) (   )

ZIP CODE   TELEPHONE (INCLUDE AREA CODE) (   )

9. OTHER INSURED'S NAME (Last Name, First Name, Middle Initial)

10. IS PATIENT'S CONDITION RELATED TO:

11. INSURED'S POLICY GROUP OR FECA NUMBER

a. OTHER INSURED'S POLICY OR GROUP NUMBER

a. EMPLOYMENT? (CURRENT OR PREVIOUS) ☐ YES ☐ NO

a. INSURED'S DATE OF BIRTH MM | DD | YY   SEX M ☐ F ☐

b. OTHER INSURED'S DATE OF BIRTH MM | DD | YY   SEX M ☐ F ☐

b. AUTO ACCIDENT?   PLACE (State) ☐ YES ☐ NO

b. EMPLOYER'S NAME OR SCHOOL NAME

c. EMPLOYER'S NAME OR SCHOOL NAME

c. OTHER ACCIDENT? ☐ YES ☐ NO

c. INSURANCE PLAN NAME OR PROGRAM NAME

d. INSURANCE PLAN NAME OR PROGRAM NAME

10d. RESERVED FOR LOCAL USE

d. IS THERE ANOTHER HEALTH BENEFIT PLAN? ☐ YES ☐ NO If yes, return to and complete item 9 a – d.

READ BACK OF FORM BEFORE COMPLETING & SIGNING THIS FORM.
12. PATIENT'S OR AUTHORIZED PERSON'S SIGNATURE I authorize the release of any medical or other information necessary to process this claim. I also request payment of government benefits either to myself or to the party who accepts assignment below.

SIGNED _____   DATE _____

13. INSURED'S OR AUTHORIZED PERSON'S SIGNATURE I authorize payment of medical benefits to the undersigned physician or supplier for services described below.

SIGNED _____

PATIENT AND INSURED INFORMATION

14. DATE OF CURRENT: MM | DD | YY   ◄ ILLNESS (First symptom) OR INJURY (Accident) OR PREGNANCY (LMP)

15. IF PATIENT HAS HAD SAME OR SIMILAR ILLNESS, GIVE FIRST DATE MM | DD | YY

16. DATES PATIENT UNABLE TO WORK IN CURRENT OCCUPATION MM | DD | YY FROM   TO MM | DD | YY

17. NAME OF REFERRING PHYSICIAN OR OTHER SOURCE

17a. I.D. NUMBER OF REFERRING PHYSICIAN

18. HOSPITALIZATION DATES RELATED TO CURRENT SERVICES MM | DD | YY FROM   TO MM | DD | YY

19. RESERVED FOR LOCAL USE

20. OUTSIDE LAB? ☐ YES ☐ NO $ CHARGES

21. DIAGNOSIS OR NATURE OF ILLNESS OR INJURY. (RELATE ITEMS 1, 2, 3, OR 4 TO ITEM 24E BY LINE)

1. ____ . __   3. ____ . __
2. ____ . __   4. ____ . __

22. MEDICAID RESUBMISSION CODE   ORIGINAL REF. NO.

23. PRIOR AUTHORIZATION NUMBER

24. A DATE(S) OF SERVICE						B Place of Service	C Type of Service	D PROCEDURES, SERVICES, OR SUPPLIES (Explain Unusual Circumstances)		E DIAGNOSIS CODE	F $ CHARGES	G DAYS OR UNITS	H EPSDT Family Plan	I EMG	J COB	K RESERVED FOR LOCAL USE
From MM	DD	YY	To MM	DD	YY			CPT/HCPCS	MODIFIER							
1																
2																
3																
4																
5																
6																

25. FEDERAL TAX I.D. NUMBER SSN ☐ EIN ☐

26. PATIENT'S ACCOUNT NO.

27. ACCEPT ASSIGNMENT? (For govt. claims, see back) ☐ YES ☐ NO

28. TOTAL CHARGE $

29. AMOUNT PAID $

30. BALANCE DUE $

31. SIGNATURE OF PHYSICIAN OR SUPPLIER INCLUDING DEGREES OR CREDENTIALS (I certify that the statements on the reverse apply to this bill and are made a part thereof.)

SIGNED _____   DATE _____

32. NAME AND ADDRESS OF FACILITY WHERE SERVICES WERE RENDERED (If other than home or office)

33. PHYSICIAN'S, SUPPLIER'S BILLING NAME, ADDRESS, ZIP CODE & PHONE #

PIN#   GRP#

PHYSICIAN OR SUPPLIER INFORMATION

(SAMPLE ONLY - NOT APPROVED FOR USE)

PLEASE PRINT OR TYPE

SAMPLE FORM 1500
SAMPLE FORM 1500 SAMPLE FORM 1500

153

DATE	REMARKS			
10/03/XX	Dr. Mason is NonPAR with Medicare			

PATIENT		CHART #	SEX	BIRTHDATE
Samual T. Mahoney Jr. 312-78-5894		14-g	M	09/04/30

MAILING ADDRESS	CITY	STATE	ZIP	HOME PHONE	WORK PHONE
498 Meadow Lane	Anywhere	US	12345	(101) 333-5555	

EMPLOYER	ADDRESS	PATIENT STATUS
	Anywhere US	X MARRIED DIVORCED SINGLE STUDENT OTHER

INSURANCE: PRIMARY	ID#	GROUP	SECONDARY POLICY
Medicare	312-78-5894A		

POLICYHOLDER NAME	BIRTHDATE	RELATIONSHIP	POLICYHOLDER NAME	BIRTHDATE	RELATIONSHIP
		Self			

SUPPLEMENTAL PLAN	EMPLOYER

POLICYHOLDER NAME	BIRTHDATE	RELATIONSHIP	DIAGNOSIS	CODE
			1. Asthma, unspecified	493.90
EMPLOYER			2. URI	465.9
			3.	
REFERRING PHYSICIAN UPIN/SSN			4.	

PLACE OF SERVICE   Office

PROCEDURES	CODE	CHARGE
1. Est. Pt. OV Level II	99212	$25.16
2.		
3.		
4.		
5.		
6.		

SPECIAL NOTES

TOTAL CHARGES	PAYMENTS	ADJUSTMENTS	BALANCE
$25.16	$25.16	0	$0.00

RETURN VISIT	PHYSICIAN SIGNATURE
	Lisa M. Mason, M.D.

MEDICARE # L1234 MEDICAID # LMM1234 BCBS # 39994	**LISA M. MASON, M.D. FAMILY PRACTICE** **547 ANTIGUA ROAD, ANYWHERE, US 12345** **PHONE NUMBER (101)111-5555**	EIN # 11495867 SSN # 333-12-9484 UPIN # LM4234 GRP # LM29883

(SAMPLE ONLY - NOT APPROVED FOR USE)

CARRIER

| | PICA

HEALTH INSURANCE CLAIM FORM

PICA | |

1. MEDICARE   MEDICAID   CHAMPUS   CHAMPVA   GROUP HEALTH PLAN   FECA BLK LUNG   OTHER
☐ (Medicare #) ☐ (Medicaid #) ☐ (Sponsor's SSN) ☐ (VA File #) ☐ (SSN or ID) ☐ (SSN) ☐ (ID)

1a. INSURED'S I.D. NUMBER   (FOR PROGRAM IN ITEM 1)

2. PATIENT'S NAME (Last Name, First Name, Middle Initial)

3. PATIENT'S BIRTH DATE   SEX
MM   DD   YY   M ☐   F ☐

4. INSURED'S NAME (Last Name, First Name, Middle Initial)

5. PATIENT'S ADDRESS (No. Street)

6. PATIENT RELATIONSHIP TO INSURED
Self ☐   Spouse ☐   Child ☐   Other ☐

7. INSURED'S ADDRESS (No. Street)

CITY   STATE

8. PATIENT STATUS
Single ☐   Married ☐   Other ☐
Employed ☐   Full-Time Student ☐   Part-Time Student ☐

CITY   STATE

ZIP CODE   TELEPHONE (Include Area Code)
(   )

ZIP CODE   TELEPHONE (INCLUDE AREA CODE)
(   )

9. OTHER INSURED'S NAME (Last Name, First Name, Middle Initial)

10. IS PATIENT'S CONDITION RELATED TO:

11. INSURED'S POLICY GROUP OR FECA NUMBER

a. OTHER INSURED'S POLICY OR GROUP NUMBER

a. EMPLOYMENT? (CURRENT OR PREVIOUS)
☐ YES   ☐ NO

a. INSURED'S DATE OF BIRTH   SEX
MM   DD   YY   M ☐   F ☐

b. OTHER INSURED'S DATE OF BIRTH   SEX
MM   DD   YY   M ☐   F ☐

b. AUTO ACCIDENT?   PLACE (State)
☐ YES   ☐ NO

b. EMPLOYER'S NAME OR SCHOOL NAME

c. EMPLOYER'S NAME OR SCHOOL NAME

c. OTHER ACCIDENT?
☐ YES   ☐ NO

c. INSURANCE PLAN NAME OR PROGRAM NAME

d. INSURANCE PLAN NAME OR PROGRAM NAME

10d. RESERVED FOR LOCAL USE

d. IS THERE ANOTHER HEALTH BENEFIT PLAN?
☐ YES   ☐ NO   If yes, return to and complete item 9 a – d.

READ BACK OF FORM BEFORE COMPLETING & SIGNING THIS FORM.
12. PATIENT'S OR AUTHORIZED PERSON'S SIGNATURE I authorize the release of any medical or other information necessary to process this claim. I also request payment of government benefits either to myself or to the party who accepts assignment below.

SIGNED _____   DATE _____

13. INSURED'S OR AUTHORIZED PERSON'S SIGNATURE I authorize payment of medical benefits to the undersigned physician or supplier for services described below.

SIGNED _____

PATIENT AND INSURED INFORMATION

14. DATE OF CURRENT: ILLNESS (First symptom) OR
MM   DD   YY   INJURY (Accident) OR PREGNANCY (LMP)

15. IF PATIENT HAS HAD SAME OR SIMILAR ILLNESS, GIVE FIRST DATE   MM   DD   YY

16. DATES PATIENT UNABLE TO WORK IN CURRENT OCCUPATION
MM   DD   YY   MM   DD   YY
FROM   TO

17. NAME OF REFERRING PHYSICIAN OR OTHER SOURCE

17a. I.D. NUMBER OF REFERRING PHYSICIAN

18. HOSPITALIZATION DATES RELATED TO CURRENT SERVICES
MM   DD   YY   MM   DD   YY
FROM   TO

19. RESERVED FOR LOCAL USE

20. OUTSIDE LAB? $ CHARGES
☐ YES   ☐ NO

21. DIAGNOSIS OR NATURE OF ILLNESS OR INJURY. (RELATE ITEMS 1, 2, 3, OR 4 TO ITEM 24E BY LINE)
1. |___ . ___   3. |___ . ___
2. |___ . ___   4. |___ . ___

22. MEDICAID RESUBMISSION
CODE   ORIGINAL REF. NO.

23. PRIOR AUTHORIZATION NUMBER

24.	A					B	C	D			E	F	G	H	I	J	K
	DATE(S) OF SERVICE					Place of Service	Type of Service	PROCEDURES, SERVICES, OR SUPPLIES (Explain Unusual Circumstances)			DIAGNOSIS CODE	$ CHARGES	DAYS OR UNITS	EPSDT Family Plan	EMG	COB	RESERVED FOR LOCAL USE
	From			To				CPT/HCPCS		MODIFIER							
	MM	DD	YY	MM	DD	YY												
1																	
2																	
3																	
4																	
5																	
6																	

25. FEDERAL TAX I.D. NUMBER   SSN ☐ EIN ☐

26. PATIENT'S ACCOUNT NO.

27. ACCEPT ASSIGNMENT? (For govt. claims, see back)
☐ YES   ☐ NO

28. TOTAL CHARGE $

29. AMOUNT PAID $

30. BALANCE DUE $

31. SIGNATURE OF PHYSICIAN OR SUPPLIER INCLUDING DEGREES OR CREDENTIALS
(I certify that the statements on the reverse apply to this bill and are made a part thereof.)

SIGNED _____ DATE _____

32. NAME AND ADDRESS OF FACILITY WHERE SERVICES WERE RENDERED (If other than home or office)

33. PHYSICIAN'S, SUPPLIER'S BILLING NAME, ADDRESS, ZIP CODE & PHONE #

PIN#   GRP#

PHYSICIAN OR SUPPLIER INFORMATION

(SAMPLE ONLY - NOT APPROVED FOR USE)

PLEASE PRINT OR TYPE

SAMPLE FORM 1500
SAMPLE FORM 1500 SAMPLE FORM 1500

155

DATE	REMARKS			
03/07/XX	Medigap Payer Identification Number 123456994			

PATIENT			CHART #	SEX	BIRTHDATE
Abraham N. Freed 645-45-4545			14-h	M	10/03/22

MAILING ADDRESS	CITY	STATE	ZIP	HOME PHONE	WORK PHONE
12 Nottingham Circle	Anywhere	US	12345	(101) 333-5555	

EMPLOYER	ADDRESS		PATIENT STATUS
	Anywhere US		X MARRIED DIVORCED SINGLE STUDENT OTHER

INSURANCE: PRIMARY	ID#	GROUP	SECONDARY POLICY
Medicare	645-45-4545A		

POLICYHOLDER NAME	BIRTHDATE	RELATIONSHIP	POLICYHOLDER NAME	BIRTHDATE	RELATIONSHIP
		Self			

SUPPLEMENTAL PLAN	EMPLOYER
BCBS Medigap NXY645-45-4545 987	

POLICYHOLDER NAME	BIRTHDATE	RELATIONSHIP	DIAGNOSIS	CODE
		Self	1. Hypertension, malignant	401.0
EMPLOYER			2. Dizziness	780.2
Retired Johnson Steel			3.	
REFERRING PHYSICIAN UPIN/SSN			4.	

PLACE OF SERVICE   Office

PROCEDURES	CODE	CHARGE
1. New PT OV Level IV	99204	$100.00
2. EKG	93000	$50.00
3. Venipuncture	36415	$8.00
4.		
5.		
6.		

SPECIAL NOTES

TOTAL CHARGES	PAYMENTS	ADJUSTMENTS	BALANCE
$158.00	-0-	-0-	$158.00

RETURN VISIT	PHYSICIAN SIGNATURE
2 Weeks	Donald L. Givings, M.D.

MEDICARE # D1234 MEDICAID # DLG1234 BCBS # 12345	DONALD L. GIVINGS, M.D. 11350 MEDICAL DRIVE, ANYWHERE, US 12345 PHONE NUMBER (101)111-5555	EIN # 11123456 SSN # 123-12-1234 UPIN # DG1234 GRP # DG12345

CARRIER

| | PICA | | **HEALTH INSURANCE CLAIM FORM** | PICA | | |

1. MEDICARE	MEDICAID	CHAMPUS	CHAMPVA	GROUP HEALTH PLAN	FECA BLK LUNG	OTHER	1a. INSURED'S I.D. NUMBER	(FOR PROGRAM IN ITEM 1)
(Medicare #)	(Medicaid #)	(Sponsor's SSN)	(VA File #)	(SSN or ID)	(SSN)	(ID)		

2. PATIENT'S NAME (Last Name, First Name, Middle Initial)	3. PATIENT'S BIRTH DATE MM DD YY SEX M☐ F☐	4. INSURED'S NAME (Last Name, First Name, Middle Initial)

5. PATIENT'S ADDRESS (No. Street)	6. PATIENT RELATIONSHIP TO INSURED Self☐ Spouse☐ Child☐ Other☐	7. INSURED'S ADDRESS (No. Street)

CITY	STATE	8. PATIENT STATUS Single☐ Married☐ Other☐	CITY	STATE

ZIP CODE	TELEPHONE (Include Area Code) ( )	Employed☐ Full-Time Student☐ Part-Time Student☐	ZIP CODE	TELEPHONE (INCLUDE AREA CODE) ( )

9. OTHER INSURED'S NAME (Last Name, First Name, Middle Initial)	10. IS PATIENT'S CONDITION RELATED TO:	11. INSURED'S POLICY GROUP OR FECA NUMBER
a. OTHER INSURED'S POLICY OR GROUP NUMBER	a. EMPLOYMENT? (CURRENT OR PREVIOUS) ☐YES ☐NO	a. INSURED'S DATE OF BIRTH MM DD YY SEX M☐ F☐
b. OTHER INSURED'S DATE OF BIRTH MM DD YY SEX M☐ F☐	b. AUTO ACCIDENT? PLACE (State) ☐YES ☐NO	b. EMPLOYER'S NAME OR SCHOOL NAME
c. EMPLOYER'S NAME OR SCHOOL NAME	c. OTHER ACCIDENT? ☐YES ☐NO	c. INSURANCE PLAN NAME OR PROGRAM NAME
d. INSURANCE PLAN NAME OR PROGRAM NAME	10d. RESERVED FOR LOCAL USE	d. IS THERE ANOTHER HEALTH BENEFIT PLAN? ☐YES ☐NO If yes, return to and complete item 9 a – d.

READ BACK OF FORM BEFORE COMPLETING & SIGNING THIS FORM.
12. PATIENT'S OR AUTHORIZED PERSON'S SIGNATURE I authorize the release of any medical or other information necessary to process this claim. I also request payment of government benefits either to myself or to the party who accepts assignment below.

SIGNED _____ DATE _____

13. INSURED'S OR AUTHORIZED PERSON'S SIGNATURE I authorize payment of medical benefits to the undersigned physician or supplier for services described below.

SIGNED _____

PATIENT AND INSURED INFORMATION

14. DATE OF CURRENT: MM DD YY ILLNESS (First symptom) OR INJURY (Accident) OR PREGNANCY (LMP)	15. IF PATIENT HAS HAD SAME OR SIMILAR ILLNESS, GIVE FIRST DATE MM DD YY	16. DATES PATIENT UNABLE TO WORK IN CURRENT OCCUPATION MM DD YY MM DD YY FROM TO
17. NAME OF REFERRING PHYSICIAN OR OTHER SOURCE	17a. I.D. NUMBER OF REFERRING PHYSICIAN	18. HOSPITALIZATION DATES RELATED TO CURRENT SERVICES MM DD YY MM DD YY FROM TO
19. RESERVED FOR LOCAL USE		20. OUTSIDE LAB? $ CHARGES ☐YES ☐NO

21. DIAGNOSIS OR NATURE OF ILLNESS OR INJURY. (RELATE ITEMS 1, 2, 3, OR 4 TO ITEM 24E BY LINE) 1. ___ 2. ___ 3. ___ 4. ___	22. MEDICAID RESUBMISSION CODE ORIGINAL REF. NO.
	23. PRIOR AUTHORIZATION NUMBER

24. A DATE(S) OF SERVICE						B Place of Service	C Type of Service	D PROCEDURES, SERVICES, OR SUPPLIES (Explain Unusual Circumstances) CPT/HCPCS MODIFIER	E DIAGNOSIS CODE	F $ CHARGES	G DAYS OR UNITS	H EPSDT Family Plan	I EMG	J COB	K RESERVED FOR LOCAL USE
	From MM DD YY		To MM DD YY												
1															
2															
3															
4															
5															
6															

25. FEDERAL TAX I.D. NUMBER SSN☐ EIN☐	26. PATIENT'S ACCOUNT NO.	27. ACCEPT ASSIGNMENT? (For govt. claims, see back) ☐YES ☐NO	28. TOTAL CHARGE $	29. AMOUNT PAID $	30. BALANCE DUE $

31. SIGNATURE OF PHYSICIAN OR SUPPLIER INCLUDING DEGREES OR CREDENTIALS (I certify that the statements on the reverse apply to this bill and are made a part thereof.) SIGNED DATE	32. NAME AND ADDRESS OF FACILITY WHERE SERVICES WERE RENDERED (If other than home or office)	33. PHYSICIAN'S, SUPPLIER'S BILLING NAME, ADDRESS, ZIP CODE & PHONE # PIN# GRP#

PHYSICIAN OR SUPPLIER INFORMATION

PLEASE PRINT OR TYPE

SAMPLE FORM 1500
SAMPLE FORM 1500 SAMPLE FORM 1500

PLEASE
DO NOT
STAPLE
IN THIS
AREA

CARRIER

| | PICA

HEALTH INSURANCE CLAIM FORM

PICA | |

1. MEDICARE MEDICAID CHAMPUS CHAMPVA GROUP HEALTH PLAN FECA BLK LUNG OTHER	1a. INSURED'S I.D. NUMBER (FOR PROGRAM IN ITEM 1)
☐ (Medicare #) ☐ (Medicaid #) ☐ (Sponsor's SSN) ☐ (VA File #) ☐ (SSN or ID) ☐ (SSN) ☐ (ID)	

2. PATIENT'S NAME (Last Name, First Name, Middle Initial)	3. PATIENT'S BIRTH DATE MM DD YY SEX M☐ F☐	4. INSURED'S NAME (Last Name, First Name, Middle Initial)
5. PATIENT'S ADDRESS (No. Street)	6. PATIENT RELATIONSHIP TO INSURED Self☐ Spouse☐ Child☐ Other☐	7. INSURED'S ADDRESS (No. Street)
CITY STATE	8. PATIENT STATUS Single☐ Married☐ Other☐	CITY STATE
ZIP CODE TELEPHONE (Include Area Code) ( )	Employed☐ Full-Time Student☐ Part-Time Student☐	ZIP CODE TELEPHONE (INCLUDE AREA CODE) ( )

9. OTHER INSURED'S NAME (Last Name, First Name, Middle Initial)	10. IS PATIENT'S CONDITION RELATED TO:	11. INSURED'S POLICY GROUP OR FECA NUMBER
a. OTHER INSURED'S POLICY OR GROUP NUMBER	a. EMPLOYMENT? (CURRENT OR PREVIOUS) ☐ YES ☐ NO	a. INSURED'S DATE OF BIRTH MM DD YY SEX M☐ F☐
b. OTHER INSURED'S DATE OF BIRTH MM DD YY SEX M☐ F☐	b. AUTO ACCIDENT? PLACE (State) ☐ YES ☐ NO	b. EMPLOYER'S NAME OR SCHOOL NAME
c. EMPLOYER'S NAME OR SCHOOL NAME	c. OTHER ACCIDENT? ☐ YES ☐ NO	c. INSURANCE PLAN NAME OR PROGRAM NAME
d. INSURANCE PLAN NAME OR PROGRAM NAME	10d. RESERVED FOR LOCAL USE	d. IS THERE ANOTHER HEALTH BENEFIT PLAN? ☐ YES ☐ NO If yes, return to and complete item 9 a – d.

PATIENT AND INSURED INFORMATION

READ BACK OF FORM BEFORE COMPLETING & SIGNING THIS FORM.

12. PATIENT'S OR AUTHORIZED PERSON'S SIGNATURE I authorize the release of any medical or other information necessary to process this claim. I also request payment of government benefits either to myself or to the party who accepts assignment below. SIGNED _____ DATE _____	13. INSURED'S OR AUTHORIZED PERSON'S SIGNATURE I authorize payment of medical benefits to the undersigned physician or supplier for services described below. SIGNED _____

14. DATE OF CURRENT: MM DD YY ILLNESS (First symptom) OR INJURY (Accident) OR PREGNANCY (LMP)	15. IF PATIENT HAS HAD SAME OR SIMILAR ILLNESS, GIVE FIRST DATE MM DD YY	16. DATES PATIENT UNABLE TO WORK IN CURRENT OCCUPATION MM DD YY MM DD YY FROM TO
17. NAME OF REFERRING PHYSICIAN OR OTHER SOURCE	17a. I.D. NUMBER OF REFERRING PHYSICIAN	18. HOSPITALIZATION DATES RELATED TO CURRENT SERVICES MM DD YY MM DD YY FROM TO
19. RESERVED FOR LOCAL USE		20. OUTSIDE LAB? $ CHARGES ☐ YES ☐ NO

21. DIAGNOSIS OR NATURE OF ILLNESS OR INJURY. (RELATE ITEMS 1, 2, 3, OR 4 TO ITEM 24E BY LINE) 1. ⌊__ __ 3. ⌊__ __ 2. ⌊__ __ 4. ⌊__ __	22. MEDICAID RESUBMISSION CODE ORIGINAL REF. NO.
	23. PRIOR AUTHORIZATION NUMBER

24. A DATE(S) OF SERVICE				B Place of Service	C Type of Service	D PROCEDURES, SERVICES, OR SUPPLIES (Explain Unusual Circumstances) CPT/HCPCS MODIFIER	E DIAGNOSIS CODE	F $ CHARGES	G DAYS OR UNITS	H EPSDT Family Plan	I EMG	J COB	K RESERVED FOR LOCAL USE
From MM DD YY	To MM DD YY												
1													
2													
3													
4													
5													
6													

25. FEDERAL TAX I.D. NUMBER SSN☐ EIN☐	26. PATIENT'S ACCOUNT NO.	27. ACCEPT ASSIGNMENT? (For govt. claims, see back) ☐ YES ☐ NO	28. TOTAL CHARGE $	29. AMOUNT PAID $	30. BALANCE DUE $
31. SIGNATURE OF PHYSICIAN OR SUPPLIER INCLUDING DEGREES OR CREDENTIALS (I certify that the statements on the reverse apply to this bill and are made a part thereof.) SIGNED _____ DATE _____	32. NAME AND ADDRESS OF FACILITY WHERE SERVICES WERE RENDERED (If other than home or office)	33. PHYSICIAN'S, SUPPLIER'S BILLING NAME, ADDRESS, ZIP CODE & PHONE # PIN# GRP#

PHYSICIAN OR SUPPLIER INFORMATION

(SAMPLE ONLY - NOT APPROVED FOR USE)   *PLEASE PRINT OR TYPE*

SAMPLE FORM 1500
SAMPLE FORM 1500 SAMPLE FORM 1500

DATE	REMARKS			
03/07/XX	Medigap Payer Identification Number 123456994			

PATIENT			CHART #	SEX	BIRTHDATE
Esther K. Freed	777-66-4444		14-i	F	03/26/25

MAILING ADDRESS	CITY	STATE	ZIP	HOME PHONE	WORK PHONE
12 Nottingham Circle	Anywhere	US	12345	(101) 333-5555	

EMPLOYER	ADDRESS		PATIENT STATUS		
	Anywhere	US	X MARRIED DIVORCED SINGLE STUDENT OTHER		

INSURANCE: PRIMARY	ID#	GROUP	SECONDARY POLICY
Medicare	777-66-4444A		

POLICYHOLDER NAME	BIRTHDATE	RELATIONSHIP	POLICYHOLDER NAME	BIRTHDATE	RELATIONSHIP
		Self			

SUPPLEMENTAL PLAN	EMPLOYER
BCBS Medigap NXY645-45-4545 987	

POLICYHOLDER NAME	BIRTHDATE	RELATIONSHIP	DIAGNOSIS	CODE
Abraham N. Freed	10/03/22	Spouse	1. Bronchopneumonia	485

EMPLOYER: Retired Johnson Steel

2. Hemoptysis — 786.3
3. Hematuria — 599.7
4.

REFERRING PHYSICIAN UPIN/SSN

PLACE OF SERVICE Office

PROCEDURES	CODE	CHARGE
1. New PT OV Level IV	99204	$100.00
2. Chest x-ray 2 views	71020	$50.00
3. Urinalysis, with micro	81001	$10.00
4.		
5.		
6.		

SPECIAL NOTES

TOTAL CHARGES	PAYMENTS	ADJUSTMENTS	BALANCE
$160.00	0	0	$160.00

RETURN VISIT	PHYSICIAN SIGNATURE
2 Weeks	Donald L. Givings, M.D.

DONALD L. GIVINGS, M.D.
11350 MEDICAL DRIVE, ANYWHERE, US 12345
PHONE NUMBER (101)111-5555

MEDICARE # D1234
MEDICAID # DLG1234
BCBS # 12345

EIN # 11123456
SSN # 123-12-1234
UPIN # DG1234
GRP # DG12345

(SAMPLE ONLY - NOT APPROVED FOR USE)

CARRIER

[ ][ ] PICA

HEALTH INSURANCE CLAIM FORM

PICA [ ][ ]

1. MEDICARE	MEDICAID	CHAMPUS	CHAMPVA	GROUP HEALTH PLAN	FECA BLK LUNG	OTHER	1a. INSURED'S I.D. NUMBER	(FOR PROGRAM IN ITEM 1)
[ ] (Medicare #)	[ ] (Medicaid #)	[ ] (Sponsor's SSN)	[ ] (VA File #)	[ ] (SSN or ID)	[ ] (SSN)	[ ] (ID)		

2. PATIENT'S NAME (Last Name, First Name, Middle Initial)

3. PATIENT'S BIRTH DATE MM | DD | YY   SEX M [ ] F [ ]

4. INSURED'S NAME (Last Name, First Name, Middle Initial)

5. PATIENT'S ADDRESS (No. Street)

6. PATIENT RELATIONSHIP TO INSURED
Self [ ] Spouse [ ] Child [ ] Other [ ]

7. INSURED'S ADDRESS (No. Street)

CITY   STATE

8. PATIENT STATUS
Single [ ] Married [ ] Other [ ]

CITY   STATE

ZIP CODE   TELEPHONE (Include Area Code)
(   )

Employed [ ]   Full-Time Student [ ]   Part-Time Student [ ]

ZIP CODE   TELEPHONE (INCLUDE AREA CODE)
(   )

9. OTHER INSURED'S NAME (Last Name, First Name, Middle Initial)

10. IS PATIENT'S CONDITION RELATED TO:

11. INSURED'S POLICY GROUP OR FECA NUMBER

a. OTHER INSURED'S POLICY OR GROUP NUMBER

a. EMPLOYMENT? (CURRENT OR PREVIOUS)
[ ] YES [ ] NO

a. INSURED'S DATE OF BIRTH MM | DD | YY   SEX M [ ] F [ ]

b. OTHER INSURED'S DATE OF BIRTH MM | DD | YY   SEX M [ ] F [ ]

b. AUTO ACCIDENT?   PLACE (State)
[ ] YES [ ] NO

b. EMPLOYER'S NAME OR SCHOOL NAME

c. EMPLOYER'S NAME OR SCHOOL NAME

c. OTHER ACCIDENT?
[ ] YES [ ] NO

c. INSURANCE PLAN NAME OR PROGRAM NAME

d. INSURANCE PLAN NAME OR PROGRAM NAME

10d. RESERVED FOR LOCAL USE

d. IS THERE ANOTHER HEALTH BENEFIT PLAN?
[ ] YES [ ] NO   If yes, return to and complete item 9 a – d.

READ BACK OF FORM BEFORE COMPLETING & SIGNING THIS FORM.
12. PATIENT'S OR AUTHORIZED PERSON'S SIGNATURE I authorize the release of any medical or other information necessary to process this claim. I also request payment of government benefits either to myself or to the party who accepts assignment below.

SIGNED _____   DATE _____

13. INSURED'S OR AUTHORIZED PERSON'S SIGNATURE I authorize payment of medical benefits to the undersigned physician or supplier for services described below.

SIGNED _____

PATIENT AND INSURED INFORMATION

14. DATE OF CURRENT: MM | DD | YY ◄ ILLNESS (First symptom) OR INJURY (Accident) OR PREGNANCY (LMP)

15. IF PATIENT HAS HAD SAME OR SIMILAR ILLNESS, GIVE FIRST DATE MM | DD | YY

16. DATES PATIENT UNABLE TO WORK IN CURRENT OCCUPATION MM | DD | YY   MM | DD | YY
FROM   TO

17. NAME OF REFERRING PHYSICIAN OR OTHER SOURCE

17a. I.D. NUMBER OF REFERRING PHYSICIAN

18. HOSPITALIZATION DATES RELATED TO CURRENT SERVICES MM | DD | YY   MM | DD | YY
FROM   TO

19. RESERVED FOR LOCAL USE

20. OUTSIDE LAB? $ CHARGES
[ ] YES [ ] NO

21. DIAGNOSIS OR NATURE OF ILLNESS OR INJURY. (RELATE ITEMS 1, 2, 3, OR 4 TO ITEM 24E BY LINE)
1. [___ . ___]   3. [___ . ___]
2. [___ . ___]   4. [___ . ___]

22. MEDICAID RESUBMISSION CODE   ORIGINAL REF. NO.

23. PRIOR AUTHORIZATION NUMBER

24. A DATE(S) OF SERVICE						B Place of Service	C Type of Service	D PROCEDURES, SERVICES, OR SUPPLIES (Explain Unusual Circumstances) CPT/HCPCS	MODIFIER	E DIAGNOSIS CODE	F $ CHARGES	G DAYS OR UNITS	H EPSDT Family Plan	I EMG	J COB	K RESERVED FOR LOCAL USE
From MM	DD	YY	To MM	DD	YY											
1																
2																
3																
4																
5																
6																

25. FEDERAL TAX I.D. NUMBER   SSN [ ] EIN [ ]

26. PATIENT'S ACCOUNT NO.

27. ACCEPT ASSIGNMENT? (For govt. claims, see back)
[ ] YES [ ] NO

28. TOTAL CHARGE $

29. AMOUNT PAID $

30. BALANCE DUE $

31. SIGNATURE OF PHYSICIAN OR SUPPLIER INCLUDING DEGREES OR CREDENTIALS (I certify that the statements on the reverse apply to this bill and are made a part thereof.)

SIGNED _____ DATE _____

32. NAME AND ADDRESS OF FACILITY WHERE SERVICES WERE RENDERED (If other than home or office)

33. PHYSICIAN'S, SUPPLIER'S BILLING NAME, ADDRESS, ZIP CODE & PHONE #

PIN#   GRP#

PHYSICIAN OR SUPPLIER INFORMATION

(SAMPLE ONLY - NOT APPROVED FOR USE)

PLEASE PRINT OR TYPE

SAMPLE FORM 1500
SAMPLE FORM 1500 SAMPLE FORM 1500

(SAMPLE ONLY - NOT APPROVED FOR USE)

CARRIER

HEALTH INSURANCE CLAIM FORM

PICA | | |

PICA | | |

1. MEDICARE	MEDICAID	CHAMPUS	CHAMPVA	GROUP HEALTH PLAN	FECA BLK.LUNG	OTHER	1a. INSURED'S I.D. NUMBER	(FOR PROGRAM IN ITEM 1)
(Medicare #)	(Medicaid #)	(Sponsor's SSN)	(VA File #)	(SSN or ID)	(SSN)	(ID)		

2. PATIENT'S NAME (Last Name, First Name, Middle Initial)

3. PATIENT'S BIRTH DATE   MM   DD   YY   SEX   M   F

4. INSURED'S NAME (Last Name, First Name, Middle Initial)

5. PATIENT'S ADDRESS (No. Street)

6. PATIENT RELATIONSHIP TO INSURED   Self   Spouse   Child   Other

7. INSURED'S ADDRESS (No. Street)

CITY   STATE

8. PATIENT STATUS   Single   Married   Other

Employed   Full-Time Student   Part-Time Student

CITY   STATE

ZIP CODE   TELEPHONE (Include Area Code) ( )

ZIP CODE   TELEPHONE (INCLUDE AREA CODE) ( )

9. OTHER INSURED'S NAME (Last Name, First Name, Middle Initial)

10. IS PATIENT'S CONDITION RELATED TO:

11. INSURED'S POLICY GROUP OR FECA NUMBER

a. OTHER INSURED'S POLICY OR GROUP NUMBER

a. EMPLOYMENT? (CURRENT OR PREVIOUS)   YES   NO

a. INSURED'S DATE OF BIRTH   MM   DD   YY   SEX   M   F

b. OTHER INSURED'S DATE OF BIRTH   MM   DD   YY   SEX   M   F

b. AUTO ACCIDENT?   PLACE (State)   YES   NO

b. EMPLOYER'S NAME OR SCHOOL NAME

c. EMPLOYER'S NAME OR SCHOOL NAME

c. OTHER ACCIDENT?   YES   NO

c. INSURANCE PLAN NAME OR PROGRAM NAME

d. INSURANCE PLAN NAME OR PROGRAM NAME

10d. RESERVED FOR LOCAL USE

d. IS THERE ANOTHER HEALTH BENEFIT PLAN?   YES   NO   If yes, return to and complete item 9 a – d.

READ BACK OF FORM BEFORE COMPLETING & SIGNING THIS FORM.
12. PATIENT'S OR AUTHORIZED PERSON'S SIGNATURE I authorize the release of any medical or other information necessary to process this claim. I also request payment of government benefits either to myself or to the party who accepts assignment below.

SIGNED _____   DATE _____

13. INSURED'S OR AUTHORIZED PERSON'S SIGNATURE I authorize payment of medical benefits to the undersigned physician or supplier for services described below.

SIGNED _____

14. DATE OF CURRENT: MM   DD   YY   ILLNESS (First symptom) OR INJURY (Accident) OR PREGNANCY (LMP)

15. IF PATIENT HAS HAD SAME OR SIMILAR ILLNESS, GIVE FIRST DATE   MM   DD   YY

16. DATES PATIENT UNABLE TO WORK IN CURRENT OCCUPATION   MM   DD   YY   FROM   TO   MM   DD   YY

17. NAME OF REFERRING PHYSICIAN OR OTHER SOURCE

17a. I.D. NUMBER OF REFERRING PHYSICIAN

18. HOSPITALIZATION DATES RELATED TO CURRENT SERVICES   MM   DD   YY   FROM   TO   MM   DD   YY

19. RESERVED FOR LOCAL USE

20. OUTSIDE LAB?   YES   NO $ CHARGES

21. DIAGNOSIS OR NATURE OF ILLNESS OR INJURY. (RELATE ITEMS 1, 2, 3, OR 4 TO ITEM 24E BY LINE)

1. _____ . _____   3. _____ . _____

2. _____ . _____   4. _____ . _____

22. MEDICAID RESUBMISSION CODE   ORIGINAL REF. NO.

23. PRIOR AUTHORIZATION NUMBER

24. A DATE(S) OF SERVICE						B Place of Service	C Type of Service	D PROCEDURES, SERVICES, OR SUPPLIES (Explain Unusual Circumstances)		E DIAGNOSIS CODE	F $ CHARGES	G DAYS OR UNITS	H EPSDT Family Plan	I EMG	J COB	K RESERVED FOR LOCAL USE
From MM	DD	YY	To MM	DD	YY			CPT/HCPCS	MODIFIER							
1																
2																
3																
4																
5																
6																

25. FEDERAL TAX I.D. NUMBER   SSN   EIN

26. PATIENT'S ACCOUNT NO.

27. ACCEPT ASSIGNMENT? (For govt. claims, see back)   YES   NO

28. TOTAL CHARGE $

29. AMOUNT PAID $

30. BALANCE DUE $

31. SIGNATURE OF PHYSICIAN OR SUPPLIER INCLUDING DEGREES OR CREDENTIALS (I certify that the statements on the reverse apply to this bill and are made a part thereof.)

SIGNED _____   DATE _____

32. NAME AND ADDRESS OF FACILITY WHERE SERVICES WERE RENDERED (If other than home or office)

33. PHYSICIAN'S, SUPPLIER'S BILLING NAME, ADDRESS, ZIP CODE & PHONE #

PIN#   GRP#

PATIENT AND INSURED INFORMATION

PHYSICIAN OR SUPPLIER INFORMATION

(SAMPLE ONLY - NOT APPROVED FOR USE)

PLEASE PRINT OR TYPE

SAMPLE FORM 1500
SAMPLE FORM 1500 SAMPLE FORM 1500

DATE	REMARKS				
03/17/XX	Medigap Payer Identification Number 334455993				

PATIENT				CHART #	SEX	BIRTHDATE
Mary R. Booth	212-77-4444			14-j	F	10/14/33

MAILING ADDRESS	CITY	STATE	ZIP	HOME PHONE	WORK PHONE
1007 Bond Avenue	Anywhere	US	12345	(101) 333-5555	X

EMPLOYER	ADDRESS	PATIENT STATUS
	Anywhere US	X
		MARRIED DIVORCED SINGLE STUDENT OTHER

INSURANCE: PRIMARY	ID#	GROUP	SECONDARY POLICY
Medicare	212-77-4444A		

POLICYHOLDER NAME	BIRTHDATE	RELATIONSHIP	POLICYHOLDER NAME	BIRTHDATE	RELATIONSHIP
		Self			

SUPPLEMENTAL PLAN	EMPLOYER
AARP Medigap 212-77-4444	

POLICYHOLDER NAME	BIRTHDATE	RELATIONSHIP	DIAGNOSIS	CODE
			1. Hypertension, benign	401.1
EMPLOYER			2.	
Retired Mt. Royal Drugs			3.	
REFERRING PHYSICIAN UPIN/SSN			4.	

PLACE OF SERVICE   Office

PROCEDURES	CODE	CHARGE
1. Est. Pt. OV Level I	99211	$55.00
2.		
3.		
4.		
5.		
6.		

SPECIAL NOTES

TOTAL CHARGES	PAYMENTS	ADJUSTMENTS	BALANCE
$55.00	0	0	$55.00

RETURN VISIT	PHYSICIAN SIGNATURE
3 Months	Donald L. Givings, M.D.

MEDICARE # D1234	**DONALD L. GIVINGS, M.D.**	EIN # 11123456
MEDICAID # DLG1234	**11350 MEDICAL DRIVE, ANYWHERE, US 12345**	SSN # 123-12-1234
BCBS # 12345	**PHONE NUMBER (101)111-5555**	UPIN # DG1234
		GRP # DG12345

PLEASE
DO NOT
STAPLE
IN THIS
AREA

CARRIER

| | PICA

HEALTH INSURANCE CLAIM FORM

PICA | |

1. MEDICARE	MEDICAID	CHAMPUS	CHAMPVA	GROUP HEALTH PLAN	FECA BLK LUNG	OTHER	1a. INSURED'S I.D. NUMBER	(FOR PROGRAM IN ITEM 1)
(Medicare #)	(Medicaid #)	(Sponsor's SSN)	(VA File #)	(SSN or ID)	(SSN)	(ID)		

2. PATIENT'S NAME (Last Name, First Name, Middle Initial)

3. PATIENT'S BIRTH DATE MM | DD | YY   SEX M [ ] F [ ]

4. INSURED'S NAME (Last Name, First Name, Middle Initial)

5. PATIENT'S ADDRESS (No. Street)

6. PATIENT RELATIONSHIP TO INSURED Self [ ] Spouse [ ] Child [ ] Other [ ]

7. INSURED'S ADDRESS (No. Street)

CITY   STATE

8. PATIENT STATUS Single [ ] Married [ ] Other [ ]

CITY   STATE

ZIP CODE   TELEPHONE (Include Area Code) (   )

Employed [ ] Full-Time Student [ ] Part-Time Student [ ]

ZIP CODE   TELEPHONE (INCLUDE AREA CODE) (   )

9. OTHER INSURED'S NAME (Last Name, First Name, Middle Initial)

10. IS PATIENT'S CONDITION RELATED TO:

11. INSURED'S POLICY GROUP OR FECA NUMBER

a. OTHER INSURED'S POLICY OR GROUP NUMBER

a. EMPLOYMENT? (CURRENT OR PREVIOUS) YES [ ] NO [ ]

a. INSURED'S DATE OF BIRTH MM | DD | YY   SEX M [ ] F [ ]

b. OTHER INSURED'S DATE OF BIRTH MM | DD | YY   SEX M [ ] F [ ]

b. AUTO ACCIDENT?   PLACE (State) YES [ ] NO [ ]

b. EMPLOYER'S NAME OR SCHOOL NAME

c. EMPLOYER'S NAME OR SCHOOL NAME

c. OTHER ACCIDENT? YES [ ] NO [ ]

c. INSURANCE PLAN NAME OR PROGRAM NAME

d. INSURANCE PLAN NAME OR PROGRAM NAME

10d. RESERVED FOR LOCAL USE

d. IS THERE ANOTHER HEALTH BENEFIT PLAN? YES [ ] NO [ ] If yes, return to and complete item 9 a – d.

READ BACK OF FORM BEFORE COMPLETING & SIGNING THIS FORM.
12. PATIENT'S OR AUTHORIZED PERSON'S SIGNATURE   I authorize the release of any medical or other information necessary to process this claim. I also request payment of government benefits either to myself or to the party who accepts assignment below.

SIGNED _____   DATE _____

13. INSURED'S OR AUTHORIZED PERSON'S SIGNATURE   I authorize payment of medical benefits to the undersigned physician or supplier for services described below.

SIGNED _____

PATIENT AND INSURED INFORMATION

14. DATE OF CURRENT: MM | DD | YY   ◄ ILLNESS (First symptom) OR INJURY (Accident) OR PREGNANCY (LMP)

15. IF PATIENT HAS HAD SAME OR SIMILAR ILLNESS, GIVE FIRST DATE   MM | DD | YY

16. DATES PATIENT UNABLE TO WORK IN CURRENT OCCUPATION MM | DD | YY   MM | DD | YY FROM   TO

17. NAME OF REFERRING PHYSICIAN OR OTHER SOURCE

17a. I.D. NUMBER OF REFERRING PHYSICIAN

18. HOSPITALIZATION DATES RELATED TO CURRENT SERVICES MM | DD | YY   MM | DD | YY FROM   TO

19. RESERVED FOR LOCAL USE

20. OUTSIDE LAB? YES [ ] NO [ ] $ CHARGES

21. DIAGNOSIS OR NATURE OF ILLNESS OR INJURY. (RELATE ITEMS 1, 2, 3, OR 4 TO ITEM 24E BY LINE) ─────

1. |__ . __| 3. |__ . __|

2. |__ . __| 4. |__ . __|

22. MEDICAID RESUBMISSION CODE   ORIGINAL REF. NO.

23. PRIOR AUTHORIZATION NUMBER

24. A DATE(S) OF SERVICE						B Place of Service	C Type of Service	D PROCEDURES, SERVICES, OR SUPPLIES (Explain Unusual Circumstances) CPT/HCPCS	MODIFIER	E DIAGNOSIS CODE	F $ CHARGES	G DAYS OR UNITS	H EPSDT Family Plan	I EMG	J COB	K RESERVED FOR LOCAL USE
From MM	DD	YY	To MM	DD	YY											
1																
2																
3																
4																
5																
6																

25. FEDERAL TAX I.D. NUMBER   SSN [ ] EIN [ ]

26. PATIENT'S ACCOUNT NO.

27. ACCEPT ASSIGNMENT? (For govt. claims, see back) YES [ ] NO [ ]

28. TOTAL CHARGE $

29. AMOUNT PAID $

30. BALANCE DUE $

31. SIGNATURE OF PHYSICIAN OR SUPPLIER INCLUDING DEGREES OR CREDENTIALS (I certify that the statements on the reverse apply to this bill and are made a part thereof.)

SIGNED _____ DATE _____

32. NAME AND ADDRESS OF FACILITY WHERE SERVICES WERE RENDERED (If other than home or office)

33. PHYSICIAN'S, SUPPLIER'S BILLING NAME, ADDRESS, ZIP CODE & PHONE #

PIN#   GRP#

PHYSICIAN OR SUPPLIER INFORMATION

163

(SAMPLE ONLY - NOT APPROVED FOR USE)

CARRIER

[ ][ ] PICA

HEALTH INSURANCE CLAIM FORM

PICA [ ][ ]

1.	MEDICARE	MEDICAID	CHAMPUS	CHAMPVA	GROUP HEALTH PLAN	FECA BLK LUNG	OTHER	1a. INSURED'S I.D. NUMBER	(FOR PROGRAM IN ITEM 1)
	(Medicare #)	(Medicaid #)	(Sponsor's SSN)	(VA File #)	(SSN or ID)	(SSN)	(ID)		

2. PATIENT'S NAME (Last Name, First Name, Middle Initial)

3. PATIENT'S BIRTH DATE MM | DD | YY   SEX   M [ ] F [ ]

4. INSURED'S NAME (Last Name, First Name, Middle Initial)

5. PATIENT'S ADDRESS (No. Street)

6. PATIENT RELATIONSHIP TO INSURED
Self [ ] Spouse [ ] Child [ ] Other [ ]

7. INSURED'S ADDRESS (No. Street)

CITY   STATE

8. PATIENT STATUS
Single [ ] Married [ ] Other [ ]
Employed [ ] Full-Time Student [ ] Part-Time Student [ ]

CITY   STATE

ZIP CODE   TELEPHONE (Include Area Code) ( )

ZIP CODE   TELEPHONE (INCLUDE AREA CODE) ( )

9. OTHER INSURED'S NAME (Last Name, First Name, Middle Initial)

10. IS PATIENT'S CONDITION RELATED TO:

11. INSURED'S POLICY GROUP OR FECA NUMBER

a. OTHER INSURED'S POLICY OR GROUP NUMBER

a. EMPLOYMENT? (CURRENT OR PREVIOUS)
[ ] YES [ ] NO

a. INSURED'S DATE OF BIRTH MM | DD | YY   SEX M [ ] F [ ]

b. OTHER INSURED'S DATE OF BIRTH MM | DD | YY   SEX M [ ] F [ ]

b. AUTO ACCIDENT?   PLACE (State)
[ ] YES [ ] NO

b. EMPLOYER'S NAME OR SCHOOL NAME

c. EMPLOYER'S NAME OR SCHOOL NAME

c. OTHER ACCIDENT?
[ ] YES [ ] NO

c. INSURANCE PLAN NAME OR PROGRAM NAME

d. INSURANCE PLAN NAME OR PROGRAM NAME

10d. RESERVED FOR LOCAL USE

d. IS THERE ANOTHER HEALTH BENEFIT PLAN?
[ ] YES [ ] NO   If yes, return to and complete item 9 a – d.

READ BACK OF FORM BEFORE COMPLETING & SIGNING THIS FORM.
12. PATIENT'S OR AUTHORIZED PERSON'S SIGNATURE I authorize the release of any medical or other information necessary to process this claim. I also request payment of government benefits either to myself or to the party who accepts assignment below.

SIGNED _____ DATE _____

13. INSURED'S OR AUTHORIZED PERSON'S SIGNATURE I authorize payment of medical benefits to the undersigned physician or supplier for services described below.

SIGNED _____

14. DATE OF CURRENT: MM | DD | YY   ILLNESS (First symptom) OR INJURY (Accident) OR PREGNANCY (LMP)

15. IF PATIENT HAS HAD SAME OR SIMILAR ILLNESS, GIVE FIRST DATE MM | DD | YY

16. DATES PATIENT UNABLE TO WORK IN CURRENT OCCUPATION MM | DD | YY
FROM _____ TO _____ MM | DD | YY

17. NAME OF REFERRING PHYSICIAN OR OTHER SOURCE

17a. I.D. NUMBER OF REFERRING PHYSICIAN

18. HOSPITALIZATION DATES RELATED TO CURRENT SERVICES MM | DD | YY
FROM _____ TO _____ MM | DD | YY

19. RESERVED FOR LOCAL USE

20. OUTSIDE LAB? $ CHARGES
[ ] YES [ ] NO

21. DIAGNOSIS OR NATURE OF ILLNESS OR INJURY. (RELATE ITEMS 1, 2, 3, OR 4 TO ITEM 24E BY LINE)

1. |___.___| 3. |___.___|

2. |___.___| 4. |___.___|

22. MEDICAID RESUBMISSION CODE _____ ORIGINAL REF. NO. _____

23. PRIOR AUTHORIZATION NUMBER

24. A DATE(S) OF SERVICE						B Place of Service	C Type of Service	D PROCEDURES, SERVICES, OR SUPPLIES (Explain Unusual Circumstances)		E DIAGNOSIS CODE	F $ CHARGES	G DAYS OR UNITS	H EPSDT Family Plan	I EMG	J COB	K RESERVED FOR LOCAL USE
From MM	DD	YY	To MM	DD	YY			CPT/HCPCS	MODIFIER							
1																
2																
3																
4																
5																
6																

25. FEDERAL TAX I.D. NUMBER   SSN [ ] EIN [ ]

26. PATIENT'S ACCOUNT NO.

27. ACCEPT ASSIGNMENT? (For govt. claims, see back)
[ ] YES [ ] NO

28. TOTAL CHARGE $

29. AMOUNT PAID $

30. BALANCE DUE $

31. SIGNATURE OF PHYSICIAN OR SUPPLIER INCLUDING DEGREES OR CREDENTIALS (I certify that the statements on the reverse apply to this bill and are made a part thereof.)

SIGNED _____ DATE _____

32. NAME AND ADDRESS OF FACILITY WHERE SERVICES WERE RENDERED (If other than home or office)

33. PHYSICIAN'S, SUPPLIER'S BILLING NAME, ADDRESS, ZIP CODE & PHONE #

PIN# _____   GRP# _____

(SAMPLE ONLY - NOT APPROVED FOR USE)

PLEASE PRINT OR TYPE

SAMPLE FORM 1500
SAMPLE FORM 1500 SAMPLE FORM 1500

DATE	REMARKS			
12/15/XX				

PATIENT			CHART #	SEX	BIRTHDATE
Patricia S. Delaney 485375869			14-k	F	04/12/31

MAILING ADDRESS	CITY	STATE	ZIP	HOME PHONE	WORK PHONE
485 Garden Lane	Anywhere	US	12345	(101) 333-5555	

EMPLOYER	ADDRESS	PATIENT STATUS					
	Anywhere US			X			
		MARRIED	DIVORCED	SINGLE	STUDENT	OTHER	

INSURANCE: PRIMARY	ID#	GROUP	SECONDARY POLICY
Medicare	485375869A		

POLICYHOLDER NAME	BIRTHDATE	RELATIONSHIP	POLICYHOLDER NAME	BIRTHDATE	RELATIONSHIP
		Self			

SUPPLEMENTAL PLAN		EMPLOYER
Medicaid	22886644XT	

POLICYHOLDER NAME	BIRTHDATE	RELATIONSHIP	DIAGNOSIS	CODE
		Self	1. Rosacea	695.3
EMPLOYER			2.	
			3.	
REFERRING PHYSICIAN UPIN/SSN			4.	

PLACE OF SERVICE	Office

PROCEDURES	CODE	CHARGE
1. Ext. Pt. OV Level I	99211	$55.00
2.		
3.		
4.		
5.		
6.		

SPECIAL NOTES

Refer patient to a Dermatologist

TOTAL CHARGES	PAYMENTS	ADJUSTMENTS	BALANCE
$55.00	-0-	-0-	$55.00

RETURN VISIT	PHYSICIAN SIGNATURE
PRN	Donald L. Givings, M.D.

MEDICARE # D1234
MEDICAID # DLG1234
BCBS # 12345

DONALD L. GIVINGS, M.D.
11350 MEDICAL DRIVE, ANYWHERE, US 12345
PHONE NUMBER (101)111-5555

EIN # 11123456
SSN # 123-12-1234
UPIN # DG1234
GRP # DG12345

PLEASE
DO NOT
STAPLE
IN THIS
AREA

CARRIER

☐☐☐ PICA

HEALTH INSURANCE CLAIM FORM

PICA ☐☐☐

| 1. MEDICARE ☐ (Medicare #)   MEDICAID ☐ (Medicaid #)   CHAMPUS ☐ (Sponsor's SSN)   CHAMPVA ☐ (VA File #)   GROUP HEALTH PLAN ☐ (SSN or ID)   FECA BLK LUNG ☐ (SSN)   OTHER ☐ (ID) | 1a. INSURED'S I.D. NUMBER   (FOR PROGRAM IN ITEM 1) |

2. PATIENT'S NAME (Last Name, First Name, Middle Initial)

3. PATIENT'S BIRTH DATE   MM ┊ DD ┊ YY   SEX   M ☐   F ☐

4. INSURED'S NAME (Last Name, First Name, Middle Initial)

5. PATIENT'S ADDRESS (No. Street)

6. PATIENT RELATIONSHIP TO INSURED   Self ☐   Spouse ☐   Child ☐   Other ☐

7. INSURED'S ADDRESS (No. Street)

CITY   STATE

8. PATIENT STATUS   Single ☐   Married ☐   Other ☐

CITY   STATE

ZIP CODE   TELEPHONE (Include Area Code)   ( )

Employed ☐   Full-Time Student ☐   Part-Time Student ☐

ZIP CODE   TELEPHONE (INCLUDE AREA CODE)   ( )

9. OTHER INSURED'S NAME (Last Name, First Name, Middle Initial)

10. IS PATIENT'S CONDITION RELATED TO:

11. INSURED'S POLICY GROUP OR FECA NUMBER

a. OTHER INSURED'S POLICY OR GROUP NUMBER

a. EMPLOYMENT? (CURRENT OR PREVIOUS)   ☐ YES   ☐ NO

a. INSURED'S DATE OF BIRTH   MM ┊ DD ┊ YY   SEX   M ☐   F ☐

b. OTHER INSURED'S DATE OF BIRTH   MM ┊ DD ┊ YY   SEX   M ☐   F ☐

b. AUTO ACCIDENT?   PLACE (State)   ☐ YES   ☐ NO

b. EMPLOYER'S NAME OR SCHOOL NAME

c. EMPLOYER'S NAME OR SCHOOL NAME

c. OTHER ACCIDENT?   ☐ YES   ☐ NO

c. INSURANCE PLAN NAME OR PROGRAM NAME

d. INSURANCE PLAN NAME OR PROGRAM NAME

10d. RESERVED FOR LOCAL USE

d. IS THERE ANOTHER HEALTH BENEFIT PLAN?   ☐ YES   ☐ NO   If yes, return to and complete item 9 a – d.

READ BACK OF FORM BEFORE COMPLETING & SIGNING THIS FORM.

12. PATIENT'S OR AUTHORIZED PERSON'S SIGNATURE. I authorize the release of any medical or other information necessary to process this claim. I also request payment of government benefits either to myself or to the party who accepts assignment below.

SIGNED _____ DATE _____

13. INSURED'S OR AUTHORIZED PERSON'S SIGNATURE. I authorize payment of medical benefits to the undersigned physician or supplier for services described below.

SIGNED _____

14. DATE OF CURRENT: MM ┊ DD ┊ YY   ILLNESS (First symptom) OR INJURY (Accident) OR PREGNANCY (LMP)

15. IF PATIENT HAS HAD SAME OR SIMILAR ILLNESS, GIVE FIRST DATE   MM ┊ DD ┊ YY

16. DATES PATIENT UNABLE TO WORK IN CURRENT OCCUPATION   MM ┊ DD ┊ YY   MM ┊ DD ┊ YY   FROM   TO

17. NAME OF REFERRING PHYSICIAN OR OTHER SOURCE

17a. I.D. NUMBER OF REFERRING PHYSICIAN

18. HOSPITALIZATION DATES RELATED TO CURRENT SERVICES   MM ┊ DD ┊ YY   MM ┊ DD ┊ YY   FROM   TO

19. RESERVED FOR LOCAL USE

20. OUTSIDE LAB?   ☐ YES   ☐ NO $ CHARGES

21. DIAGNOSIS OR NATURE OF ILLNESS OR INJURY. (RELATE ITEMS 1, 2, 3, OR 4 TO ITEM 24E BY LINE)

1. ┗___ ┊ ___   3. ┗___ ┊ ___

2. ┗___ ┊ ___   4. ┗___ ┊ ___

22. MEDICAID RESUBMISSION CODE   ORIGINAL REF. NO.

23. PRIOR AUTHORIZATION NUMBER

24. A DATE(S) OF SERVICE						B Place of Service	C Type of Service	D PROCEDURES, SERVICES, OR SUPPLIES (Explain Unusual Circumstances) CPT/HCPCS MODIFIER	E DIAGNOSIS CODE	F $ CHARGES	G DAYS OR UNITS	H EPSDT Family Plan	I EMG	J COB	K RESERVED FOR LOCAL USE
From			To												
MM	DD	YY	MM	DD	YY										
1															
2															
3															
4															
5															
6															

25. FEDERAL TAX I.D. NUMBER   SSN ☐   EIN ☐

26. PATIENT'S ACCOUNT NO.

27. ACCEPT ASSIGNMENT? (For govt. claims, see back)   YES ☐   NO ☐

28. TOTAL CHARGE $

29. AMOUNT PAID $

30. BALANCE DUE $

31. SIGNATURE OF PHYSICIAN OR SUPPLIER INCLUDING DEGREES OR CREDENTIALS (I certify that the statements on the reverse apply to this bill and are made a part thereof.)

SIGNED _____ DATE _____

32. NAME AND ADDRESS OF FACILITY WHERE SERVICES WERE RENDERED (If other than home or office)

33. PHYSICIAN'S, SUPPLIER'S BILLING NAME, ADDRESS, ZIP CODE & PHONE #

PIN# _____ GRP# _____

PATIENT AND INSURED INFORMATION   PHYSICIAN OR SUPPLIER INFORMATION

DATE		REMARKS				
12/15/XX						

PATIENT			CHART #	SEX	BIRTHDATE
Patricia S. Delaney 485375869			14-1	F	04/12/31

MAILING ADDRESS	CITY	STATE	ZIP	HOME PHONE	WORK PHONE
485 Garden Lane	Anywhere	US	12345	(101) 333-5555	

EMPLOYER	ADDRESS	PATIENT STATUS
	Anywhere US	X
		MARRIED DIVORCED SINGLE STUDENT OTHER

INSURANCE: PRIMARY	ID#	GROUP	SECONDARY POLICY
Medicare	485375869A		

POLICYHOLDER NAME	BIRTHDATE	RELATIONSHIP	POLICYHOLDER NAME	BIRTHDATE	RELATIONSHIP
		Self			

SUPPLEMENTAL PLAN		EMPLOYER
Medicaid	22886644XT	

POLICYHOLDER NAME	BIRTHDATE	RELATIONSHIP	DIAGNOSIS	CODE
		Self	1. Rosacea	695.3
EMPLOYER			2.	
			3.	
REFERRING PHYSICIAN UPIN/SSN			4.	
Donald L. Givings, M.D.	123-12-1234			

PLACE OF SERVICE   Office

PROCEDURES	CODE	CHARGE
1. Office Consult Level III	99243	$85.00
2.		
3.		
4.		
5.		
6.		

SPECIAL NOTES

TOTAL CHARGES	PAYMENTS	ADJUSTMENTS	BALANCE
$85.00	-0-	-0-	$85.00

RETURN VISIT	PHYSICIAN SIGNATURE
PRN	*Claire M. Skinner, M.D.*

	CLAIRE M. SKINNER, M.D. DERMATOLOGY	EIN # 11555555
MEDICARE # C1234	50 CLEAR VIEW DRIVE, ANYWHERE, US 12345	SSN # 333-44-1234
MEDICAID # CMS1234	PHONE NUMBER (101)111-5555	UPIN # CS1234
BCBS # 94949		GRP # CS12345

PLEASE
DO NOT
STAPLE
IN THIS
AREA

(SAMPLE ONLY - NOT APPROVED FOR USE)

CARRIER

☐☐ PICA

HEALTH INSURANCE CLAIM FORM

PICA ☐☐☐

1. MEDICARE ☐ (Medicare #) MEDICAID ☐ (Medicaid #) CHAMPUS ☐ (Sponsor's SSN) CHAMPVA ☐ (VA File #) GROUP HEALTH PLAN ☐ (SSN or ID) FECA BLK LUNG ☐ (SSN) OTHER ☐ (ID)

1a. INSURED'S I.D. NUMBER   (FOR PROGRAM IN ITEM 1)

2. PATIENT'S NAME (Last Name, First Name, Middle Initial)

3. PATIENT'S BIRTH DATE   SEX
   MM ¦ DD ¦ YY   M ☐   F ☐

4. INSURED'S NAME (Last Name, First Name, Middle Initial)

5. PATIENT'S ADDRESS (No. Street)

6. PATIENT RELATIONSHIP TO INSURED
   Self ☐ Spouse ☐ Child ☐ Other ☐

7. INSURED'S ADDRESS (No. Street)

CITY   STATE

8. PATIENT STATUS
   Single ☐ Married ☐ Other ☐
   Employed ☐ Full-Time Student ☐ Part-Time Student ☐

CITY   STATE

ZIP CODE   TELEPHONE (Include Area Code)
             (   )

ZIP CODE   TELEPHONE (INCLUDE AREA CODE)
             (   )

9. OTHER INSURED'S NAME (Last Name, First Name, Middle Initial)

10. IS PATIENT'S CONDITION RELATED TO:

11. INSURED'S POLICY GROUP OR FECA NUMBER

a. OTHER INSURED'S POLICY OR GROUP NUMBER

a. EMPLOYMENT? (CURRENT OR PREVIOUS)
   ☐ YES   ☐ NO

a. INSURED'S DATE OF BIRTH   SEX
   MM ¦ DD ¦ YY   M ☐ F ☐

b. OTHER INSURED'S DATE OF BIRTH   SEX
   MM ¦ DD ¦ YY   M ☐ F ☐

b. AUTO ACCIDENT?   PLACE (State)
   ☐ YES   ☐ NO

b. EMPLOYER'S NAME OR SCHOOL NAME

c. EMPLOYER'S NAME OR SCHOOL NAME

c. OTHER ACCIDENT?
   ☐ YES   ☐ NO

c. INSURANCE PLAN NAME OR PROGRAM NAME

d. INSURANCE PLAN NAME OR PROGRAM NAME

10d. RESERVED FOR LOCAL USE

d. IS THERE ANOTHER HEALTH BENEFIT PLAN?
   ☐ YES   ☐ NO   If yes, return to and complete item 9 a – d.

READ BACK OF FORM BEFORE COMPLETING & SIGNING THIS FORM.
12. PATIENT'S OR AUTHORIZED PERSON'S SIGNATURE I authorize the release of any medical or other information necessary to process this claim. I also request payment of government benefits either to myself or to the party who accepts assignment below.

SIGNED _____   DATE _____

13. INSURED'S OR AUTHORIZED PERSON'S SIGNATURE I authorize payment of medical benefits to the undersigned physician or supplier for services described below.

SIGNED _____

14. DATE OF CURRENT: ILLNESS (First symptom) OR
   MM ¦ DD ¦ YY   INJURY (Accident) OR
                      PREGNANCY (LMP)

15. IF PATIENT HAS HAD SAME OR SIMILAR ILLNESS,
    GIVE FIRST DATE   MM ¦ DD ¦ YY

16. DATES PATIENT UNABLE TO WORK IN CURRENT OCCUPATION
    FROM MM ¦ DD ¦ YY   TO MM ¦ DD ¦ YY

17. NAME OF REFERRING PHYSICIAN OR OTHER SOURCE

17a. I.D. NUMBER OF REFERRING PHYSICIAN

18. HOSPITALIZATION DATES RELATED TO CURRENT SERVICES
    FROM MM ¦ DD ¦ YY   TO MM ¦ DD ¦ YY

19. RESERVED FOR LOCAL USE

20. OUTSIDE LAB? $ CHARGES
    ☐ YES   ☐ NO

21. DIAGNOSIS OR NATURE OF ILLNESS OR INJURY. (RELATE ITEMS 1, 2, 3, OR 4 TO ITEM 24E BY LINE)
   1. ☐___ . ___   3. ☐___ . ___
   2. ☐___ . ___   4. ☐___ . ___

22. MEDICAID RESUBMISSION CODE   ORIGINAL REF. NO.

23. PRIOR AUTHORIZATION NUMBER

24. A DATE(S) OF SERVICE						B Place of Service	C Type of Service	D PROCEDURES, SERVICES, OR SUPPLIES (Explain Unusual Circumstances)		E DIAGNOSIS CODE	F $ CHARGES	G DAYS OR UNITS	H EPSDT Family Plan	I EMG	J COB	K RESERVED FOR LOCAL USE
From MM	DD	YY	To MM	DD	YY			CPT/HCPCS	MODIFIER							
1																
2																
3																
4																
5																
6																

25. FEDERAL TAX I.D. NUMBER   SSN ☐ EIN ☐

26. PATIENT'S ACCOUNT NO.

27. ACCEPT ASSIGNMENT? (For govt. claims, see back)
    ☐ YES   ☐ NO

28. TOTAL CHARGE $

29. AMOUNT PAID $

30. BALANCE DUE $

31. SIGNATURE OF PHYSICIAN OR SUPPLIER INCLUDING DEGREES OR CREDENTIALS (I certify that the statements on the reverse apply to this bill and are made a part thereof.)

SIGNED _____   DATE _____

32. NAME AND ADDRESS OF FACILITY WHERE SERVICES WERE RENDERED (If other than home or office)

33. PHYSICIAN'S, SUPPLIER'S BILLING NAME, ADDRESS, ZIP CODE & PHONE #

PIN#   GRP#

(SAMPLE ONLY - NOT APPROVED FOR USE)

PLEASE PRINT OR TYPE

SAMPLE FORM 1500
SAMPLE FORM 1500 SAMPLE FORM 1500

PATIENT AND INSURED INFORMATION

PHYSICIAN OR SUPPLIER INFORMATION

168

Complete the Medical Necessity Statement for Danielle H. Ford, Case Study 14-m.

Practice Letterhead

To My Medicare Patients:

My primary concern as your physician is to provide you with the best possible care. Medicare does not pay for all services and will only allow those which it determines, under the guidelines spelled out in the Omnibus Reconciliation Act of 1986 Section 1862(a)(1), to be reasonable and necessary. Under this law, a procedure or service deemed to be medically unreasonable or unnecessary will be denied. Since I believe each scheduled visit or planned procedure is both reasonable and necessary, I am required to notify you in advance that the following procedures or services listed below, which we have mutually agreed on, may be denied by Medicare.

Date of Service _____

Description of Service   Charge

_____   _____

_____   _____

_____   _____

Denial may be for the following reasons:

1. Medicare does not usually pay for this many visits or treatments,

2. Medicare does not usually pay for this many services within this period of time, and/or

3. Medicare does not usually pay for this type of service for your condition.

I, however, believe these procedures/services to be both reasonable and necessary for your condition, and will assist you in collecting payment from Medicare. In order for me to assist you in this matter, the law requires that you read the following agreement and sign it.

I have been informed by _____ that he/she believes, in my case, Medicare is likely to deny payment for the services and reasons stated above. If Medicare denies payment, I agree to be personally and fully responsible for payment.

Beneficiary's Name: _____ Medicare ID # _____ or

Beneficiary's Signature _____

or

Authorized Representative's Signature _____

DATE	REMARKS			
08/09/XX	Have the patient sign a Medicare Medical Necessity form			

PATIENT		CHART #	SEX	BIRTHDATE
Danielle H. Ford 756-66-7878		14-m	F	12/10/22

MAILING ADDRESS	CITY	STATE	ZIP	HOME PHONE	WORK PHONE
28 Delightful Drive	Anywhere	US	12345	(101) 333-5555	

EMPLOYER	ADDRESS	PATIENT STATUS
	Anywhere US	X MARRIED DIVORCED SINGLE STUDENT OTHER

INSURANCE: PRIMARY	ID#	GROUP	SECONDARY POLICY
Medicare	756-66-7878W		

POLICYHOLDER NAME	BIRTHDATE	RELATIONSHIP	POLICYHOLDER NAME	BIRTHDATE	RELATIONSHIP

SUPPLEMENTAL PLAN	EMPLOYER

POLICYHOLDER NAME	BIRTHDATE	RELATIONSHIP	DIAGNOSIS	CODE
			1. Routine examination	V70.0
EMPLOYER			2.	
			3.	
REFERRING PHYSICIAN UPIN/SSN			4.	

PLACE OF SERVICE   Office

PROCEDURES	CODE	CHARGE
1. Preventive medicine, 65 years and over	99397	$65.00
2.		
3.		
4.		
5.		
6.		

SPECIAL NOTES

TOTAL CHARGES	PAYMENTS	ADJUSTMENTS	BALANCE
$65.00	$65.00	0	$0.00

RETURN VISIT	PHYSICIAN SIGNATURE
PRN	Donald L. Givings, M.D.

DONALD L. GIVINGS, M.D.
11350 MEDICAL DRIVE, ANYWHERE, US 12345
PHONE NUMBER (101)111-5555

MEDICARE # D1234
MEDICAID # DLG1234
BCBS # 12345

EIN # 11123456
SSN # 123-12-1234
UPIN # DG1234
GRP # DG12345

(SAMPLE ONLY - NOT APPROVED FOR USE)

CARRIER

| | PICA |

HEALTH INSURANCE CLAIM FORM

PICA | | |

| 1. MEDICARE | MEDICAID | CHAMPUS | CHAMPVA | GROUP HEALTH PLAN | FECA BLK LUNG | OTHER | 1a. INSURED'S I.D. NUMBER (FOR PROGRAM IN ITEM 1) |

☐ (Medicare #) ☐ (Medicaid #) ☐ (Sponsor's SSN) ☐ (VA File #) ☐ (SSN or ID) ☐ (SSN) ☐ (ID)

2. PATIENT'S NAME (Last Name, First Name, Middle Initial)

3. PATIENT'S BIRTH DATE   MM ┊ DD ┊ YY   SEX   M ☐   F ☐

4. INSURED'S NAME (Last Name, First Name, Middle Initial)

5. PATIENT'S ADDRESS (No. Street)

6. PATIENT RELATIONSHIP TO INSURED
Self ☐   Spouse ☐   Child ☐   Other ☐

7. INSURED'S ADDRESS (No. Street)

CITY   STATE

8. PATIENT STATUS
Single ☐   Married ☐   Other ☐
Employed ☐   Full-Time Student ☐   Part-Time Student ☐

CITY   STATE

ZIP CODE   TELEPHONE (Include Area Code)   (   )

ZIP CODE   TELEPHONE (INCLUDE AREA CODE)   (   )

9. OTHER INSURED'S NAME (Last Name, First Name, Middle Initial)

10. IS PATIENT'S CONDITION RELATED TO:

11. INSURED'S POLICY GROUP OR FECA NUMBER

a. OTHER INSURED'S POLICY OR GROUP NUMBER

a. EMPLOYMENT? (CURRENT OR PREVIOUS)   ☐ YES   ☐ NO

a. INSURED'S DATE OF BIRTH   MM ┊ DD ┊ YY   SEX   M ☐   F ☐

b. OTHER INSURED'S DATE OF BIRTH   MM ┊ DD ┊ YY   SEX   M ☐   F ☐

b. AUTO ACCIDENT?   PLACE (State)   ☐ YES   ☐ NO

b. EMPLOYER'S NAME OR SCHOOL NAME

c. EMPLOYER'S NAME OR SCHOOL NAME

c. OTHER ACCIDENT?   ☐ YES   ☐ NO

c. INSURANCE PLAN NAME OR PROGRAM NAME

d. INSURANCE PLAN NAME OR PROGRAM NAME

10d. RESERVED FOR LOCAL USE

d. IS THERE ANOTHER HEALTH BENEFIT PLAN?
☐ YES   ☐ NO   If yes, return to and complete item 9 a – d.

READ BACK OF FORM BEFORE COMPLETING & SIGNING THIS FORM.
12. PATIENT'S OR AUTHORIZED PERSON'S SIGNATURE I authorize the release of any medical or other information necessary to process this claim. I also request payment of government benefits either to myself or to the party who accepts assignment below.

SIGNED _____   DATE _____

13. INSURED'S OR AUTHORIZED PERSON'S SIGNATURE I authorize payment of medical benefits to the undersigned physician or supplier for services described below.

SIGNED _____

PATIENT AND INSURED INFORMATION

14. DATE OF CURRENT: MM ┊ DD ┊ YY   ◄ ILLNESS (First symptom) OR INJURY (Accident) OR PREGNANCY (LMP)

15. IF PATIENT HAS HAD SAME OR SIMILAR ILLNESS, GIVE FIRST DATE   MM ┊ DD ┊ YY

16. DATES PATIENT UNABLE TO WORK IN CURRENT OCCUPATION   MM ┊ DD ┊ YY   FROM   TO   MM ┊ DD ┊ YY

17. NAME OF REFERRING PHYSICIAN OR OTHER SOURCE

17a. I.D. NUMBER OF REFERRING PHYSICIAN

18. HOSPITALIZATION DATES RELATED TO CURRENT SERVICES   MM ┊ DD ┊ YY   FROM   TO   MM ┊ DD ┊ YY

19. RESERVED FOR LOCAL USE

20. OUTSIDE LAB?   ☐ YES   ☐ NO $ CHARGES

21. DIAGNOSIS OR NATURE OF ILLNESS OR INJURY. (RELATE ITEMS 1, 2, 3, OR 4 TO ITEM 24E BY LINE)
1. └___ . __
2. └___ . __
3. └___ . __
4. └___ . __

22. MEDICAID RESUBMISSION CODE   ORIGINAL REF. NO.

23. PRIOR AUTHORIZATION NUMBER

| 24. | A DATE(S) OF SERVICE | | | | | B Place of Service | C Type of Service | D PROCEDURES, SERVICES, OR SUPPLIES (Explain Unusual Circumstances) CPT/HCPCS ┊ MODIFIER | E DIAGNOSIS CODE | F $ CHARGES | G DAYS OR UNITS | H EPSDT Family Plan | I EMG | J COB | K RESERVED FOR LOCAL USE |
	From MM ┊ DD ┊ YY			To MM ┊ DD ┊ YY											
1															
2															
3															
4															
5															
6															

25. FEDERAL TAX I.D. NUMBER   SSN ☐   EIN ☐

26. PATIENT'S ACCOUNT NO.

27. ACCEPT ASSIGNMENT? (For govt. claims, see back)   ☐ YES   ☐ NO

28. TOTAL CHARGE $

29. AMOUNT PAID $

30. BALANCE DUE $

31. SIGNATURE OF PHYSICIAN OR SUPPLIER INCLUDING DEGREES OR CREDENTIALS (I certify that the statements on the reverse apply to this bill and are made a part thereof.)

SIGNED _____ DATE _____

32. NAME AND ADDRESS OF FACILITY WHERE SERVICES WERE RENDERED (If other than home or office)

33. PHYSICIAN'S, SUPPLIER'S BILLING NAME, ADDRESS, ZIP CODE & PHONE #

PIN#   GRP#

PHYSICIAN OR SUPPLIER INFORMATION

(SAMPLE ONLY - NOT APPROVED FOR USE)

PLEASE PRINT OR TYPE

SAMPLE FORM 1500
SAMPLE FORM 1500   SAMPLE FORM 1500

Medicaid

FEDERAL ELIGIBILITY REQUIREMENTS

1. List several persons who currently qualify for federal Medicaid assistance.

_____

_____

_____

_____

2. Are individual states allowed to establish income-level eligibility guidelines for Medicaid? _____

3. Each state established its own eligibility standards within the _____ _____
guidelines.

4. When a patient claims to receive Medicaid, what must be presented as proof? _____

_____

5. In many cases, what does eligibility depend upon? _____

6. What do most states use for verification of eligibility? _____

FEDERAL BENEFITS

7. List several services covered by the federal portion of Medicaid.

_____

_____

_____

_____

8. What does the EPSDT legislation mandate? _____

_____

STATE SERVICES

9. Define *medically needy*. _____

_____

10. If a Medicaid patient is being admitted to the hospital for a non-emergency service what is required by most states? _____

11. Many states have implemented a _____ _____ to track over-utilization of services.

12. List six medical situations that require preauthorization from Medicaid.

a. _____

b. _____

c. _____

d. _____

e. _____

f. _____

MEDICAID AS A SECONDARY PAYER

13. Medicaid is always the ___. (Circle the correct answer.)

a. primary insurance

b. secondary insurance

c. payer of last resort

d. none of the above

14. Medicaid is billed only ___. (Circle the correct answer.)

a. if other coverage denies responsibility for payment

b. if other coverage pays less than the Medicaid fee schedule

c. if Medicaid covers a procedure not covered by another policy

d. all of the above

PARTICIPATING PROVIDERS

15. If a patient has Medicaid and a service was performed that is a Medicaid-covered benefit, can the provider balance bill the patient? _____

16. Can a Medicaid patient be billed for a service that is not a Medicaid-covered benefit? _____

MEDICAID AND MANAGED CARE

17. Many states have requested federal permission to integrate persons receiving Medicaid into ___. (Circle the correct answer)

a. HMO programs

b. PPO programs

c. POS programs

d. all of the above

18. Most Medicaid HMO programs offer capitated services to ___. (Circle the correct answer.)
    a. chronically ill members
    b. healthier members
    c. members in rural communities
    d. any of the above

19. All Medicaid HMO patients have a ___. (Circle the correct answer.)
    a. primary care physician
    b. case manager
    c. gatekeeper
    d. any of the above

BILLING INFORMATION NOTES

20. In most states the required form for submitting Medicaid claims is the ___. (Circle the correct answer.)
    a. UB92   c. HCFA-1500
    b. HCFA-1450   d. none of the above

21. In most states the deadline for filing claims for Medicaid patients is ___. (Circle the correct answer.)
    a. variable from state to state
    b. 30 days
    c. 60 days
    d. 90 days

22. Medicaid crossover claims follow the ___ deadlines for claims. (Circle the correct answer.)
    a. Medicaid   c. Medicare
    b. secondary   d. none of the above

23. State why collection of fees for uncovered services is difficult. _____

_____

24. If the assignment of benefits is not marked on the HCFA-1500 form, what can happen to reimbursement? _____

25. The answer to each of the following statements is either yes or no. Indicate your choice by placing **Y** for yes or **N** for no on the line provided.

_____ a. Can a provider attempt to collect the difference between the Medicaid payment and the fee charged if the patient did not reveal that he/she was a Medicaid recipient at the time of service?

_____ b. Can there be a deductible for persons in the medically indigent classification?

_____ c. Are copayments required for some categories of Medicaid recipients?

_____ d. Does the Medicaid recipient pay a premium for medical coverage?

_____ e. If the patient's condition warrants extension of authorized inpatient days, should the hospital seek authorization for additional inpatient days?

_____ f. Can Medicaid patients be eligible for Medicaid benefits one month and not the next?

_____ g. Are cards issued for the "Unborn child of..." good for services as soon as the child is born?

Know Your Acronyms

26. Define the following acronyms:

   a. SSI _____

   b. AFDC _____

   c. EPSDT _____

   d. TANF _____

   e. SCHIP _____

EXERCISES

1. Complete the Case Studies, 15-a through 15-f, using the blank claim form provided. Follow the step-by-step instructions in the textbook to properly complete the claim form. You may choose to use a pencil so corrections can be made.

Case Study 15-a

DATE 11/13/XX	REMARKS			
PATIENT Sharon W. Casey 333-55-7979		CHART # 15-a	SEX F	BIRTHDATE 10/06/70

MAILING ADDRESS	CITY	STATE	ZIP	HOME PHONE	WORK PHONE
483 Oakdale Avenue	Anywhere	US	12345	(101) 333-5555	

EMPLOYER	ADDRESS	PATIENT STATUS
		X MARRIED DIVORCED SINGLE STUDENT OTHER

INSURANCE: PRIMARY Medicaid	ID# 22334455	GROUP	SECONDARY POLICY

POLICYHOLDER NAME	BIRTHDATE	RELATIONSHIP	POLICYHOLDER NAME	BIRTHDATE	RELATIONSHIP

SUPPLEMENTAL PLAN	EMPLOYER

POLICYHOLDER NAME	BIRTHDATE	RELATIONSHIP	DIAGNOSIS	CODE
			1. Excessive menstruation	626.2
EMPLOYER			2. Irregular menstrual cycle	626.4
			3.	
REFERRING PHYSICIAN UPIN/SSN			4.	

PLACE OF SERVICE Office		
PROCEDURES	CODE	CHARGE
1. Est. Pt. Ov Level III	99213	$75.00
2.		
3.		
4.		
5.		
6.		

SPECIAL NOTES
Refer patient to GYN

TOTAL CHARGES $75.00	PAYMENTS -0-	ADJUSTMENTS -0-	BALANCE $75.00

RETURN VISIT PRN	PHYSICIAN SIGNATURE *Donald L. Givings, M.D.*

MEDICARE # D1234 MEDICAID # DLG1234 BCBS # 12345	DONALD L. GIVINGS, M.D. 11350 MEDICAL DRIVE, ANYWHERE, US 12345 PHONE NUMBER (101)111-5555	EIN # 11123456 SSN # 123-12-1234 UPIN # DG1234 GRP # DG12345

(SAMPLE ONLY - NOT APPROVED FOR USE)

CARRIER

HEALTH INSURANCE CLAIM FORM

PICA ☐☐☐   PICA ☐☐☐

1. MEDICARE	MEDICAID	CHAMPUS	CHAMPVA	GROUP HEALTH PLAN	FECA BLK LUNG	OTHER	1a. INSURED'S I.D. NUMBER	(FOR PROGRAM IN ITEM 1)
☐ (Medicare #)	☐ (Medicaid #)	☐ (Sponsor's SSN)	☐ (VA File #)	☐ (SSN or ID)	☐ (SSN)	☐ (ID)		

2. PATIENT'S NAME (Last Name, First Name, Middle Initial)

3. PATIENT'S BIRTH DATE   MM | DD | YY   SEX   M ☐   F ☐

4. INSURED'S NAME (Last Name, First Name, Middle Initial)

5. PATIENT'S ADDRESS (No. Street)

6. PATIENT RELATIONSHIP TO INSURED   Self ☐   Spouse ☐   Child ☐   Other ☐

7. INSURED'S ADDRESS (No. Street)

CITY   STATE

8. PATIENT STATUS   Single ☐   Married ☐   Other ☐

   Employed ☐   Full-Time Student ☐   Part-Time Student ☐

CITY   STATE

ZIP CODE   TELEPHONE (Include Area Code) ( )

ZIP CODE   TELEPHONE (INCLUDE AREA CODE) ( )

9. OTHER INSURED'S NAME (Last Name, First Name, Middle Initial)

10. IS PATIENT'S CONDITION RELATED TO:

11. INSURED'S POLICY GROUP OR FECA NUMBER

a. OTHER INSURED'S POLICY OR GROUP NUMBER

a. EMPLOYMENT? (CURRENT OR PREVIOUS)   ☐ YES   ☐ NO

a. INSURED'S DATE OF BIRTH   MM | DD | YY   SEX   M ☐   F ☐

b. OTHER INSURED'S DATE OF BIRTH   MM | DD | YY   SEX   M ☐   F ☐

b. AUTO ACCIDENT?   PLACE (State)   ☐ YES   ☐ NO

b. EMPLOYER'S NAME OR SCHOOL NAME

c. EMPLOYER'S NAME OR SCHOOL NAME

c. OTHER ACCIDENT?   ☐ YES   ☐ NO

c. INSURANCE PLAN NAME OR PROGRAM NAME

d. INSURANCE PLAN NAME OR PROGRAM NAME

10d. RESERVED FOR LOCAL USE

d. IS THERE ANOTHER HEALTH BENEFIT PLAN?   ☐ YES   ☐ NO   If yes, return to and complete item 9 a – d.

READ BACK OF FORM BEFORE COMPLETING & SIGNING THIS FORM.

12. PATIENT'S OR AUTHORIZED PERSON'S SIGNATURE I authorize the release of any medical or other information necessary to process this claim. I also request payment of government benefits either to myself or to the party who accepts assignment below.

SIGNED _____ DATE _____

13. INSURED'S OR AUTHORIZED PERSON'S SIGNATURE I authorize payment of medical benefits to the undersigned physician or supplier for services described below.

SIGNED _____

PATIENT AND INSURED INFORMATION

14. DATE OF CURRENT: MM | DD | YY   ILLNESS (First symptom) OR INJURY (Accident) OR PREGNANCY (LMP)

15. IF PATIENT HAS HAD SAME OR SIMILAR ILLNESS, GIVE FIRST DATE   MM | DD | YY

16. DATES PATIENT UNABLE TO WORK IN CURRENT OCCUPATION   MM | DD | YY   FROM   TO   MM | DD | YY

17. NAME OF REFERRING PHYSICIAN OR OTHER SOURCE

17a. I.D. NUMBER OF REFERRING PHYSICIAN

18. HOSPITALIZATION DATES RELATED TO CURRENT SERVICES   MM | DD | YY   FROM   TO   MM | DD | YY

19. RESERVED FOR LOCAL USE

20. OUTSIDE LAB?   ☐ YES   ☐ NO $ CHARGES

21. DIAGNOSIS OR NATURE OF ILLNESS OR INJURY. (RELATE ITEMS 1, 2, 3, OR 4 TO ITEM 24E BY LINE)

1. _____ . _____   3. _____ . _____

2. _____ . _____   4. _____ . _____

22. MEDICAID RESUBMISSION CODE   ORIGINAL REF. NO.

23. PRIOR AUTHORIZATION NUMBER

24. A DATE(S) OF SERVICE						B Place of Service	C Type of Service	D PROCEDURES, SERVICES, OR SUPPLIES (Explain Unusual Circumstances)		E DIAGNOSIS CODE	F $ CHARGES	G DAYS OR UNITS	H EPSDT Family Plan	I EMG	J COB	K RESERVED FOR LOCAL USE
From MM	DD	YY	To MM	DD	YY			CPT/HCPCS	MODIFIER							
1																
2																
3																
4																
5																
6																

25. FEDERAL TAX I.D. NUMBER   SSN ☐   EIN ☐

26. PATIENT'S ACCOUNT NO.

27. ACCEPT ASSIGNMENT? (For govt. claims, see back)   ☐ YES   ☐ NO

28. TOTAL CHARGE $

29. AMOUNT PAID $

30. BALANCE DUE $

31. SIGNATURE OF PHYSICIAN OR SUPPLIER INCLUDING DEGREES OR CREDENTIALS (I certify that the statements on the reverse apply to this bill and are made a part thereof.)

SIGNED _____ DATE _____

32. NAME AND ADDRESS OF FACILITY WHERE SERVICES WERE RENDERED (If other than home or office)

33. PHYSICIAN'S, SUPPLIER'S BILLING NAME, ADDRESS, ZIP CODE & PHONE #

PIN#   GRP#

PHYSICIAN OR SUPPLIER INFORMATION

PLEASE PRINT OR TYPE

SAMPLE FORM 1500
SAMPLE FORM 1500 SAMPLE FORM 1500

DATE	REMARKS				
11/20/XX					

PATIENT			CHART #	SEX	BIRTHDATE
Sharon W. Casey 333-55-7979			15-b	F	10/06/70

MAILING ADDRESS	CITY	STATE	ZIP	HOME PHONE	WORK PHONE
483 Oakdale Avenue	Anywhere	US	12345	(101) 333-5555	

EMPLOYER	ADDRESS	PATIENT STATUS
		X
		MARRIED DIVORCED SINGLE STUDENT OTHER

INSURANCE: PRIMARY	ID#	GROUP	SECONDARY POLICY
Medicaid	22334455		

POLICYHOLDER NAME	BIRTHDATE	RELATIONSHIP	POLICYHOLDER NAME	BIRTHDATE	RELATIONSHIP

SUPPLEMENTAL PLAN	EMPLOYER

POLICYHOLDER NAME	BIRTHDATE	RELATIONSHIP	DIAGNOSIS		CODE
			1. Excessive menstruation		626.2
EMPLOYER			2. Irregular menstrual cycle		626.4
			3.		
REFERRING PHYSICIAN UPIN/SSN			4.		
Donald L. Givings, M.D. DLG1234					

PLACE OF SERVICE   Office

PROCEDURES	CODE	CHARGE
1. Office Consult Level III	99243	$85.00
2.		
3.		
4.		
5.		
6.		

SPECIAL NOTES

TOTAL CHARGES	PAYMENTS	ADJUSTMENTS	BALANCE
$85.00	0	0	$85.00

RETURN VISIT	PHYSICIAN SIGNATURE
One month	*Maria C Section, M.D.*

MEDICARE # M1234
MEDICAID # MCS1234
BCBS # 11223

MARIA C. SECTION, M.D. OB/GYN
11 MADEN LANE, ANYWHERE, US 12345
PHONE NUMBER (101)111-5555

EIN # 11669977
SSN # 444-22-1234
UPIN # MS1234

(SAMPLE ONLY - NOT APPROVED FOR USE)

CARRIER

| | PICA | | **HEALTH INSURANCE CLAIM FORM** | PICA | | |

1. MEDICARE	MEDICAID	CHAMPUS	CHAMPVA	GROUP HEALTH PLAN	FECA BLK LUNG	OTHER	1a. INSURED'S I.D. NUMBER	(FOR PROGRAM IN ITEM 1)
☐ (Medicare #)	☐ (Medicaid #)	☐ (Sponsor's SSN)	☐ (VA File #)	☐ (SSN or ID)	☐ (SSN)	☐ (ID)		

2. PATIENT'S NAME (Last Name, First Name, Middle Initial)

3. PATIENT'S BIRTH DATE MM DD YY SEX M ☐ F ☐

4. INSURED'S NAME (Last Name, First Name, Middle Initial)

5. PATIENT'S ADDRESS (No. Street)

6. PATIENT RELATIONSHIP TO INSURED Self ☐ Spouse ☐ Child ☐ Other ☐

7. INSURED'S ADDRESS (No. Street)

CITY   STATE

8. PATIENT STATUS Single ☐ Married ☐ Other ☐

CITY   STATE

ZIP CODE   TELEPHONE (Include Area Code) (   )

Employed ☐ Full-Time Student ☐ Part-Time Student ☐

ZIP CODE   TELEPHONE (INCLUDE AREA CODE) (   )

9. OTHER INSURED'S NAME (Last Name, First Name, Middle Initial)

10. IS PATIENT'S CONDITION RELATED TO:

11. INSURED'S POLICY GROUP OR FECA NUMBER

a. OTHER INSURED'S POLICY OR GROUP NUMBER

a. EMPLOYMENT? (CURRENT OR PREVIOUS) ☐ YES ☐ NO

a. INSURED'S DATE OF BIRTH MM DD YY SEX M ☐ F ☐

b. OTHER INSURED'S DATE OF BIRTH MM DD YY SEX M ☐ F ☐

b. AUTO ACCIDENT? PLACE (State) ☐ YES ☐ NO

b. EMPLOYER'S NAME OR SCHOOL NAME

c. EMPLOYER'S NAME OR SCHOOL NAME

c. OTHER ACCIDENT? ☐ YES ☐ NO

c. INSURANCE PLAN NAME OR PROGRAM NAME

d. INSURANCE PLAN NAME OR PROGRAM NAME

10d. RESERVED FOR LOCAL USE

d. IS THERE ANOTHER HEALTH BENEFIT PLAN? ☐ YES ☐ NO If yes, return to and complete item 9 a – d.

READ BACK OF FORM BEFORE COMPLETING & SIGNING THIS FORM.
12. PATIENT'S OR AUTHORIZED PERSON'S SIGNATURE I authorize the release of any medical or other information necessary to process this claim. I also request payment of government benefits either to myself or to the party who accepts assignment below.

SIGNED _____ DATE _____

13. INSURED'S OR AUTHORIZED PERSON'S SIGNATURE I authorize payment of medical benefits to the undersigned physician or supplier for services described below.

SIGNED _____

PATIENT AND INSURED INFORMATION

14. DATE OF CURRENT: MM DD YY ◄ ILLNESS (First symptom) OR INJURY (Accident) OR PREGNANCY (LMP)

15. IF PATIENT HAS HAD SAME OR SIMILAR ILLNESS, GIVE FIRST DATE MM DD YY

16. DATES PATIENT UNABLE TO WORK IN CURRENT OCCUPATION MM DD YY FROM TO MM DD YY

17. NAME OF REFERRING PHYSICIAN OR OTHER SOURCE

17a. I.D. NUMBER OF REFERRING PHYSICIAN

18. HOSPITALIZATION DATES RELATED TO CURRENT SERVICES MM DD YY FROM TO MM DD YY

19. RESERVED FOR LOCAL USE

20. OUTSIDE LAB? ☐ YES ☐ NO $ CHARGES

21. DIAGNOSIS OR NATURE OF ILLNESS OR INJURY. (RELATE ITEMS 1, 2, 3, OR 4 TO ITEM 24E BY LINE)

1. |___.___   3. |___.___

2. |___.___   4. |___.___

22. MEDICAID RESUBMISSION CODE   ORIGINAL REF. NO.

23. PRIOR AUTHORIZATION NUMBER

24. A DATE(S) OF SERVICE						B Place of Service	C Type of Service	D PROCEDURES, SERVICES, OR SUPPLIES (Explain Unusual Circumstances) CPT/HCPCS MODIFIER		E DIAGNOSIS CODE	F $ CHARGES	G DAYS OR UNITS	H EPSDT Family Plan	I EMG	J COB	K RESERVED FOR LOCAL USE
From MM	DD	YY	To MM	DD	YY											
1																
2																
3																
4																
5																
6																

25. FEDERAL TAX I.D. NUMBER SSN ☐ EIN ☐

26. PATIENT'S ACCOUNT NO.

27. ACCEPT ASSIGNMENT? (For govt. claims, see back) YES ☐ NO ☐

28. TOTAL CHARGE $

29. AMOUNT PAID $

30. BALANCE DUE $

31. SIGNATURE OF PHYSICIAN OR SUPPLIER INCLUDING DEGREES OR CREDENTIALS (I certify that the statements on the reverse apply to this bill and are made a part thereof.)

SIGNED _____ DATE _____

32. NAME AND ADDRESS OF FACILITY WHERE SERVICES WERE RENDERED (If other than home or office)

33. PHYSICIAN'S, SUPPLIER'S BILLING NAME, ADDRESS, ZIP CODE & PHONE #

PIN#   GRP#

PHYSICIAN OR SUPPLIER INFORMATION

PLEASE PRINT OR TYPE

SAMPLE FORM 1500
SAMPLE FORM 1500 SAMPLE FORM 1500

DATE	REMARKS			
06/19/XX				

PATIENT			CHART #	SEX	BIRTHDATE
Fred R. Jones 384-66-4535			15-c	M	01/05/49

MAILING ADDRESS	CITY	STATE	ZIP	HOME PHONE	WORK PHONE
444 Taylor Avenue	Anywhere	US	12345	(101) 333-5555	

EMPLOYER	ADDRESS	PATIENT STATUS
		X
		MARRIED DIVORCED SINGLE STUDENT OTHER

INSURANCE: PRIMARY	ID#	GROUP	SECONDARY POLICY
Medicaid	55771122		

POLICYHOLDER NAME	BIRTHDATE	RELATIONSHIP	POLICYHOLDER NAME	BIRTHDATE	RELATIONSHIP

SUPPLEMENTAL PLAN	EMPLOYER

POLICYHOLDER NAME	BIRTHDATE	RELATIONSHIP	DIAGNOSIS	CODE
			1. Difficulty in walking	719.70
EMPLOYER			2.	
			3.	
REFERRING PHYSICIAN UPIN/SSN			4.	

PLACE OF SERVICE   Office

PROCEDURES	CODE	CHARGE
1. Est. Pt. OV Level III	99213	$75.00
2.		
3.		
4.		
5.		
6.		

SPECIAL NOTES

Refer patient to a Podiatrist

TOTAL CHARGES	PAYMENTS	ADJUSTMENTS	BALANCE
$75.00	0	0	$75.00

RETURN VISIT	PHYSICIAN SIGNATURE
3 months	Donald L. Givings, M.D.

MEDICARE # D1234 MEDICAID # DLG1234 BCBS # 12345	**DONALD L. GIVINGS, M.D.** 11350 MEDICAL DRIVE, ANYWHERE, US 12345 **PHONE NUMBER (101)111-5555**	EIN # 11123456 SSN # 123-12-1234 UPIN # DG1234 GRP # DG12345

(SAMPLE ONLY - NOT APPROVED FOR USE)

CARRIER

HEALTH INSURANCE CLAIM FORM

PICA [ ] [ ]

[ ] [ ] PICA

1. MEDICARE MEDICAID CHAMPUS CHAMPVA GROUP HEALTH PLAN FECA BLK LUNG OTHER	1a. INSURED'S I.D. NUMBER (FOR PROGRAM IN ITEM 1)

1. MEDICARE [ ] (Medicare #) MEDICAID [ ] (Medicaid #) CHAMPUS [ ] (Sponsor's SSN) CHAMPVA [ ] (VA File #) GROUP HEALTH PLAN [ ] (SSN or ID) FECA BLK LUNG [ ] (SSN) OTHER [ ] (ID) | 1a. INSURED'S I.D. NUMBER   (FOR PROGRAM IN ITEM 1)

2. PATIENT'S NAME (Last Name, First Name, Middle Initial) | 3. PATIENT'S BIRTH DATE MM | DD | YY   SEX M [ ] F [ ] | 4. INSURED'S NAME (Last Name, First Name, Middle Initial)

5. PATIENT'S ADDRESS (No. Street) | 6. PATIENT RELATIONSHIP TO INSURED Self [ ] Spouse [ ] Child [ ] Other [ ] | 7. INSURED'S ADDRESS (No. Street)

CITY ____ STATE ____ | 8. PATIENT STATUS Single [ ] Married [ ] Other [ ] | CITY ____ STATE ____

ZIP CODE ____ TELEPHONE (Include Area Code) ( ) | Employed [ ] Full-Time Student [ ] Part-Time Student [ ] | ZIP CODE ____ TELEPHONE (INCLUDE AREA CODE) ( )

9. OTHER INSURED'S NAME (Last Name, First Name, Middle Initial) | 10. IS PATIENT'S CONDITION RELATED TO: | 11. INSURED'S POLICY GROUP OR FECA NUMBER

a. OTHER INSURED'S POLICY OR GROUP NUMBER | a. EMPLOYMENT? (CURRENT OR PREVIOUS) YES [ ] NO [ ] | a. INSURED'S DATE OF BIRTH MM | DD | YY   SEX M [ ] F [ ]

b. OTHER INSURED'S DATE OF BIRTH MM | DD | YY   SEX M [ ] F [ ] | b. AUTO ACCIDENT? PLACE (State) YES [ ] NO [ ] | b. EMPLOYER'S NAME OR SCHOOL NAME

c. EMPLOYER'S NAME OR SCHOOL NAME | c. OTHER ACCIDENT? YES [ ] NO [ ] | c. INSURANCE PLAN NAME OR PROGRAM NAME

d. INSURANCE PLAN NAME OR PROGRAM NAME | 10d. RESERVED FOR LOCAL USE | d. IS THERE ANOTHER HEALTH BENEFIT PLAN? YES [ ] NO [ ] If yes, return to and complete item 9 a – d.

READ BACK OF FORM BEFORE COMPLETING & SIGNING THIS FORM.
12. PATIENT'S OR AUTHORIZED PERSON'S SIGNATURE I authorize the release of any medical or other information necessary to process this claim. I also request payment of government benefits either to myself or to the party who accepts assignment below.

SIGNED _____ DATE _____

13. INSURED'S OR AUTHORIZED PERSON'S SIGNATURE I authorize payment of medical benefits to the undersigned physician or supplier for services described below.

SIGNED _____

PATIENT AND INSURED INFORMATION

14. DATE OF CURRENT: MM | DD | YY ◄ ILLNESS (First symptom) OR INJURY (Accident) OR PREGNANCY (LMP) | 15. IF PATIENT HAS HAD SAME OR SIMILAR ILLNESS, GIVE FIRST DATE MM | DD | YY | 16. DATES PATIENT UNABLE TO WORK IN CURRENT OCCUPATION MM | DD | YY   FROM _____ TO _____ MM | DD | YY

17. NAME OF REFERRING PHYSICIAN OR OTHER SOURCE | 17a. I.D. NUMBER OF REFERRING PHYSICIAN | 18. HOSPITALIZATION DATES RELATED TO CURRENT SERVICES MM | DD | YY   FROM _____ TO _____ MM | DD | YY

19. RESERVED FOR LOCAL USE | | 20. OUTSIDE LAB? YES [ ] NO [ ] $ CHARGES

21. DIAGNOSIS OR NATURE OF ILLNESS OR INJURY. (RELATE ITEMS 1, 2, 3, OR 4 TO ITEM 24E BY LINE)
1. |___ . ___| 3. |___ . ___|
2. |___ . ___| 4. |___ . ___|

22. MEDICAID RESUBMISSION CODE _____ ORIGINAL REF. NO. _____

23. PRIOR AUTHORIZATION NUMBER

24. A. DATE(S) OF SERVICE		B. Place of Service	C. Type of Service	D. PROCEDURES, SERVICES, OR SUPPLIES (Explain Unusual Circumstances)		E. DIAGNOSIS CODE	F. $ CHARGES	G. DAYS OR UNITS	H. EPSDT Family Plan	I. EMG	J. COB	K. RESERVED FOR LOCAL USE
From MM DD YY	To MM DD YY			CPT/HCPCS	MODIFIER							
1												
2												
3												
4												
5												
6												

| 25. FEDERAL TAX I.D. NUMBER   SSN [ ] EIN [ ] | 26. PATIENT'S ACCOUNT NO. | 27. ACCEPT ASSIGNMENT? (For govt. claims, see back) YES [ ] NO [ ] | 28. TOTAL CHARGE $ | 29. AMOUNT PAID $ | 30. BALANCE DUE $ |

31. SIGNATURE OF PHYSICIAN OR SUPPLIER INCLUDING DEGREES OR CREDENTIALS (I certify that the statements on the reverse apply to this bill and are made a part thereof.)

SIGNED _____ DATE _____

32. NAME AND ADDRESS OF FACILITY WHERE SERVICES WERE RENDERED (If other than home or office)

33. PHYSICIAN'S, SUPPLIER'S BILLING NAME, ADDRESS, ZIP CODE & PHONE #

PIN# _____ GRP# _____

PHYSICIAN OR SUPPLIER INFORMATION

PLEASE PRINT OR TYPE

SAMPLE FORM 1500
SAMPLE FORM 1500 SAMPLE FORM 1500

181

DATE	REMARKS			
06/23/XX				

PATIENT		CHART #	SEX	BIRTHDATE
Fred R. Jones 384-66-4535		15-d	M	01/05/49

MAILING ADDRESS	CITY	STATE	ZIP	HOME PHONE	WORK PHONE
444 Taylor Avenue	Anywhere	US	12345	(101) 333-5555	

EMPLOYER	ADDRESS	PATIENT STATUS
		X
		MARRIED DIVORCED SINGLE STUDENT OTHER

INSURANCE: PRIMARY	ID#	GROUP	SECONDARY POLICY
Medicaid	55771122		

POLICYHOLDER NAME	BIRTHDATE	RELATIONSHIP	POLICYHOLDER NAME	BIRTHDATE	RELATIONSHIP

SUPPLEMENTAL PLAN	EMPLOYER

POLICYHOLDER NAME	BIRTHDATE	RELATIONSHIP	DIAGNOSIS	CODE
			1. Fracture, great toe	826.0
EMPLOYER			2.	
			3.	
REFERRING PHYSICIAN UPIN/SSN			4.	
Donald L. Givings, M.D. DLG1234				

PLACE OF SERVICE   Office

PROCEDURES	CODE	CHARGE
1. Office Consult Level II	99242	$75.00
2. Toe x-ray 2 views	73660	$50.00
3. Closed treatment of fracture, great toe	28490	$65.00
4.		
5.		
6.		

SPECIAL NOTES

TOTAL CHARGES	PAYMENTS	ADJUSTMENTS	BALANCE
$190.00	-0-	-0-	$190.00

RETURN VISIT	PHYSICIAN SIGNATURE
	John F. Walker, D.P.M.

MEDICARE # J2234
MEDICAID # JFW1234
BCBS # 12345

JOHN F. WALKER, D.P.M. PODIATRY
546 FOOTHILL PLACE, ANYWHERE, US 12345
PHONE NUMBER (101)111-5555

EIN # 11993377
SSN # 657-12-4454
UPIN # JW1234
GRP # JW12345

(SAMPLE ONLY - NOT APPROVED FOR USE)

CARRIER

HEALTH INSURANCE CLAIM FORM

PICA ☐☐

☐☐ PICA

1. MEDICARE MEDICAID CHAMPUS CHAMPVA GROUP HEALTH PLAN FECA BLK LUNG OTHER	1a. INSURED'S I.D. NUMBER (FOR PROGRAM IN ITEM 1)

☐ (Medicare #) ☐ (Medicaid #) ☐ (Sponsor's SSN) ☐ (VA File #) ☐ (SSN or ID) ☐ (SSN) ☐ (ID)

2. PATIENT'S NAME (Last Name, First Name, Middle Initial)

3. PATIENT'S BIRTH DATE MM | DD | YY   SEX M ☐ F ☐

4. INSURED'S NAME (Last Name, First Name, Middle Initial)

5. PATIENT'S ADDRESS (No. Street)

6. PATIENT RELATIONSHIP TO INSURED Self ☐ Spouse ☐ Child ☐ Other ☐

7. INSURED'S ADDRESS (No. Street)

CITY   STATE

8. PATIENT STATUS Single ☐ Married ☐ Other ☐ Employed ☐ Full-Time Student ☐ Part-Time Student ☐

CITY   STATE

ZIP CODE   TELEPHONE (Include Area Code) (   )

ZIP CODE   TELEPHONE (INCLUDE AREA CODE) (   )

9. OTHER INSURED'S NAME (Last Name, First Name, Middle Initial)

10. IS PATIENT'S CONDITION RELATED TO:

11. INSURED'S POLICY GROUP OR FECA NUMBER

a. OTHER INSURED'S POLICY OR GROUP NUMBER

a. EMPLOYMENT? (CURRENT OR PREVIOUS) ☐ YES ☐ NO

a. INSURED'S DATE OF BIRTH MM | DD | YY   SEX M ☐ F ☐

b. OTHER INSURED'S DATE OF BIRTH MM | DD | YY   SEX M ☐ F ☐

b. AUTO ACCIDENT?   PLACE (State) ☐ YES ☐ NO

b. EMPLOYER'S NAME OR SCHOOL NAME

c. EMPLOYER'S NAME OR SCHOOL NAME

c. OTHER ACCIDENT? ☐ YES ☐ NO

c. INSURANCE PLAN NAME OR PROGRAM NAME

d. INSURANCE PLAN NAME OR PROGRAM NAME

10d. RESERVED FOR LOCAL USE

d. IS THERE ANOTHER HEALTH BENEFIT PLAN? ☐ YES ☐ NO If yes, return to and complete item 9 a – d.

READ BACK OF FORM BEFORE COMPLETING & SIGNING THIS FORM.

12. PATIENT'S OR AUTHORIZED PERSON'S SIGNATURE I authorize the release of any medical or other information necessary to process this claim. I also request payment of government benefits either to myself or to the party who accepts assignment below.

SIGNED _____ DATE _____

13. INSURED'S OR AUTHORIZED PERSON'S SIGNATURE I authorize payment of medical benefits to the undersigned physician or supplier for services described below.

SIGNED _____

PATIENT AND INSURED INFORMATION

14. DATE OF CURRENT: MM | DD | YY ◄ ILLNESS (First symptom) OR INJURY (Accident) OR PREGNANCY (LMP)

15. IF PATIENT HAS HAD SAME OR SIMILAR ILLNESS, GIVE FIRST DATE MM | DD | YY

16. DATES PATIENT UNABLE TO WORK IN CURRENT OCCUPATION MM | DD | YY   MM | DD | YY FROM   TO

17. NAME OF REFERRING PHYSICIAN OR OTHER SOURCE

17a. I.D. NUMBER OF REFERRING PHYSICIAN

18. HOSPITALIZATION DATES RELATED TO CURRENT SERVICES MM | DD | YY   MM | DD | YY FROM   TO

19. RESERVED FOR LOCAL USE

20. OUTSIDE LAB? ☐ YES ☐ NO $ CHARGES

21. DIAGNOSIS OR NATURE OF ILLNESS OR INJURY. (RELATE ITEMS 1, 2, 3, OR 4 TO ITEM 24E BY LINE)

1. ____ . ____   3. ____ . ____

2. ____ . ____   4. ____ . ____

22. MEDICAID RESUBMISSION CODE   ORIGINAL REF. NO.

23. PRIOR AUTHORIZATION NUMBER

24. A DATE(S) OF SERVICE						B Place of Service	C Type of Service	D PROCEDURES, SERVICES, OR SUPPLIES (Explain Unusual Circumstances) CPT/HCPCS MODIFIER	E DIAGNOSIS CODE	F $ CHARGES	G DAYS OR UNITS	H EPSDT Family Plan	I EMG	J COB	K RESERVED FOR LOCAL USE
From MM	DD	YY	To MM	DD	YY										
1															
2															
3															
4															
5															
6															

25. FEDERAL TAX I.D. NUMBER SSN ☐ EIN ☐

26. PATIENT'S ACCOUNT NO.

27. ACCEPT ASSIGNMENT? (For govt. claims, see back) ☐ YES ☐ NO

28. TOTAL CHARGE $

29. AMOUNT PAID $

30. BALANCE DUE $

31. SIGNATURE OF PHYSICIAN OR SUPPLIER INCLUDING DEGREES OR CREDENTIALS (I certify that the statements on the reverse apply to this bill and are made a part thereof.) SIGNED _____ DATE _____

32. NAME AND ADDRESS OF FACILITY WHERE SERVICES WERE RENDERED (if other than home or office)

33. PHYSICIAN'S, SUPPLIER'S BILLING NAME, ADDRESS, ZIP CODE & PHONE # PIN#   GRP#

PHYSICIAN OR SUPPLIER INFORMATION

PLEASE PRINT OR TYPE

SAMPLE FORM 1500
SAMPLE FORM 1500 SAMPLE FORM 1500

DATE 07/18/XX			REMARKS				

PATIENT				CHART #	SEX	BIRTHDATE	
Richard J. Davis 123-55-7979				15-e	M	03/10/94	

MAILING ADDRESS	CITY	STATE	ZIP	HOME PHONE	WORK PHONE
3764 Ravenwood Ave	Anywhere	US	12345	(101) 333-5555	

EMPLOYER	ADDRESS	PATIENT STATUS
		MARRIED DIVORCED SINGLE STUDENT OTHER

INSURANCE: PRIMARY	ID#	GROUP	SECONDARY POLICY
Medicaid	77557755		

POLICYHOLDER NAME	BIRTHDATE	RELATIONSHIP	POLICYHOLDER NAME	BIRTHDATE	RELATIONSHIP

SUPPLEMENTAL PLAN	EMPLOYER

POLICYHOLDER NAME	BIRTHDATE	RELATIONSHIP	DIAGNOSIS	CODE
			1. Routine child health check	V20.2
EMPLOYER			2.	
			3.	
REFERRING PHYSICIAN UPIN/SSN			4.	

PLACE OF SERVICE   Office

PROCEDURES	CODE	CHARGE
1. Preventive medicine Est. Pt. 5-11 years	99393	$60.00
2. DTaP	90700	$40.00
3. MMR	90707	$55.00
4. OPV	90712	$25.00
5. Immunization administration	90472	$25.00
6.		

SPECIAL NOTES

TOTAL CHARGES	PAYMENTS	ADJUSTMENTS	BALANCE
$205.00	0	0	$205.00

RETURN VISIT	PHYSICIAN SIGNATURE
	Donald L. Givings, M.D.

MEDICARE # D1234
MEDICAID # DLG1234
BCBS # 12345

DONALD L. GIVINGS, M.D.
11350 MEDICAL DRIVE, ANYWHERE, US 12345
PHONE NUMBER (101)111-5555

EIN # 11123456
SSN # 123-12-1234
UPIN # DG1234
GRP # DG12345

PLEASE
DO NOT
STAPLE
IN THIS
AREA

CARRIER

☐☐ PICA

HEALTH INSURANCE CLAIM FORM

PICA ☐☐☐

1. MEDICARE ☐ (Medicare #)	MEDICAID ☐ (Medicaid #)	CHAMPUS ☐ (Sponsor's SSN)	CHAMPVA ☐ (VA File #)	GROUP HEALTH PLAN ☐ (SSN or ID)	FECA BLK LUNG ☐ (SSN)	OTHER ☐ (ID)	1a. INSURED'S I.D. NUMBER (FOR PROGRAM IN ITEM 1)

2. PATIENT'S NAME (Last Name, First Name, Middle Initial)	3. PATIENT'S BIRTH DATE MM ┆ DD ┆ YY SEX M ☐ F ☐	4. INSURED'S NAME (Last Name, First Name, Middle Initial)

5. PATIENT'S ADDRESS (No. Street)	6. PATIENT RELATIONSHIP TO INSURED Self ☐ Spouse ☐ Child ☐ Other ☐	7. INSURED'S ADDRESS (No. Street)

CITY	STATE	8. PATIENT STATUS Single ☐ Married ☐ Other ☐	CITY	STATE

ZIP CODE	TELEPHONE (Include Area Code) ( )	Employed ☐ Full-Time Student ☐ Part-Time Student ☐	ZIP CODE	TELEPHONE (INCLUDE AREA CODE) ( )

9. OTHER INSURED'S NAME (Last Name, First Name, Middle Initial)	10. IS PATIENT'S CONDITION RELATED TO:	11. INSURED'S POLICY GROUP OR FECA NUMBER

a. OTHER INSURED'S POLICY OR GROUP NUMBER	a. EMPLOYMENT? (CURRENT OR PREVIOUS) YES ☐ NO ☐	a. INSURED'S DATE OF BIRTH MM ┆ DD ┆ YY SEX M ☐ F ☐

b. OTHER INSURED'S DATE OF BIRTH MM ┆ DD ┆ YY SEX M ☐ F ☐	b. AUTO ACCIDENT? PLACE (State) YES ☐ NO ☐	b. EMPLOYER'S NAME OR SCHOOL NAME

c. EMPLOYER'S NAME OR SCHOOL NAME	c. OTHER ACCIDENT? YES ☐ NO ☐	c. INSURANCE PLAN NAME OR PROGRAM NAME

d. INSURANCE PLAN NAME OR PROGRAM NAME	10d. RESERVED FOR LOCAL USE	d. IS THERE ANOTHER HEALTH BENEFIT PLAN? YES ☐ NO ☐ If yes, return to and complete item 9 a – d.

READ BACK OF FORM BEFORE COMPLETING & SIGNING THIS FORM.

12. PATIENT'S OR AUTHORIZED PERSON'S SIGNATURE I authorize the release of any medical or other information necessary to process this claim. I also request payment of government benefits either to myself or to the party who accepts assignment below.

SIGNED _____ DATE _____

13. INSURED'S OR AUTHORIZED PERSON'S SIGNATURE I authorize payment of medical benefits to the undersigned physician or supplier for services described below.

SIGNED _____

PATIENT AND INSURED INFORMATION

14. DATE OF CURRENT: MM ┆ DD ┆ YY ◀ ILLNESS (First symptom) OR INJURY (Accident) OR PREGNANCY (LMP)	15. IF PATIENT HAS HAD SAME OR SIMILAR ILLNESS, GIVE FIRST DATE MM ┆ DD ┆ YY	16. DATES PATIENT UNABLE TO WORK IN CURRENT OCCUPATION MM ┆ DD ┆ YY MM ┆ DD ┆ YY FROM TO

17. NAME OF REFERRING PHYSICIAN OR OTHER SOURCE	17a. I.D. NUMBER OF REFERRING PHYSICIAN	18. HOSPITALIZATION DATES RELATED TO CURRENT SERVICES MM ┆ DD ┆ YY MM ┆ DD ┆ YY FROM TO

19. RESERVED FOR LOCAL USE		20. OUTSIDE LAB? $ CHARGES YES ☐ NO ☐

21. DIAGNOSIS OR NATURE OF ILLNESS OR INJURY. (RELATE ITEMS 1, 2, 3, OR 4 TO ITEM 24E BY LINE)

1. ┗___ . ___ 3. ┗___ . ___

2. ┗___ . ___ 4. ┗___ . ___

22. MEDICAID RESUBMISSION CODE   ORIGINAL REF. NO.

23. PRIOR AUTHORIZATION NUMBER

24. A. DATE(S) OF SERVICE						B. Place of Service	C. Type of Service	D. PROCEDURES, SERVICES, OR SUPPLIES (Explain Unusual Circumstances) CPT/HCPCS ┆ MODIFIER	E. DIAGNOSIS CODE	F. $ CHARGES	G. DAYS OR UNITS	H. EPSDT Family Plan	I. EMG	J. COB	K. RESERVED FOR LOCAL USE
From MM	DD	YY	To MM	DD	YY										
1															
2															
3															
4															
5															
6															

25. FEDERAL TAX I.D. NUMBER SSN ☐ EIN ☐	26. PATIENT'S ACCOUNT NO.	27. ACCEPT ASSIGNMENT? (For govt. claims, see back) YES ☐ NO ☐	28. TOTAL CHARGE $	29. AMOUNT PAID $	30. BALANCE DUE $

31. SIGNATURE OF PHYSICIAN OR SUPPLIER INCLUDING DEGREES OR CREDENTIALS (I certify that the statements on the reverse apply to this bill and are made a part thereof.) SIGNED _____ DATE _____	32. NAME AND ADDRESS OF FACILITY WHERE SERVICES WERE RENDERED (If other than home or office)	33. PHYSICIAN'S, SUPPLIER'S BILLING NAME, ADDRESS, ZIP CODE & PHONE # PIN# _____ GRP# _____

PHYSICIAN OR SUPPLIER INFORMATION

(SAMPLE ONLY - NOT APPROVED FOR USE)

PLEASE PRINT OR TYPE

SAMPLE FORM 1500
SAMPLE FORM 1500 SAMPLE FORM 1500

185

DATE	REMARKS				
09/17/XX					

PATIENT			CHART #	SEX	BIRTHDATE
Dolores Giovanni 234-56-7891			15-f	F	10/22/66

MAILING ADDRESS	CITY	STATE	ZIP	HOME PHONE	WORK PHONE
384 Beverly Avenue	Anywhere	US	12345	(101) 333-5555	

EMPLOYER	ADDRESS	PATIENT STATUS
		X
		MARRIED DIVORCED SINGLE STUDENT OTHER

INSURANCE: PRIMARY	ID#	GROUP	SECONDARY POLICY
Medicare	88776655		

POLICYHOLDER NAME	BIRTHDATE	RELATIONSHIP	POLICYHOLDER NAME	BIRTHDATE	RELATIONSHIP

SUPPLEMENTAL PLAN	EMPLOYER

POLICYHOLDER NAME	BIRTHDATE	RELATIONSHIP	DIAGNOSIS	CODE
			1. E. coli, unspecified	008.00
EMPLOYER			2.	
			3.	
REFERRING PHYSICIAN UPIN/SSN			4.	

PLACE OF SERVICE   Mercy Hospital, Anywhere St., Anywhere, US 12345, Medicaid PIN# MHS2244

PROCEDURES	CODE	CHARGE
1. Initial Hosp. Level IV 09/13/XX	99224	$175.00
2. Subsq. Hosp. Level III 09/14/XX, 09/15/XX, 09/16/XX	99233	Each @ $85.00
3. Hosp. Discharge more than 30 min. 09/17/XX	99239	$100.00
4.		
5.		
6.		

SPECIAL NOTES

TOTAL CHARGES	PAYMENTS	ADJUSTMENTS	BALANCE
$530.00	-0-	-0-	$530.00

RETURN VISIT	PHYSICIAN SIGNATURE
	Donald L. Givings, M.D.

MEDICARE # D1234	**DONALD L. GIVINGS, M.D.**	EIN # 11-123456
MEDICAID # DLG1234	**11350 MEDICAL DRIVE, ANYWHERE, US 12345**	SSN # 123-12-1234
BCBS # 12345	**PHONE NUMBER (101)111-5555**	UPIN # DG1234
		GRP # DG12345

(SAMPLE ONLY - NOT APPROVED FOR USE)

CARRIER

HEALTH INSURANCE CLAIM FORM

PICA [ ] [ ]   PICA [ ] [ ]

1. MEDICARE	MEDICAID	CHAMPUS	CHAMPVA	GROUP HEALTH PLAN	FECA BLK LUNG	OTHER	1a. INSURED'S I.D. NUMBER	(FOR PROGRAM IN ITEM 1)
[ ] (Medicare #)	[ ] (Medicaid #)	[ ] (Sponsor's SSN)	[ ] (VA File #)	[ ] (SSN or ID)	[ ] (SSN)	[ ] (ID)		

2. PATIENT'S NAME (Last Name, First Name, Middle Initial)

3. PATIENT'S BIRTH DATE MM | DD | YY   SEX M [ ]   F [ ]

4. INSURED'S NAME (Last Name, First Name, Middle Initial)

5. PATIENT'S ADDRESS (No. Street)

6. PATIENT RELATIONSHIP TO INSURED Self [ ] Spouse [ ] Child [ ] Other [ ]

7. INSURED'S ADDRESS (No. Street)

CITY   STATE

8. PATIENT STATUS Single [ ] Married [ ] Other [ ]   Employed [ ] Full-Time Student [ ] Part-Time Student [ ]

CITY   STATE

ZIP CODE   TELEPHONE (Include Area Code) (   )

ZIP CODE   TELEPHONE (INCLUDE AREA CODE) (   )

9. OTHER INSURED'S NAME (Last Name, First Name, Middle Initial)

10. IS PATIENT'S CONDITION RELATED TO:

11. INSURED'S POLICY GROUP OR FECA NUMBER

a. OTHER INSURED'S POLICY OR GROUP NUMBER

a. EMPLOYMENT? (CURRENT OR PREVIOUS) [ ] YES [ ] NO

a. INSURED'S DATE OF BIRTH MM | DD | YY   SEX M [ ] F [ ]

b. OTHER INSURED'S DATE OF BIRTH MM | DD | YY   SEX M [ ] F [ ]

b. AUTO ACCIDENT?   PLACE (State) [ ] YES [ ] NO

b. EMPLOYER'S NAME OR SCHOOL NAME

c. EMPLOYER'S NAME OR SCHOOL NAME

c. OTHER ACCIDENT? [ ] YES [ ] NO

c. INSURANCE PLAN NAME OR PROGRAM NAME

d. INSURANCE PLAN NAME OR PROGRAM NAME

10d. RESERVED FOR LOCAL USE

d. IS THERE ANOTHER HEALTH BENEFIT PLAN? [ ] YES [ ] NO   If yes, return to and complete item 9 a – d.

READ BACK OF FORM BEFORE COMPLETING & SIGNING THIS FORM.
12. PATIENT'S OR AUTHORIZED PERSON'S SIGNATURE I authorize the release of any medical or other information necessary to process this claim. I also request payment of government benefits either to myself or to the party who accepts assignment below.

SIGNED _____ DATE _____

13. INSURED'S OR AUTHORIZED PERSON'S SIGNATURE I authorize payment of medical benefits to the undersigned physician or supplier for services described below.

SIGNED _____

PATIENT AND INSURED INFORMATION

14. DATE OF CURRENT: MM | DD | YY   ILLNESS (First symptom) OR INJURY (Accident) OR PREGNANCY (LMP)

15. IF PATIENT HAS HAD SAME OR SIMILAR ILLNESS, GIVE FIRST DATE MM | DD | YY

16. DATES PATIENT UNABLE TO WORK IN CURRENT OCCUPATION MM | DD | YY FROM   TO   MM | DD | YY

17. NAME OF REFERRING PHYSICIAN OR OTHER SOURCE

17a. I.D. NUMBER OF REFERRING PHYSICIAN

18. HOSPITALIZATION DATES RELATED TO CURRENT SERVICES MM | DD | YY FROM   TO   MM | DD | YY

19. RESERVED FOR LOCAL USE

20. OUTSIDE LAB? [ ] YES [ ] NO $ CHARGES

21. DIAGNOSIS OR NATURE OF ILLNESS OR INJURY. (RELATE ITEMS 1, 2, 3, OR 4 TO ITEM 24E BY LINE)

1. |___.___|
2. |___.___|
3. |___.___|
4. |___.___|

22. MEDICAID RESUBMISSION CODE   ORIGINAL REF. NO.

23. PRIOR AUTHORIZATION NUMBER

24. A. DATE(S) OF SERVICE						B. Place of Service	C. Type of Service	D. PROCEDURES, SERVICES, OR SUPPLIES (Explain Unusual Circumstances)		E. DIAGNOSIS CODE	F. $ CHARGES	G. DAYS OR UNITS	H. EPSDT Family Plan	I. EMG	J. COB	K. RESERVED FOR LOCAL USE
From MM	DD	YY	To MM	DD	YY			CPT/HCPCS	MODIFIER							
1																
2																
3																
4																
5																
6																

25. FEDERAL TAX I.D. NUMBER   SSN [ ] EIN [ ]

26. PATIENT'S ACCOUNT NO.

27. ACCEPT ASSIGNMENT? (For govt. claims, see back) [ ] YES [ ] NO

28. TOTAL CHARGE $

29. AMOUNT PAID $

30. BALANCE DUE $

31. SIGNATURE OF PHYSICIAN OR SUPPLIER INCLUDING DEGREES OR CREDENTIALS (I certify that the statements on the reverse apply to this bill and are made a part thereof.)

SIGNED _____ DATE _____

32. NAME AND ADDRESS OF FACILITY WHERE SERVICES WERE RENDERED (If other than home or office)

33. PHYSICIAN'S, SUPPLIER'S BILLING NAME, ADDRESS, ZIP CODE & PHONE #

PIN#   GRP#

PHYSICIAN OR SUPPLIER INFORMATION

(SAMPLE ONLY - NOT APPROVED FOR USE)

PLEASE PRINT OR TYPE

SAMPLE FORM 1500
SAMPLE FORM 1500 SAMPLE FORM 1500

TRICARE/ CHAMPUS

TRICARE OVERVIEW

1. List four medical treatment plans from which active duty and retired beneficiaries can choose.

   a. _____

   b. _____

   c. _____

   d. _____

2. Match the insurance terms in the first column with the definitions in the second column. Write the correct letter in each blank.

   _____ TRICARE Prime   a. PPO-type program

   _____ TRICARE Extra   b. replaces old CHAMPUS

   _____ TRICARE Standard   c. policyholder

   _____ TRICARE Sponsor   d. full-service HMO

3. Which TRICARE plan will automatically enroll all active-duty personnel? _____

4. Active-duty dependents who enroll in the TRICARE Prime program are charged a ___. (Circle the correct answer.)

   a. deductible

   b. copayment

   c. premium

   d. all of the above

5. TRICARE-eligible dependents electing TRICARE Prime must agree to remain in the program for at least ___. (Circle the correct answer.)

   a. 12 months

   b. 18 months

   c. 9 months

   d. 6 months

6. All beneficiaries in TRICARE Prime are required to obtain a _____ _____ _____ who will maintain their medical records and authorize all specialty care.

7. If a TRICARE Prime beneficiary needs to see a specialist what must he/she obtain from their primary care manager? _____

8. If a TRICARE Prime beneficiary elects to seek nonemergency care from an out-of-network provider without PCM authorization, what option can he/she exercise and what result will this have on the beneficiary? _____

_____

9. If a TRICARE Prime patient goes to the nearest hospital in an emergency situation, what must he/she do within 24 hours? _____

10. What are the advantages to TRICARE Extra patients who elect to use a network provider?

_____

_____

11. Is the Point-of-Service option available for TRICARE Extra beneficiaries? _____

12. Which TRICARE option is simply a name change for the regular CHAMPUS program?

_____

13. Which TRICARE option gives beneficiaries the most freedom to choose their health care provider?

_____

14. Briefly define the following terms.
    a. TRICARE Sponsor   _____
    b. TRICARE Service Center _____
    c. Health Care Finders   _____
    d. TRICARE Management Activity _____

TRICARE ELIGIBILITY

15. Indicate whether the following patients are eligible for the TRICARE program by placing **Y** for yes or **N** for no on the line provided.

    _____ a. The 22-year-old unmarried daughter of an active duty military person who is not a full-time student

    _____ b. The wife of a retired person in the uniformed service

    _____ c. A 21-year-old disabled child of an active duty person who requires continuous hospitalization

    _____ d. The widow of an active duty person who has married someone who is not in the service

    _____ e. A preadoptive child living with active duty personnel who has not been granted custody

16. What system must all TRICARE-eligible persons be enrolled in?

_____

TRICARE PREAUTHORIZATION

17. If a TRICARE patient were in need of a cystoscopy, would this procedure require authorization?

    _____

18. When a particular health care service cannot be performed at a military treatment facility, the required preauthorization takes the form of a _____ _____ .

Critical Thinking

19. Write a paragraph describing a situation that would be considered to be a medical emergency by TRICARE.

    _____

    _____

    _____

    _____

20. Write a paragraph describing a situation that TRICARE would consider to be an urgent medical problem.

    _____

    _____

    _____

    _____

COVERED SERVICES

21. On the line provided, indicate whether the following procedures are covered by TRICARE.

    _____ a. Mental health and substance abuse

    _____ b. Acupuncture

    _____ c. Mail-order prescriptions

    _____ d. Over-the-counter drugs

    _____ e. Domiciliary or custodial care

    _____ f. Hospice care

    _____ g. Breast augmentation

    _____ h. Sterilization reversals

    _____ i. Catastrophic coverage

    _____ j. Experimental procedures

TRICARE AS A SECONDARY PAYOR

22. Briefly describe when TRICARE is used as a secondary payor. _____

    _____

TRICARE LIMITING CHARGES

23. All TRICARE nonPAR providers are subject to a _____ _____ of fifteen percent above the TRICARE Fee Schedule for PAR providers.

24. List two exceptions to the fifteen percent limiting charge.

    a. _____

    b. _____

TRICARE BILLING INFORMATION

25. When sending claims to the TRICARE carrier, be sure to use both the _____ _____ _____ number and its associated zip code.

26. TRICARE is based in ___. (Circle the correct answer.)

    a. California

    b. Colorado

    c. New York

    d. None of the above

27. Changes in general benefits are enacted by ___. (Circle the correct answer.)

    a. HCFA

    b. the military

    c. the United States Congress

    d. none of the above

28. The form used to file a TRICARE claim is ___. (Circle the correct answer.)

    a. HCFA-1450

    b. HCFA-1500

    c. different for each catchment area

    d. any of the above

29. For mental health cases, a TRICARE treatment report must be filed with a claim for more than ___ outpatient visits in any calendar year. (Circle the correct answer.)

    a. 25

    b. 30

    c. 45

    d. none of the above

30. Claims will be denied if they are filed more than ___ months after the date of service for outpatient care. (Circle the correct answer.)

    a. 6

    b. 9

    c. 12

    d. 18

31. Which of the following TRICARE plans require payment of a premium? (Circle the correct answer.)

    a. TRICARE Prime

    b. TRICARE Standard

    c. TRICARE Extra

    d. all of the above

32. All deductibles are applied in the government's fiscal year which runs from ___. (Circle the correct answer.)

    a. July 1 of one year to June 30 of the next

    b. October 1 of one year to September 30 of the next

    c. January 1 to December 31 of the same year

Critical Thinking

33. Write a paragraph describing the **Good Faith Policy**.

    _____

    _____

    _____

34. If a TRICARE patient is being transferred within six months, should yes or no be checked in Block 27 of the HCFA-1500 form? _____ Why? _____

    _____

35. What words should be written across the top of the claim form when filing services that fall under the special handicap benefits? _____

36. What words should be written on the envelope when filing services for hospice care?

    _____

37. If a TRICARE claim has been filed with no response for 45 days, who should be contacted?

    _____

Know Your Acronyms

38. Define the following acronyms:

    a. PCM   _____

    b. POS   _____

    c. TSC   _____

    d. HCF   _____

    e. TMA   _____

    f. DEERS _____

    g. MTF   _____

    h. NAS   _____

    i. TC   _____

EXERCISES

....

1. Complete Case Studies 16-a through 16-e using the blank claim form provided. Follow the step-by-step instructions in the textbook to properly complete the claim form. If a patient has a secondary carrier, complete an additional claim form using secondary directions in the textbook. You may choose to use a pencil so corrections can be made.

Case Study 16-a

DATE 11/05/XX	REMARKS Duty Station Address 111 Army Base, Aberdeen MD 21040			
PATIENT Jeffrey D. Heem 234-55-6789		CHART # 16-a	SEX M	BIRTHDATE 05/05/64

MAILING ADDRESS 333 Heavenly Place	CITY Anywhere	STATE US	ZIP 12345	HOME PHONE (101) 333-5555	WORK PHONE

EMPLOYER US Army	ADDRESS See Remarks	PATIENT STATUS X MARRIED DIVORCED SINGLE STUDENT OTHER

INSURANCE: PRIMARY TRICARE Standard	ID# 234-55-6789	GROUP	SECONDARY POLICY

POLICYHOLDER NAME	BIRTHDATE	RELATIONSHIP Self	POLICYHOLDER NAME	BIRTHDATE	RELATIONSHIP

SUPPLEMENTAL PLAN	EMPLOYER

POLICYHOLDER NAME	BIRTHDATE	RELATIONSHIP	DIAGNOSIS	CODE
			1. Acute sinusitis, frontal	461.1
EMPLOYER			2. Sore throat	784.1
			3.	
REFERRING PHYSICIAN UPIN/SSN			4.	

PLACE OF SERVICE   Office

PROCEDURES	CODE	CHARGE
1. New Pt. OV Level II	99202	$70.00
2.		
3.		
4.		
5.		
6.		

SPECIAL NOTES

TOTAL CHARGES $70.00	PAYMENTS -0-	ADJUSTMENTS -0-	BALANCE $70.00

RETURN VISIT	PHYSICIAN SIGNATURE *Donald L. Givings, M.D.*

MEDICARE # D1234 MEDICAID # DLG1234 BCBS # 12345	DONALD L. GIVINGS, M.D. 11350 MEDICAL DRIVE, ANYWHERE, US 12345 PHONE NUMBER (101)111-5555	EIN # 11123456 SSN # 123-12-1234 UPIN # DG1234 GRP # DG12345

(SAMPLE ONLY - NOT APPROVED FOR USE)

CARRIER

| | PICA | | | **HEALTH INSURANCE CLAIM FORM** | PICA | | |

| 1. MEDICARE ☐ (Medicare #) | MEDICAID ☐ (Medicaid #) | CHAMPUS ☐ (Sponsor's SSN) | CHAMPVA ☐ (VA File #) | GROUP HEALTH PLAN ☐ (SSN or ID) | FECA BLK LUNG ☐ (SSN) | OTHER ☐ (ID) | 1a. INSURED'S I.D. NUMBER (FOR PROGRAM IN ITEM 1) |

2. PATIENT'S NAME (Last Name, First Name, Middle Initial)

3. PATIENT'S BIRTH DATE MM ╎ DD ╎ YY   SEX   M ☐   F ☐

4. INSURED'S NAME (Last Name, First Name, Middle Initial)

5. PATIENT'S ADDRESS (No. Street)

6. PATIENT RELATIONSHIP TO INSURED   Self ☐   Spouse ☐   Child ☐   Other ☐

7. INSURED'S ADDRESS (No. Street)

CITY   STATE

8. PATIENT STATUS   Single ☐   Married ☐   Other ☐
Employed ☐   Full-Time Student ☐   Part-Time Student ☐

CITY   STATE

ZIP CODE   TELEPHONE (Include Area Code) (   )

ZIP CODE   TELEPHONE (INCLUDE AREA CODE) (   )

9. OTHER INSURED'S NAME (Last Name, First Name, Middle Initial)

10. IS PATIENT'S CONDITION RELATED TO:

11. INSURED'S POLICY GROUP OR FECA NUMBER

a. OTHER INSURED'S POLICY OR GROUP NUMBER

a. EMPLOYMENT? (CURRENT OR PREVIOUS)   YES ☐   NO ☐

a. INSURED'S DATE OF BIRTH MM ╎ DD ╎ YY   SEX   M ☐   F ☐

b. OTHER INSURED'S DATE OF BIRTH MM ╎ DD ╎ YY   SEX   M ☐   F ☐

b. AUTO ACCIDENT?   PLACE (State)   YES ☐   NO ☐

b. EMPLOYER'S NAME OR SCHOOL NAME

c. EMPLOYER'S NAME OR SCHOOL NAME

c. OTHER ACCIDENT?   YES ☐   NO ☐

c. INSURANCE PLAN NAME OR PROGRAM NAME

d. INSURANCE PLAN NAME OR PROGRAM NAME

10d. RESERVED FOR LOCAL USE

d. IS THERE ANOTHER HEALTH BENEFIT PLAN?   YES ☐   NO ☐   If yes, return to and complete item 9 a – d.

READ BACK OF FORM BEFORE COMPLETING & SIGNING THIS FORM.
12. PATIENT'S OR AUTHORIZED PERSON'S SIGNATURE I authorize the release of any medical or other information necessary to process this claim. I also request payment of government benefits either to myself or to the party who accepts assignment below.

SIGNED _____   DATE _____

13. INSURED'S OR AUTHORIZED PERSON'S SIGNATURE I authorize payment of medical benefits to the undersigned physician or supplier for services described below.

SIGNED _____

PATIENT AND INSURED INFORMATION

14. DATE OF CURRENT: MM ╎ DD ╎ YY ◄ ILLNESS (First symptom) OR INJURY (Accident) OR PREGNANCY (LMP)

15. IF PATIENT HAS HAD SAME OR SIMILAR ILLNESS, GIVE FIRST DATE MM ╎ DD ╎ YY

16. DATES PATIENT UNABLE TO WORK IN CURRENT OCCUPATION MM ╎ DD ╎ YY   FROM   TO   MM ╎ DD ╎ YY

17. NAME OF REFERRING PHYSICIAN OR OTHER SOURCE

17a. I.D. NUMBER OF REFERRING PHYSICIAN

18. HOSPITALIZATION DATES RELATED TO CURRENT SERVICES MM ╎ DD ╎ YY   FROM   TO   MM ╎ DD ╎ YY

19. RESERVED FOR LOCAL USE

20. OUTSIDE LAB? $ CHARGES   YES ☐   NO ☐

21. DIAGNOSIS OR NATURE OF ILLNESS OR INJURY. (RELATE ITEMS 1, 2, 3, OR 4 TO ITEM 24E BY LINE)
1. ∟____.____   3. ∟____.____
2. ∟____.____   4. ∟____.____

22. MEDICAID RESUBMISSION CODE   ORIGINAL REF. NO.

23. PRIOR AUTHORIZATION NUMBER

24. A DATE(S) OF SERVICE						B Place of Service	C Type of Service	D PROCEDURES, SERVICES, OR SUPPLIES (Explain Unusual Circumstances)		E DIAGNOSIS CODE	F $ CHARGES	G DAYS OR UNITS	H EPSDT Family Plan	I EMG	J COB	K RESERVED FOR LOCAL USE
From MM	DD	YY	To MM	DD	YY			CPT/HCPCS	MODIFIER							
1																
2																
3																
4																
5																
6																

25. FEDERAL TAX I.D. NUMBER   SSN ☐   EIN ☐

26. PATIENT'S ACCOUNT NO.

27. ACCEPT ASSIGNMENT? (For govt. claims, see back)   YES ☐   NO ☐

28. TOTAL CHARGE $

29. AMOUNT PAID $

30. BALANCE DUE $

31. SIGNATURE OF PHYSICIAN OR SUPPLIER INCLUDING DEGREES OR CREDENTIALS (I certify that the statements on the reverse apply to this bill and are made a part thereof.)

SIGNED _____   DATE _____

32. NAME AND ADDRESS OF FACILITY WHERE SERVICES WERE RENDERED (If other than home or office)

33. PHYSICIAN'S, SUPPLIER'S BILLING NAME, ADDRESS, ZIP CODE & PHONE #

PIN#   GRP#

PHYSICIAN OR SUPPLIER INFORMATION

(SAMPLE ONLY - NOT APPROVED FOR USE)   *PLEASE PRINT OR TYPE*   SAMPLE FORM 1500
SAMPLE FORM 1500 SAMPLE FORM 1500

DATE	REMARKS			
06/22/XX	Duty Station Address Dept. 21 Naval Station, Anywhere US 23456			

PATIENT		CHART #	SEX	BIRTHDATE
Dana S. Bright	456-77-2345	16-b	F	07/05/71

MAILING ADDRESS	CITY	STATE	ZIP	HOME PHONE	WORK PHONE
28 Upton Circle	Anywhere	US	12345	(101) 333-5555	

EMPLOYER	ADDRESS	PATIENT STATUS
		X MARRIED DIVORCED SINGLE STUDENT OTHER

INSURANCE: PRIMARY	ID#	GROUP	SECONDARY POLICY
TRICARE Extra	567-56-5757		

POLICYHOLDER NAME	BIRTHDATE	RELATIONSHIP	POLICYHOLDER NAME	BIRTHDATE	RELATIONSHIP
Ron L. Bright	8/12/70	Spouse			

SUPPLEMENTAL PLAN	EMPLOYER

POLICYHOLDER NAME	BIRTHDATE	RELATIONSHIP	DIAGNOSIS	CODE
			1. Chronic cholecystitis	575.11

EMPLOYER	
US Navy (See duty address in remarks)	2.

REFERRING PHYSICIAN UPIN/SSN	3.
	4.

PLACE OF SERVICE	Office

PROCEDURES	CODE	CHARGE
1. Est. Pt. Level IV	99214	$85.00
2.		
3.		
4.		
5.		
6.		

SPECIAL NOTES
Refer patient to Dr. Kutter

TOTAL CHARGES	PAYMENTS	ADJUSTMENTS	BALANCE
$85.00	0	0	$85.00

RETURN VISIT	PHYSICIAN SIGNATURE
	Donald L. Givings, M.D.

	DONALD L. GIVINGS, M.D.	EIN # 11123456
MEDICARE # D1234	11350 MEDICAL DRIVE, ANYWHERE, US 12345	SSN # 123-12-1234
MEDICAID # DLG1234	PHONE NUMBER (101)111-5555	UPIN # DG1234
BCBS # 12345		GRP # DG12345

PLEASE
DO NOT
STAPLE
IN THIS
AREA

CARRIER

[ ] [ ] PICA

HEALTH INSURANCE CLAIM FORM

PICA [ ] [ ]

1.	MEDICARE	MEDICAID	CHAMPUS	CHAMPVA	GROUP HEALTH PLAN	FECA BLK LUNG	OTHER	1a. INSURED'S I.D. NUMBER	(FOR PROGRAM IN ITEM 1)
	(Medicare #)	(Medicaid #)	(Sponsor's SSN)	(VA File #)	(SSN or ID)	(SSN)	(ID)		

2. PATIENT'S NAME (Last Name, First Name, Middle Initial)

3. PATIENT'S BIRTH DATE MM | DD | YY   SEX M [ ] F [ ]

4. INSURED'S NAME (Last Name, First Name, Middle Initial)

5. PATIENT'S ADDRESS (No. Street)

6. PATIENT RELATIONSHIP TO INSURED
Self [ ] Spouse [ ] Child [ ] Other [ ]

7. INSURED'S ADDRESS (No. Street)

CITY   STATE

8. PATIENT STATUS
Single [ ] Married [ ] Other [ ]
Employed [ ] Full-Time Student [ ] Part-Time Student [ ]

CITY   STATE

ZIP CODE   TELEPHONE (Include Area Code) (   )

ZIP CODE   TELEPHONE (INCLUDE AREA CODE) (   )

9. OTHER INSURED'S NAME (Last Name, First Name, Middle Initial)

10. IS PATIENT'S CONDITION RELATED TO:

11. INSURED'S POLICY GROUP OR FECA NUMBER

a. OTHER INSURED'S POLICY OR GROUP NUMBER

a. EMPLOYMENT? (CURRENT OR PREVIOUS)
[ ] YES [ ] NO

a. INSURED'S DATE OF BIRTH MM | DD | YY   SEX M [ ] F [ ]

b. OTHER INSURED'S DATE OF BIRTH MM | DD | YY   SEX M [ ] F [ ]

b. AUTO ACCIDENT?   PLACE (State)
[ ] YES [ ] NO

b. EMPLOYER'S NAME OR SCHOOL NAME

c. EMPLOYER'S NAME OR SCHOOL NAME

c. OTHER ACCIDENT?
[ ] YES [ ] NO

c. INSURANCE PLAN NAME OR PROGRAM NAME

d. INSURANCE PLAN NAME OR PROGRAM NAME

10d. RESERVED FOR LOCAL USE

d. IS THERE ANOTHER HEALTH BENEFIT PLAN?
[ ] YES [ ] NO If yes, return to and complete item 9 a – d.

READ BACK OF FORM BEFORE COMPLETING & SIGNING THIS FORM.
12. PATIENT'S OR AUTHORIZED PERSON'S SIGNATURE I authorize the release of any medical or other information necessary to process this claim. I also request payment of government benefits either to myself or to the party who accepts assignment below.

SIGNED _____ DATE _____

13. INSURED'S OR AUTHORIZED PERSON'S SIGNATURE I authorize payment of medical benefits to the undersigned physician or supplier for services described below.

SIGNED _____

PATIENT AND INSURED INFORMATION

14. DATE OF CURRENT: ILLNESS (First symptom) OR INJURY (Accident) OR PREGNANCY (LMP) MM | DD | YY

15. IF PATIENT HAS HAD SAME OR SIMILAR ILLNESS, GIVE FIRST DATE MM | DD | YY

16. DATES PATIENT UNABLE TO WORK IN CURRENT OCCUPATION MM | DD | YY FROM   TO MM | DD | YY

17. NAME OF REFERRING PHYSICIAN OR OTHER SOURCE

17a. I.D. NUMBER OF REFERRING PHYSICIAN

18. HOSPITALIZATION DATES RELATED TO CURRENT SERVICES MM | DD | YY FROM   TO MM | DD | YY

19. RESERVED FOR LOCAL USE

20. OUTSIDE LAB? [ ] YES [ ] NO $ CHARGES

21. DIAGNOSIS OR NATURE OF ILLNESS OR INJURY. (RELATE ITEMS 1, 2, 3, OR 4 TO ITEM 24E BY LINE)
1. _____ . _____
2. _____ . _____
3. _____ . _____
4. _____ . _____

22. MEDICAID RESUBMISSION CODE   ORIGINAL REF. NO.

23. PRIOR AUTHORIZATION NUMBER

24. A DATE(S) OF SERVICE						B Place of Service	C Type of Service	D PROCEDURES, SERVICES, OR SUPPLIES (Explain Unusual Circumstances) CPT/HCPCS MODIFIER	E DIAGNOSIS CODE	F $ CHARGES	G DAYS OR UNITS	H EPSDT Family Plan	I EMG	J COB	K RESERVED FOR LOCAL USE
From MM	DD	YY	To MM	DD	YY											
1															
2															
3															
4															
5															
6															

25. FEDERAL TAX I.D. NUMBER SSN [ ] EIN [ ]

26. PATIENT'S ACCOUNT NO.

27. ACCEPT ASSIGNMENT? (For govt. claims, see back) [ ] YES [ ] NO

28. TOTAL CHARGE $

29. AMOUNT PAID $

30. BALANCE DUE $

31. SIGNATURE OF PHYSICIAN OR SUPPLIER INCLUDING DEGREES OR CREDENTIALS (I certify that the statements on the reverse apply to this bill and are made a part thereof.)

SIGNED _____ DATE _____

32. NAME AND ADDRESS OF FACILITY WHERE SERVICES WERE RENDERED (If other than home or office)

33. PHYSICIAN'S, SUPPLIER'S BILLING NAME, ADDRESS, ZIP CODE & PHONE #

PIN#   GRP#

PHYSICIAN OR SUPPLIER INFORMATION

PLEASE PRINT OR TYPE

SAMPLE FORM 1500
SAMPLE FORM 1500 SAMPLE FORM 1500

197

DATE	REMARKS			
06/29/XX	Duty Station Address Dept. 21 Naval Station, Anywhere US 23456			

PATIENT		CHART #	SEX	BIRTHDATE
Dana S. Bright 456-77-2345		16-c	F	07/05/71

MAILING ADDRESS	CITY	STATE	ZIP	HOME PHONE	WORK PHONE
28 Upton Circle	Anywhere	US	12345	(101) 333-5555	

EMPLOYER	ADDRESS	PATIENT STATUS
		X MARRIED DIVORCED SINGLE STUDENT OTHER

INSURANCE: PRIMARY	ID#	GROUP	SECONDARY POLICY
TRICARE Extra	567-56-5757		

POLICYHOLDER NAME	BIRTHDATE	RELATIONSHIP	POLICYHOLDER NAME	BIRTHDATE	RELATIONSHIP
Ron L. Bright	8/12/70	Spouse			

SUPPLEMENTAL PLAN	EMPLOYER

POLICYHOLDER NAME	BIRTHDATE	RELATIONSHIP	DIAGNOSIS	CODE
			1. Chronic cholecystitis	575.11
EMPLOYER			2.	
US Navy (See duty address in remarks)			3.	
REFERRING PHYSICIAN UPIN/SSN			4.	
Donald L. Givings, M.D. 11-123456				

PLACE OF SERVICE Mercy Hospital, Anywhere St., Anywhere, US 12345 (Outpatient)		
PROCEDURES	CODE	CHARGE
1. Laparoscopic cholecystectomy 6/29/XX	56340	$2,300.00
2.		
3.		
4.		
5.		
6.		

SPECIAL NOTES
Send a letter to Dr. Givings thanking him for this referral

TOTAL CHARGES	PAYMENTS	ADJUSTMENTS	BALANCE
$2,300.00	-0-	-0-	$2,300.00

RETURN VISIT	PHYSICIAN SIGNATURE
	Jonathan B. Kutter, M.D.

MEDICARE # J1234 MEDICAID # JBK1234 BCBS # 12885	JONATHAN B. KUTTER, M.D. SURGEON 339 WOODLAND PLACE, ANYWHERE, US 12345 PHONE NUMBER (101)111-5555	EIN # 11556677 SSN # 245-12-1234 UPIN # JK1234 GRP # JK12345

(SAMPLE ONLY - NOT APPROVED FOR USE)

CARRIER

HEALTH INSURANCE CLAIM FORM

PICA [ ] [ ]   PICA [ ] [ ]

1. MEDICARE MEDICAID CHAMPUS CHAMPVA GROUP HEALTH PLAN FECA BLK LUNG OTHER	1a. INSURED'S I.D. NUMBER (FOR PROGRAM IN ITEM 1)

[ ] (Medicare #)   [ ] (Medicaid #)   [ ] (Sponsor's SSN)   [ ] (VA File #)   [ ] (SSN or ID)   [ ] (SSN)   [ ] (ID)

2. PATIENT'S NAME (Last Name, First Name, Middle Initial)

3. PATIENT'S BIRTH DATE   MM | DD | YY   SEX   M [ ] F [ ]

4. INSURED'S NAME (Last Name, First Name, Middle Initial)

5. PATIENT'S ADDRESS (No. Street)

6. PATIENT RELATIONSHIP TO INSURED
Self [ ]   Spouse [ ]   Child [ ]   Other [ ]

7. INSURED'S ADDRESS (No. Street)

CITY   STATE

8. PATIENT STATUS
Single [ ]   Married [ ]   Other [ ]
Employed [ ]   Full-Time Student [ ]   Part-Time Student [ ]

CITY   STATE

ZIP CODE   TELEPHONE (Include Area Code)   (   )

ZIP CODE   TELEPHONE (INCLUDE AREA CODE)   (   )

9. OTHER INSURED'S NAME (Last Name, First Name, Middle Initial)

10. IS PATIENT'S CONDITION RELATED TO:

11. INSURED'S POLICY GROUP OR FECA NUMBER

a. OTHER INSURED'S POLICY OR GROUP NUMBER

a. EMPLOYMENT? (CURRENT OR PREVIOUS)   YES [ ]   NO [ ]

a. INSURED'S DATE OF BIRTH   MM | DD | YY   SEX   M [ ] F [ ]

b. OTHER INSURED'S DATE OF BIRTH   MM | DD | YY   SEX   M [ ] F [ ]

b. AUTO ACCIDENT?   PLACE (State)   YES [ ]   NO [ ]

b. EMPLOYER'S NAME OR SCHOOL NAME

c. EMPLOYER'S NAME OR SCHOOL NAME

c. OTHER ACCIDENT?   YES [ ]   NO [ ]

c. INSURANCE PLAN NAME OR PROGRAM NAME

d. INSURANCE PLAN NAME OR PROGRAM NAME

10d. RESERVED FOR LOCAL USE

d. IS THERE ANOTHER HEALTH BENEFIT PLAN?
YES [ ]   NO [ ]   If yes, return to and complete item 9 a – d.

READ BACK OF FORM BEFORE COMPLETING & SIGNING THIS FORM.
12. PATIENT'S OR AUTHORIZED PERSON'S SIGNATURE I authorize the release of any medical or other information necessary to process this claim. I also request payment of government benefits either to myself or to the party who accepts assignment below.

SIGNED _____   DATE _____

13. INSURED'S OR AUTHORIZED PERSON'S SIGNATURE I authorize payment of medical benefits to the undersigned physician or supplier for services described below.

SIGNED _____

PATIENT AND INSURED INFORMATION

14. DATE OF CURRENT: ILLNESS (First symptom) OR   INJURY (Accident) OR   PREGNANCY (LMP)   MM | DD | YY

15. IF PATIENT HAS HAD SAME OR SIMILAR ILLNESS, GIVE FIRST DATE   MM | DD | YY

16. DATES PATIENT UNABLE TO WORK IN CURRENT OCCUPATION   MM | DD | YY   FROM   TO   MM | DD | YY

17. NAME OF REFERRING PHYSICIAN OR OTHER SOURCE

17a. I.D. NUMBER OF REFERRING PHYSICIAN

18. HOSPITALIZATION DATES RELATED TO CURRENT SERVICES   MM | DD | YY   FROM   TO   MM | DD | YY

19. RESERVED FOR LOCAL USE

20. OUTSIDE LAB? $ CHARGES   YES [ ]   NO [ ]

21. DIAGNOSIS OR NATURE OF ILLNESS OR INJURY. (RELATE ITEMS 1, 2, 3, OR 4 TO ITEM 24E BY LINE)
1. ____   3. ____
2. ____   4. ____

22. MEDICAID RESUBMISSION CODE   ORIGINAL REF. NO.

23. PRIOR AUTHORIZATION NUMBER

24. A. DATE(S) OF SERVICE						B. Place of Service	C. Type of Service	D. PROCEDURES, SERVICES, OR SUPPLIES (Explain Unusual Circumstances) CPT/HCPCS	MODIFIER	E. DIAGNOSIS CODE	F. $ CHARGES	G. DAYS OR UNITS	H. EPSDT Family Plan	I. EMG	J. COB	K. RESERVED FOR LOCAL USE
From MM	DD	YY	To MM	DD	YY											
1																
2																
3																
4																
5																
6																

25. FEDERAL TAX I.D. NUMBER   SSN [ ] EIN [ ]

26. PATIENT'S ACCOUNT NO.

27. ACCEPT ASSIGNMENT? (For govt. claims, see back)   YES [ ]   NO [ ]

28. TOTAL CHARGE $

29. AMOUNT PAID $

30. BALANCE DUE $

31. SIGNATURE OF PHYSICIAN OR SUPPLIER INCLUDING DEGREES OR CREDENTIALS (I certify that the statements on the reverse apply to this bill and are made a part thereof.)

SIGNED _____   DATE _____

32. NAME AND ADDRESS OF FACILITY WHERE SERVICES WERE RENDERED (If other than home or office)

33. PHYSICIAN'S, SUPPLIER'S BILLING NAME, ADDRESS, ZIP CODE & PHONE #

PIN#   GRP#

PHYSICIAN OR SUPPLIER INFORMATION

(SAMPLE ONLY - NOT APPROVED FOR USE)

PLEASE PRINT OR TYPE

SAMPLE FORM 1500
SAMPLE FORM 1500 SAMPLE FORM 1500

DATE	REMARKS			
04/12/XX				

PATIENT		CHART #	SEX	BIRTHDATE
Odel M. Ryer Jr. 464-44-4646		16-d	M	04/28/49

MAILING ADDRESS	CITY	STATE	ZIP	HOME PHONE	WORK PHONE
484 Pinewood Ave.	Anywhere	US	12345	(101) 333-5555	

EMPLOYER	ADDRESS		PATIENT STATUS
US Air Force Retired	Anywhere	US	X MARRIED DIVORCED SINGLE STUDENT OTHER

INSURANCE: PRIMARY	ID#	GROUP	SECONDARY POLICY
TRICARE Standard	464-44-4646		

POLICYHOLDER NAME	BIRTHDATE	RELATIONSHIP	POLICYHOLDER NAME	BIRTHDATE	RELATIONSHIP
		Self			

SUPPLEMENTAL PLAN	EMPLOYER

POLICYHOLDER NAME	BIRTHDATE	RELATIONSHIP	DIAGNOSIS	CODE
			1. Heartburn	787.1
EMPLOYER			2.	
			3.	
REFERRING PHYSICIAN UPIN/SSN			4.	

PLACE OF SERVICE   Office

PROCEDURES	CODE	CHARGE
1. Est. Pt. OV Level I	99211	$55.00
2.		
3.		
4.		
5.		
6.		

SPECIAL NOTES

TOTAL CHARGES	PAYMENTS	ADJUSTMENTS	BALANCE
$55.00	0	0	$55.00

RETURN VISIT	PHYSICIAN SIGNATURE
PRN	Donald L. Givings, M.D.

DONALD L. GIVINGS, M.D.
11350 MEDICAL DRIVE, ANYWHERE, US 12345
PHONE NUMBER (101)111-5555

MEDICARE # D1234
MEDICAID # DLG1234
BCBS # 12345

EIN # 11123456
SSN # 123-12-1234
UPIN # DG1234
GRP # DG12345

PLEASE
DO NOT
STAPLE
IN THIS
AREA

CARRIER

| | PICA |

HEALTH INSURANCE CLAIM FORM

PICA | |

| 1. MEDICARE | MEDICAID | CHAMPUS | CHAMPVA | GROUP HEALTH PLAN | FECA BLK LUNG | OTHER | 1a. INSURED'S I.D. NUMBER (FOR PROGRAM IN ITEM 1) |
| (Medicare #) | (Medicaid #) | (Sponsor's SSN) | (VA File #) | (SSN or ID) | (SSN) | (ID) | |

2. PATIENT'S NAME (Last Name, First Name, Middle Initial)

3. PATIENT'S BIRTH DATE
MM   DD   YY   SEX   M □   F □

4. INSURED'S NAME (Last Name, First Name, Middle Initial)

5. PATIENT'S ADDRESS (No. Street)

6. PATIENT RELATIONSHIP TO INSURED
Self □   Spouse □   Child □   Other □

7. INSURED'S ADDRESS (No. Street)

CITY   STATE

8. PATIENT STATUS
Single □   Married □   Other □

CITY   STATE

ZIP CODE   TELEPHONE (Include Area Code) (   )

Employed □   Full-Time Student □   Part-Time Student □

ZIP CODE   TELEPHONE (INCLUDE AREA CODE) (   )

9. OTHER INSURED'S NAME (Last Name, First Name, Middle Initial)

10. IS PATIENT'S CONDITION RELATED TO:

11. INSURED'S POLICY GROUP OR FECA NUMBER

a. OTHER INSURED'S POLICY OR GROUP NUMBER

a. EMPLOYMENT? (CURRENT OR PREVIOUS)
□ YES   □ NO

a. INSURED'S DATE OF BIRTH
MM   DD   YY   SEX   M □   F □

b. OTHER INSURED'S DATE OF BIRTH
MM   DD   YY   SEX   M □   F □

b. AUTO ACCIDENT?   PLACE (State)
□ YES   □ NO

b. EMPLOYER'S NAME OR SCHOOL NAME

c. EMPLOYER'S NAME OR SCHOOL NAME

c. OTHER ACCIDENT?
□ YES   □ NO

c. INSURANCE PLAN NAME OR PROGRAM NAME

d. INSURANCE PLAN NAME OR PROGRAM NAME

10d. RESERVED FOR LOCAL USE

d. IS THERE ANOTHER HEALTH BENEFIT PLAN?
□ YES   □ NO   If yes, return to and complete item 9 a – d.

READ BACK OF FORM BEFORE COMPLETING & SIGNING THIS FORM.
12. PATIENT'S OR AUTHORIZED PERSON'S SIGNATURE I authorize the release of any medical or other information necessary to process this claim. I also request payment of government benefits either to myself or to the party who accepts assignment below.

SIGNED _____   DATE _____

13. INSURED'S OR AUTHORIZED PERSON'S SIGNATURE I authorize payment of medical benefits to the undersigned physician or supplier for services described below.

SIGNED _____

PATIENT AND INSURED INFORMATION

14. DATE OF CURRENT: ILLNESS (First symptom) OR
MM   DD   YY   INJURY (Accident) OR PREGNANCY (LMP)

15. IF PATIENT HAS HAD SAME OR SIMILAR ILLNESS, GIVE FIRST DATE   MM   DD   YY

16. DATES PATIENT UNABLE TO WORK IN CURRENT OCCUPATION
MM   DD   YY   MM   DD   YY
FROM   TO

17. NAME OF REFERRING PHYSICIAN OR OTHER SOURCE

17a. I.D. NUMBER OF REFERRING PHYSICIAN

18. HOSPITALIZATION DATES RELATED TO CURRENT SERVICES
MM   DD   YY   MM   DD   YY
FROM   TO

19. RESERVED FOR LOCAL USE

20. OUTSIDE LAB? $ CHARGES
□ YES   □ NO

21. DIAGNOSIS OR NATURE OF ILLNESS OR INJURY. (RELATE ITEMS 1, 2, 3, OR 4 TO ITEM 24E BY LINE)

1. |___ . ___   3. |___ . ___

2. |___ . ___   4. |___ . ___

22. MEDICAID RESUBMISSION
CODE   ORIGINAL REF. NO.

23. PRIOR AUTHORIZATION NUMBER

24. A					B	C	D	E	F	G	H	I	J	K
DATE(S) OF SERVICE					Place of Service	Type of Service	PROCEDURES, SERVICES, OR SUPPLIES (Explain Unusual Circumstances)	DIAGNOSIS CODE	$ CHARGES	DAYS OR UNITS	EPSDT Family Plan	EMG	COB	RESERVED FOR LOCAL USE
From			To				CPT/HCPCS MODIFIER							
MM	DD	YY	MM	DD	YY										
1														
2														
3														
4														
5														
6														

25. FEDERAL TAX I.D. NUMBER   SSN □   EIN □

26. PATIENT'S ACCOUNT NO.

27. ACCEPT ASSIGNMENT? (For govt. claims, see back)
□ YES   □ NO

28. TOTAL CHARGE $

29. AMOUNT PAID $

30. BALANCE DUE $

31. SIGNATURE OF PHYSICIAN OR SUPPLIER INCLUDING DEGREES OR CREDENTIALS (I certify that the statements on the reverse apply to this bill and are made a part thereof.)

SIGNED _____   DATE _____

32. NAME AND ADDRESS OF FACILITY WHERE SERVICES WERE RENDERED (If other than home or office)

33. PHYSICIAN'S, SUPPLIER'S BILLING NAME, ADDRESS, ZIP CODE & PHONE #

PIN#   GRP#

PHYSICIAN OR SUPPLIER INFORMATION

DATE	REMARKS			
06/11/XX	Father is stationed at 555 Regiment Way, Anywhere US 12345			

PATIENT			CHART #	SEX	BIRTHDATE
Annalisa M. Faris	456-77-5555		16-e	F	04/04/99

MAILING ADDRESS	CITY	STATE	ZIP	HOME PHONE	WORK PHONE
394 Myriam Court	Anywhere	US	12345	(101) 333-5555	

EMPLOYER	ADDRESS	PATIENT STATUS
		X
		MARRIED DIVORCED SINGLE STUDENT OTHER

INSURANCE: PRIMARY	ID#	GROUP	SECONDARY POLICY
TRICARE Prime	323-23-3333		

POLICYHOLDER NAME	BIRTHDATE	RELATIONSHIP	POLICYHOLDER NAME	BIRTHDATE	RELATIONSHIP
Nacir R. Faris	6/21/75	Father			

SUPPLEMENTAL PLAN	EMPLOYER

POLICYHOLDER NAME	BIRTHDATE	RELATIONSHIP

DIAGNOSIS	CODE
1. Chills with fever	780.6
2. Lethargy	780.7
3. Loss of appetite	783.0
4. Loss of weight	783.2

EMPLOYER
US Army (See duty address in remarks)

REFERRING PHYSICIAN UPIN/SSN

PLACE OF SERVICE   Mercy Hospital, Anywhere Street, Anywhere, US 12345

PROCEDURES		CODE	CHARGE
1. Initial Hosp. Level V	06/02/XX	99225	$200.00
2. Subsq. Hosp. Level III	06/03/XX	99233	85.00
3. Subsq. Hosp. Level III	06/04/XX	99233	85.00
4. Subsq. Hosp. Level III	06/06/XX	99233	85.00
5. Subsq. Hosp. Level II	06/07/XX	99232	75.00
6. Subsq. Hosp. Level II	06/09/XX	99232	75.00
7. Subsq. Hosp. Level II	06/10/XX	99232	75.00

SPECIAL NOTES
Admission authorization # D50123
Patient was discharged 06/11/XX but not seen

TOTAL CHARGES	PAYMENTS	ADJUSTMENTS	BALANCE
$680.00	0	0	$680.00

RETURN VISIT	PHYSICIAN SIGNATURE
	Donald L. Givings, M.D.

	DONALD L. GIVINGS, M.D.	
MEDICARE # D1234	11350 MEDICAL DRIVE, ANYWHERE, US 12345	EIN # 11123456
MEDICAID # DLG1234	PHONE NUMBER (101)111-5555	SSN # 123-12-1234
BCBS # 12345		UPIN # DG1234
		GRP # DG12345

(SAMPLE ONLY - NOT APPROVED FOR USE)

CARRIER

[ ][ ] PICA

HEALTH INSURANCE CLAIM FORM

PICA [ ][ ]

1. MEDICARE	MEDICAID	CHAMPUS	CHAMPVA	GROUP HEALTH PLAN	FECA BLK LUNG	OTHER	1a. INSURED'S I.D. NUMBER	(FOR PROGRAM IN ITEM 1)
[ ] (Medicare #)	[ ] (Medicaid #)	[ ] (Sponsor's SSN)	[ ] (VA File #)	[ ] (SSN or ID)	[ ] (SSN)	[ ] (ID)		

2. PATIENT'S NAME (Last Name, First Name, Middle Initial)

3. PATIENT'S BIRTH DATE
MM | DD | YY   SEX
M [ ]   F [ ]

4. INSURED'S NAME (Last Name, First Name, Middle Initial)

5. PATIENT'S ADDRESS (No. Street)

6. PATIENT RELATIONSHIP TO INSURED
Self [ ] Spouse [ ] Child [ ] Other [ ]

7. INSURED'S ADDRESS (No. Street)

CITY   STATE

8. PATIENT STATUS
Single [ ] Married [ ] Other [ ]
Employed [ ] Full-Time Student [ ] Part-Time Student [ ]

CITY   STATE

ZIP CODE   TELEPHONE (Include Area Code)
(   )

ZIP CODE   TELEPHONE (INCLUDE AREA CODE)
(   )

9. OTHER INSURED'S NAME (Last Name, First Name, Middle Initial)

10. IS PATIENT'S CONDITION RELATED TO:

11. INSURED'S POLICY GROUP OR FECA NUMBER

a. OTHER INSURED'S POLICY OR GROUP NUMBER

a. EMPLOYMENT? (CURRENT OR PREVIOUS)
[ ] YES [ ] NO

a. INSURED'S DATE OF BIRTH
MM | DD | YY   SEX
M [ ]   F [ ]

b. OTHER INSURED'S DATE OF BIRTH
MM | DD | YY   SEX
M [ ]   F [ ]

b. AUTO ACCIDENT?   PLACE (State)
[ ] YES [ ] NO

b. EMPLOYER'S NAME OR SCHOOL NAME

c. EMPLOYER'S NAME OR SCHOOL NAME

c. OTHER ACCIDENT?
[ ] YES [ ] NO

c. INSURANCE PLAN NAME OR PROGRAM NAME

d. INSURANCE PLAN NAME OR PROGRAM NAME

10d. RESERVED FOR LOCAL USE

d. IS THERE ANOTHER HEALTH BENEFIT PLAN?
[ ] YES [ ] NO If yes, return to and complete item 9 a – d.

READ BACK OF FORM BEFORE COMPLETING & SIGNING THIS FORM.
12. PATIENT'S OR AUTHORIZED PERSON'S SIGNATURE I authorize the release of any medical or other information necessary to process this claim. I also request payment of government benefits either to myself or to the party who accepts assignment below.

SIGNED _____   DATE _____

13. INSURED'S OR AUTHORIZED PERSON'S SIGNATURE I authorize payment of medical benefits to the undersigned physician or supplier for services described below.

SIGNED _____

14. DATE OF CURRENT:
MM | DD | YY
ILLNESS (First symptom) OR
INJURY (Accident) OR
PREGNANCY (LMP)

15. IF PATIENT HAS HAD SAME OR SIMILAR ILLNESS, GIVE FIRST DATE   MM | DD | YY

16. DATES PATIENT UNABLE TO WORK IN CURRENT OCCUPATION
MM | DD | YY   MM | DD | YY
FROM   TO

17. NAME OF REFERRING PHYSICIAN OR OTHER SOURCE

17a. I.D. NUMBER OF REFERRING PHYSICIAN

18. HOSPITALIZATION DATES RELATED TO CURRENT SERVICES
MM | DD | YY   MM | DD | YY
FROM   TO

19. RESERVED FOR LOCAL USE

20. OUTSIDE LAB? $ CHARGES
[ ] YES [ ] NO

21. DIAGNOSIS OR NATURE OF ILLNESS OR INJURY. (RELATE ITEMS 1, 2, 3, OR 4 TO ITEM 24E BY LINE)

1. |___|___| 3. |___|___|

2. |___|___| 4. |___|___|

22. MEDICAID RESUBMISSION CODE   ORIGINAL REF. NO.

23. PRIOR AUTHORIZATION NUMBER

24. A DATE(S) OF SERVICE						B Place of Service	C Type of Service	D PROCEDURES, SERVICES, OR SUPPLIES (Explain Unusual Circumstances) CPT/HCPCS	MODIFIER	E DIAGNOSIS CODE	F $ CHARGES	G DAYS OR UNITS	H EPSDT Family Plan	I EMG	J COB	K RESERVED FOR LOCAL USE
From MM	DD	YY	To MM	DD	YY											
1																
2																
3																
4																
5																
6																

25. FEDERAL TAX I.D. NUMBER   SSN [ ] EIN [ ]

26. PATIENT'S ACCOUNT NO.

27. ACCEPT ASSIGNMENT? (For govt. claims, see back)
YES [ ] NO [ ]

28. TOTAL CHARGE
$

29. AMOUNT PAID
$

30. BALANCE DUE
$

31. SIGNATURE OF PHYSICIAN OR SUPPLIER INCLUDING DEGREES OR CREDENTIALS (I certify that the statements on the reverse apply to this bill and are made a part thereof.)

SIGNED _____   DATE _____

32. NAME AND ADDRESS OF FACILITY WHERE SERVICES WERE RENDERED (If other than home or office)

33. PHYSICIAN'S, SUPPLIER'S BILLING NAME, ADDRESS, ZIP CODE & PHONE #

PIN# _____   GRP# _____

(SAMPLE ONLY - NOT APPROVED FOR USE)   *PLEASE PRINT OR TYPE*

SAMPLE FORM 1500
SAMPLE FORM 1500 SAMPLE FORM 1500

Workers' Compensation

INTRODUCTION

1. Describe what it was like before the enactment of Workers' Compensation laws.

_____

_____

_____

_____

_____

2. State the threefold philosophy behind the establishment of Workers' Compensation laws.

a. _____

b. _____

c. _____

FEDERAL COMPENSATION PROGRAMS

3. The program for coal miners is better known as the _____ _____ _____ .

4. If a patient has been injured at work, how can the provider find the mailing address of the district office for submission of injury reports and claims? _____

STATE-SPONSORED COVERAGE

5. List four types of coverage that have emerged from state legislatures.

a. _____

b. _____

c. _____

d. _____

6. The cost of Workers' Compensation has skyrocketed, causing many employers to turn long-term cases over to ___. (Circle the correct answer.)

    a. Medicare

    b. Medicaid

    c. managed care programs

    d. none of the above

7. What is the name of the government agency responsible for administering the Workers' Compensation law and handling appeals for claims that have been denied? (Circle the correct answer.)

    a. State Compensation Fund

    b. State Compensation Department

    c. State Compensation Division

    d. none of the above

ELIGIBILITY

8. List three occupations in which coverage for stress-related disorders has been awarded.

    a. _____

    b. _____

    c. _____

9. Give two situations of when an employee would qualify for Workers' Compensation even though he/she was not physically on company property. (Do not use examples given in the textbook.)

_____

_____

_____

_____

_____

_____

_____

_____

CLASSIFICATION OF ON-THE-JOB INJURIES

10. List five classifications of Workers' Compensation cases mandated by federal law.

    a. _____

    b. _____

    c. _____

    d. _____

    e. _____

11. The answer to each of the following statements is either true or false. Indicate your choice by placing **T** for a true statement or **F** for a false statement on the line provided.

    _____ a. Medical claims with no disability are filed for minor injuries when the worker is treated and able to return to work within a few days.

    _____ b. Temporary disability claims cover medical treatment for injuries and disorders but not payment for lost income.

    _____ c. Permanent disability refers to the employee's degree of injury.

    _____ d. Vocational rehabilitation claims cover the expense of vocational retraining.

12. Describe the difference between **disability precluding heavy lifting** and **disability precluding very heavy lifting**. _____

    _____

13. Match the terminology describing pain in the first column with the definitions in the second column. Write the correct letter in each blank.

    _____ Minimal pain   a. tolerable, but there may be some limitations in performance of assigned duties

    _____ Slight pain   b. precludes any activity that precipitates pain

    _____ Moderate pain   c. tolerable, but there may be marked handicapping of performance

    _____ Severe pain   d. annoyance, but will not handicap the performance of the patient's work

14. How are death benefits computed? _____

OSHA ACT OF 1970

15. Why was OSHA enacted by Congress? _____

16. What is the name of the vaccination that must be administered to each worker who might be exposed to infectious materials? _____

17. Comprehensive records of all vaccinations received and any accidental exposure incidents must be kept for ___. (Circle the correct answer.)

    a. 5 years

    b. 10 years

    c. 15 years

    d. 20 years

SPECIAL HANDLING OF WORKERS' COMPENSATION CASES

18. If a patient has Workers' Compensation and the amount charged for the treatment is greater than the approved reimbursement for the treatment, can the provider balance bill the patient? _____

Critical Thinking

19. Why is it important to maintain separate files on patients who receive treatment from the same provider for both work-related disorders and regular medical care?

_____

_____

_____

_____

_____

FIRST REPORT OF INJURY

20. When should the First Report of Injury form be completed? _____

_____

21. List four parties who should receive a copy of a First Report of Injury form.

    a. _____

    b. _____

    c. _____

    d. _____

22. Explain why there is no patient signature line on the First Report of Injury form.

_____

_____

_____

23. What is the time limit for filing the First Report of Injury form? _____

_____

24. If an employer disputes the legitimacy of a claim, should the provider still file the First Report of Injury form? _____

25. When a patient receives written notice of denial of the claim from the employer, the patient is required to file an appeal with the ___. (Circle the correct answer.)

    a. employer

    b. state Workers' Compensation Commission/Board

    c. insurance carrier

    d. all of the above

PROGRESS REPORTS

26. What is the purpose of the Progress Report? _____

_____

27. What should be done with a file or case number once it is assigned by the carrier or the Workers' Compensation Commission/Board? _____

_____

ILLING INFORMATION NOTES

28. Which of the following injured workers may be eligible for federal compensation plans? (Circle the correct answer/answers.)

    a. coal miners

    b. military employees

    c. federal employees

    d. all of the above

29. Which of the following can be designated a fiscal agent by state law and the corporation involved? (Circle the correct answer.)

    a. the State Compensation Fund

    b. a private, commercial insurance carrier

    c. the employer's special company capital funds set aside for compensation cases

    d. any of the above

30. What is the deductible for Workers' Compensation claims? _____

31. What is the copayment for Workers' Compensation claims? _____

Know Your Acronyms

32. Define the following acronyms:

    a. OSHA   _____

    b. MSDS   _____

EXERCISES

1. Complete Case Studies 17-a through 17-f using the blank claim form provided. Follow the step-by-step instructions in the textbook to properly complete the claim form. If a patient has a secondary carrier, complete an additional claim form using secondary directions in the textbook. You may choose to use a pencil so corrections can be made.

DATE	REMARKS			
02/03/XX	Injured today at work, no assigned claim number			

PATIENT			CHART #	SEX	BIRTHDATE
Sandy S. Grand	444-55-6666		17-a	F	12/03/72

MAILING ADDRESS	CITY	STATE	ZIP	HOME PHONE	WORK PHONE
109 Darling Road	Anywhere	US	12345	(101) 333-5555	(101) 444-5555

EMPLOYER	ADDRESS		PATIENT STATUS	
Starport Fitness Center	Anywhere	US		X	
			MARRIED DIVORCED SINGLE STUDENT OTHER	

INSURANCE: PRIMARY	ID#	GROUP	SECONDARY POLICY
Workers Trust			

POLICYHOLDER NAME	BIRTHDATE	RELATIONSHIP	POLICYHOLDER NAME	BIRTHDATE	RELATIONSHIP
		Self			

SUPPLEMENTAL PLAN	EMPLOYER

POLICYHOLDER NAME	BIRTHDATE	RELATIONSHIP	DIAGNOSIS	CODE
			1. Wrist fracture, closed	814.00
EMPLOYER			2. Fall from chair	E884.2
			3.	
REFERRING PHYSICIAN UPIN/SSN			4.	

PLACE OF SERVICE	Office

PROCEDURES	CODE	CHARGE
1. New Pt. OV Level IV	99204	$100.00
2.		
3.		
4.		
5.		
6.		
7.		

SPECIAL NOTES
Patient cannot return to work until seen by the Orthopedist, Dr. Breaker

TOTAL CHARGES	PAYMENTS	ADJUSTMENTS	BALANCE
$100.00	-0-	-0-	$100.00

RETURN VISIT	PHYSICIAN SIGNATURE
	Donald L. Givings, M.D.

MEDICARE # D1234	**DONALD L. GIVINGS, M.D.**	EIN # 11123456
MEDICAID # DLG1234	**11350 MEDICAL DRIVE, ANYWHERE, US 12345**	SSN # 123-12-1234
BCBS # 12345	**PHONE NUMBER (101)111-5555**	UPIN # DG1234
		GRP # DG12345

(SAMPLE ONLY - NOT APPROVED FOR USE)

CARRIER

HEALTH INSURANCE CLAIM FORM

| | PICA | | | | PICA | |

1. MEDICARE ☐ (Medicare #)   MEDICAID ☐ (Medicaid #)   CHAMPUS ☐ (Sponsor's SSN)   CHAMPVA ☐ (VA File #)   GROUP HEALTH PLAN ☐ (SSN or ID)   FECA BLK LUNG ☐ (SSN)   OTHER ☐ (ID)

1a. INSURED'S I.D. NUMBER   (FOR PROGRAM IN ITEM 1)

2. PATIENT'S NAME (Last Name, First Name, Middle Initial)

3. PATIENT'S BIRTH DATE   MM | DD | YY   SEX   M ☐   F ☐

4. INSURED'S NAME (Last Name, First Name, Middle Initial)

5. PATIENT'S ADDRESS (No. Street)

6. PATIENT RELATIONSHIP TO INSURED   Self ☐   Spouse ☐   Child ☐   Other ☐

7. INSURED'S ADDRESS (No. Street)

CITY   STATE

8. PATIENT STATUS   Single ☐   Married ☐   Other ☐

   Employed ☐   Full-Time Student ☐   Part-Time Student ☐

CITY   STATE

ZIP CODE   TELEPHONE (Include Area Code)   ( )

ZIP CODE   TELEPHONE (INCLUDE AREA CODE)   ( )

9. OTHER INSURED'S NAME (Last Name, First Name, Middle Initial)

10. IS PATIENT'S CONDITION RELATED TO:

11. INSURED'S POLICY GROUP OR FECA NUMBER

a. OTHER INSURED'S POLICY OR GROUP NUMBER

a. EMPLOYMENT? (CURRENT OR PREVIOUS)   YES ☐   NO ☐

a. INSURED'S DATE OF BIRTH   MM | DD | YY   SEX   M ☐   F ☐

b. OTHER INSURED'S DATE OF BIRTH   MM | DD | YY   SEX   M ☐   F ☐

b. AUTO ACCIDENT?   PLACE (State)   YES ☐   NO ☐

b. EMPLOYER'S NAME OR SCHOOL NAME

c. EMPLOYER'S NAME OR SCHOOL NAME

c. OTHER ACCIDENT?   YES ☐   NO ☐

c. INSURANCE PLAN NAME OR PROGRAM NAME

d. INSURANCE PLAN NAME OR PROGRAM NAME

10d. RESERVED FOR LOCAL USE

d. IS THERE ANOTHER HEALTH BENEFIT PLAN?   YES ☐   NO ☐   If yes, return to and complete item 9 a – d.

READ BACK OF FORM BEFORE COMPLETING & SIGNING THIS FORM.
12. PATIENT'S OR AUTHORIZED PERSON'S SIGNATURE I authorize the release of any medical or other information necessary to process this claim. I also request payment of government benefits either to myself or to the party who accepts assignment below.

SIGNED _____ DATE _____

13. INSURED'S OR AUTHORIZED PERSON'S SIGNATURE I authorize payment of medical benefits to the undersigned physician or supplier for services described below.

SIGNED _____

PATIENT AND INSURED INFORMATION

14. DATE OF CURRENT: MM | DD | YY   ILLNESS (First symptom) OR INJURY (Accident) OR PREGNANCY (LMP)

15. IF PATIENT HAS HAD SAME OR SIMILAR ILLNESS, GIVE FIRST DATE   MM | DD | YY

16. DATES PATIENT UNABLE TO WORK IN CURRENT OCCUPATION   MM | DD | YY   FROM   TO   MM | DD | YY

17. NAME OF REFERRING PHYSICIAN OR OTHER SOURCE

17a. I.D. NUMBER OF REFERRING PHYSICIAN

18. HOSPITALIZATION DATES RELATED TO CURRENT SERVICES   MM | DD | YY   FROM   TO   MM | DD | YY

19. RESERVED FOR LOCAL USE

20. OUTSIDE LAB?   YES ☐   NO ☐ $ CHARGES

21. DIAGNOSIS OR NATURE OF ILLNESS OR INJURY. (RELATE ITEMS 1, 2, 3, OR 4 TO ITEM 24E BY LINE)

1. L___ . ___   3. L___ . ___
2. L___ . ___   4. L___ . ___

22. MEDICAID RESUBMISSION CODE   ORIGINAL REF. NO.

23. PRIOR AUTHORIZATION NUMBER

24. A. DATE(S) OF SERVICE						B. Place of Service	C. Type of Service	D. PROCEDURES, SERVICES, OR SUPPLIES (Explain Unusual Circumstances) CPT/HCPCS	MODIFIER	E. DIAGNOSIS CODE	F. $ CHARGES	G. DAYS OR UNITS	H. EPSDT Family Plan	I. EMG	J. COB	K. RESERVED FOR LOCAL USE
From MM	DD	YY	To MM	DD	YY											
1																
2																
3																
4																
5																
6																

25. FEDERAL TAX I.D. NUMBER   SSN ☐ EIN ☐

26. PATIENT'S ACCOUNT NO.

27. ACCEPT ASSIGNMENT? (For govt. claims, see back)   YES ☐   NO ☐

28. TOTAL CHARGE $

29. AMOUNT PAID $

30. BALANCE DUE $

31. SIGNATURE OF PHYSICIAN OR SUPPLIER INCLUDING DEGREES OR CREDENTIALS (I certify that the statements on the reverse apply to this bill and are made a part thereof.)

SIGNED _____ DATE _____

32. NAME AND ADDRESS OF FACILITY WHERE SERVICES WERE RENDERED (If other than home or office)

33. PHYSICIAN'S, SUPPLIER'S BILLING NAME, ADDRESS, ZIP CODE & PHONE #

PIN#   GRP#

PHYSICIAN OR SUPPLIER INFORMATION

(SAMPLE ONLY - NOT APPROVED FOR USE)

PLEASE PRINT OR TYPE

SAMPLE FORM 1500
SAMPLE FORM 1500   SAMPLE FORM 1500

DATE	REMARKS			
02/05/XX	Patient may return to work 2/12/XX			

PATIENT			CHART #	SEX	BIRTHDATE
Sandy S. Grand	444-55-6666		17-b	F	12/03/72

MAILING ADDRESS	CITY	STATE	ZIP	HOME PHONE	WORK PHONE
109 Darling Road	Anywhere	US	12345	(101) 333-5555	(101) 444-5555

EMPLOYER	ADDRESS		PATIENT STATUS				
Starport Fitness Center	Anywhere	US	MARRIED	DIVORCED	SINGLE X	STUDENT	OTHER

INSURANCE: PRIMARY	ID#	GROUP	SECONDARY POLICY
Workers Trust	CLR5457		

POLICYHOLDER NAME	BIRTHDATE	RELATIONSHIP	POLICYHOLDER NAME	BIRTHDATE	RELATIONSHIP
		Self			

SUPPLEMENTAL PLAN	EMPLOYER

POLICYHOLDER NAME	BIRTHDATE	RELATIONSHIP	DIAGNOSIS	CODE
			1. Wrist fracture, closed	814.00
EMPLOYER			2. Fall from chair	E884.2
			3.	
REFERRING PHYSICIAN UPIN/SSN			4.	
Donald L. Givings, M.D.	123-12-1234			

PLACE OF SERVICE	Office

PROCEDURES	CODE	CHARGE
1. Office consult Level IV	99244	$95.00
2. X-ray wrist, complete	73110	$75.00
3. Application of cast, hand and lower forearm	29085	$50.00
4.		
5.		
6.		
7.		

SPECIAL NOTES

Date of injury: 02/03/XX

TOTAL CHARGES	PAYMENTS	ADJUSTMENTS	BALANCE
$220.00	0	0	$220.00

RETURN VISIT	PHYSICIAN SIGNATURE
2 weeks	Elliot A. Breaker, M.D.

MEDICARE # E1234 MEDICAID # EAB1234 BCBS # 48489	**Elliot A. Breaker, M.D. Orthopedist** **5124 PHARMACY DRIVE, ANYWHERE, US 12345** **PHONE NUMBER (101)111-5555**	EIN # 11997755 SSN # 223-22-1222 UPIN # EB1234 GRP # EB12345

(SAMPLE ONLY - NOT APPROVED FOR USE)

CARRIER

| | PICA

HEALTH INSURANCE CLAIM FORM

PICA | |

| 1. MEDICARE [ ] (Medicare #) | MEDICAID [ ] (Medicaid #) | CHAMPUS [ ] (Sponsor's SSN) | CHAMPVA [ ] (VA File #) | GROUP HEALTH PLAN [ ] (SSN or ID) | FECA BLK LUNG [ ] (SSN) | OTHER [ ] (ID) | 1a. INSURED'S I.D. NUMBER | (FOR PROGRAM IN ITEM 1) |

| 2. PATIENT'S NAME (Last Name, First Name, Middle Initial) | 3. PATIENT'S BIRTH DATE MM | DD | YY   SEX   M [ ]   F [ ] | 4. INSURED'S NAME (Last Name, First Name, Middle Initial) |

5. PATIENT'S ADDRESS (No. Street)

6. PATIENT RELATIONSHIP TO INSURED
Self [ ]   Spouse [ ]   Child [ ]   Other [ ]

7. INSURED'S ADDRESS (No. Street)

CITY | STATE

8. PATIENT STATUS
Single [ ]   Married [ ]   Other [ ]

CITY | STATE

ZIP CODE | TELEPHONE (Include Area Code) ( )

Employed [ ]   Full-Time Student [ ]   Part-Time Student [ ]

ZIP CODE | TELEPHONE (INCLUDE AREA CODE) ( )

9. OTHER INSURED'S NAME (Last Name, First Name, Middle Initial)

10. IS PATIENT'S CONDITION RELATED TO:

11. INSURED'S POLICY GROUP OR FECA NUMBER

a. OTHER INSURED'S POLICY OR GROUP NUMBER

a. EMPLOYMENT? (CURRENT OR PREVIOUS)
[ ] YES   [ ] NO

a. INSURED'S DATE OF BIRTH MM | DD | YY   SEX M [ ]   F [ ]

b. OTHER INSURED'S DATE OF BIRTH MM | DD | YY   SEX M [ ]   F [ ]

b. AUTO ACCIDENT?   PLACE (State)
[ ] YES   [ ] NO

b. EMPLOYER'S NAME OR SCHOOL NAME

c. EMPLOYER'S NAME OR SCHOOL NAME

c. OTHER ACCIDENT?
[ ] YES   [ ] NO

c. INSURANCE PLAN NAME OR PROGRAM NAME

d. INSURANCE PLAN NAME OR PROGRAM NAME

10d. RESERVED FOR LOCAL USE

d. IS THERE ANOTHER HEALTH BENEFIT PLAN?
[ ] YES   [ ] NO   If yes, return to and complete item 9 a – d.

READ BACK OF FORM BEFORE COMPLETING & SIGNING THIS FORM.
12. PATIENT'S OR AUTHORIZED PERSON'S SIGNATURE I authorize the release of any medical or other information necessary to process this claim. I also request payment of government benefits either to myself or to the party who accepts assignment below.

SIGNED _____   DATE _____

13. INSURED'S OR AUTHORIZED PERSON'S SIGNATURE I authorize payment of medical benefits to the undersigned physician or supplier for services described below.

SIGNED _____

PATIENT AND INSURED INFORMATION

14. DATE OF CURRENT: MM | DD | YY   ◄ ILLNESS (First symptom) OR INJURY (Accident) OR PREGNANCY (LMP)

15. IF PATIENT HAS HAD SAME OR SIMILAR ILLNESS, GIVE FIRST DATE MM | DD | YY

16. DATES PATIENT UNABLE TO WORK IN CURRENT OCCUPATION MM | DD | YY   MM | DD | YY
FROM   TO

17. NAME OF REFERRING PHYSICIAN OR OTHER SOURCE

17a. I.D. NUMBER OF REFERRING PHYSICIAN

18. HOSPITALIZATION DATES RELATED TO CURRENT SERVICES MM | DD | YY   MM | DD | YY
FROM   TO

19. RESERVED FOR LOCAL USE

20. OUTSIDE LAB? $ CHARGES
[ ] YES   [ ] NO

21. DIAGNOSIS OR NATURE OF ILLNESS OR INJURY. (RELATE ITEMS 1, 2, 3, OR 4 TO ITEM 24E BY LINE)

1. |___|.|___| 3. |___|.|___|

2. |___|.|___| 4. |___|.|___|

22. MEDICAID RESUBMISSION CODE   ORIGINAL REF. NO.

23. PRIOR AUTHORIZATION NUMBER

24. A DATE(S) OF SERVICE			B Place of Service	C Type of Service	D PROCEDURES, SERVICES, OR SUPPLIES (Explain Unusual Circumstances)		E DIAGNOSIS CODE	F $ CHARGES	G DAYS OR UNITS	H EPSDT Family Plan	I EMG	J COB	K RESERVED FOR LOCAL USE
From MM DD YY	To MM DD YY				CPT/HCPCS	MODIFIER							
1													
2													
3													
4													
5													
6													

PHYSICIAN OR SUPPLIER INFORMATION

25. FEDERAL TAX I.D. NUMBER   SSN [ ] EIN [ ]

26. PATIENT'S ACCOUNT NO.

27. ACCEPT ASSIGNMENT? (For govt. claims, see back)
[ ] YES   [ ] NO

28. TOTAL CHARGE $

29. AMOUNT PAID $

30. BALANCE DUE $

31. SIGNATURE OF PHYSICIAN OR SUPPLIER INCLUDING DEGREES OR CREDENTIALS (I certify that the statements on the reverse apply to this bill and are made a part thereof.)

SIGNED _____   DATE _____

32. NAME AND ADDRESS OF FACILITY WHERE SERVICES WERE RENDERED (If other than home or office)

33. PHYSICIAN'S, SUPPLIER'S BILLING NAME, ADDRESS, ZIP CODE & PHONE #

PIN# _____   GRP# _____

(SAMPLE ONLY - NOT APPROVED FOR USE)

PLEASE PRINT OR TYPE

SAMPLE FORM 1500
SAMPLE FORM 1500 SAMPLE FORM 1500

DATE	REMARKS			
05/12/XX	Patient injured at end of shift today			

PATIENT			CHART #	SEX	BIRTHDATE
Marianna D. Holland		494-55-6969	17-c	F	11/05/77

MAILING ADDRESS	CITY	STATE	ZIP	HOME PHONE	WORK PHONE
509 Dutch Street	Anywhere	US	12345	(101) 333-5555	(101) 444-5555

EMPLOYER	ADDRESS		PATIENT STATUS
Hair Etc.	Anywhere	US	X MARRIED DIVORCED SINGLE STUDENT OTHER

INSURANCE: PRIMARY	ID#	GROUP	SECONDARY POLICY
Workers Shield	BA6788		

POLICYHOLDER NAME	BIRTHDATE	RELATIONSHIP	POLICYHOLDER NAME	BIRTHDATE	RELATIONSHIP
		Self			

SUPPLEMENTAL PLAN	EMPLOYER

POLICYHOLDER NAME	BIRTHDATE	RELATIONSHIP	DIAGNOSIS	CODE
			1. Fracture, nasal bones, closed	802.0
EMPLOYER			2.	
			3.	
REFERRING PHYSICIAN UPIN/SSN			4.	

PLACE OF SERVICE   Office

PROCEDURES	CODE	CHARGE
1. New Pt. OV Level III	99203	$80.00
2.		
3.		
4.		
5.		
6.		

SPECIAL NOTES

Patient may return to work 5/16/XX

TOTAL CHARGES	PAYMENTS	ADJUSTMENTS	BALANCE
$80.00	0	0	$80.00

RETURN VISIT	PHYSICIAN SIGNATURE
PRN	Donald L. Givings, M.D.

MEDICARE # D1234
MEDICAID # DLG1234
BCBS # 12345

DONALD L. GIVINGS, M.D.
11350 MEDICAL DRIVE, ANYWHERE, US 12345
PHONE NUMBER (101)111-5555

EIN # 11123456
SSN # 123-12-1234
UPIN # DG1234
GRP # DG12345

PLEASE
DO NOT
STAPLE
IN THIS
AREA

CARRIER

HEALTH INSURANCE CLAIM FORM

| | | PICA | | | | PICA | | |

1. MEDICARE   MEDICAID   CHAMPUS   CHAMPVA   GROUP HEALTH PLAN   FECA BLK LUNG   OTHER

(Medicare #)   (Medicaid #)   (Sponsor's SSN)   (VA File #)   (SSN or ID)   (SSN)   (ID)

1a. INSURED'S I.D. NUMBER   (FOR PROGRAM IN ITEM 1)

2. PATIENT'S NAME (Last Name, First Name, Middle Initial)

3. PATIENT'S BIRTH DATE   MM   DD   YY   SEX   M   F

4. INSURED'S NAME (Last Name, First Name, Middle Initial)

5. PATIENT'S ADDRESS (No. Street)

6. PATIENT RELATIONSHIP TO INSURED   Self   Spouse   Child   Other

7. INSURED'S ADDRESS (No. Street)

CITY   STATE

8. PATIENT STATUS   Single   Married   Other

CITY   STATE

ZIP CODE   TELEPHONE (Include Area Code)   ( )

Employed   Full-Time Student   Part-Time Student

ZIP CODE   TELEPHONE (INCLUDE AREA CODE)   ( )

9. OTHER INSURED'S NAME (Last Name, First Name, Middle Initial)

10. IS PATIENT'S CONDITION RELATED TO:

11. INSURED'S POLICY GROUP OR FECA NUMBER

a. OTHER INSURED'S POLICY OR GROUP NUMBER

a. EMPLOYMENT? (CURRENT OR PREVIOUS)   YES   NO

a. INSURED'S DATE OF BIRTH   MM   DD   YY   SEX   M   F

b. OTHER INSURED'S DATE OF BIRTH   MM   DD   YY   SEX   M   F

b. AUTO ACCIDENT?   PLACE (State)   YES   NO

b. EMPLOYER'S NAME OR SCHOOL NAME

c. EMPLOYER'S NAME OR SCHOOL NAME

c. OTHER ACCIDENT?   YES   NO

c. INSURANCE PLAN NAME OR PROGRAM NAME

d. INSURANCE PLAN NAME OR PROGRAM NAME

10d. RESERVED FOR LOCAL USE

d. IS THERE ANOTHER HEALTH BENEFIT PLAN?   YES   NO   If yes, return to and complete item 9 a – d.

READ BACK OF FORM BEFORE COMPLETING & SIGNING THIS FORM.

12. PATIENT'S OR AUTHORIZED PERSON'S SIGNATURE I authorize the release of any medical or other information necessary to process this claim. I also request payment of government benefits either to myself or to the party who accepts assignment below.

SIGNED _____ DATE _____

13. INSURED'S OR AUTHORIZED PERSON'S SIGNATURE I authorize payment of medical benefits to the undersigned physician or supplier for services described below.

SIGNED _____

PATIENT AND INSURED INFORMATION

14. DATE OF CURRENT: MM DD YY   ILLNESS (First symptom) OR INJURY (Accident) OR PREGNANCY (LMP)

15. IF PATIENT HAS HAD SAME OR SIMILAR ILLNESS, GIVE FIRST DATE   MM DD YY

16. DATES PATIENT UNABLE TO WORK IN CURRENT OCCUPATION   MM DD YY   FROM   TO   MM DD YY

17. NAME OF REFERRING PHYSICIAN OR OTHER SOURCE

17a. I.D. NUMBER OF REFERRING PHYSICIAN

18. HOSPITALIZATION DATES RELATED TO CURRENT SERVICES   MM DD YY   FROM   TO   MM DD YY

19. RESERVED FOR LOCAL USE

20. OUTSIDE LAB?   YES   NO $ CHARGES

21. DIAGNOSIS OR NATURE OF ILLNESS OR INJURY. (RELATE ITEMS 1, 2, 3, OR 4 TO ITEM 24E BY LINE)

1. ___ . ___   3. ___ . ___

2. ___ . ___   4. ___ . ___

22. MEDICAID RESUBMISSION CODE   ORIGINAL REF. NO.

23. PRIOR AUTHORIZATION NUMBER

24. A DATE(S) OF SERVICE						B Place of Service	C Type of Service	D PROCEDURES, SERVICES, OR SUPPLIES (Explain Unusual Circumstances) CPT/HCPCS | MODIFIER	E DIAGNOSIS CODE	F $ CHARGES	G DAYS OR UNITS	H EPSDT Family Plan	I EMG	J COB	K RESERVED FOR LOCAL USE
From MM	DD	YY	To MM	DD	YY										
1															
2															
3															
4															
5															
6															

25. FEDERAL TAX I.D. NUMBER   SSN EIN

26. PATIENT'S ACCOUNT NO.

27. ACCEPT ASSIGNMENT? (For govt. claims, see back)   YES   NO

28. TOTAL CHARGE $

29. AMOUNT PAID $

30. BALANCE DUE $

31. SIGNATURE OF PHYSICIAN OR SUPPLIER INCLUDING DEGREES OR CREDENTIALS (I certify that the statements on the reverse apply to this bill and are made a part thereof.)

SIGNED _____ DATE _____

32. NAME AND ADDRESS OF FACILITY WHERE SERVICES WERE RENDERED (If other than home or office)

33. PHYSICIAN'S, SUPPLIER'S BILLING NAME, ADDRESS, ZIP CODE & PHONE #

PIN#   GRP#

PHYSICIAN OR SUPPLIER INFORMATION

DATE	REMARKS			
10/10/XX	Injured yesterday at work			

PATIENT			CHART #	SEX	BIRTHDATE
Thomas J. Buffett	363-44-5858		17-d	M	12/03/65

MAILING ADDRESS	CITY	STATE	ZIP	HOME PHONE	WORK PHONE
12 Hauser Drive	Anywhere	US	12345	(101) 333-5555	(101) 444-5555

EMPLOYER	ADDRESS		PATIENT STATUS X
Start Packing Real Estate	Anywhere	US	MARRIED DIVORCED SINGLE STUDENT OTHER

INSURANCE: PRIMARY	ID#	GROUP	SECONDARY POLICY
Workers Guard	WC4958		

POLICYHOLDER NAME	BIRTHDATE	RELATIONSHIP	POLICYHOLDER NAME	BIRTHDATE	RELATIONSHIP
		Self			

SUPPLEMENTAL PLAN	EMPLOYER

POLICYHOLDER NAME	BIRTHDATE	RELATIONSHIP	DIAGNOSIS	CODE
			1. Ankle sprain, deltoid	845.01
EMPLOYER			2.	
			3.	
REFERRING PHYSICIAN UPIN/SSN			4.	

PLACE OF SERVICE Office

PROCEDURES	CODE	CHARGE
1. New Pt. OV Level II	99202	$70.00
2.		
3.		
4.		
5.		
6.		

SPECIAL NOTES

Patient may return to work tomorrow

TOTAL CHARGES	PAYMENTS	ADJUSTMENTS	BALANCE
$70.00	$0.00	$0.00	$70.00

RETURN VISIT	PHYSICIAN SIGNATURE
PRN	Donald L. Givings, M.D.

MEDICARE # D1234 MEDICAID # DLG1234 BCBS # 12345	**DONALD L. GIVINGS, M.D.** **11350 MEDICAL DRIVE, ANYWHERE, US 12345** **PHONE NUMBER (101)111-5555**	EIN # 11123456 SSN # 123-12-1234 UPIN # DG1234 GRP # DG12345

(SAMPLE ONLY - NOT APPROVED FOR USE)

CARRIER

☐☐ PICA

HEALTH INSURANCE CLAIM FORM   PICA ☐☐

| 1. MEDICARE ☐ (Medicare #) | MEDICAID ☐ (Medicaid #) | CHAMPUS ☐ (Sponsor's SSN) | CHAMPVA ☐ (VA File #) | GROUP HEALTH PLAN ☐ (SSN or ID) | FECA BLK LUNG ☐ (SSN) | OTHER ☐ (ID) | 1a. INSURED'S I.D. NUMBER | (FOR PROGRAM IN ITEM 1) |

2. PATIENT'S NAME (Last Name, First Name, Middle Initial)

3. PATIENT'S BIRTH DATE MM DD YY   SEX M ☐ F ☐

4. INSURED'S NAME (Last Name, First Name, Middle Initial)

5. PATIENT'S ADDRESS (No. Street)

6. PATIENT RELATIONSHIP TO INSURED Self ☐ Spouse ☐ Child ☐ Other ☐

7. INSURED'S ADDRESS (No. Street)

CITY   STATE

8. PATIENT STATUS Single ☐ Married ☐ Other ☐
Employed ☐ Full-Time Student ☐ Part-Time Student ☐

CITY   STATE

ZIP CODE   TELEPHONE (Include Area Code) (   )

ZIP CODE   TELEPHONE (INCLUDE AREA CODE) (   )

9. OTHER INSURED'S NAME (Last Name, First Name, Middle Initial)

10. IS PATIENT'S CONDITION RELATED TO:

11. INSURED'S POLICY GROUP OR FECA NUMBER

a. OTHER INSURED'S POLICY OR GROUP NUMBER

a. EMPLOYMENT? (CURRENT OR PREVIOUS) YES ☐ NO ☐

a. INSURED'S DATE OF BIRTH MM DD YY   SEX M ☐ F ☐

b. OTHER INSURED'S DATE OF BIRTH MM DD YY SEX M ☐ F ☐

b. AUTO ACCIDENT? YES ☐ NO ☐ PLACE (State)

b. EMPLOYER'S NAME OR SCHOOL NAME

c. EMPLOYER'S NAME OR SCHOOL NAME

c. OTHER ACCIDENT? YES ☐ NO ☐

c. INSURANCE PLAN NAME OR PROGRAM NAME

d. INSURANCE PLAN NAME OR PROGRAM NAME

10d. RESERVED FOR LOCAL USE

d. IS THERE ANOTHER HEALTH BENEFIT PLAN? YES ☐ NO ☐ If yes, return to and complete item 9 a – d.

READ BACK OF FORM BEFORE COMPLETING & SIGNING THIS FORM.
12. PATIENT'S OR AUTHORIZED PERSON'S SIGNATURE I authorize the release of any medical or other information necessary to process this claim. I also request payment of government benefits either to myself or to the party who accepts assignment below.

SIGNED _____ DATE _____

13. INSURED'S OR AUTHORIZED PERSON'S SIGNATURE I authorize payment of medical benefits to the undersigned physician or supplier for services described below.

SIGNED _____

PATIENT AND INSURED INFORMATION

14. DATE OF CURRENT: MM DD YY ILLNESS (First symptom) OR INJURY (Accident) OR PREGNANCY (LMP)

15. IF PATIENT HAS HAD SAME OR SIMILAR ILLNESS, GIVE FIRST DATE MM DD YY

16. DATES PATIENT UNABLE TO WORK IN CURRENT OCCUPATION MM DD YY FROM TO MM DD YY

17. NAME OF REFERRING PHYSICIAN OR OTHER SOURCE

17a. I.D. NUMBER OF REFERRING PHYSICIAN

18. HOSPITALIZATION DATES RELATED TO CURRENT SERVICES MM DD YY FROM TO MM DD YY

19. RESERVED FOR LOCAL USE

20. OUTSIDE LAB? YES ☐ NO ☐ $ CHARGES

21. DIAGNOSIS OR NATURE OF ILLNESS OR INJURY. (RELATE ITEMS 1, 2, 3, OR 4 TO ITEM 24E BY LINE)
1. ____ . ____   3. ____ . ____
2. ____ . ____   4. ____ . ____

22. MEDICAID RESUBMISSION CODE _____ ORIGINAL REF. NO.

23. PRIOR AUTHORIZATION NUMBER

24. A DATE(S) OF SERVICE						B Place of Service	C Type of Service	D PROCEDURES, SERVICES, OR SUPPLIES (Explain Unusual Circumstances) CPT/HCPCS MODIFIER	E DIAGNOSIS CODE	F $ CHARGES	G DAYS OR UNITS	H EPSDT Family Plan	I EMG	J COB	K RESERVED FOR LOCAL USE
From MM	DD	YY	To MM	DD	YY										
1															
2															
3															
4															
5															
6															

| 25. FEDERAL TAX I.D. NUMBER SSN ☐ EIN ☐ | 26. PATIENT'S ACCOUNT NO. | 27. ACCEPT ASSIGNMENT? (For govt. claims, see back) YES ☐ NO ☐ | 28. TOTAL CHARGE $ | 29. AMOUNT PAID $ | 30. BALANCE DUE $ |

31. SIGNATURE OF PHYSICIAN OR SUPPLIER INCLUDING DEGREES OR CREDENTIALS (I certify that the statements on the reverse apply to this bill and are made a part thereof.)

SIGNED _____ DATE _____

32. NAME AND ADDRESS OF FACILITY WHERE SERVICES WERE RENDERED (If other than home or office)

33. PHYSICIAN'S, SUPPLIER'S BILLING NAME, ADDRESS, ZIP CODE & PHONE #

PIN# _____ GRP# _____

PHYSICIAN OR SUPPLIER INFORMATION

(SAMPLE ONLY - NOT APPROVED FOR USE)

PLEASE PRINT OR TYPE

SAMPLE FORM 1500
SAMPLE FORM 1500 SAMPLE FORM 1500

DATE	REMARKS				
07/16/XX	Patient was seen in the ER today. Injury occurred at work this morning				

PATIENT			CHART #	SEX	BIRTHDATE
Priscilla R. Shepard	456-78-9999		17-e	F	07/15/56

MAILING ADDRESS	CITY	STATE	ZIP	HOME PHONE	WORK PHONE
23 Easy Street	Anywhere	US	12345	(101) 333-5555	(101) 444-5555

EMPLOYER	ADDRESS		PATIENT STATUS		
Ultimate Cleaners	Anywhere	US		X	
			MARRIED DIVORCED SINGLE STUDENT OTHER		

INSURANCE: PRIMARY	ID#	GROUP	SECONDARY POLICY
Workers Prompt	MA4958		

POLICYHOLDER NAME	BIRTHDATE	RELATIONSHIP	POLICYHOLDER NAME	BIRTHDATE	RELATIONSHIP
		Self			

SUPPLEMENTAL PLAN	EMPLOYER

POLICYHOLDER NAME	BIRTHDATE	RELATIONSHIP	DIAGNOSIS		CODE
			1. Open wound shoulder complicated		880.10
EMPLOYER			2.		
			3.		
REFERRING PHYSICIAN UPIN/SSN			4.		

PLACE OF SERVICE	Mercy Hospital, Anywhere Street, Anywhere, US 12345

PROCEDURES	CODE	CHARGE
1. ER Visit Level III	99283	$150.00
2.		
3.		
4.		
5.		
6.		

SPECIAL NOTES
Patient is to be admitted in the morning

TOTAL CHARGES	PAYMENTS	ADJUSTMENTS	BALANCE
$150.00	$0.00	$0.00	$150.00

RETURN VISIT	PHYSICIAN SIGNATURE
	Donald L. Givings, M.D.

MEDICARE # D1234 MEDICAID # DLG1234 BCBS # 12345	**DONALD L. GIVINGS, M.D.** **11350 MEDICAL DRIVE, ANYWHERE, US 12345** **PHONE NUMBER (101)111-5555**	EIN # 11123456 SSN # 123-12-1234 UPIN # DG1234 GRP # DG12345

PLEASE
DO NOT
STAPLE
IN THIS
AREA

⬆ CARRIER

HEALTH INSURANCE CLAIM FORM

☐☐ PICA

PICA ☐☐☐

1. MEDICARE	MEDICAID	CHAMPUS	CHAMPVA	GROUP HEALTH PLAN	FECA BLK LUNG	OTHER	1a. INSURED'S I.D. NUMBER	(FOR PROGRAM IN ITEM 1)
☐ (Medicare #)	☐ (Medicaid #)	☐ (Sponsor's SSN)	☐ (VA File #)	☐ (SSN or ID)	☐ (SSN)	☐ (ID)		

2. PATIENT'S NAME (Last Name, First Name, Middle Initial)

3. PATIENT'S BIRTH DATE
MM ┆ DD ┆ YY   SEX
M ☐   F ☐

4. INSURED'S NAME (Last Name, First Name, Middle Initial)

5. PATIENT'S ADDRESS (No. Street)

6. PATIENT RELATIONSHIP TO INSURED
Self ☐ Spouse ☐ Child ☐ Other ☐

7. INSURED'S ADDRESS (No. Street)

CITY   STATE

8. PATIENT STATUS
Single ☐   Married ☐   Other ☐

CITY   STATE

ZIP CODE   TELEPHONE (Include Area Code)
(   )

Employed ☐   Full-Time Student ☐   Part-Time Student ☐

ZIP CODE   TELEPHONE (INCLUDE AREA CODE)
(   )

9. OTHER INSURED'S NAME (Last Name, First Name, Middle Initial)

10. IS PATIENT'S CONDITION RELATED TO:

11. INSURED'S POLICY GROUP OR FECA NUMBER

a. OTHER INSURED'S POLICY OR GROUP NUMBER

a. EMPLOYMENT? (CURRENT OR PREVIOUS)
☐ YES   ☐ NO

a. INSURED'S DATE OF BIRTH
MM ┆ DD ┆ YY   SEX
M ☐   F ☐

b. OTHER INSURED'S DATE OF BIRTH
MM ┆ DD ┆ YY   SEX
M ☐   F ☐

b. AUTO ACCIDENT?   PLACE (State)
☐ YES   ☐ NO

b. EMPLOYER'S NAME OR SCHOOL NAME

c. EMPLOYER'S NAME OR SCHOOL NAME

c. OTHER ACCIDENT?
☐ YES   ☐ NO

c. INSURANCE PLAN NAME OR PROGRAM NAME

d. INSURANCE PLAN NAME OR PROGRAM NAME

10d. RESERVED FOR LOCAL USE

d. IS THERE ANOTHER HEALTH BENEFIT PLAN?
☐ YES   ☐ NO   If yes, return to and complete item 9 a – d.

READ BACK OF FORM BEFORE COMPLETING & SIGNING THIS FORM.
12. PATIENT'S OR AUTHORIZED PERSON'S SIGNATURE I authorize the release of any medical or other information necessary to process this claim. I also request payment of government benefits either to myself or to the party who accepts assignment below.

SIGNED _____ DATE _____

13. INSURED'S OR AUTHORIZED PERSON'S SIGNATURE I authorize payment of medical benefits to the undersigned physician or supplier for services described below.

SIGNED _____

⬆ PATIENT AND INSURED INFORMATION

14. DATE OF CURRENT: ◀ ILLNESS (First symptom) OR
MM ┆ DD ┆ YY   INJURY (Accident) OR
                   PREGNANCY (LMP)

15. IF PATIENT HAS HAD SAME OR SIMILAR ILLNESS,
GIVE FIRST DATE   MM ┆ DD ┆ YY

16. DATES PATIENT UNABLE TO WORK IN CURRENT OCCUPATION
MM ┆ DD ┆ YY   MM ┆ DD ┆ YY
FROM   TO

17. NAME OF REFERRING PHYSICIAN OR OTHER SOURCE

17a. I.D. NUMBER OF REFERRING PHYSICIAN

18. HOSPITALIZATION DATES RELATED TO CURRENT SERVICES
MM ┆ DD ┆ YY   MM ┆ DD ┆ YY
FROM   TO

19. RESERVED FOR LOCAL USE

20. OUTSIDE LAB? $ CHARGES
☐ YES   ☐ NO

21. DIAGNOSIS OR NATURE OF ILLNESS OR INJURY. (RELATE ITEMS 1, 2, 3, OR 4 TO ITEM 24E BY LINE)

1. ┖___ . __
2. ┖___ . __
3. ┖___ . __
4. ┖___ . __

22. MEDICAID RESUBMISSION
CODE   ORIGINAL REF. NO.

23. PRIOR AUTHORIZATION NUMBER

24. A DATE(S) OF SERVICE						B Place of Service	C Type of Service	D PROCEDURES, SERVICES, OR SUPPLIES (Explain Unusual Circumstances) CPT/HCPCS ┆ MODIFIER	E DIAGNOSIS CODE	F $ CHARGES	G DAYS OR UNITS	H EPSDT Family Plan	I EMG	J COB	K RESERVED FOR LOCAL USE
From MM ┆ DD ┆ YY			To MM ┆ DD ┆ YY												
1															
2															
3															
4															
5															
6															

25. FEDERAL TAX I.D. NUMBER   SSN ☐ EIN ☐

26. PATIENT'S ACCOUNT NO.

27. ACCEPT ASSIGNMENT?
(For govt. claims, see back)
☐ YES   ☐ NO

28. TOTAL CHARGE
$

29. AMOUNT PAID
$

30. BALANCE DUE
$

31. SIGNATURE OF PHYSICIAN OR SUPPLIER INCLUDING DEGREES OR CREDENTIALS
(I certify that the statements on the reverse apply to this bill and are made a part thereof.)

SIGNED _____ DATE _____

32. NAME AND ADDRESS OF FACILITY WHERE SERVICES WERE RENDERED (If other than home or office)

33. PHYSICIAN'S, SUPPLIER'S BILLING NAME, ADDRESS, ZIP CODE & PHONE #

PIN#   GRP#

⬆ PHYSICIAN OR SUPPLIER INFORMATION

PLEASE PRINT OR TYPE

SAMPLE FORM 1500
SAMPLE FORM 1500 SAMPLE FORM 1500

DATE 07/21/XX	REMARKS			

PATIENT			CHART #	SEX	BIRTHDATE
Priscilla R. Shepard	456-78-9999		17-f	F	07/15/56

MAILING ADDRESS	CITY	STATE	ZIP	HOME PHONE	WORK PHONE
23 Easy Street	Anywhere	US	12345	(101) 333-5555	(101) 444-5555

EMPLOYER	ADDRESS		PATIENT STATUS	
Ultimate Cleaners	Anywhere	US	X MARRIED DIVORCED SINGLE STUDENT OTHER	

INSURANCE: PRIMARY	ID#	GROUP	SECONDARY POLICY
Workers Prompt	MA4958		

POLICYHOLDER NAME	BIRTHDATE	RELATIONSHIP	POLICYHOLDER NAME	BIRTHDATE	RELATIONSHIP
		Self			

SUPPLEMENTAL PLAN	EMPLOYER

POLICYHOLDER NAME	BIRTHDATE	RELATIONSHIP	DIAGNOSIS	CODE
			1. Open wound, shoulder, complicated	880.10
EMPLOYER			2.	
			3.	
REFERRING PHYSICIAN UPIN/SSN			4.	

PLACE OF SERVICE	Mercy Hospital, Anywhere Street, Anywhere, US 12345

PROCEDURES		CODE	CHARGE
1. Initial Visit Level III	07/17/XX	99223	$150.00
2. Subsq. Hosp. Level II	07/18/XX	99232	$75.00
3. Subsq. Hosp. Level II	07/19/XX	99232	$75.00
4. Hosp. Discharge 45 min.	07/20/XX	99239	$75.00
5.			
6.			

SPECIAL NOTES
Date of injury 07/16/XX

TOTAL CHARGES	PAYMENTS	ADJUSTMENTS	BALANCE
$375.00	$0.00	$0.00	$375.00

RETURN VISIT	PHYSICIAN SIGNATURE
	Donald L. Givings, M.D.

MEDICARE # D1234 MEDICAID # DLG1234 BCBS # 12345	DONALD L. GIVINGS, M.D. 11350 MEDICAL DRIVE, ANYWHERE, US 12345 PHONE NUMBER (101)111-5555	EIN # 11123456 SSN # 123-12-1234 UPIN # DG1234 GRP # DG12345

(SAMPLE ONLY - NOT APPROVED FOR USE)

CARRIER

| | PICA | | **HEALTH INSURANCE CLAIM FORM** | PICA | |

1. MEDICARE	MEDICAID	CHAMPUS	CHAMPVA	GROUP HEALTH PLAN	FECA BLK LUNG	OTHER	1a. INSURED'S I.D. NUMBER	(FOR PROGRAM IN ITEM 1)
(Medicare #)	(Medicaid #)	(Sponsor's SSN)	(VA File #)	(SSN or ID)	(SSN)	(ID)		

2. PATIENT'S NAME (Last Name, First Name, Middle Initial)	3. PATIENT'S BIRTH DATE MM DD YY SEX M F	4. INSURED'S NAME (Last Name, First Name, Middle Initial)

5. PATIENT'S ADDRESS (No. Street)	6. PATIENT RELATIONSHIP TO INSURED Self Spouse Child Other	7. INSURED'S ADDRESS (No. Street)

CITY	STATE	8. PATIENT STATUS Single Married Other	CITY	STATE

ZIP CODE	TELEPHONE (Include Area Code) ( )	Employed Full-Time Student Part-Time Student	ZIP CODE	TELEPHONE (INCLUDE AREA CODE) ( )

9. OTHER INSURED'S NAME (Last Name, First Name, Middle Initial)	10. IS PATIENT'S CONDITION RELATED TO:	11. INSURED'S POLICY GROUP OR FECA NUMBER

a. OTHER INSURED'S POLICY OR GROUP NUMBER	a. EMPLOYMENT? (CURRENT OR PREVIOUS) YES NO	a. INSURED'S DATE OF BIRTH MM DD YY SEX M F

b. OTHER INSURED'S DATE OF BIRTH MM DD YY SEX M F	b. AUTO ACCIDENT? PLACE (State) YES NO	b. EMPLOYER'S NAME OR SCHOOL NAME

c. EMPLOYER'S NAME OR SCHOOL NAME	c. OTHER ACCIDENT? YES NO	c. INSURANCE PLAN NAME OR PROGRAM NAME

d. INSURANCE PLAN NAME OR PROGRAM NAME	10d. RESERVED FOR LOCAL USE	d. IS THERE ANOTHER HEALTH BENEFIT PLAN? YES NO If yes, return to and complete item 9 a – d.

READ BACK OF FORM BEFORE COMPLETING & SIGNING THIS FORM.
12. PATIENT'S OR AUTHORIZED PERSON'S SIGNATURE I authorize the release of any medical or other information necessary to process this claim. I also request payment of government benefits either to myself or to the party who accepts assignment below.

SIGNED _____ DATE _____

13. INSURED'S OR AUTHORIZED PERSON'S SIGNATURE I authorize payment of medical benefits to the undersigned physician or supplier for services described below.

SIGNED _____

PATIENT AND INSURED INFORMATION

14. DATE OF CURRENT: MM DD YY ◄ ILLNESS (First symptom) OR INJURY (Accident) OR PREGNANCY (LMP)	15. IF PATIENT HAS HAD SAME OR SIMILAR ILLNESS, GIVE FIRST DATE MM DD YY	16. DATES PATIENT UNABLE TO WORK IN CURRENT OCCUPATION MM DD YY MM DD YY FROM TO

17. NAME OF REFERRING PHYSICIAN OR OTHER SOURCE	17a. I.D. NUMBER OF REFERRING PHYSICIAN	18. HOSPITALIZATION DATES RELATED TO CURRENT SERVICES MM DD YY MM DD YY FROM TO

19. RESERVED FOR LOCAL USE		20. OUTSIDE LAB? YES NO $ CHARGES

21. DIAGNOSIS OR NATURE OF ILLNESS OR INJURY. (RELATE ITEMS 1, 2, 3, OR 4 TO ITEM 24E BY LINE)

1. ____ . ____   3. ____ . ____
2. ____ . ____   4. ____ . ____

22. MEDICAID RESUBMISSION CODE	ORIGINAL REF. NO.

23. PRIOR AUTHORIZATION NUMBER

24. A DATE(S) OF SERVICE		B Place of Service	C Type of Service	D PROCEDURES, SERVICES, OR SUPPLIES (Explain Unusual Circumstances)		E DIAGNOSIS CODE	F $ CHARGES	G DAYS OR UNITS	H EPSDT Family Plan	I EMG	J COB	K RESERVED FOR LOCAL USE
From MM DD YY	To MM DD YY			CPT/HCPCS	MODIFIER							
1												
2												
3												
4												
5												
6												

25. FEDERAL TAX I.D. NUMBER SSN EIN	26. PATIENT'S ACCOUNT NO.	27. ACCEPT ASSIGNMENT? (For govt. claims, see back) YES NO	28. TOTAL CHARGE $	29. AMOUNT PAID $	30. BALANCE DUE $

31. SIGNATURE OF PHYSICIAN OR SUPPLIER INCLUDING DEGREES OR CREDENTIALS (I certify that the statements on the reverse apply to this bill and are made a part thereof.) SIGNED _____ DATE _____	32. NAME AND ADDRESS OF FACILITY WHERE SERVICES WERE RENDERED (If other than home or office)	33. PHYSICIAN'S, SUPPLIER'S BILLING NAME, ADDRESS, ZIP CODE & PHONE # PIN# GRP#

PHYSICIAN OR SUPPLIER INFORMATION

PLEASE PRINT OR TYPE

SAMPLE FORM 1500
SAMPLE FORM 1500 SAMPLE FORM 1500